United Kingdom Association for European Law

University Association for Contemporary European Studies

LEGAL ISSUES OF THE MAASTRICHT TREATY

Edited by

David O'Keeffe, BCL, LLM (NUI), LLM (Yale),
Doctorandus (Leyden)

Solicitor
Professor of European Law, University College London

Patrick M Twomey, BCL (NUI), LLM (London)

Barrister of the King's Inns
Lecturer in Law, University of Liverpool

Wiley Chancery Law

A Division of John Wiley & Sons

London · New York · Chichester · Brisbane · Toronto · Singapore

Published in the United Kingdom by
Chancery Law Publishing Ltd
Baffins Lane, Chichester
West Sussex PO19 1UD

Published in North America by
John Wiley & Sons Inc
7222 Commerce Center Drive
Colorado Springs, CO 80919
USA

Typeset by
Create Publishing Services Ltd
Bath

Printed in Great Britain by
Bookcraft (Bath) Ltd

First published in paperback 1994

Reprinted February 1995

ISBN 0 471 94199 9 (cloth)

ISBN 0 471 95567 1 (paper)

A copy of the CIP entry for this book
is available from the British Library

Contents

CONTENTS

CONTENTS

Part 9: SOCIAL POLICY

Part 10: THE BRITISH AND DANISH POSITIONS

Preface

After all the debates in Parliament, on television and in the press, it might be wondered whether further discussion about the Maastricht Treaty could have, or even by the beginning of 1993 could have had, any interest or freshness.

The papers presented at the conference organised by the United Kingdom Association for European Law together with the University Association for Contemporary European Studies in March 1993 at King's College, and the discussion which followed, showed how much there was to say on vital topics from the lawyer's point of view. Indeed I do not recall a more lively or constructive one-day conference. I am particularly glad that it should have taken place as one of the activities of the UKAEL.

The decision to publish those papers and others on allied topics is much to be welcomed. Even those who thought that Maastricht had to be ratified lock, stock and barrel by the United Kingdom do not claim that the Treaty is a perfect, a simple, or a final document. It gave formal recognition to some principles and practices already recognised by the European Court; it adopted fundamental decisions in regard to the structure of the Union and the Community, even if the principles on which they were based had already been set out in the Treaty of Rome and the Single European Act; it expressly recognised the importance of technological development, of education, of the environment; it laid down a programme for monetary union which, as the British Government recognised, was optimistic if not premature. And much, much more.

Almost all of these developments have proved to be controversial in principle (see at a relatively lowly level of public interest the amendments put down in the House of Lords in relation to the decision to give the Court of Justice power, on a proposal from the Commission, to fine Member States for breaches of the Treaty) or have provoked much discussion as to whether, even if right in principle, they have been adopted in a way which is practically viable or right.

The papers in this book do not set out to develop a particular theme. They approach individualistically separate topics. They are written by lawyers of considerable experience and standing in the different spheres. They are often highly critical of what has been done – that is the function and the joy of the academic lawyer – yet they are written, as I see it, by lawyers who are wholly in favour of the aims of the Community and of developing integration ("union") and this must be kept in mind by those who read their criticisms of what has been agreed. The criticism is fundamentally constructive and forward-looking. How difficult is it going to be to make the Social Protocol work, with the United Kingdom not part of it – what are the legal issues raised? What, if any, is the role of the Court of Justice in deciding whether the principle of subsidiarity has been complied with, indeed what is the meaning of the principle? Can the

Three Pillar structure really work? Is such a structure (especially with "opt-outs" and reservations) fundamentally dangerous for the kind of Community we ought to be creating? Should at least some of the provisions of the chapter on Justice and Home Affairs (The Third Pillar) be transferred to the Community? Is "co-decision", rather than "co-operation", going to lead to greater problems between the Council and the Parliament – has the latter been given enough, or too much, of a role? Has the protection of Human Rights been sufficiently safeguarded? Are we now committed to "variable geometry", to a two-speed Europe? Can the provisions on monetary union survive the present economic and monetary problems — or can they be amended in a way which is still compatible with the principle of the Union? Again, and much, much more.

The electric atmosphere in the House of Commons during the debates on the Social Protocol, and in the House of Lords during the referendum debate (with, apparently, a record turn out in the lobbies), the serious attention given to all aspects of the Treaty showed the great interest and concern (both ways, for and against the Treaty) which exists. There is a great deal still to be worked out – much by the Court of Justice, more no doubt by the 1996 conference and the next one after that. Maastricht does not purport to be final (how could it?) and the more we consider the result of Maastricht, the more ready shall we be to prepare for and understand the next round. This book, both where the authors approve and where they challenge or condemn what has been done provides a valuable critical analysis from which further debate can proceed.

The Rt Hon The Lord Slynn of Hadley

Introduction

The idea for this book had its origin in a conference on the legal aspects of the Maastricht Treaty organised by David O'Keeffe for the United Kingdom Association for European Law, which was held in conjunction with the University Association for Contemporary European Studies at King's College London on 5 March 1993. Given the interest in the topic, we thought that it would be useful to publish the six papers presented at the conference, together with contributions from a number of other experts in the field, drawn from those who participated in the conference as well as one or two who were unable to attend. Not every subject in the Treaty is covered, as we concentrate on those topics of particular interest to lawyers, and even then the myriad of issues raised by the Treaty called for selectivity. There are one or two subjects which we would have liked to include, but were unable to do so. Where we felt it justified, we invited several articles on the same topic, albeit from different viewpoints, as in the case of subsidiarity.

The book has ten sections. As far as possible, the order of the subjects follows that of the Treaty on the European Union (TEU) itself. In Part One, dealing with the Treaty framework and constitutional change, *Paul Demaret* gives an outline of the structure of the Maastricht Treaty and its relationship with the Community Treaties. He notes the lack of unity in the institutional and substantive provisions and highlights the variable geometry which is a feature of the Treaty. *Stephen Weatherill* analyses the problem of the division of competence within the Community, and maintains that the Maastricht Treaty may have set up even more battlegrounds for constitutional challenge.

Part Two contains three articles on subsidiarity, by *Akos Toth, Josephine Steiner* and *Nicholas Emiliou*. Toth argues that the distinction between exclusive and non-exclusive competence introduced by the TEU is alien to the EEC Treaty. He also highlights the difficulties inherent in the double test set for the application of the subsidiarity principle. Finally he poses the question of who is to decide, and by what procedure, whether the principle is applicable in individual cases. Steiner maintains that the principle should be interpreted strictly in order to control the drift to centralization; it could also give the Community a new impetus to reorder its priorities. Emiliou argues that subsidiarity can only be understood within the context of federalism. As centralising models are rejected, a model of federalism based on the subsidiarity principle is attractive, maintaining strong central institutions and a high degree of administrative decentralization.

Part Three contains articles on Union citizenship by *David O'Keeffe* and *Carlos Closa* and on human rights by *Patrick Twomey*. O'Keeffe's is a general introduction to the subject whereas Closa deals with the specific issue of the role played by the nationality of the Member States in the concept of Union citizenship. Twomey discusses the absence of a coherent human rights dimension in the Treaty.

Part Four contains an analysis of the legal and institutional issues affecting Economic and Monetary Union by *D R R Dunnett*. He observes that the essential concept of EMU as expressed in the Delors report is sound, but that the Treaty provisions on the means for attaining it and the powers of the institutions to administer it, are imperfect.

In Part Five, *Martin Hession* and *Richard Macrory* examine the new environmental policy established by the TEU, one of the most important areas in the substantive law changes wrought by the Treaty. They point out that although the TEU strengthens and deepens the role of environmental policy at Community level, the Treaty provisions themselves may compound rather than resolve difficulties.

In Part Six, *Donald Macrae* deals with the TEU provisions relating to institutional and decision-making changes. This is followed by articles on the role of the Court of Justice and the European Parliament in the light of the TEU by *William Robinson* and *Kieran Bradley* respectively.

Part Seven contains three articles on the Common Foreign and Security Policy (CFSP). *Martin Eaton* gives an overall analysis of the CFSP provisions. *Nanette Neuwahl* discusses the requirement of consistency, a guiding principle governing the relations between the various actors (Community, largely intergovernmental CFSP, Member States) concerned in the increasingly complex decision-making process. *Marise Cremona* analyses the relationship between the CFSP and the external relations powers of the Community, in particular its economic relations and common commercial policy.

The Third Pillar of the TEU is dealt with in Part Eight. *Hans Ulrich Jessurun d'Oliveira* gives a critical analysis of the provisions on free movement, immigration and asylum. *Monica den Boer* deals with the issue of European police co-operation as provided under the TEU.

Part Nine contains three articles covering different aspects of the Social Policy provisions of the TEU. *Jo Shaw* discusses the changes made by the TEU to the social policy provisions contained in the main body of the EC Treaty, but concludes that as a result of the minimalist attitude of some Member States to social policy when drafting the Treaties, changes in the effectiveness of Community social policy are more likely to come from future case-law of the Court of Justice than from this source. *Erika Szyszczak* analyses the novel provisions of the TEU annexing a Protocol and Agreement on Social Policy to the Treaty. She takes the view that the development is unfortunate, both for the coherence of European integration and for the protection of individual rights in the context of a changing economic climate. *Tamara Hervey* discusses the legal issues arising from Protocol 2 on Article 119, the so-called *Barber* Protocol.

Part Ten analyses the issues raised by the TEU in two Member States, the United Kingdom and Denmark, both of which acceded to the Community in 1973, and in both of which the ratification of the Treaty caused notable problems. *Baroness Elles* discusses the constitutional and parliamentary aspects of the

TEU in the United Kingdom. Finally *Deirdre Curtin* discusses the "concessions" made to Denmark at the Edinburgh European Council. She argues that the TEU was not amended by the inter-governmental agreement reached at Edinburgh, but that Denmark's rights and obligations under the TEU were merely spelled out or clarified. In the case of the right not to participate in the third stage of EMU, she observes that Denmark already had a latent right under the TEU which was merely "activated".

We are grateful to the Right Hon The Lord Slynn of Hadley, President of the United Kingdom Association for European Law, for contributing the Preface to this book.

We would like to thank the Right Hon The Baroness Elles, Vice-President of the United Kingdom Association for European Law, who first suggested the theme of the conference, and the subsequent publication.

Since the book had its origin in a conference, we think that it is appropriate to thank those who contributed to that conference, including Lord Slynn who opened the conference and chaired several sessions, Professor David Vaughan QC, who chaired one of the sessions, and the two commentators who led the discussions following the papers, Baroness Elles and Professor Alan Dashwood.

We would also like to thank Eva Evans, Executive Secretary of the United Kingdom Association for European Law, for her help in organising the conference.

We would like to thank our colleagues at the European Law Institute of the University of Durham, where we worked on this book. Our thanks go in particular to Dr Tamara Hervey, its Assistant Director, and to Ms Susan George, for her administrative and secretarial help. We would also like to thank our publisher, Jane Belford, for her pleasant cooperation and her enthusiasm for the project.

Finally, we would like to thank the contributors. We hoped to produce a timely book, and we appreciate that despite their numerous other obligations, they were able to meet the very tight deadlines.

DAVID O'KEEFFE
PATRICK M TWOMEY
26 July 1993

List of Contributors

Monica den Boer — Research Fellow, Department of Politics, University of Edinburgh.

Kieran St C Bradley — Member of the Legal Service, European Parliament.

Carlos Closa — Profesor Asociado, Universidad Complutense, Madrid.

Marise Cremona — Senior Fellow, Centre for Commercial Law Studies, Queen Mary and Westfield College, London.

Deirdre Curtin — Professor of the Law of International Organizations, University of Utrecht.

Paul Demaret — Professor, Director, Institut d'Etudes Juridiques Européennes Fernand Dehousse, University of Liège; Director of Legal Studies, College of Europe, Bruges.

D R R Dunnett — Head of Division, Legal Directorate, European Investment Bank.

M R Eaton — Deputy Legal Adviser, Foreign and Commonwealth Office.

Baroness Elles — Member of Select Committee and Sub-Committee E (Law and Institutions, House of Lords).

Nicholas Emiliou — Lecturer in European Law, Queen Mary and Westfield College, London.

Tamara K Hervey — Jean Monnet Lecturer in European Law; Assistant Director, European Law Institute, University of Durham.

Martin Hession — Research Associate, Centre for Environmental Technology, Imperial College, London.

Hans Ulrich Jessurun d'Oliveira — Professor, European University Institute, Florence, and University of Amsterdam.

Donald Macrae — Deputy Legal Adviser to the Cabinet Office (European Secretariat).

Richard Macrory — Denton Hall Professor of Environmental Law, Centre for Environmental Technology, Imperial College, London.

Nanette Neuwahl — Lecturer in Law, University of Leicester.

Ronald van Ooik	Lecturer, Europa Institute, University of Utrecht.
David O'Keeffe	Professor of European Law, University College London.
William Robinson	Associate, European Law Institute, University of Durham.
Jo Shaw	Senior Lecturer in Law, Keele University.
Lord Slynn of Hadley	Lord of Appeal in Ordinary; President, United Kingdom Association for European Law.
Josephine Steiner	Senior Lecturer in Law, University of Sheffield.
Erika Szyszczak	Senior Lecturer in Law, London School of Economics and Political Science.
A G Toth	Professor of European Law, University of Strathclyde in Glasgow.
Patrick M Twomey	Lecturer in Law, University of Liverpool.
Stephen Weatherill	Reader in European Community Law, University of Nottingham.

Tables

DECISIONS

PROPOSED LEGISLATION

CONVENTIONS

CONSTITUTIONS

NATIONAL LEGISLATION

Part 1

Treaty Framework and Constitutional Change

Chapter 1
The Treaty Framework

Introduction

The Maastricht Treaty comprises two main groups of provisions. The first group is designed to revise the EEC, ECSC and EAEC Treaties either by amending some of their present provisions or by adding new ones. The EEC Treaty would henceforth be called the "Treaty establishing the European Community". The latter forms the essential part of the first pillar of the European Union. The second group of provisions is meant to supplement the existing treaties through the establishment of a detailed framework for intergovernmental co-operation in the field of foreign and security policy and in the fields of justice and home affairs. Intergovernmental co-operation in these two sectors would constitute the second and third pillars of the European Union. The two groups of provisions just mentioned are followed by a great number of protocols and declarations.

To the untrained reader, the international instrument signed at Maastricht in early 1992 must seem a legal maze, particularly as it failed to provide a complete and co-ordinated version of the new Treaty establishing a European Community, the successor to the EEC Treaty. *The Economist*[1] thus reported half-jokingly that a lot of Danes and French had voted against the Maastricht Treaty because their Governments gave them the original version to read, whereas, in contrast, the Irish Government issued a booklet summarising Maastricht in plain language and won a two-thirds vote in favour. Hereafter, the Irish approach shall be followed as much as possible.

Two questions will be addressed. The first question is whether the European Union shall truly be served by "a single institutional framework" as the Maastricht Treaty proclaims.[2] The second is whether, in terms of substance, the Maastricht Treaty shall effectively lead to greater consistency in the internal and external relations of the European Union.[3]

The Institutional framework

Does Maastricht provide for a single institutional framework? To such question, there is no simple answer. There are arguments in favour and against a positive answer. In the author's opinion, the latter outweighs the former.

---

[1] 17 October 1992.
[2] See Art C.
[3] See Arts A, B and C.

Homogeneity : the European Union

As already mentioned, the Maastricht Treaty rests on three pillars. The first pillar consists of the former EEC, ECSC and EAEC Treaties as amended, the second deals with foreign and security policy and the third with justice and home affairs. That three-part edifice is, however, topped by a common roof, the European Union, which is headed by the European Council.[4] The four main Community institutions, *i.e.* the Council, the Commission, the European Parliament and the Court of Justice, are also the four main institutions of the European Union.[5] The three parts of the Treaty on European Union are subject to the same revision procedure.[6] Moreover, if a European State wants to become a member of the Union, it shall have to adhere to the entire Treaty.[7]

Heterogeneity : the Community method v the intergovernmental method

The European Union relies on two different institutional methods. The Community method characterises the first pillar, whereas the intergovernmental method applies to the second and third pillars.

Maastricht and the Community method

The Community method means granting powers not only to the Council, where the Member States meet, but also to the Commission and the Court of Justice, as well as gradually enlarging the powers of the European Parliament. Its essential features are majority voting in the Council and the important role given to supranational institutions.

The Community method makes progress in several areas. The Treaty establishing the European Community increases the number of cases where qualified majority voting applies in the Council.[8] It sets up a new legislative procedure, which gives a greater role to the European Parliament.[9] The Court of Justice is granted power to impose fines on Member States that do not comply with its rulings.[10] On the other hand, the subsidiarity principle inserted in the Treaty establishing the European Community[11] is intended to act as a brake on the Commission's legislative initiatives.

The major advance with respect to the Community method is in the monetary field. Viewed from an institutional perspective, monetary matters stand somewhat apart in the Treaty establishing the European Community.[12] This can be explained by their specificity and by the desire to make the European Central Bank fully independent.

---

[4] See Art D.
[5] See Art E.
[6] See Art N.
[7] See Art O.
[8] For an example, see Art 130s.
[9] See Art 189 (b) and, for an example, Art 100a.
[10] See Art 171 para 2.
[11] See Art 3b.
[12] See Art 109a to Art 109d.

The most important actors are the Council and the European Central Bank whose primary task is to conduct the Community monetary policy. The Commission keeps its traditional role, although at times it must share its power of initiative with the European Central Bank[13] or with the Member States.[14] The Parliament's assent is needed for the adoption of important legislative measures.[15] The Court of Justice is to interpret and to review acts taken by the European Central Bank.[16] The latter is given the status of a fully-fledged Community institution. It will exert normative powers[17] and, under certain circumstances, may impose fines on undertakings.[18] It is also entitled to bring a national central bank before the Court of Justice for failure to fulfil its obligations under the EMU.[19]

Maastricht and the intergovernmental method

The second and third pillars of the Maastricht Treaty will be implemented according to the intergovernmental method. Here, the most important institution, by far, is the Council, assisted at times by new intergovernmental committees, the Political Committee (with respect to foreign and security policy) and the Co-ordinating Committee (with respect to justice and home affairs). Under the second and third pillars, Council decisions are, as a rule, taken unanimously.

The Commission is competent to make proposals, but not always, and it must share that function with the Member States.[20] The Parliament is at best consulted. Furthermore, measures adopted by the Council within the scope of the second and third pillars are normally not subject to interpretation or review by the Court of Justice.[21]

Maastricht and the uncertain dividing line between the Community method and the intergovernmental method

The Maastricht Treaty cannot be said to provide for a single institutional framework since its implementation rests on two different sets of legal mechanisms. However, the distinction between the Community method and the intergovernmental method should not be overstated. Under the Maastricht Treaty, the dividing line between the two types of mechanisms and between their respective fields of application is, in several instances, less than clear-cut. It may also change in the future.

(a) Intergovernmental co-operation, which applies to foreign and security policy, as well as to justice and home affairs, is not always of the same nature. At times, it may take a strong Community flavour. For example, under the second

---

[13] See Art 106 (5) and (6).
[14] See Art 109d.
[15] See Art 106 (5).
[16] See Arts 173 and 177.
[17] See Art 108a (1) and (2).
[18] See Art 108a (3).
[19] See Art 180.
[20] See Arts J.8 (3) and K.3.
[21] See Art L.

pillar, qualified majority voting is not altogether excluded, at least outside de-fence matters.[22] Majority voting may also be envisaged under the third pillar.[23] As important, the Court of Justice could be given jurisdiction to interpret con-ventions concluded by the Member States and to rule on disputes regarding their application.[24]

In addition, administrative expenses incurred as a result of the implementa-tion of the second and third pillars are to be supported by the Community budget. Operational expenses will be supported either by the Member States or, if the Council unanimously so decides, by the Community itself.[25]

(b) Conversely, under the Treaty establishing the European Community, *i.e.* the first pillar, the intergovernmental spirit is not far away when decisions re-quire unanimous voting in the Council. Consideration should, for instance, be given to the fact that in the fields of culture, education or public health the Community has only limited powers and that co-operation between the Member States is the rule. It should also be observed that no infringement proceedings may be brought before the Court of Justice against Member States that might be guilty of excessive budgetary deficits.[26]

There are also links between matters falling within the scope of Community law and matters assigned to intergovernmental co-operation. Economic sanc-tions[27] and visa policies[28] provide interesting examples.

(c) Several provisions of the Maastricht Treaty imply that the line dividing matters falling within the Community competencies, and those which remain the province of Member States, and the subject of intergovernmental co-oper-ation may shift in the future. First, the opening provision of the Maastricht Treaty acknowledges the dynamic nature of the European union. According to Article A, "the Treaty marks a new stage in the process of creating an ever closer union among the peoples of Europe". Second, in 1996 a conference shall be convened, which will examine "to what extent the policies and forms of co-operation introduced by this Treaty may need to be revised with the aim of ensuring the effectiveness of the mechanisms and the institutions of the Com-munity".[29] This is a rather convoluted way of stating that an extension of the competences of the Community may be envisaged. Third, Article K.9 is more precise. It explicitly contemplates, albeit under very strict conditions, the trans-fer of certain matters relating to justice and home affairs from the third pillar to Article 100c of the Treaty establishing a European Community.[30] Similarly, Article 8e defines the conditions to be met in order to give more substance to the concept of European citizenship.

---

[22] See Art J.3 (2).

[23] See Art K.3 (2).

[24] See Art K.3 (2), *in fine.*

[25] See Arts J.11 (2) and K.8 (2).

[26] See Art 104c (10).

[27] See Art 228a.

[28] See Arts 100c and d.

[29] See Arts B and N.2.

[30] The matters in question are listed in Arts K.1(1) to (6). They include asylum policy, external border cross-ing, immigration policy and policy regarding third country nationals, drug addiction and fraud on an inter-national scale. Asylum policy was identified as a matter of priority, see Final Act, Declaration on asylum.

What Denmark obtained at the Edinburgh summit[31] was in large part a form of reassurance : that, under the Maastricht Treaty, it could not be forced to take such further steps on the road towards a "closer union". Indeed, they would require not only a unanimous vote in the Council, but also their ratification by the Member States in accordance with their respective constitutional requirements. The point made here is simply that the Maastricht Treaty itself, admittedly in a very guarded way, leaves the door open to a transfer of matters from the realm of intergovernmental co-operation to that of Community law.

(d) In any event, the Maastricht Treaty commits the Member States to maintain the *acquis communautaire*.[32] This is subject to the control of the Court of Justice.[33] Assuming the Maastricht Treaty enters into force, one of the most interesting legal, but also political issue, is how and to what extent matters dealt with in the first pillar and those dealt with in the second and third pillar will be kept separate. A recent case before the Court of Justice provides an illustration. It related to the granting of humanitarian aid to Bangladesh. The decision to grant the aid was taken by the Member States meeting within the Council. That decision was challenged by the European Parliament on the ground that it should have been adopted on the basis of Article 203 of the EEC Treaty.[34]

Cases such as the one just mentioned are most likely to arise with respect to the free movement of persons. The latter is an integral part of the internal market and as such is to a significant extent already governed by Community law. But important questions relating directly to the free movement of persons form part of the third pillar. If, under the prodding of the Commission and the European Parliament, the Court of Justice were to broadly interpret the *acquis communautaire*, the third pillar could be emptied of part of its content. It is worth recalling here that some Member States tried, without success, to bring into the first pillar matters now found in the third.

The Substantive framework

As already mentioned, the Maastricht Treaty refers to the "process of creating an ever closer union"[35] and stresses the need for consistency in the economic, social and political fields.[36] However, an examination of the substantive aspects of the Treaty reveals that if the latter indeed is intended to promote greater consistency in both the internal and external relations of the Union, it also sanctions the spread of "variable geometry". These two characteristics of the Maastricht Treaty are closely linked.

---

[31] See Denmark and the Treaty on European Union, OJ 1992 C348/1.
[32] See Arts B and M.
[33] See Art L (c).
[34] Joint cases C-181/91 and C-248/91 *European Parliament v Council and Commission*, OJ 1991 C-217, OJ 1991 C-307/7. Judgment 30 June 1993, however, against the Parliament.
[35] See Art A.
[36] See Arts A, B and C.

Consistency

The most important substantive change that the Maastricht Treaty would bring about is of course the establishment of a Monetary Union, with a single currency under the control of a European Central Bank.[37] This in turn requires that Member States reach a high degree of convergence in the conduct of their economic policies.[38] The EMU appears as the logical step to be taken after the completion of the internal market, particularly to those who see in the EMU the springboard towards a more politically integrated Europe.

The establishment of a common visa policy[39] and greater intergovernmental co-operation in the fields of justice and home affairs may help to achieve the free movement of natural persons between the Member States. The latter constitutes an essential feature of the internal market, which has not yet been fully implemented.

The Maastricht Treaty seeks to foster greater social, economic and political cohesion in several other ways. Among these, mention should be made of the granting of certain political rights and diplomatic protection to citizens of the Union,[40] the agreement on social policy,[41] the establishment of trans-European networks[42] and the setting-up of a Cohesion Fund.[43] Greater external consistency could of course result from the implementation of a common foreign and security policy, particularly if it were to extend to the defence field.[44]

Fragmentation

Member States have in several instances been allowed to proceed at different speeds on the road towards greater integration on account of their varying degree of social and economic development. The implementation of the Directive on the free circulation of capital[45] is a typical example. Variable geometry or "l'Europe à la carte" means something else, in that the Member States are not required to move towards the same objective. The Treaty of Maastricht offers concrete examples of both the variable speed and variable geometry concepts. The spread of the latter has some troublesome implications for the future of the Community as a coherent entity.

Illustrations

(a) The provisions of the Maastricht Treaty concerning the EMU could lead to a three-tiered monetary Europe. The first tier would consist of the Member States

---

[37] See Arts 105 *et seq.*
[38] See in particular Art 109j, Art 104c, the Protocol on the excessive deficit procedure and the Protocol on the convergence criteria.
[39] See Art 100c.
[40] See Arts 8b and 8c.
[41] See Agreement on social policy concluded between the Member States of the European Community with the exception of the United Kingdom.
[42] See Art 129b *et seq.*
[43] See Art 130d.
[44] See Art J4.
[45] See Council Dir of June 24, 1988, Art 6, OJ 1988 L178/5.

who succeeded in meeting the criteria for economic convergence.[46] Such a group would probably include some former EFTA countries. The second tier would comprise those Member States wishing to share in a common currency, but who have not yet fulfilled the economic conditions.[47] Likely candidates for that group are southern Member States, who could be joined by some central European countries. A third tier would be made up of what might be called the "hold-outs". Denmark has already signified that it would not take part in the third and last stage of the EMU.[48] The United Kingdom was granted the right to keep its options open.[49]

The status of Denmark and the United Kingdom in the economic and monetary field is a good illustration of variable geometry. The Treaty provides other examples. The Protocol on social policy, in effect, allows the United Kingdom not to take part in the implementation of the Social Charter of 1989. In defence matters, Member States who are parties to the WEU are invited to move ahead and no guarantee is given that the other Member States will join them at a later stage. To the contrary, the Edinburgh summit recorded Denmark's decision not to participate in the preparation and the implementation of decisions concerning defence. Finally, in the fields of justice and home affairs, "the establishment or development of closer co-operation between two or more Member States" on the Schengen pattern is explicitly allowed.[50] Denmark, Ireland and the United Kingdom are not parties to the Schengen agreements.

Potential implications

Here again the argument should not be overstated. The Maastricht Treaty is of course not designed to encourage the development of a fragmented Europe. However, in some important areas a degree of fragmentation had to be permitted as the price to be paid for allowing a majority of Member States to move forward down the road towards greater social, economic and political integration. Variable geometry may become a permanent feature of the European Union. The crucial issue then, is to identify where, the extent to which and for how long variable geometry can be tolerated without putting into jeopardy the *acquis communautaire*. Such an inquiry cannot be undertaken here. A few questions are nevertheless worth raising.

(a) Several European countries have applied to become members of the European Community. Is it really conceivable that new members could be refused the kind of derogations that existing members, such as the United Kingdom and Denmark obtained under the Maastricht Treaty? That was at any rate the position taken by the European Council at the Edinburgh summit when it dealt with the situation of Denmark. It is, however, somewhat inconsistent to declare, on the one hand, that provisions adopted with respect to Denmark are fully

---

[46] See Art 109j.
[47] See Art 109k.
[48] See Protocol on certain provisions relating to Denmark and the Treaty on European Union, *supra*, n 31.
[49] See Protocol on certain provisions relating to the United Kingdom.
[50] See Art K.7.

compatible with the Maastricht Treaty and to decide, on the other hand, that such provisions may not apply to any other, existing or future, Member States.[51]

(b) The internal market is undoubtedly the core of the European Union. But will that core hold together if variable geometry is not a transient phenomenon? A hypothetical case may serve to illustrate the point. Alone among the Member States, a State has steadfastly refused both to join the EMU and to participate in the harmonization of social policy. As a result of both the deliberate depreciation of its currency and its lower level of social protection, that State enjoys for a while a competitive advantage when trading with the other Member States. Some of the latter States take countervailing measures. Would the Community institutions be capable of upholding the free circulation of goods or services in such a case?

(c) In order to free the circulation of natural persons between their territories, as the concept of a single market requires, Member States who are parties to the Schengen agreements need to strengthen controls at their external borders. However, since all the Member States are not parties to the Schengen agreements, the implementation of the latter could have the effect of making the crossing of certain internal borders more difficult for third country nationals. This in turn is not entirely consistent with the idea of an internal market extending to 12 Member States.

(d) In the years ahead, some form of common defence policy could take shape in the framework of the WEU. Based on past events, the need to deploy military means in order to protect the Community's oil supplies cannot be excluded. Assuming such need occurs, that would mean that only Member States who are parties to the WEU would bear the burden of protecting the European Union's interests. This is bound to affect the inner working of the European Union. Conceivably, the voice of those Member States who behave like free riders in the field of defence will count less than that of the other Member States when the Community is to formulate its commercial or energy policy.

(e) Under the Protocol on Social Policy, British Members of the European Parliament keep the right to intervene and to vote on social policy matters from which the United Kingdom has decided to exclude itself. This can be accepted if it remains an isolated instance. It is, however, difficult to imagine that bizarre institutional arrangements such as the Protocol on Social Policy could be multiplied without putting a strain on the Community institutional framework.

Conclusion

The Maastricht Treaty's institutional framework, as well as its substantive framework, is characterised by a certain lack of unity. The Treaty provides for two different types of institutional mechanism depending on the nature of the subject matter. However, the exact frontier between the Commmunity method

---

[51] See *supra*, n 31.

and the intergovernmental method or between their respective fields of application is not always easy to define. In several respects, the Maastricht Treaty may help the Community or a majority of its members to achieve greater internal and external consistency. In certain areas, most notably in the monetary and social fields, variable geometry was the price to be paid in exchange. In the future, much will probably depend on whether the EMU turns out to be a success or a failure. In the former case, variable geometry is likely to recede, whereas in the latter it is likely to expand.

Throughout this article, it has been assumed that the Maastricht Treaty will enter into force. A failure to ratify the Maastricht Treaty would certainly leave a Community less united than under the Maastricht framework, despite the latter's weaknesses.

PAUL DEMARET

Chapter 2

Beyond Preemption? Shared Competence and Constitutional Change in the European Community

The Problem of competence

The European Community enjoys no general competence, but rather the specific competences or enumerated powers conferred on it by its constitutive Treaties. The "problem of competence" arises in two linked aspects. First, the Treaty does not explicitly share out or set boundaries between the competences of the Community and the Member States, in contrast to, for example, the relationship between federal and *Länder* authorities explicitly mapped out in the German *Grundgesetz*. Secondly, the Treaty offers no statement of the consequences for national competence of Community competence in a particular field.

It is well known that the Court has assumed a key role in this area. It has construed the Treaties "in a constitutional mode rather than employing the traditional international law methodology. Proceeding from its fragile jurisdictional base, the Court has arrogated to itself the ultimate authority to draw the line between Community law and national law".[1] Writers have long been accustomed to remarking on the Court's constitutionalization of the Treaty[2] and the Court itself has increasingly and vividly made explicit its commitments in this direction. In *Les Verts* v *Parliament*[3] it referred to the Treaty as a "basic constitutional charter", a perception confirmed *inter alia* in Opinion 1/91, where the Treaty was acclaimed as "the constitutional charter of a Community based on the rule of law".[4] What, then, does the Community's constitution, interpreted by its Court, have to say about the problem of competence?

---

[1] Stein, 'Lawyers, judges and the making of a transnational constitution', (1981) 75 American J Intl L, 1.
[2] *e.g.* Weiler, 'The Community system: the dual character of supranationalism' (1981) 1 YEL 267 and 'The Transformation of Europe' (1991) 100 Yale LJ 2403; Lenaerts, 'Constitutionalism and the many faces of federalism' (1990) 38 AJCL 205; Mancini, 'The making of a constitution for Europe' (1989) 26 CML Rev 595.
[3] Case 294/83 [1986] ECR 1339.
[4] [1992] 1 CMLR 245.

The Allocation of competence

The Court has determined that in some areas the Community is exclusively competent. Perhaps the most celebrated example is provided by the areas subject to the Common Commercial Policy under Article 113.[5] Member States may not act in this field, irrespective of whether or not the Community has itself acted.

Elsewhere, the Community and the Member States are concurrently competent, in the sense that the Community enjoys competence, but until such time as it acts, the Member States may act within the limits set by the Treaty relating to, for example, free movement under Articles 30 and 59, non-discrimination on grounds of nationality under Article 7 and, more broadly still, the general obligation of Community solidarity under Article 5.[6] Concurrence thus implies the supremacy of Community norms in case of conflict. Once the Community has acted, if it acts, it then assumes exclusive competence in the field which it has occupied, thereby transforming concurrent State/Community competence into exclusive Community competence – the doctrine of preemption.

Finally, in some areas Member States retain exclusive competence. The existence of residual areas of exclusive Member State competence seems to be a logical corollary of the limited competence conferred on the Community by the Treaty, but the breadth of Community competence greatly confines the scope of these areas. They are occasionally revealed by the Court in decisions which hold fact patterns to be unaffected by Community law, such as "purely internal" matters, but the logic of the integrating market dictates that few such areas persist. A State can in principle regulate the composition of cheese made by producers on its own territory without facing challenge drawn from primary EC law, but it is misleading to describe regulation of cheese making as a matter of exclusive national competence, for an importer will be able to invoke primary Community law to challenge national technical standards which obstruct cross-border trade and, moreover, the Community is competent to legislate in the field.[7] Member States remain competent to apply domestic competition policy to deals which do not affect inter-State trade, but this freedom is circumscribed by the demands of Article 5.[8] National law determines the procedures for ensuring protection of directly effective Community law rights before national courts – subject to increasingly prominent obligations under Article 5.[9]

In the realm of secondary rather than primary Community law, it is equally logical that under the principle of enumerated powers, the Community must lack competence to legislate in some fields, which therefore remain within the protected jurisdiction of the national legislator. Such areas are few, because the

---

[5] Opinion 1/75 [1975] ECR 1355.

[6] For discussion of how far general principles of Community law such as fundamental human rights bind Member States acting in areas touched by Community law see Jacobs in O'Reilly (ed), *Human Rights and Constitutional Law* (1992) 243–250.

[7] *Cf* Case 237/82 *Jongeneel Kaas* [1984] ECR 483.

[8] Case 14/68 *Walt Wilhelm* [1969] ECR 1.

[9] From Case 45/76 *Comet* [1976] ECR 2043 to Cases C-6 & 9/90 *Francovich* v *Italian State* judgment of 19 November 1991 via, *inter alia*, Case 199/82 *San Giorgio* [1983] ECR 3595 and Case C-213/89 *Factortame* [1990] ECR I-2433.

Community's enumerated powers are actually very wide. Article 235, linked to Articles 2 and 3, in particular, but also Article 100 and later Article 100a, have been used to push Community competence into some rather unlikely corners.[10] The validity of using Article 235 to enlarge Community competence in a particular field has never been challenged before the Court,[11] largely because Article 235 in any event contains protection for dissentient States in its requirement of unanimity. Viewed from this perspective, it is difficult to envisage the Court ever holding a sphere to lie beyond the Community's strict legal competence, once a measure based on Article 235 has invaded that sphere. The end of Community competence, the start of exclusive national competence, is in this sense not static and is determined in law by the ability to secure unanimity in the Community's principal political institution, the Council.

The Court has no history of reining in the growth of Community competence. It has never upheld a challenge to Community competence, which is rather important background knowledge when one comes to assess a major unresolved legal issue of the Maastricht Treaty, the capacity of Article 3b to act as, at last, that strict rule which will set bounds to Community legislative competence. Community competence has expanded by virtue of Treaty amendments, most significantly in the Single European Act and now in the Treaty on European Union, although to some extent those amendments merely confirmed expansion which had occurred as a result of judicial and legislative practice.[12] Far from confining the practical expansion of Community competence, the Court itself has a record of contributing to the assertion of Community competence in areas apparently outwith the Treaty. For example, the Single European Act inserted a title on Environmental Protection, but the Court in *ADBHU*[13] had already declared environmental protection to be "one of the Community's essential objectives". The Treaty on European Union introduces a Consumer Protection Title, but the Court in *GB-INNO* v *CCL*[14] had already found that "under Community law concerning consumer protection the provision of information to the consumer is considered one of the principal requirements." Whereas in 1963 the Court referred in *Van Gend en Loos*[15] to states joining the Community having limited their powers "albeit in limited fields", in 1991, in Opinion 1/91, it chose to refer instead to "ever wider fields" a reference to dynamic expansion towards a general jurisdiction for which the Court itself is in no small part responsible.

This description already suggests a blurring of competence allocation between Community and Member States, and the Maastricht Treaty has further contributed to the blur, not least by including the subsidiarity principle

---

[10] Usher, *The Continuing Development of Law and Institutions* in Academy of European Law (ed.), *Collected Courses* Vol II, Book I, 148–150, 163–165 (Art 100), 160–162 (Art 100A), pp150–153, 163–165 (Art 235).
[11] Although its use in preference to other more specific provisions of the Treaty was challenged in Case 45/86 *Commission* v *Council* [1987] ECR 1493.
[12] Usher in Smythe and White (eds), *Current Issues in European and International Law* (1990) Ch 1.
[13] Case 240/83 [1985] ECR 531.
[14] Case C-362/88 [1990] ECR I-667.
[15] Case 26/62 [1963] ECR 1.

which, loosely described, impinges on issues of competence, albeit without offering much clarity. Yet it is questions of "allocation of competence" between States and the Community which are central to the political debate about the future of the Community. This article will portray the present state of Community law as one where exclusive competence, whether of Community or of Member States, is increasingly rare. This leaves concurrent competence, but whereas under classic notions of preemption one would expect this to be whittled away by the spread of Community legislative activity, the idea that Community action in a field of concurrent competence confers exclusive competence on the Community will be shown to be undermined to the point where it can hardly be claimed any longer as a basic principle of the Community legal order. Community action no longer cleanly preempts national competence. Nor can it, in an increasingly heterogenous Community.

Since analysis of the preemption doctrine has long located it firmly in the fundamental constitutional principles of the Community legal order, any adjustment to it is constitutionally very significant. This is important as part of the assessment of the Maastricht Treaty, but is plainly incapable of resolution in that Treaty. Are we witnessing the fragmentation of EC law?

Preemption

Under the "classic" preemption doctrine, once the Community legislates in a field, it occupies that field, thereby precluding Member State action. The Community has assumed exclusive competence in the field. This pattern is the basis for the creation of a uniform body of Community law applicable in all the Member States.[16]

The attraction of this principle lies in its rigidity. The Community, having acted, sets the rule; the Member States have surrendered power to act unilaterally in that field. The Community rule becomes the common basis for economic activity on which business may rely in treating the territory of the Member States as a single market.

So the application of primary Community law, Articles 30–36 of the Treaty, is inadequate to secure the free movement of goods, because Article 36 provides an interim, albeit narrowly construed, justification for national measures which obstruct trade. It may fall to the Court to rule on whether a national measure is justified, despite its trade-inhibiting effect, which is in itself a source of unpredictability as the Court is forced to make some difficult assessments in the trade-off between market liberalization and, for example, national initiatives of environmental protection[17] and consumer protection.[18] The classic solution in the

---

[16] Discussed by Waelbroeck in Sandalow and Stein (eds), *Courts and Free Markets* (1982).

[17] Case 302/86 *Commission* v *Denmark* [1988] ECR 4607.

[18] Compare Case 286/81 *Oosthoek* [1982] ECR 4575 (marketing rule lawful) with Case C-362/88 *GB-INNO* v *CCL* [1990] ECR I-667 (marketing rule unlawful).

Treaty is the introduction of Directives on the basis of Article 100 and, after the Single European Act, measures on the basis of Article 100a which establish common rules in the field, applicable throughout the territory of the Community. Member States may no longer invoke Article 36 to justify derogation from the Community rule, because they have transferred regulatory power to the Community. The Community rule has occupied the field.[19]

Applying this model, the Court found the United Kingdom in breach of its Community obligations in *Commission* v *United Kingdom* .[20] The United Kingdom had required motor vehicles sold on its territory to carry "dim dip" devices. Yet the field had already been occupied by Community rules imposing no such requirement. The Court ruled that ". . . the Member States cannot unilaterally require manufacturers who have complied with the harmonised technical requirements set out in Directive 76/756/EEC to comply with a requirement which is not imposed by that directive, since motor vehicles complying with the technical requirements laid down therein must be able to move freely within the common market." The Court interpreted the list of devices permitted by the Directive as exhaustive, this being consistent with the objective of abolishing "hindrances to trade within the Community resulting from the fact that mandatory technical requirements differ from one Member State to another . . . ." The Directive had a blocking effect on national competence to act. The same pattern applies to the law governing the free movement of persons, well illustrated by M Auer, who was qualified as a veterinary surgeon in Italy but who wished to practise in France. Pending Community legislative action in the field of professional qualifications, France was entitled to deny him access to the French market. Once a Directive had been introduced, establishing criteria which M Auer met, France lost the power to exclude him from the market.[21]

This is "total" or "exhaustive" harmonization. Were States permitted unilaterally to derogate from the Community norm, the notion of market integration under a common legal order would seem illusory. Constitutionally, preemption appears to lie very close to the heart of the objectives of the Community. Regulations are directly applicable according to Article 189 and prevail over conflicting national law.[22] The rigorous application of these principles has been further enhanced by the Court's ruling that even wrongfully unimplemented Directives may achieve this preemptive effect, directly[23] or perhaps even, albeit less satisfactorily, indirectly,[24] despite the limitations on the reach of Directives into the national legal order suggested by Article 189's reference to implementation according to national choice of form and methods.

---

[19] *e.g.* Case 5/77 *Tedeschi* [1977] ECR 1555; Case 251/78 *Denkavit* [1979] ECR 3369; Case C-246/91 *Commission* v *France* judgment of 5 May 1993.

[20] Case 60/86 [1988] ECR 3921.

[21] Case 136/78 [1979] ECR 437; Case 271/82 [1983] ECR 2727.

[22] Case 106/77 *Simmenthal* [1978] ECR 629.

[23] *e.g.* Case 148/78 *Ratti* [1979] ECR 1629; Case 271/82 *supra* n 21.

[24] Case C-106/89 *Marleasing* [1990] ECR I-4135; on the scope of the indirect route, Stuyck and Wytinck (1991) 28 CML Rev 205.

The Nuances of preemption

Given the key constitutional role of preemption, it is remarkable that Cross was able recently to allege, with some justification, that analysis of preemption is surrounded by obscurity and inconsistency.[25] In part this confusion is attributable to varying terminology used in the literature.[26] But, more fundamentally, it is also attributable to the fact that there are several ways in which this clear-cut picture of total harmonization does not occur consequent on the Community having legislated. It is always necessary to examine closely a Community act in order to determine its proper scope. A measure may occupy a field, preempting national competence; but outwith its field, States remain free to act, subject always to the rules of primary Community law. The Court has a role to play in determining carefully the precise extent to which Member State competence, concurrent prior to Community action, has been ousted.[27] So in *Jongeneel Kaas*[28] the Court ruled that a Regulation occupied a neighbouring field, but not the matter at hand, control of the quality of cheese produced on Dutch territory, thereby preserving national competence. *Commission* v *Germany*[29] shows a similar approach in relation to the free movement of insurance services, where existing Community legislative initiatives were of inadequate breadth to preclude the application of some national measures, which then fell for consideration in the light of primary Community law. The issue has also arisen regularly before the Court in relation to the scope of Member State competence in agricultural markets which have been subjected to Community rules.[30]

However, in cases where it decides on the scope of the occupied field, the Court is not choosing between the merits of competing regulatory regimes. It is interpreting the Community provisions to determine whether they have occupied the field. If they have, they are the applicable provisions and Member States, preempted, may not depart from them.[31] If they have not occupied the field, then Member States retain competence, subject to the application of primary Community law.

The unfeasibility and undesirability of preemption

There are enormous advantages for commercial certainty in fixing a Community rule, susceptible to neither unilateral national alteration nor the judicial weighing exercise inherent in the *Cassis* approach to Article 30. Yet preemption in its traditional form has flaws, arising from the broad perception that it may be

---

[25] (1992) 29 CML Rev 447.

[26] Bieber (1988) 13 EL Rev 147, 154–155, trying to dispel confusion.

[27] *e.g.* Temple Lang (1986) 6 YEL 183; Bieber *supra* n 26 154–157; Lenaerts (including comparison with US practice) *supra* n 2.

[28] *Supra*, n 7.

[29] Case 205/84 [1986] ECR 3755.

[30] Louis, *The Community Legal Order* (1990) 18–21.

[31] I leave aside the relatively peripheral phenomenon of optional Directives, whereby States may continue to permit non-conforming products to be marketed within their own domestic market only.

neither feasible nor desirable to suppose that a rigid rule of preemption can serve an increasingly heterogenous Community. Preemption is difficult to achieve, given the unfeasibility of replacing 12 regimes with one. This leads to a legislative logjam, an obstacle firmly fixed, until 1987, by the practice of unanimous voting in Council which forced the Community to move at the pace of the slowest member. Even if a single Community rule is agreed, its stifling effect on national initiatives may prove undesirable. A uniform Community rule may ossify practice, discouraging innovation. In *Commission* v *United Kingdom*,[32] the United Kingdom argued that "dim dip" devices improved road safety, but once the Court had ruled that the Directive had occupied the field, the merits of this argument were quite irrelevant. Preemption, the basis of market integration, prevailed, denying States the competence unilaterally to regulate the market. The United Kingdom would have to address its arguments about road safety to its partners in an attempt to secure amendment of the Directive, but amending Community rules is a laborious business and, moreover, that process contains a natural in-built bias in favour of inertia, the preservation of established rules on the basis of which the market is already integrating. Yet failure to achieve the rapid adaptation of obsolete norms in response to technical innovation will cause inefficiency within the Community market, which will also affect the competitiveness of Community operators in world markets. Preemption risks creating a level but barren playing field.

Both unfeasibility and undesirability arise because the Community's pursuit of preemption is hindered by its own heterogeneity. This naturally becomes more acute as the Community expands, drawing in distinct cultural traditions, incapable of reduction to a single Community norm. The problem also deepens as the Community sets itself more ambitious targets, which can only be achieved by a more active approach to the adoption of legislation. Something other than classic preemption is plainly required to resolve such issues of accommodating heterogeneity in the Community. It is submitted that one is forced to accept that, while the Community may have a role to play, so too must the Member States. Competence is shared.

The modern law of preemption

The drive to avoid the stifling effect of Community uniformity has been a prominent feature of Community legislative activity in recent years. In fact, clear-cut lines were blurred long before Maastricht. Already in 1981 Weiler alerted us to the Court, astute to dangers in conferring exclusive powers on Community institutions unequal to the task, shifting from pure preemption, which yields exclusive Community competence, to pragmatism characterised by concurrent competence.[33] In 1984 Ehlermann drew attention to the amount of flexibility in the existing structure of Community law as a reason for doubting

---

[32] *Supra*, n 20.
[33] *Supra*, n 2 esp 278–279; also Waelbroeck, *supra*, n 16.

the need for any pressure towards a "two-speed" Europe.[34] He referred to, *inter alia*, transitional periods, safeguard clauses and exceptions applicable to specific Member States. These techniques, and others, are all important in an assessment of the state of the modern law of preemption.

Safeguard procedures, commonly written into Directives, permit States to take action in accordance with defined procedures in the Directive where a threat to health, not covered by the terms of the Directive, is revealed. Subsequent adjustment of the rule is thus permitted. Article 100a(5) takes this idea into the Treaty. This does not involve setting a higher *rule*, but rather relates to individual products and is provisional only – in fact, the safeguard procedure envisages adaptation to reestablish the harmonization already achieved. The procedure is not motivated by the need to respond to technical innovation. It is true that Directives also commonly provide for a Committee whose task is to adapt to technical progress. The existence of these Committees avoids the need for recourse to the full legislative procedure to achieve updating, although the workload still remains dauntingly high given the sheer scope of Community action and the speed of technological change in some fields. Fundamentally, however, even these Committees remain subject to in-built inertia and bias in favour of maintaining the status quo.

The New Approach to Technical Harmonization[35] injects flexibility into Directives, by setting harmonised norms in terms of conformity, with essential safety requirements instead of more specific technical specifications. Conformity with the essential safety requirements is demonstrated by adherence to standards or, alternatively, by securing approval of a particular model even where it does not meet the standards. This ensures greater flexibility within the Community measure. However, this flexibility is afforded to the trader within the occupied field, not to the State. The State is bound to accept products conforming to the rule, subject to the limited safeguard procedure. New Approach Directives conform in this sense to "classic" preemption theory.

Recent developments testify to greater readiness to accept derogations in Directives, in order to secure progress in the face of unbridgeable disagreement. The approximation formula under the Product Liability Directive provides that "The producer shall be liable for damage caused by a defect in his product".[36] Yet there was intense disagreement about the desirability of this regime, with the United Kingdom in particular adhering to the view that such a "strict liability" system would inhibit producers from innovation for fear of vast financial liability. The Directive, as adopted, dilutes the system of strict liability by the inclusion of a so-called development risk defence in Article 7(e). A producer of a defective product is able to escape liability by proving "that the state of scientific and technical knowledge at the time when he put the product into circulation was not such as to enable the existence of the defect to be discovered". This reflects the British view, but, reflecting the contrary view that the development risk defence undermines consumer protection, Article 15(1)(b) grants Member

---

[34] (1984) 82 Michigan Law Rev 1274.
[35] OJ 1985 C136/1.
[36] Dir 85/374 (OJ 1985 L210/29).

States the option of extending liability even to defects of this type. There are, accordingly, differing liability rules in different States depending on whether the Article 15(1)(b) option has been taken. The search for uniformity has been compromised, but without such compromise there may have been no Directive in the first place, or at best only a minimalist, anodyne measure. Instinctively one might suppose that half a loaf is better than none, but this may not apply in the Community context, where compromise may weaken the very ambitious goals of the legal order. The option may induce forum shopping, for consumers will prefer to sue in States which have opted to exclude the defence. Business choices about where to locate plant and market goods may be distorted by preference for States which maintain the defence. The very nature of Directives is such as to yield a certain differentiated integration, through their (not always timeous) transposition into national law in accordance with national techniques, but the Product Liability Directive goes some way further, in yielding on its face to the impossibility of securing agreement on a rather important facet of the harmoniscd rule. Although this structure can be accommodated within classic preemption theory in the sense that the Community rule, not national law, sets the parameters of the option, in substance the level playing field has been compromised. It remains contentious how far such options granted in Directives, from wine taxation to worker participation, constitute an acceptable recognition of national peculiarities and how far they undermine the very fabric of the common/ internal market and its level playing field, by depriving legislation of the qualities necessary to achieve integration and regulation.

The need for shared competence

These several techniques address the problem of the unfeasibility and undesirability of classic preemption. However, they remain largely within the grip of the framework of classic total harmonization, by which Community legislation transforms concurrent competence into exclusive Community competence. All view unilateral national initiatives as essentially threatening to a Community legal order dominated by the perspective of market integration. The objective of this article is to suggest fundamental readjustment of appreciation of the role of national initiatives and the limits of Community action.

The Community will benefit from sharing competence with the Member States. The Community *cannot* deal with everything and is weakening itself by closing off national and regional support. Given that, first, preemption denies Member States the power to fulfil their constitutional responsibilities to their own citizens, and that, second, the Community does not/cannot take over that responsibility effectively, whether substantively or institutionally,[37] a model of shared competence is both necessary and desirable. The abandonment of total harmonization carries with it a recognition that regulating the Community market is a task not only for the Community, but also for national and regional

---

[37] For the same perspective on human rights in the Community, see Clapham (1990) 10 YEL 309.

authorities. It also emphasizes that there is more to the Community and its doctrine of preemption than simple market liberalization.

The significance of this has already been drawn out in discussion of the Product Liability Directive. In casting aside total harmonization as a model which cannot reflect the diversity of interests in the modern Community, one is welcoming flexibility and innovation and enshrining greater sensitivity to national preferences. The other side of the coin is the potential loss of commercial certainty consequent on the erosion of the uniform Community rule; fundamentally a potential disintegration in the Community legal order. This broad policy issue readily brings to mind questions about the structure of the Maastricht Treaty, a Europe of "bits and pieces",[38] and indeed the debate will inevitably intensify as the Community expands further. Can one recognise and accommodate diversity within the common market without irretrievably compromising and fragmenting the integrity of the legal order?

Article 100a(4)

The Single European Act injected qualified majority voting into the Treaty, as a practical means of securing fulfilment of the political commitment to complete the internal market by the end of 1992. Removal of the national veto brought into sharper focus the consequences of preemption for outvoted States and provoked a rupture in the constitutional orthodoxy of preemption. According to Article 100a(4) EEC, even after the adoption of a harmonization measure under Article 100a(1), a State is permitted to apply national provisions where it deems it necessary on grounds of major needs referred to in Article 36, or relating to protection of the environment or the working environment, subject to notification to and approval by the Commission. The provision subverts the traditional doctrine of preemption under Article 100, because it envisages that even after the adoption of a Community rule, Member States may depart from that norm, albeit after a specified Commission management procedure, in a way which may lead to persisting market segregation. Does Article 100a(4) recognise the agreement to disagree as a Community act?

The political, imprecise flavour of Article 100a(4) allowed discussion of its precise scope of application.[39] Is it, for example, open to all states or only to outvoted states? Some pragmatists urged a generous approach to its invocation as an inducement to states to agree to measures in Council; it was after all the absence of such agreement, pre-Single European Act, which had brought the Community to stagnation. More interestingly, one's preferred interpretation of Article 100a(4) may in part reflect one's constitutional standpoint. A view which is wedded to classic preemption would maintain that Article 100a(4), perceived by most commentators with gloom as formalising an alarming retreat

---

[38] Curtin (1993) 30 CML Rev 17.
[39] See, *e.g.* Ehlermann (1987) 24 CML Rev 361; Flynn *ibid* 689.

in the *acquis communautaire* in yielding competence to States even post-harmonization, can be invoked only in strictly limited circumstances. By contrast, a view which is more sceptical about the feasibility/desirability of classic preemption, and more sanguine about the value of national competence to act, even in fields where the Community too has acted, would tend towards a more generous view of Article 100a(4). The provision would be regarded as reflective of the view that free trade is not automatically accepted as the overriding Community objective by the Member States where that may lead to a surrender of power to the Community to regulate the national market in pursuit of the objectives referred to in Article 100a(4). By undermining Community preemption, Article 100a(4) establishes within the Treaty the legitimate importance of national regulatory measures within the Community legislative framework; shared competence.

The academic who makes a living out of observing what happens when a spanner is thrown into the works will regret that the Court has never had the chance to display its notion of the constitutional relationship between Community and Member State competence in the specific context of determining how Article 100a(4) operates. Article 100a(4) has been invoked very infrequently[40] and has never been the subject of litigation. That fact is in itself of interest. Pescatore was the sternest critic of the "verbose vagueness" of the Single European Act[41] but the gloom which greeted Article 100a(4)'s rupture of the *acquis communautaire* on preemption can now be placed in context. True, only extended empirical examination of Council practice would reveal how the availability of recourse to Article 100a(4) has affected negotiation, but at least the infrequency with which Article 100a(4) has been formally invoked suggests that the political will of the Member States, and the momentum of 1992, has kept the Community structure more or less intact and that shared competence is not destructive of progress in the Community. Ultimately the most remarked on practical consequence of Article 100a has been the clearing of the air caused by opportunities for qualified majority voting in Council following the abandonment of the practice of unanimity, not the differentiation offered by Article 100a(4).

Minimum harmonization

Minimum harmonization found a place in the Treaty after the amendments effected by the Single European Act. The new Article 130t provided that "The [environmental] protective measures adopted . . . shall not prevent any Member State from maintaining or introducing more stringent measures compatible with this Treaty." Article 118a(3) applies a similar formula to protection of working conditions. The minimum harmonization technique is also to be found in a

---

[40] For comment see Kramer (1993) 30 CML Rev 125, 133.
[41] (1987) 24 CML Rev 9.

wide range of individual Directives, adopted before and after the Single European Act "constitutionalised" the technique in some areas of Community legislative competence. In the field of consumer protection, for example, the minimum harmonization formula is familiar.[42] Directive 84/450, relating to the approximation of national laws concerning misleading advertising,[43] provides in Article 7 that the Directive does not preclude the application of provisions of "more extensive protection". Directive 85/577, regulating the protection of the consumer in respect of contracts negotiated away from business premises ("doorstep selling"),[44] makes a similar concession in Article 8. Stricter controls are not excluded by such Directives, although they must conform to Article 30.

The Treaty on European Union agreed at Maastricht lends further prominence to the technique of minimum harmonization. The new Title on Consumer Protection provides in Article 129a(3) EC that "Action adopted [by the Council] pursuant to paragraph 2 shall not prevent any Member State from maintaining or introducing more stringent protective measures. Such measures must be compatible with this Treaty. The Commission shall be notified of them."[45] At Edinburgh in December 1992, the Conclusions of the Presidency declared a yet deeper commitment to the technique; ". . . where it is necessary to set standards at Community level, consideration should be given to setting minimum standards, with freedom for Member States to set higher standards, not only in the areas where the treaty so requires . . . but also in other areas where this would not conflict with the objectives of the proposed measure or with the Treaty."

Minimum harmonization is plainly an element in a strategy of emphasising a lighter regulatory touch by the Community and of showing deeper sensitivity to national regulatory initiatives. In the field of environmental policy, characterised by the minimum harmonization formula under Article 130t, Kramer describes a "system of shared competence . . . set up under the Treaty [which] aims at optimising protection."[46] Both states and the Community share responsibilities even after the Community has acted, whereas rigid preemption would dictate that the Community obtains exclusive competence in a field in which it has acted. The technique confronts the risk of the unregulated market, where the Community preempts State competence without fully having the capacity to act in replacement, by admitting that regulatory competence rests with the Member States as well as the Community, even after the Community has acted in a field.

Minimum harmonization too may mean an agreement to disagree. Just as Pescatore was critical of the fragmenting effect of Article 100a(4), so Taschner has referred to minimum harmonization evading the inconvenience of reaching agreement.[47] It is certainly true that minimum harmonization does not comply

---

[42] Mortelmans, 'Minimum harmonization and consumer law' (1988) ECLJ 2.

[43] OJ 1984 L250/17.

[44] OJ 1985 L372/31.

[45] Discussed by Weatherill and Micklitz, 'Consumer Policy in the EC before and after Maastricht' (1993) 16 JCP forthcoming.

[46] (1993) 30 CML Rev 111, 114.

[47] See discussion by Kramer, *EEC Consumer Law* (1986) paras 84–88.

with "classic" notions of preemption, because the field in which the Community acts becomes subject to shared occupation, by the Community rule and, potentially, by stricter Member State rules. Yet, precisely because the minimum harmonization formula envisages the setting of a Community rule which will not totally replace national tradition, it appears the only way to secure agreement on Community intervention in a field where States will not give up their competence to set stricter standards. Minimum harmonization is simply realistic in a heterogenous Community where States are unwilling to permit a deterioration in their standards despite the pursuit of common Community rules. Moreover, although potentially detrimental to market integration, it respects the role of national regulatory initiatives within the framework of Community legislative activity.

Minimum harmonization emphasises the continuing importance of Court of Justice scrutiny under Articles 30–36. Previously, these provisions used to be important where the Community had not acted in a field, irrelevant where it had. Under minimum harmonization they apply even where the Community has acted, where the State decides to use its room for manoeuvre by introducing stricter rules. Whereas, under old-style preemption, the Community rule provided both floor and ceiling, now, under minimum harmonization, the rule provides the floor but Articles 30–36 provide the ceiling. Directive 85/577 on "doorstep selling",[48] introduces a harmonised Community-wide regime which will permit the consumer a minimum seven-day period in which to withdraw from a contract concluded in such circumstances, but in *Buet* v *Ministère Public*[49] the Court, following the Directive's minimum status, ruled that the applicability of a French law which went so far as to prohibit "doorstep selling" of educational material was not excluded by the Directive, nor was it incompatible with Article 30 of the Treaty, despite its restrictive effect on cross-border trade. The reference in the *Cassis de Dijon* formula to "in the absence of common rules . . . it is for the Member States to regulate [subject to the requirements of Article 30]" may increasingly have to be recast as "even in the presence of common rules . . .."

The wider pattern of regulation

Constitutionally, something rather significant is happening here. Under classic preemption the Community sets the rules and individual rights to the pursuit of free trade enforceable against States arise thereunder. Those rights, typically enjoyed by traders, are qualified under a minimum harmonization formula, as the "automaticity" of free trade consequential on preemption diminishes. Article 100a(4) was a step along this road; the minimum harmonization formula is more fully realised in the sense that the opportunities for its invocation are subject to fewer restrictions. Both Article 100a(4) and minimum harmonization

---

[48] *Supra*, n 44.
[49] Case 328/87 [1989] ECR 1235.

demonstrate an increasing recognition that Community legislative activity is multi-functional. It promotes free trade, but it also recognises the legitimate role played by national regulation within the Community framework of market regulation. National regulation can no longer be taken simply as an obstruction to Community market integration, as an awkward interruption to preemption. National authorities now become a key part of the *Community* institutional structure.

Economic rights to integration, enforceable by traders, are adjusted because these rights are increasingly qualified by the development of rights to regulation, whether in the fields of consumer protection, worker protection, (the practical relevance of which *Francovich* provides a good example,) or environmental protection, all of which are "constitutionalised" in Titles separate from Article 100a. The structure of *Community* law, even after legislative intervention under Articles 100/100a, recognises not just market liberalization and not just Community regulation, but also the proper role of *national* initiatives in regulating the internal market. Via minimum harmonization and differentiated integration, we are seeing a new legal concept of the internal market, in which national responsibilities to citizens are not simply tolerated, but instead accepted within a Community framework of shared responsibilities for market regulation.[50] Articles 8a and 100a(1), with their emphasis on free trade, must be read alongside (not above) other provisions of the Treaty which emphasise regulated trade – regulated by Community, national, regional and local authorities.

If this describes a process whereby the proper contours of national identity within a common market may become visible, it may serve to reassure all citizens of the appeal of the Community enterprise, not just the minority actively involved in trading across borders. It could be rather more attractive than the counterproductive idea of Citizenship of the Union, which – admittedly because it was misunderstood[51] – repelled the Danes; and which – because it was all too well understood – leaves many non-EC Europeans simultaneously frustrated and incensed by its presumption.

Subsidiarity

Too much has already been written about the principle of Subsidiarity for extended analysis to be justified here.[52] However, it deserves brief attention, for it too has been represented as an attempt to give practical shape to the general perception that the structure of EC policy making requires adjustment, specifically in respect of competence allocation, and, moreover, it too has aroused fears that the process may undermine the *acquis communautaire* and cause

---

[50] So the regulation of the internal market is not a matter of exclusive Community competence; *contra*, vigorously, Toth (1992) 29 CMLRev 1079 esp 1094.

[51] Weatherill and Beaumont, *EC Law* (1993) 774–779.

[52] See Toth, 'A legal analysis of subsidiarity', Steiner, 'Subsidiarity under the Maastricht Treaty', Emilou, 'Subsidiarity: panacea or fig leaf?' in this volume at 37, 49 and 65 respectively.

a fragmentation of the EC legal order. Toth stands as the critic of subsidiarity from this perspective in the same way as Pescatore criticised Article 100a(4) and Taschner criticised minimum harmonization.[53]

Formally, Article 3b seems justiciable as a competence threshold to Community action, which must be crossed before the Community can go on to find a specific Treaty base on which to legislate. Article 3b would confine the Community's competence to legislate, theoretically even under Article 235. The Article 3b threshold, enforced through an Article 173 application for annulment, could be an attractive protection for a State outvoted under a qualified majority base. It is, however, hard to see how the principle of subsidiarity adds anything to the legal issue. It can be predicted that, assuming an adequate (for the purposes of Article 190) explanation of the reasons why Community competence in the light of Article 3b is asserted, the Court will not find the Community to have acted *ultra vires*. To this extent, one may expect that the Court will effectively ensure that the assembly of sufficient political support for a measure in Council will be enough as a matter of institutional practice to ensure it falls within the Community's *vires*.This has been the case in the past under Articles 100 and 235, although admittedly thereunder States enjoy the protection of the unanimity requirement. In a combative contribution to the Delors Colloquium in 1991, Lord Mackenzie Stuart focused on the principle's lack of legal precision in expressing fears about the Court's credibility if it engaged in active application of the subsidiarity principle as a legal norm.[54] Judicial reluctance to interfere with the limits of Community competence set by the political institutions remains the best guess. Whatever its political impact, Article 3b is not the *legal* rule which will, at last, provide a brake on expanding Community competence.

It is submitted that although subsidiarity may act as a useful starting point for debate about competence allocation, it cannot by itself resolve any such debate. It lacks precision beyond its role as shorthand for concern about the Problem of Competence. In fact subsidiarity, like Article 100a(4) before it and the Social Policy Protocol after it, was a deliberately obscure notion designed to facilitate agreement among the Member States. It would not have done its job had reservoirs of academic and journalistic ink *not* been spilt on its behalf.

The message is that subsidiarity is open-ended in its impact on the allocation of competence. It is, as Sir Leon Brittan has observed, about fixing the "best level" for action.[55] It does not make assumptions about protecting State "sovereignty". In some circumstances, it may point to renationalization – where efficiency so dictates. In other circumstances, it may have precisely the opposite impact, as a Community-enabling provision – where efficiency so dictates. Sir Leon made this point vividly, and perhaps mischievously, in his evidence to the House of Commons Foreign Affairs Select Committee in March 1993, when he proposed the pursuit of Economic and Monetary Union among the Member States as an application of the principle of subsidiarity, in view of

---

[53] (1992) 29 CML Rev 1079.
[54] *Subsidiarity: the Challenge of Change* (1991).
[55] (1992) *Public Law* 567, 574.

its contribution to reducing costs and increasing stability.[56] A well-balanced portrayal of subsidiarity was provided at the Edinburgh European Council in December 1992, where the Conclusions of the Presidency included the statement that "subsidiarity is a dynamic concept and should be applied in the light of the objectives set out in the Treaty. It allows Community action to be expanded where circumstances so require, and conversely, to be restricted or discontinued where it is no longer justified."

Once it is appreciated that subsidiarity cuts both ways, its legal or political value as a solution diminishes. In a climate of concern about the suppression of the contribution of national and local experience to the development of the Community, which has fuelled a resistance to transfer of powers, subsidiarity would be welcome were it to generate a creative debate about competence allocation in the Community. Regrettably, the evidence that it may help to sharpen the debate is not encouraging. Subsidiarity seems to have joined federalism on the list of terminology, unharmonised and culturally unharmonisable, which confuses rather than clarifies.

If its elevation to a significant legal rule seems unfeasible, subsidiarity will (or has) become part of the political fabric of the Community's institutional structure. The Commission submitted a report to the Edinburgh European Council in which it reviewed existing and proposed legislation in the light of the subsidiarity principle. The question arises, how far subsidiarity is an excuse for jettisoning issues found to be too tricky or too politically controversial, rather than really forming part of a principled review of the limits of Community intervention required to achieve the objectives of the Treaty. At present subsidiarity seems a rather blunt instrument for making decisions about the Problem of Competence. Its essentially political context was emphasised at Edinburgh by the plan to draw up an inter-institutional agreement on its application. That immediately suggests that it will sink into the intransparent culture of the Community's political infighting, emerging as an excuse rather than as an explanation and doing little to appeal to the citizen.

Competition between regulators

This analysis has attempted to present a positive perspective on the adjustment of established constitutional principles. In a Community of, say, 20 Member States, traditional preemption leading to exclusive Community competence would be both unfeasible (the rules could not be agreed) and undesirable (because of the suppression of diversity). Reich[57] points out that, the wider the Community's competence, the less exclusive its jurisdiction, the deeper the "interbrand" competition between legal orders. In an expanding heterogenous Community, regulatory competition is irresistibly on the rise. Subsidiarity is a

---

[56] HC 642-II 213.

[57] (1992) 29 CML Rev 895; also developed by Joerges, *European Economic Law, the Nation-state and the Maastricht Treaty* in Dehousse (ed), *The European Union Treaty* (1993).

slogan for this. More concretely, minimum harmonization acts as a technique for establishing a Community framework as a base, within which diversity can be accommodated – and managed, in a process of competitive improvement. Community and Member States share in the regulatory process, a realistic reflection of a growing heterogeneity which precludes old-style preemption. The constitution is changing, not collapsing, in pursuit of the construction of a general theory of "workable" competition between public regulators, to control the process of regulatory competition.

Much more dangerous is the treatment at Maastricht of the UK's position in relation to Social Policy. It is not necessary here to delve into the complex legal arguments surrounding the nature of the Social Policy Protocol, where there is indeed doubt whether it is *Community* law at all.[58] It is a further example of the Community being unable to progress according to a common Community model, yet it goes far beyond the matters discussed above, for it envisages a State playing no part in whole blocks of Community common policy making. The Protocol is not an attempt to manage diversity within a basic Community framework in the manner of minimum harmonization. It arises from objections to the existence of a Community framework. It does not share competence, it denies it. It envisages a particular State competing against other States outside the control of even a minimum Community rule. This is a very serious matter from the perspective of the cohesiveness of the Community legal order and the fulfilment of the objectives in, *inter alia*, Articles 2 and 3 of the Treaty.

The background perception lies in a scepticism whether the level playing field is in fact desirable and a preference for mutual recognition of divergent regulatory standards; home country control plus market freedom, with a distaste for a Community-imposed minimum. "Competition between regulators" will be driven by consumers of regulation – firms, the market – voting with their feet by corporate relocation. That market will lead to the efficient rule being "bought" and thus settled. The Social Policy field was a battleground for this ideology before, at and, doubtless will be so, after Maastricht. The United Kingdom has not succeeded in ensuring competition between all 12 regulators, but it believes that the Social Policy Protocol will allow it to compete against one other regulator in the market for consumers of regulatory regimes. That other regulator is the rest of the Community and already John Major has gleefully welcomed Hoover as a satisfied customer at the UK's bazaar.[59]

Regulatory competition is creeping out from behind the uniformity of preemption. It is submitted that where a Community rule has been set as a starting point, a floor, the process can be reconciled with the evolution of the Community. Where the Community is excluded from the field, the structure is fundamentally alien to the common market, for it implies a purely one-dimensional insistence on market access. Social Policy has not yet travelled the full distance down that road, but the Hoover affair provides a glimpse of the

---

[58] Curtin *supra*, n 38.
[59] See, bitterly, (1993) 30 CML Rev 445 (editorial).

operation of a market where even minimum Community standards are not uniform.

Managing fragmentation

It is far beyond the scope of this article to offer broad prescriptions for the future. It is a truism to say that much will rest with political will. However, it seems fundamental that the diversity which follows the decline of preemption implies a need for management of the process. This is certainly recognised. Fear of the process of fragmentation underlies the robust comments that States aspiring to Community membership will have to accept the full package, aside from the normal transitional period on accession, and will not have the luxury, afforded to some extent to existing members, to pick and choose from the Maastricht menu. The message at the moment is that Maastricht will not be a basis for accelerating fragmentation. Perhaps no would-be member will have the political clout to argue for special rules, but the process has a momentum of its own and it will be a surprise if Maastricht is not seen as having set some sort of precedent for further *à la carte* selection in imminent accession negotiation and, *a fortiori*, at the intergovernmental conferences of 1996.

The management of areas where the Community prefers to set minimum rules is already developing. A major pragmatic element in the management of minimum harmonization must involve notification to the Commission of rules introduced by Member States above the Community norm. Directive 83/189[60] made an important start in establishing such a system of notification. Notification requirements are increasingly being written into the Treaty. Commission management under Article 100a(4) was part of this agenda. In the Treaty on European Union, the minimum harmonization formula in Article 129a, the new Title on Consumer Protection, explicitly requires more stringent national measures to be notified to the Commission. The Treaty also amends Article 130t, concerning minimum harmonization in environmental protection, by explicitly requiring notification to the Commission of stricter rules. Notification allows the Commission to judge whether the Article 30 ceiling has been breached but also, where it has not, the notified higher national standard may provide the basis for improving the level set by the Community's own minimum standard. In this way national regulatory initiatives may provide a creative impulse in the continuing process of developing the Community's regulatory structure towards, *inter alia*, the high level of protection of the consumer and the environment referred to in Articles 129a and 130r EC respectively – a race to the ceiling. Only by abandoning exclusive Community competence in favour of shared competence can this desirable possibility be opened up, because previously, new standards could be introduced only after approval by the Community, a laborious process with an uncertainty of outcome which would inhibit investment in innovation.

---

[60] OJ 1983 L109/8.

The Court has, in Article 5 of the Treaty of Rome, a basis for directing the management of shared competence within the Community framework. Although the diminishing scope of the preemptive effect of Community law suggests a loosening of the Community structure, at the constitutional level decisions such as *Francovich* demonstrate the Court's readiness to preserve and enforce the impact of obligations accepted under Community law.[61] Article 5 provides the means for establishing that both Community and Member States share responsibilities for developing the Community market framework, which embraces responsibilities for both market integration and market regulation. Article 5 directs that once the Community has acted, States are responsible for furthering Community policy. The wider the Community competence; the deeper the impact of Article 5, an observation which is clearly pertinent in assessing the vitality of the extensions of Community competence attributable to the Treaty on European Union. The specific impact of Article 5 on national authorities varies according to competence distribution in the sector concerned,[62] but the key point is that Article 5 bridges the State/ Community gap by stressing the Community context in which national action occurs. This is well developed in relation to the role of the national judiciary, but it also applies to national administrative agencies.

Article 5 directs State authorities to co-operate with the Community institutions and States to co-operate with each other,[63] but Article 5 also draws Community institutions into support for national agencies responsible for application of Community law.[64] The Court's insistence that Article 5 binds Community institutions, not simply Member States, runs contrary to the specific words of the provision and demonstrates forcibly the broad policy role of Article 5 in drawing all relevant institutions into the job of effectively sustaining Community policy. In areas touched by Community competence, Member State and Community competence becomes ever more closely linked. Article 5 blurs the rigid competence division. No attempt is made here exhaustively to classify the use of Article 5 in developing shared competence; the impossibility of that task is in fact an indication of why Article 5 is brimming with potential for the future.

The Court's shaping of Article 5 into a general constitutional principle, far beyond its explicit wording, is emblematic of the Court's self-evolution into a general constitutional court possessed of inherent jurisdiction to ensure the observance of the rule of law in the Community, beyond the Treaty structure of enumerated powers.[65] This may be seen as a response to the fragmentation of Community law in that the Court itself is strengthening its own capacity to supervise the overall structure of the Community, just as, in a specific case of fragmentation, the Court has energetically controlled failure to implement Directives. Justification for the Court's activism lies in the overall aims of the Treaty – the constitutional rule of law.[66]

Accordingly, Article 5 is likely to be vigorously employed by the Court as a

---

[61] The intergovernmental/supranational dichotomy famously explored by Weiler *supra*, n 2.
[62] For a survey see Temple Lang (1990) 27 CML Rev 645.
[63] *e.g.* Case 272/80 *Biologische Producten* [1981] ECR 3277.
[64] *e.g.* Case C-2/88Imm *Zwartveld* [1990] ECR I-3365.
[65] *Cf* Arnull (1990) 27 CML Rev 683.
[66] *Cf* Mancini *supra*, n 2.

basis for an obligation to manage the varying patterns of integration so that the Community structure does not fragment. Where competence is shared, as under the minimum harmonization formula, this can readily take the concrete form of, for example, obligations to co-operate and notify. Critically, it is much more difficult to extend this idea into the fields of the "opt-outs", which represent a denial of Community competence. The Court may have to make a choice about how far it is prepared to go beyond supervising management of shared competence into the realm of invalidating denial of competence. This is a major test for the Court, in that it implies action to prevent a fragmentation of the Community structure on which the Member States have unanimously agreed. This is an enormous leap, yet it may be tested in the Social Policy field. Curtin has been especially fierce in attacking the Member States, as has Herren der Vertrage, for meddling with the Constitution, the charter of individual rights, and argues that where the *acquis communautaire* is violated, Treaty amendments may be held unconstitutional.[67] Opinion 1/91[68] surprised many with its assertiveness in this direction, but this would be several steps further. The Court would risk a loss of legitimacy – yet politicians who have littered the Treaty with remnants of their own inability to settle disagreement and who have played fast and loose with individual constitutional rights could hardly claim the high moral or legal ground.

Conclusion

The overall policy question which underlies this article asks whether the EC is fragmenting or evolving. It is a theme which can be traced through many areas, including options in individual Directives, Article 100a(4), minimum harmonization, subsidiarity, and the variable structures of EMU and the Social Policy Protocol in the Treaty on European Union. There are unavoidable pressures for flexibility which arise out of the diversity of national experience and tradition among the Member States, yet there remains a need to locate these adjustments within an overall, workable Community framework. The Maastricht Treaty in no sense solves these problems. If anything it sets up more battlegrounds, such as the legality of the Social Policy Protocol and the opportunity for constitutional challenge under Article 3b.

The objective of accommodating diversity within a useful, albeit often loose, agreement is familiar in the law and practice of international treaties. States may, for example, be permitted to make reservations to an international treaty, which modify the effect on that State of provisions of the treaty, thereby accommodating diversity of aspiration within a viable overall structure. This pattern appears increasingly appealing to the Member States of the Community. Yet, there must come a point where the process becomes an agreement to disagree, in which the breadth of participation undermines the depth of commitments

---

[67] *Supra*, n 38; also Whiteford (1993) 18 EL Rev 202.
[68] *Supra*, n 4.

undertaken. In international law, this may arise as a legal point in determining the validity of a reservation.[69] This may prove analogous to the European Court's assessment of the validity of the Social Policy Protocol in the shadow of the question whether such arrangements deprive the Community of the *sui generis* constitutional foundation which sets it apart from more traditional treaties.

More generally, the international law comparison helps in identifying the consequences for the Community of pursuing the path of "opt-outs" as its version of the flexibility permitted by reservations to treaties. Shaw explains that "[t]he capacity of a state to make reservations to an international treaty illustrates the principle of sovereignty of states, whereby a state may refuse its consent to particular provisions so that they do not become binding upon it."[70] This notion of reservations, as the exercise of State sovereignty, poses direct questions for the structure of the Community, which has powers stemming from a limitation of sovereignty by the Member States in pursuit of more effective power exercised through the wider structure.[71] The opt-out as reservation, retaining national sovereignty and denying Community competence, may undermine the whole essence of the Community as a body to which powers have been transferred, in turn jeopardising the nature of the Community's uniform legal order.

Where is the momentum? At present, the Community seems to be in danger of limping from one intergovernmental conference to the next, with key decisions increasingly drifting out with the established Community structure, circumventing the Court. How long must we wait until the Community becomes a state not just a market?

STEPHEN WEATHERILL

---

[69] Vienna Convention on the Law of Treaties 1969, Arts 19–21; Bowett, 'Reservations to non-restricted multilateral treaties' (1976–77) 48 BYIL 67.

[70] Shaw, *International Law* 3rd ed (1991) 571.

[71] Case 6/64 *Costa* v *ENEL* [1964] ECR 585.

Part 2

Subsidiarity

Chapter 3
A Legal Analysis of Subsidiarity

Introduction

It is no exaggeration to say that there are few concepts in the Maastricht Treaty, or indeed in Community law as a whole, which are more elusive than the concept of subsidiarity. This was clearly demonstrated in 1992 when President Jacques Delors offered a prize to anyone who could define subsidiarity. I am not sure if anybody succeeded, but certainly it is not the purpose of my article to try to win that prize. On the contrary, my aim is to show that subsidiarity, at least as it appears in the Maastricht Treaty, presents a number of legal pitfalls and ambiguities which, in spite of the rapidly growing literature on the subject,[1] have not been clarified so far. It is therefore entirely correct to say that subsidiarity is one of the many "unresolved" legal issues of the Maastricht Treaty.

I wish to make it clear that I intend to adhere strictly to the title of my article, which is: *a legal analysis* of subsidiarity. I do not wish to enter the debate as to whether it is a politically useful, appropriate, or even necessary part of the Maastricht package; nor do I seek to explore the origins and history of subsidiarity and its role in other contexts, for example, in the context of federal constitutions. I simply start from the fact that it has been incorporated in the Maastricht Treaty and is therefore (or will become upon ratification) a binding provision with legally relevant consequences. It is these consequences that I intend to examine, highlighting some of the obscure aspects of subsidiarity which in my opinion have not been sufficiently addressed so far.

Subsidiarity in the Maastricht Treaty

As is well known, the principle itself appears in Article 3b of the amended EC Treaty. It has not been formally incorporated in the ECSC and Euratom Treaties, nor in the provisions on a Common Foreign and Security Policy, nor – with one exception[2] – in the provisions on co-operation in the fields of justice and home affairs.

---

[1] Of the most recent literature, see *e.g.* Cass, 'The word that saves Maastricht? The principle of subsidiarity and the division of powers within the European Community' (1992) 29 CML Rev 1107; Constantinesco, 'Who's afraid of subsidiarity?' (1991) 11 YEL 33; Emiliou, 'Subsidiarity: an effective barrier against 'the enterprises of ambition'?' (1992) 17 EL Rev 383; Toth, 'The principle of subsidiarity in the Maastricht Treaty' (1992) 29 CML Rev 1079. See also Emiliou, 'Subsidiarity: panacea or fig leaf?' and Steiner, 'Subsidiarity under the Maastricht Treaty' in this volume at 65 and 49 respectively.
[2] Art K.3(2)(b) TEU.

On the other hand, there are references to subsidiarity in the Preamble and in Articles A and B of the Treaty. In particular, Article B seems to make subsidiarity applicable across the whole Union Treaty. However, these provisions are more in the nature of political statements, declarations of intent, rather than provisions with precise legal effects. For example, it is clear that the statements in the Preamble and Article A that the principle of subsidiarity is to ensure that "decisions are taken as closely as possible to the citizen" can have no legal effect in Community law. Surely, the question at what level decisions are taken within the Member States, whether at the level of the central, regional or local government, is a matter for national law to regulate in which Community law cannot interfere. Subsidiarity can only determine whether decisions should be taken at the Community or national level, no more. Moreover, since the jurisdiction of the European Court of Justice (hereinafter the Court of Justice or the Court) does not extend to the Preamble and Titles I, V and VI,[3] the principle of subsidiarity is not justiciable before the Court except in so far as it has been incorporated in the EC Treaty.[4]

Turning now to Article 3b itself, it is a more complex legal provision than it might appear at first sight. In fact, it contains not one but three distinct – although closely related – legal concepts.

The first concept, which appears in the first paragraph, is the principle of attribution of powers or the principle of conferred powers, which states that the Community can act only within the limits of the powers conferred upon it by the Treaty. This, of course, has been a basic tenet of the Community legal system from the beginning.

The second concept, appearing in the second paragraph, is the principle of subsidiarity itself, which means, in its briefest formulation, that the Community should only take action where an objective can be better achieved at the level of the Community than at the level of the individual Member States.

The third concept, incorporated in the third paragraph, is the principle of proportionality, which has been developed in the jurisprudence of the Court of Justice and according to which action by the Community shall not go beyond what is necessary to achieve the objectives of the Treaty.

One important thing to remember is that, although clearly interrelated, the three principles are legally distinct and should be kept apart. Unfortunately, there seems to be a tendency in the various documents prepared by the Commission and the European Council, to which I shall come back later, to confuse subsidiarity and proportionality in spite of the fact that the two principles have different origins, scope of application and legal effects.

Another important thing to note about the second paragraph of Article 3b, in particular, is that the principle of subsidiarity cannot create or confer competences (*i.e.* jurisdiction) on the Community – it can only be used to allocate the exercise of competences which have already been created by

---

[3] See Art L TEU subject to one exception: Art K.3(2)(c).
[4] See also the Conclusions of the Presidency on Subsidiarity, adopted at the Edinburgh European Council of 11–12 December 1992, Annex 1 to Part A, Bull EC 12–1992, 9 at 14.

other provisions of the Treaty. Article 3b therefore cannot serve as a legal basis for a Community act on its own, although, as we shall see later, it will play a part in determining the proper legal basis.

The scope of application of subsidiarity: exclusive and non-exclusive competence

If we now try to analyse Article 3b(2) further, it seems that the interpretation and application of the subsidiarity principle as defined in that article gives rise to three major problems. These are as follows.

The first, and most difficult, but at the same time perhaps least explored, problem arises from the fact that the principle is expressly stated to apply only "in areas which do not fall within [the Community's] exclusive competence". In other words, subsidiarity applies only in areas which fall within the Community's non-exclusive competence (sometimes the terms "concurrent" or "shared" competence are also used to indicate that in these areas competence is shared between the Community and the Member States).

Here the problem is that neither the original EEC Treaty nor the Maastricht Treaty makes any explicit distinction between "exclusive" and "non-exclusive" competence and the areas and matters which fall within each. Such a distinction, which is well known in federal constitutions,[5] was first introduced into Community law by the Commission's "Report on European Union" of 1975[6] (which was also the first document ever to mention subsidiarity in the context of Community law), and the distinction was later taken up by the European Parliament's draft Treaty on European Union of 1984.[7]

However, such a distinction is totally alien to, and contradicts the logic of, the structure and the actual wording of the original EEC Treaty as well as the whole jurisprudence of the Court of Justice. In fact, the division of competences between the Community and the Member States under the EEC Treaty is based on entirely different principles. The Court has confirmed time and again, in numerous decisions dealing with a wide variety of matters (such as treaty-making, tariff and commercial policy, fisheries, the common organization of the agricultural markets, free movement of goods and persons, etc) that in all matters transferred to the Community from the Member States, the Community's competence is, in principle, exclusive and leaves no room for any concurrent competence on the part of the Member States. Therefore, where the competence of the Community begins, that of the Member States ends. From then on, Member States no longer have the power unilaterally to introduce legislation. They can only act within the limits of strictly defined management/implementing powers delegated back to the national authorities by the Community institutions. As the Court of Justice has stated: "The existence of Community

[5] See *e.g.* Art 72 of the German Basic Law.
[6] Bull EC Supp 5/75.
[7] Art 12. OJ 1984 C77/53, text at C77/33.

powers excludes the possibility of concurrent powers on the part of the Member States".[8] Even the fact that during a certain period the Community fails to exercise a competence which has been transferred to it, does not create concurrent competence for the Member States during that period.[9] This principle also follows from, or is closely related to, the doctrine of the supremacy of Community law,[10] which of course is a basic tenet of Community law.

If this is so, the first conclusion that may be drawn is that, since:

(1) Article 3b expressly excludes the application of the principle of subsidiarity from areas falling within exclusive Community competence;
(2) the original EEC Treaty does not distinguish between areas falling within exclusive and those falling within non-exclusive competence; and
(3) according to the caselaw of the Court, the Community's competence is necessarily exclusive over all matters "pertaining to the pursuit of the common objectives",[11]

it follows that the principle of subsidiarity as defined in Article 3b cannot apply to any matter covered by the original EEC Treaty. Otherwise, the decision-making power which, according to the jurisprudence of the Court, has been definitively and irreversibly renounced by the Member States in favour of the Community, would be handed back to the Member States, which would be a major step backwards in the process of European integration.

This conclusion may seem a little surprising and far-fetched at first sight. However, it would appear that the Commission itself has arrived, in substance, at a similar conclusion, albeit by a different route and for different reasons. I am referring to the paper which the Commission sent to the Council and the European Parliament in October 1992 on the principle of subsidiarity.[12] In that paper, the Commission points out the absence of a clear demarcation line between exclusive and shared powers and states, among other things, that:

"Since the Treaty does not define the notion of exclusive competence or list the areas covered, it is for the institutions, and in the first place the Commission, to agree on a common approach to avoid endless demarcation disputes between exclusive competence and shared competence ...".[13]

Then, upon analysing the EEC Treaty, the Commission recognises the existence of what it calls a "block of exclusive powers joined by the common thread of an internal market". These exclusive Community powers cover, according to the Commission, the following areas and matters:

---

[8] Case 22/70 *Commission* v *Council* [1971] ECR 263 at 276 (*ERTA* case). See also Opinion 1/75 *Local Cost Standard* [1975] ECR 1355 at 1364.
[9] Case 804/79 *Commission* v *United Kingdom* [1981] ECR 1045 at 1072–76, dealing with the adoption of conservation measures as part of the Common Fisheries Policy.
[10] Particularly as it is formulated in Case 106/77 *Simmenthal* [1978] ECR 629 at 643.
[11] Case 30/59 *Steenkolenmijnen* v *High Authority* [1961] ECR 1 at 22, dealing with state aids and subsidies under the ECSC Treaty.
[12] Bull EC 10–1992, 116.
[13] *Ibid* at 120.

40

- the removal of barriers to the free movement of goods, persons, services and capital;
- the Common Commercial Policy;
- the rules on competition;
- the common organization of agricultural markets;
- the conservation of fishery resources and the common organization of the fishery markets;
- the Transport Policy.[14]

This is not an exhaustive and definitive list, but even as it is it seems to cover just about all the essential areas of the original EEC Treaty. The result is the same as the conclusion which I have reached: the principle of subsidiarity cannot apply to any matter covered by the EEC Treaty.

If we now turn to the Single European Act and the Maastricht Treaty, it is well known that these have added a number of new policy areas to those already covered by the EEC Treaty. These include:

- environmental policy;
- economic and social cohesion;
- education, vocational training, youth, culture and public health;
- consumer protection;
- trans-European networks;
- industry;
- research and technological development;
- development co-operation
- Social Policy.[15]

In most of these new areas the powers of the Community are restrictively defined, and it is apparent from the language used in the relevant articles that the new Treaties did not intend to confer exclusive competence on the Community. Nevertheless, this does not mean that the principle of subsidiarity may be applied to these new policy areas without difficulty. One problem is that many of these so-called "flanking policies" are inextricably linked with the internal market and also with one another. Thus, Article 100a of the EEC Treaty envisages that the Community will pursue health, safety, environmental and consumer protection objectives through harmonization measures relating to the establishment and functioning of the internal market. Since, as we have just seen, the development of the internal market is within exclusive Community competence, at least those aspects of health, safety, environmental and consumer protection policies which are connected with the internal market must fall within the Community's exclusive competence and therefore outside the scope of application of subsidiarity.

This also necessarily follows from the very concept of the internal market which involves the creation of a level playing field in which conditions of competition are the same for all. In other words, legislation imposing heavy financial burdens on manufacturers and traders – such as legislation implementing

---

[14] *Ibid* at 121.
[15] See Arts 21–25 of the Single European Act and Arts 126–130Y of the EC Treaty as amended by the Maastricht Treaty.

health, safety, environmental and consumer protection policies – must come from the Community and must be the same for all Member States.

But is it possible to separate those aspects of these policies which are connected with the development of the internal market from those which are not, without fragmenting the policies to the extent that they become unworkable? In other words, is it possible to apply the principle of subsidiarity to certain aspects only of these policies but not to others? This is clearly a difficulty which has been given very little consideration so far, but which has to be resolved before the principle can be applied to the new policies.

The problem outlined above is well illustrated by the Court's decision in the *Titanium dioxide* case.[16] That case involved an action brought by the Commission for the annulment of Council Directive 89/428 on procedures for harmonising the programmes for the reduction and eventual elimination of pollution caused by waste from the titanium dioxide industry. In the opinion of the Commission, the Directive lacked a valid legal basis in that it was based on Article 130s of the EEC Treaty (relating to the environment), whereas it should have been based on Article 100a (dealing with the establishment and functioning of the internal market).

The Court held that the Directive was "indissociably" concerned with both the protection of the environment and the elimination of disparities in conditions of competition which was a necessary precondition for the establishment and functioning of the internal market. However, according to Article 130r(2) of the Treaty, environmental protection was to be made a component of the Community's other policies. This requirement implied, the Court said, that a Community measure could not be covered by Article 130s merely because it also pursued objectives of environmental protection, which objectives could be effectively pursued by means of harmonising measures adopted under Article 100a. Such harmonization measures were also necessary to avoid distortion of competition which otherwise could arise from the financial burdens which environmental legislation might impose on certain undertakings. Therefore, the Court concluded that the Directive in question should have been based on Article 100a rather than Article 130s, and annulled it as illegal for that reason.

Admittedly, this case did not raise issues of subsidiarity directly.[17] Nevertheless, it does confirm the point which I have made earlier, namely, that there are situations in which an environmental, health, etc policy measure, *prima facie* governed by subsidiarity, is linked with other policies/objectives to such an extent that it has to be adopted on the basis of a Treaty article which covers an area falling within exclusive Community competence (*e.g.* the attainment of the internal market) and which therefore by definition excludes the application of the principle of subsidiarity.[18] Consequently, if in this case the main issue had been whether the Directive in question fell within the scope of subsidiarity, the

---

[16] Case C-300/89 *Commission* v *Council* [1991] ECR I-2867.

[17] The case was decided in June 1991, at a time when negotiations on the Maastricht Treaty were still in progress.

[18] See, however, Case C-155/91 *Commission* v *Council*, judgment of 17 March 1993, not yet reported, where the Court held that another environmental protection Directive (waste) was validly adopted on the sole basis of Art 130S.

Court would presumably have given a negative answer on grounds of exclusive competence generated by Article 100a, in spite of the fact that the directive was an environmental policy measure.

The application of subsidiarity in practice: the two tests

The second problem to which I have referred at the beginning arises from the way in which Article 3b determines the conditions which must be fulfilled before the subsidiarity principle may be applied. The problem here is that Article 3b lays down not one but two tests, both of which must be satisfied, which may lead to contradictory results. It provides in part that:

" ... the Community shall take action ... only if and in so far as the objectives of the proposed action cannot be sufficiently achieved by the Member States (the test of effectiveness or efficiency) and can therefore, by reason of the scale of effects of the proposed action, be better achieved by the Community" (the test of scale).

Although the two tests are clearly envisaged as two aspects of one and the same requirement (*i.e.* that something must be better achievable at the Community level to justify Community action), and therefore should lead to the same result, this is not necessarily always the case. Situations may be envisaged, particularly in the field of environmental protection, where the effectiveness test would require Community action whereas the scale test justifies national action, or vice versa.

The implementation of subsidiarity: practice and procedure

The third, but by no means the least difficult, problem is: who is to decide, and by what procedure, whether the principle of subsidiarity is applicable in individual cases? In the absence in the Maastricht Treaty of a clearly defined list of matters which are subject to the principle, and also in the absence of a decision-making mechanism for its application, these questions clearly require urgent solution.

This was recognised by the Member States at the Lisbon Summit in June 1992 when the European Council called on the Commission and the Council to look at the procedural and practical steps needed to implement the principle and to report back to the European Council in Edinburgh.[19]

The matter was again discussed at the Birmingham Special Summit in October 1992,[20] and was considered at length at the Edinburgh Summit the following December. At Edinburgh, three things happened. First, an agreement

---

[19] See Bull EC 6–1992, 8.
[20] See Bull EC 10–1992, 9.

was reached in the European Council on the overall approach to the application by the Council of the subsidiarity principle.[21] Secondly, the European Council invited the Council to seek an Inter-Institutional Agreement between the European Parliament, the Council and the Commission on the effective application of Article 3b by all institutions. At the same time, it welcomed a draft of an Inter-Institutional Agreement presented by the European Parliament.[22] Thirdly, the European Council received a report from the President of the Commission regarding the Commission's review of existing and proposed legislation in the light of the subsidiarity principle.[23]

The text produced by the European Council[24] is to some extent disappointing, particularly as regards the substantive issues.[25] For example, contrary to expectations, it contains very little on the most crucial question: what matters are covered by the subsidiarity principle (particularly in the original EEC Treaty), except stating the obvious by saying that it "does not apply to matters falling within the Community's exclusive competence".[26] Also, it tends to confuse, rather than clarify, the relationship between the three distinct and different principles set out in Article 3b, and in particular that between subsidiarity and proportionality.[27] As regards procedures and practices, it lays down the following rules to be followed by the institutions.[28]

First of all, given its right of initiative, the Commission is to play a crucial role in the implementation of Article 3b. The Commission is to consult more widely before proposing legislation, and the consultation should include the subsidiarity aspects of the proposal. The Commission is to justify, in a recital in the preamble to any new measures, the relevance of its initiative under the subsidiarity principle. This is an important requirement since Article 3b is worded in such a way ("the Community shall take action only if and in so far as . . . .") as to create a presumption in favour of Member State competence. This puts the burden of proof on the Community to justify its action. This recital will form part of the correct legal basis. The considerations of the Commission may be detailed in an explanatory memorandum attached to the proposal. The Commission will also monitor the observance of Article 3b and will submit an annual report to the European Council and the European Parliament through the General Affairs Council on the application of Article 3b.

On its part, the Council is required to examine every single Commission proposal, as well as its own amendment to such proposal, to see whether it complies with the subsidiarity principle. Such examination must form an inte-

---

[21] This is set out in Annex 1 to Part A of the Conclusions of the Presidency, see Bull EC 12–1992, 12.

[22] *Ibid* at 9.

[23] Examples of the Commission's review are set out in Annex 2 to Part A of the Conclusions of the Presidency, *ibid* at 16.

[24] *Supra* n 21.

[25] See, however, the editorial comments in (1993) 30 CMLRev 241 which generally welcome it as a 'text of substance'.

[26] Bull EC 12–1992, 14.

[27] This confusion goes back to the Commission's communication of 27 October 1992, which states that: 'The purpose of the subsidiarity principle is to give general application to the rule that the means should be proportional to the ends', Bull EC 10–1992, 122.

[28] Bull EC 12–1992, 15. These rules are without prejudice to a future Inter-Institutional Agreement.

gral part of the Council's decision-making procedure. Thus, the Council's decision on the subsidiarity aspects must be taken at the same time as the decision on the substance of the proposal and according to the same voting rules. Preliminary or parallel decision-making must be avoided. The examination will take place in the particular Council responsible for dealing with the matter, while the General Affairs Council will deal with general questions relating to the application of Article 3b. The Council must inform the European Parliament of its position concerning Article 3b in the context of the co-operation and the new co-decision procedures.[29]

As regards the form of legislation, the Guidelines adopted at Edinburgh[30] state that the Community should legislate only to the extent necessary. Where possible, Directives should be preferred to Regulations and framework Directives to detailed measures. Preference should be given, where appropriate, to non-binding measures such as recommendations and even voluntary codes of conduct. Likewise, preference should be given to the techniques of minimum standards and mutual recognition, to support programmes and programmes to co-ordinate national measures as opposed to harmonization of laws; also to co-operation between Member States accompanied by complementing, supplementing or supporting action by the Community. In other words, the application of subsidiarity will result in a general "loosening-up" of Community legislation and will possibly create a body of what is referred to as "soft-law".[31]

At the Edinburgh Summit, the Commission submitted examples of its review of existing and proposed legislation in the light of the subsidiarity principle.[32] It seems that the Commission has so far taken three kinds of action.

First, it has reviewed all proposals currently pending before the Council and Parliament and has either withdrawn or is considering withdrawing those which are not fully justified by the subsidiarity principle. These proposals cover a wide range of matters, such as food hygiene, animal welfare, radio frequencies, oil supplies, indirect taxation in different areas, various VAT matters, tax-free allowances, etc. The Commission has also concluded that certain pending proposals tend to go into excessive detail, and is planning to revise them so as to lay down general principles to be given more detailed form by the Member States. These include matters such as public takeover bids, advertising, labelling, liability of suppliers of services, data protection, etc.

Secondly, the Commission has identified several groups of existing rules and regulations which it intends to scrutinise in 1993. These cover such matters as technical standards, mutual recognition of qualifications, the environment, agriculture, animal welfare, etc. It also intends to codify and simplify the body of rules and regulations on the free movement of workers.

Thirdly, the Commission intends to abandon certain initiatives that it had planned. It will drop the harmonization of vehicle number plates, harmonization of certain technical standards and the regulation of gambling.

---

[29] Under the new Arts 189b and 189c of the EC Treaty.

[30] Bull EC 12–1992, 14.

[31] See also the Commission's communication of 27 October 1992, which justifies this development by interpreting subsidiarity as a general application of the principle of proportionality, see *supra*, n 27.

[32] *Supra*, n 23.

The Commission also intends to reject amendments proposed by the Council and Parliament which run counter to the subsidiarity principle.

Finally, the Commission indicated that it would carry out a full-scale review of existing legislation with a view to amending and adapting rules in accordance with the subsidiarity principle, as requested by the Lisbon Summit, and would submit a final report on the results to the European Council in December 1993.

Retroactivity

No-one can deny that some of the steps taken by the Commission are producing results which are desirable, reasonable and should generally be welcome. However, from a strict legal point of view, two questions arise.

First, even a cursory look at the subject-matters covered by the Commission's actions reveals that some – in fact, quite a few – of them fall within what is undoubtedly exclusive Community competence or within areas inextricably linked with the internal market which, as we have seen, comes within exclusive competence. How can these actions be justified by reliance on the subsidiarity principle which according to Article 3b does not apply to areas falling within exclusive competence?

The second question raises a much more serious issue, namely, the possible retroactive application of the subsidiarity principle. When the Commission says that it is reviewing, in accordance with the decision of the Lisbon Summit, existing legislation with a view to amending, adapting and possibly repealing acts of the institutions adopted in the past, that is nothing else than a retroactive application of subsidiarity. I myself have very grave doubts as to whether this is necessary, desirable or even possible for both legal and practical reasons.

From a legal point of view, I can find nothing in the Maastricht treaty which would enable the conclusion to be drawn that Article 3b(2) is intended to have retroactive effect. As a matter of both treaty law and Community law, retroactive application of a provision is only possible in very limited circumstances, and normally only when it is expressly spelt out. Moreover, if what I have said earlier is correct, all legislation adopted in the past under the EEC Treaty must necessarily have related to a matter falling within exclusive Community competence and therefore outside the scope of application of subsidiarity. This must be true even of measures adopted under Articles 100 and 235 and relating to such matters as consumer and environmental protection, which now fall within the "new" policy areas under the Maastricht Treaty. The reason is that both of those provisions authorise the adoption of measures only in so far as they are necessary to ensure the proper functioning of the common market – an area which is undoubtedly within exclusive Community competence. The very fact that the Council adopted a measure under either of those articles brought the subject-matter of the measure within exclusive competence and therefore removed it from the ambit of subsidiarity.

From a practical point of view, repealing or amending existing legislation under the pretext of subsidiarity would lead to highly undesirable results. It would mean relegating matters already brought within the scope of Community legislation – often as a result of very long and hard negotiations – as well as the power of supervision and enforcement relating to those matters, from Community to national competence. This could undermine the *acquis communautaire*, which according to the European Council's document should be preserved.[33] It would enable Member States to use subsidiarity to obtain repeal of (for them) inconvenient legislation on a *pick-and-choose* basis.[34]

Needless to say that any such retroactive repeal threatens to destroy hard-won achievements and would have extremely damaging effects, especially in the field of environmental legislation which is widely recognised as being one of those areas where only common action at the European/international level can be effective. Moreover, it may give rise to actions for damages under Article 215(2) EEC in respect of expenses which undertakings or Member States had to incur, for example to comply with environmental standards, which expenses would be rendered without legal basis.

Justiciability

One final question to be discussed is whether it is appropriate or advisable to involve the Court of Justice in deciding disputes arising from the application (or non-application) of the principle of subsidiarity. Most legal experts who have expressed an opinion on this question,[35] including such an eminent authority as Lord Mackenzie Stuart,[36] have come out very strongly against incorporating the principle in the EC Treaty (other than in the preamble) and against thereby making subsidiarity justiciable before the Court.

Yet, with the principle now forming part of the EC Treaty, its interpretation and application is subject to the jurisdiction of the Court in the same way as that of any other Treaty provision. This means that not only Community, but possibly also national, legislation will be open to challenge, at both Community and national levels, on the grounds that it infringes Article 3b. Such challenge may be made by Member States, Community institutions and private individuals, in both direct actions and preliminary ruling procedures, subject to the usual conditions of admissibility applicable to those actions and procedures. It is true that the conclusions of the Edinburgh Summit state that the principle of subsidiarity cannot have direct effect.[37] Even if this were true (and, given that this is a

---

[33] *Supra*, n 21, at 13.

[34] *The Times* reported on 7 August 1992 that Douglas Hurd, the British Foreign Secretary, had written to Cabinet colleagues asking them to draw up a list of EC laws that 'interfere unnecessarily with British sovereignty' with a view to repealing them. According to *The Times*, these were to include laws affecting animal welfare, food hygiene, the environment, workers' protection and the benefit system. As seen in the main text, the Commission has indeed withdrawn its proposals relating to some of these matters.

[35] See, in particular, House of Lords, Select Committee on the European Communities, Session 1989–90, 27th Report 'Economic and Monetary Union and Political Union', points 23–24, 165; *ibid*, Session 1990–91, 17th Report, 'Political Union. Law-making powers and procedures', points 52–62, 90–99, 122.

[36] See his contribution in: *Subsidiarity: the Challenge of Change*, proceedings of the Jacques Delors Colloquium organised by the European Institute of Public Administration, Maastricht (1991) at 37.

[37] *Supra*, n 21, at 14.

question of Treaty interpretation, only the Court of Justice has the power to decide whether this is true, not the European Council), it does not prevent individuals from challenging Community measures on subsidiarity grounds before national courts, and does not prevent national courts from requesting a preliminary ruling from the Court of Justice on the validity of those measures or on the interpretation of Article 3b itself with a view to testing the compatibility with it of a national legislative or administrative provision.

But the main question is: is the Court equipped to decide whether the objectives of a measure can be better achieved at the Community level than at the national level, or vice versa? This is clearly a political decision which only the political institutions can take. In the past, the Court has consistently refused to get involved in disputes of this kind by saying that these matters fall within the wide discretionary powers of the Council and the Commission which are subject to judicial review only to a limited extent.

In my opinion, it is to be expected that the Court will follow its previous practice also in the context of subsidiarity. Thus, the Court will be able to decide, on a purely legal analysis, that a matter falls within exclusive Community competence and is thus excluded from the principle's scope of application. However, in the opposite situation the Court will not be able or willing to go beyond the possible confirmation of the principle's applicability in general terms. It will not, and cannot, become the ultimate arbiter as to whether the principle of subsidiarity has been properly applied in a particular case (unless the Council or the Commission has committed a manifest error or a misuse of powers or has clearly exceeded the limits of its discretion). Otherwise, the Court would interfere with the legislative process by replacing the institutions' discretion with its own views. In any event, as we have seen, the Court will not be able to take into account the statements of the principle occurring in the Preamble and Title I of the Maastricht Treaty since those parts are excluded from the Court's jurisdiction.[38]

In conclusion, I would like to repeat what I said at the beginning. I have attempted to give a purely legal analysis of some of the least clarified aspects of subsidiarity. But I do not wish to go into the question whether its inclusion in the Maastricht Treaty has achieved, or is likely to achieve, its purpose, namely, to make the Treaty more acceptable to the peoples of Europe. Suffice it to say that I have my doubts.

A G TOTH

---

[38] Art L TEU.

Chapter 4
Subsidiarity under the Maastricht Treaty

Introduction

Despite the central importance of subsidiarity (established under the Maastricht Treaty 1991, and affirmed at the Edinburgh Summit in December 1992) as a guiding principle of Community law, the meaning and scope of this principle and its practical application are riddled with uncertainty. Discussion of the principle in the Community context, even before its incorporation into the Maastricht Treaty, reveal that it is capable of no less than 30 different meanings.[1] Designed to determine the appropriate level of action across the whole spectrum of public activity, international (in the widest sense), Community, national, regional and local,[2] it has been invoked in the Community context to assist in determining the appropriate allocation of powers as between the Community and its Member States,[3] and to control the exercise of Community powers. In this context it has been described, variously, as a principle of necessity,[4] of proportionality, of effectiveness,[5] an elementary principle of good government, or simply a principle of good sense.[6] It has been interpreted as meaning that the Community should only act:

1 where the objective cannot be achieved by regulation at national level;
2 where the objective can be better, or more effectively achieved, by action at Community level (the "efficiency by better results" criterion); or
3 where the matter in question can be more effectively regulated at Community level (the "administrative efficiency" criterion).

Furthermore, the principle of effectiveness contained in (2) and (3) can be interpreted with reference to specific criteria, that Community action is more

---

[1] Noted by Lord Mackenzie-Stuart, contribution to the Proceedings of the Jacques Delors Colloquium, *Subsidiarity and the Challenge of Change* (1991) at 39.
[2] The 'best level' principle, see Weatherill, *Subsidiarity and Responsibility* (University of Nottingham Research Paper 1992, 2).
[3] To the regret of many, who wished to see greater devolution to the regions, Art 3b EC applies only to the allocation of power as between the Community and Member States. Yet, as Emiliou points out 'Subsidiarity can only be understood and defined within the context of federalism'. See 'Subsidiarity, an effective barrier against enterprises of ambition?" 17 EL Rev (1992) 383. See also Emiliou, 'Subsidiarity: panacea or figleaf?', in this volume.
[4] The 'old meaning' see Cass 'The word that saved Maastricht: the principle of subsidiarity and the division of powers within the Community' 29 CML Rev (1992) 1107.
[5] See Santer, Delors, *Jacques Delors Colloquium, op cit*, n 1 at 17, 7; Cass, *supra*, n 4, noted the gradual watering down of the definition over three phases.
[6] Mackenzie-Stuart, *op cit*, n 1.

effective because of the scale, or cross border, or spillover effect of the matter subject to regulation; or simply in terms of administrative efficiency, in order to achieve improved "coherence".[7] The concept of cross border or spillover effect may itself be construed strictly, as meaning that the problem in question, because of its dimensions, cannot be dealt with effectively at national level, or broadly, as meaning that regulation at national level is undesirable because of its repercussions, or potential repercussions, on the single market.

If the principle of effectiveness is to be judged according to the weaker criteria of administrative efficiency or potential impact on the single market, its logic will inevitably operate in favour of increased centralization.[8] Even though many activities could be regulated (in the sense of problems dealt with) effectively at the national (or even at the regional or local) level, such regulation can interfere with the functioning of the single market, by:

(1) erecting barriers to the free movement of goods, persons, services and capital; or
(2) undermining competition within the Community by giving a competitive advantage to states with less rigorous standards.

However, the effectiveness principle must be set against another, different meaning of subsidiarity, its original, philosophical meaning, as a principle concerned with promoting social responsibility, a guarantee for individual liberty. In the words of Pope Pius XI:

"It is an injustice, a grave evil and disturbance of right order for a larger and higher association to arrogate to itself functions which can be performed efficiently by smaller and lower societies".[9]

In pursuit of this principle it is said that decisions affecting individuals should be made as closely as possible to the individual concerned.

This aspect of subsidiarity, at least as between the Community and Member States, was recognised, albeit not expressly, in the original EEC Treaty, which allowed for derogation, even from the basic Treaty freedoms, in order to preserve national autonomy in fundamental matters of public morality, public policy, public security and public health.[10] Under Article 235 the Community institutions were only empowered to act[11] where this was "necessary" in order to achieve Community objectives: the Directive itself has been cited as an example of the principle, although here it is only executive and administrative power, the "choice of form and methods" of implementation, which rests with

---

[7] Delors, *Jacques Delors Colloqium, op cit*, n 1 at 17.
[8] Noted by J S Mill *'Representative Government'* (1861) cited by Wilke & Wallace in 'Subsidiarity; approaches to power sharing in the European Community', Report for Royal Institute of International Affairs 1990, at 11, 14. Trend noted by Santer, with reference to Germany's experience (noting that the shift of power to the centre had come about 'slowly, gradually, according to efficiency demands') (*Proceedings of Jacques Delors Colloquium* 1991), at 21.
[9] Encyclical letter, *Quadragesimo Anno* (1931), cited originally in the Community context by Wilke & Wallace, *supra*, n 8 at 12.
[10] See *e.g.* Arts 36, 48(3) EEC.
[11] 'Where the Treaty has not provided the necessary powers'.

Member States: States have little discretion in matters of policy.[12] The principle can also be found in the Court of Justice's (hereinafter, the Court) jurisprudence, for example the *Cassis de Dijon*[13] "rule of reason", which allows States to derogate from the strict rules of Article 30 in order to protect certain "mandatory requirements",[14] and in the proportionality principle, adopted by the Court as a means of protecting individuals from excessive interference by public authorities.[15] Moreover, while opinions may differ as to the degree to which a "level" Community "playing field" is desirable, there is widespread agreement that certain matters should be left to Member States, even if they do affect competition in the single market. A totally level field, requiring harmonization of *ALL* matters relevant to the functioning of the single market has never been advocated,[16] nor does it exist in any mature federation.[17] With few exceptions, and regardless of the authors' integrationist leanings, references to subsidiarity point to the dangers of excessive centralization and the need to protect diversity.[18] Indeed it was the German *Länder*, which sought to invoke the principle as a means of preserving the competence of the regions against further encroachments of Community law,[19] threatened as a result of the Single European Act 1986, which rekindled the debate on subsidiarity and led to the incorporation of the principle at Maastricht.

Thus, it is clear that the principle of subsidiarity can be used, legitimately, both ways, to justify as well as to resist centralization. Moreover, given its chameleon quality, its capacity to "mean all things to all men", and the inherent conflict between criteria based on effectiveness and concern to foster social responsibility,[20] it is not surprising that it has been used, by pro- and anti-federalists alike, *sometimes in respect of the same issues*, to argue for, or against, Community, as opposed to national[21] regulation. The purpose of the present article is to examine, not the historical or theoretical aspects of subsidiarity, which have been fully documented elsewhere,[22] but its implementation by the Community under the Maastricht Treaty. Such examination seeks to discover, in the light of past interpretations and present needs, ways in which the principle may best be interpreted so as to respect and reconcile the needs of the Community, its Member States, and individual citizens. Although the principle clearly has an

---

[12] Noted by Toth 29 CML Rev (1992) 235.

[13] Case 120/78 [1979] ECR 649.

[14] Which include measures to protect national or regional socio-cultural characteristics (Case 145/88 *Torfaen BC v B&Q plc* [1989] ECR 3851), and to protect workers (Case 155/80 *Oebel* [1981] ECR 1993) and consumers (Case 120/78 *Cassis de Dijon, supra* n 13).

[15] Applied in the Community context to national as well as Community authorities see *e.g.* Case 118/75 *State v Watson & Belmann* [1976] ECR 1185.

[16] Indeed it has been suggested that 'variety in supply is a condition for economic competition. Europe derives no benefit or economic and political strength from uniformity' Hermann Hill, *Jacques Delors Colloquium, op cit* n 1 at 147.

[17] Where certain matters, particularly in the social domain, normally remain within the competence of states. See Wilke & Wallace *op cit* n 8 at 20, 29, 33, 34.

[18] *e.g.* Commission's draft report on European Union 1975, Supplement 5/75–Bull. EC; Draft Treaty on European Union OJ 1984, C 77/33; Delors, Santer, *Jacques Delors Colloquium op cit* n 1.

[19] Noted by Wilke & Wallace, *op cit,* n 8.

[20] Efficiency pulling towards centralisation, social responsibility against.

[21] Or regional or local, see comment *supra*, n 3.

[22] *e.g.* Wilke & Wallace, *op cit*, n 8; Cass (*supra*, n 4); Emiliou (*supra*, n 3), Weatherill (*supra*, n 2).

important role in determining questions of competence at the regional or local level,[23] such questions must, for reasons of time and space, lie outside the scope of this article.

Incorporation of subsidiarity principle in EC law

The principle of subsidiarity was incorporated expressly into EC law for the first time in the Single European Act 1986. Article 130r (4) EEC provides that:

"The Community shall take action relating to the environment to the extent to which the objectives referred to in paragraph 1 ('to preserve, protect and improve the quality of the environment, to contribute towards protecting human health, and to ensure a prudent and rational utilisation of natural resources') can be attained better at Community level than at the level of individual Member States."

Although the principle had been discussed in the Community context for some years, starting with the Commission's Report on European Union in 1975,[24] it is likely that the Parliament's draft Treaty on European Union, 1984,[25] provided the final spur to its introduction in the Single European Act. Article 12 (2) of the draft Treaty provided that:

"The Union shall only act to carry out those tasks which may be more effectively undertaken in common than by Member States acting separately, in particular those whose dimensions and effect extend beyond national frontiers" (para 1).

It may be noted that the subsidiarity principle was applied in the Single European Act only to matters relating to the environment, perhaps because it represented a cautious first step, perhaps because the "dimension" and spillover "effect" of many environmental problems so clearly justified a transfer of competence in these matters to the Community. It is therefore surprising that, unlike Article 12(2) of the draft Treaty,[26] the effectiveness criterion was not limited in the Single European Act by the need to show a cross border dimension or effect.

From these modest beginnings subsidiarity was elevated under the Maastricht Treaty into a general principle of Community law. A new Article 3b of the EC Treaty provided that:

"This Community shall act within the limits of the powers conferred upon it by this Treaty and of the objectives assigned to it therein. In areas which do not fall within its exclusive competence, the Community shall take action, in accordance with the principle of subsidiarity, only if and so far as the objectives of the proposed action cannot be sufficiently achieved by the Member States and can therefore, by reason of the scale or effects of the proposed action, be better achieved by the Community.

Any action by the Community shall not go beyond what is necessary to achieve the objectives of this Treaty".

---

[23] Its 'principal' use, see Emiliou (*supra*, n 3); Cass (*supra*, n 4).
[24] *Supra*, n 16.
[25] *Supra*, n 18.
[26] Ibid.

The preamble to the Treaty on European Union expresses the States' resolve:

"to continue the process of creating an ever closer union among the peoples of Europe, in which decisions are taken as closely as possible to the citizen in accordance with the principle of subsidiarity".

Title I Article A TEU reasserts the principle that "decisions [be] taken as closely as possible to the citizen". Article B, which sets out the objectives of the Union, provides that:

"the objectives of the Union shall be achieved as provided in this Treaty and in accordance with the conditions and the timetable set out therein while respecting the principle of subsidiarity as defined in Article 3b of the Treaty establishing the European Community".

Title VI (Co-operation on Justice and Home Affairs) Article K.3(2) (b) provides that the Council may:

"adopt joint action in so far as the objectives of the Union can be attained better by joint action than by the Member States acting individually on account of the scale or effects of the action envisaged."

In addition to these express provisions it has been suggested that other articles which require the Community to "support," "supplement" or "encourage" the action of Member States,[27] or which permit Member States to introduce "more stringent" measures,[28] or which provide for the adoption by the Community of "incentive measures", "excluding harmonization"[29] constitute implied examples of the subsidiarity principle.[30]

From this broad range of provisions it is clear that Member States, no doubt in a desperate bid for unanimous agreement at the 11th hour at Maastricht, sought to incorporate the principle of subsidiarity into the TEU comprehensively, in all its meanings, embracing both efficiency and social responsibility criteria, without too much regard for precision or problems of future application. However, only Article 3b expressly incorporated the principle into the EC Treaty. Thus, it is this definition of subsidiarity which will apply in the context of EC law making, and which will be subject to the jurisdiction of the Court of Justice.[31] Strictly speaking the principle expressed in the Preamble and Article A of the TEU that "decisions be taken as closely as possible to the people" applies only to intergovernmental matters decided under the TEU; it is not part of EC law. However, this aspect of subsidiarity is, it is submitted, inherent in the proportionality principle which is incorporated into Article 3b. Moreover, given that the principle of subsidiarity was intended to be central, and all embracing, at least as between the Community and Member States, it may be argued that,

---

[27] Arts 118a (Health and Safety), 126 (Education), 127 (Vocational Training), 129 (Public Health).

[28] Arts 118a (Health and Safety), 129a (Consumer protection).

[29] Arts 126, 129.

[30] All cited as examples of the subsidiarity principle in Conclusions of the Presidency, Edinburgh Summit 1992.

[31] In drawing up conventions in the field of Justice and Home Affairs under Art K.3(2) TEU the Council may stipulate that the Court of Justice shall have jurisdiction to interpret their provisions and to rule on any disputes regarding their application.

if questions of interpretation of Article 3b are raised before the Court of Justice, that Court, as a constitutional court, could take into account the original philosophical concept of subsidiarity, as expressed in the preamble and Article A of the TEU.[32] As a general principle of law, concerned with the protection of human rights,[33] it could provide valuable and much needed guidance on the interpretation and application of Article 3b.

Article 3b EC Treaty

The three paragraphs of Article 3b contain four distinct elements:

(1) The principle of conferred powers: "The Community shall act within the limits of the powers conferred upon it by this Treaty and of the objectives assigned to it therein" (Para 1);
(2) The exemption: the subsidiarity principle will only apply "in areas which do not fall within [the] exclusive competence" of the Community (para 2, first part);
(3) The subsidiarity principle; the Community shall act "only if and so far as the objectives of the proposed action cannot be sufficiently achieved by the Member States and can therefore, by reason of the scale or effects of the proposed action, be better achieved by the Community" (para 2, second part);
(4) The proportionality principle: "Any action by the Community shall not go beyond what is necessary to achieve the objectives of this Treaty" (para 3).

The Commission has suggested that (3) and (4) represent aspects of the subsidiarity principle.

These elements will be considered in turn.

The principle of conferred powers

Few difficulties should arise over this principle. There has long been unanimous agreement that the Community's powers are attributed powers. The Community can only act in areas in which it has been authorised to do so under the EC Treaty. However, given the extensive powers provided by the EC Treaty and the broad (and often vague) objectives of the Treaty, and Article 235, which allows the Community to act to achieve "one of the objectives of the Community" where the Treaty "has not provided the necessary powers", it is now,

---

[32] The Commission recognised this principle in its Communication to the Council and Parliament outlining its proposals for the application of the Subsidiarity principle (Bull. EC 10–1992 pt 2.2.1).
[33] Such principles being recognised by the Court as part of the unwritten law of the Community, see *e.g.* Case 4/73 *Nold v Commission*, [1974] ECR 491.

as Lang pointed out in 1988,[34] "difficult to see any area which will be permanently outside the scope of the Community"'s powers .... There are no clear legal limits on how far the Community can move". This observation will apply, *a fortiori*, once the Maastricht Treaty is ratified.[35] Thus Article 3b paragraph 1 offers little support to those who seek to limit the growth of Community power. If the Community is to advance, as it must, and States are to be "protected from the grip of the centralising state"[36] its progress can only be controlled by a rigorous application of paragraphs 2 and 3, hopefully leavened by the consideration expressed in the TEU that "decisions be taken as closely as possible to the people".

The exemption: areas within the Community's exclusive competence

This provision would appear to have the potential seriously to restrict the application of the subsidiarity principle. If the matter falls within the Community's exclusive competence there is no need to consider the question of subsidiarity under paragraph 2. Yet, the question of which areas fall within the Community's exclusive competence is far from clear, and has received scant critical attention since Maastricht. Where its meaning in the context of Article 3b has been considered, interpretations have been either disturbingly generous or unclear. Toth[37] has suggested that the "EC's competence is exclusive over all matters pertaining to the pursuit of the common objectives." This leads him to the "inevitable conclusion that the principle of subsidiarity cannot apply to any matter covered by the original EEC Treaty". Even the "new" areas such as public health, education and vocational training and culture introduced by the SEA and TEU, which were clearly not intended to comprise areas of exclusive Community competence, could, he suggests, be drawn into the ambit of exclusive competence, since measures in these areas often constitute "flanking" policies, inextricably connected with the single market. The Commission, outlining its views in its Communication to the Council and Parliament in 1992,[38] found the term "area of exclusive power" an "unfortunate expression"; since there was "no clear line of demarcation between exclusive and shared powers". Although the distinction was "extremely important", it had "difficulty in defining the areas of exclusive powers". Moreover, the fact that a particular area, such as agriculture, fell within the Community's exclusive power did not mean that "all responsibility for the activity in question is covered by exclusive competence. The text of the Treaty cannot be interpreted so broadly as to leave common sense out of account". The Commission suggested that exclusive powers were better defined in terms of *competence to act*, leading to the creation (once action had been taken) of "blocks of exclusive powers".

---

[34] Lang, 'EC Constitutional Law; the Division of Powers between the Community and Member States' NILQ (1988) 209.

[35] As Weatherill notes 'however anodyne the detailed provisions of the new titles introduced by the TEU may appear, their real importance lies in their existence, which generates obligations to pursue the policy sketched by the Treaty' (Research Paper, University of Nottingham 1992), *supra*, n 2 at 5.

[36] Santer *supra*, n 5.

[37] *Supra*, n 12. See also Toth, *supra*, n 1.

[38] *Supra*, n 32.

So far the arguments convince. Regrettably the Commission went on to suggest that within these blocks of competence to act, which were widely drawn to include the Common Commercial Policy, measures relating to the single market, competition, agriculture, fisheries and transport, "the Community does not have to demonstrate a need for action." Thus, whilst acknowledging that there are few areas or "blocks" in which the Community has exclusive power,[39] the Commission suggests that it is free to act within those areas without regard to subsidiarity, although there was "nothing to prevent the EC from allowing Member States to legislate" here.[40]

Commentators considering the nature and extent of the Community's exclusive powers before Maastricht have expressed widely different views. The Commission, in considering possible categories of exclusive Community powers in its 1975 report on European Union,[41] was able to suggest only Commercial Policy and Monetary Policy as potential candidates. Dahrendorf, in his Monnet lecture in 1979,[42] distinguished four main areas in which a future European Union might have exclusive competence: foreign policy, development and aid, energy and resources, and international economic agreements. He, together with Santer,[43] thought that it was time for agriculture to be removed from the field of exclusive competence. Parliament's draft Treaty on European Union 1984[44] provided that the Community should have exclusive competence in matters to complete, safeguard and develop the free movement of goods, persons, services and capital and for trade between Member States (Art 47(1)); to complete and develop Competition Policy at the level of the Union (Art 48), and for Commercial Policy (Art 64(2)).[45] On the other hand Wilke & Wallace[46] suggested that a list of the Community's exclusive powers would be "short and relatively straightforward". Similarly the Martin Report[47] considered that the Community's exclusive powers "would have to stay limited". Finally, Santer[48] singled out only currency and defence as examples of exclusive powers.

It should be noted that these commentators were addressing the question of exclusive powers in the context of the Community's progress towards European Union. The notion of "exclusive Community competence" had its origins in the Commission's report on European Union 1975.[49] The report suggested that Community competence fell into three categories; exclusive, concurrent (with Member States), and potential. It did not define precisely which matters fell within which category. The 1984 draft Treaty[50] adopted that classification as regards exclusive and concurrent powers and indicated which matters should

---

[39] 'The circumscription of powers must not be confused with the occupation of the terrain'.
[40] Idea derived from Art 12(1) of Parliament's draft Treaty 1984, cited *supra*.
[41] *Supra*, n 18.
[42] Jean Monnet lecture; 'A Third Europe' EUI Florence 1979, noted by Wilke & Wallace 1990, *op cit*, n 8.
[43] *Delors Colloquium, op cit*, n 1, p 27.
[44] *Supra*, n 18.
[45] This, together with Toth's, is the widest interpretation of the concept of exclusive competence.
[46] *Supra*, n 8.
[47] 'Parliament's strategy for European Union' (1990) cited by Santer, *Delors Colloquium, op cit*, n 1, p 23.
[48] *Ibid* at 27.
[49] *Supra*, n 18.
[50] *Supra*, n 18.

fall within each category. It also spelt out the implications of such categorization. Article 12 provided that:

"Where this Treaty confers exclusive competence on the Union, the institutions shall have sole power to act; national authorities shall only legislate to the extent laid down by the Union ..." (Art 12(l)) "Where the Treaty confers concurrent competence on the Union the Member States shall continue to act as long as the Union has not legislated." (Art 12(2) para 2)

Both the 1975 report and the 1984 draft Treaty, and indeed most opinions expressed prior to Maastricht, proceeded on the assumption that the matters designated for "exclusive" or "concurrent" competence would be listed, as under most federal systems, in an Act of Constitution. Lord Mackenzie Stuart, speaking in 1991,[51] suggested that the intergovernmental conferences in session at Maastricht should be "getting down to detailed rules of detailed competence" rather than concerning itself with the "hopelessly ill defined concept of subsidiarity". His advice was not taken. Whilst Article 3b TEU appears to have carried forward the notions and implications of exclusive and concurrent competence expressed in Article 12(1) and (2) of the 1984 draft Treaty no attempt was made in the Treaty either to define exclusive competence or to indicate any criteria by which such matters might be judged.

This is not altogether surprising. The 1975 report and the 1984 draft Treaty were based on federal models in which the respective areas of state and federal authorities are normally defined in a Constitution.[52] As Toth notes,[53] the distinction between exclusive and "non exclusive competence" is alien to, and "contradicts the logic, the structure and the actual wording of the original EEC Treaty". The EC, even at its beginnings, was not concerned with dividing competence between the Community and its Member States, but with sharing powers over a wide range of areas of activity in order to achieve certain common and mutually beneficial objectives.[54] Whilst it was clear that in some areas there would be little scope for action by Member States if the desired goal was to be achieved – a customs union is a necessary prerequisite to a single market – in most areas competence was concurrent. This did not mean that States and the Community could legislate on the same issue at the same time,[55] nor that States' competence in these matters was unrestrained, (since they are bound to comply with the rules of the EC Treaty), but that their action would be complementary, or supplementary. Once the Community has exercised its powers under the Treaty, to regulate a particular matter within a certain area of activity, clearly States are not free to enact measures which conflict with these rules.[56] As the volume and scope of Community law increases, so will States' powers diminish. But there are few areas of activity in which Member States do

---

[51] *Delors Colloquium, op cit*, n 1.
[52] Although clearly such lines cannot be strictly maintained.
[53] *Supra*, n 12.
[54] The 'partnership' approach noted by Delors, Weatherill, but with the emphasis on administrative subsidiarity. The concept of shared competence implies that states must also share responsibility for *policy*.
[55] 'simultaneous' action; see Emiliou, 17 EL Rev (1992) 383.
[56] On the principles of supremacy of EC law and the doctrine of preemption.

not retain some degree of competence. Thus it is not surprising that commentators have had difficulty in identifying areas in which the Community has exclusive competence, nor that the Heads of State refrained from doing so at Maastricht.

One is forced to the conclusion that the only areas in which the Community has exclusive competence for the purposes of Article 3b are those in which *it has already legislated*. This view draws some support from the analysis offered by the Commission[57] that the Community institutions possess *potential* competence in all the areas outlined by the Treaty. Within those areas the Community has an obligation (better described as a power) to legislate, subject to the rules and procedures of the Treaty, such action *"leading in time to blocks of exclusive powers"*. Similarly, Toth's conclusions[58] concerning the Community's exclusive powers were largely based on decisions of the Court of Justice on the supremacy of existing EC law and the principle of preemption. However the Commission's next step, its suggestion that "the subsidiarity principle cannot be invoked to question the advisability of Community action" within its blocks of potential competence, cannot be correct. Nor can it be true that Member States can only act within these areas "subject to the Commission's approval".[59] As Article 3b paragraph 1 indicates, it is the Member States which have conferred power on the Community to act, to a greater or lesser degree. Surely the competence of Member States ends, not as Toth suggests,[60] where the competence of the Community begins, but where its powers have been exercised. As Temple Lang observes,[61] "every new Community measure creates a new area of exclusive Community power." The fact that competence to act, even to act comprehensively, has been granted to the Community by the Treaty does not, and surely cannot mean that its competence to act[62] in these areas cannot be subject to the subsidiarity principle. To allow whole areas of activity to escape scrutiny under paragraph 2, simply because the Community has potential competence in these areas, would surely undermine the very purpose for which this provision was intended.

The subsidiarity principle: subsidiarity plus proportionality

It is generally agreed[63] that the principle of subsidiarity has a two-fold purpose in Community law:

(1) to assess the need for Community action. As the Commission has pointed out:[64]

---

[57] Communication to the Council and Parliament 1992, *supra*, n 32.

[58] *Supra*, n 12.

[59] Idea derived from Art 12(1) Parliament's draft Treaty 1984, *supra*, n 18.

[60] *Supra*, n 58.

[61] *Supra*, n 34.

[62] The Commission acknowledges that Art 3b para 3 may control the Community in the *exercise* of its powers (see Bull EC 10/92).

[63] See Martin Report, cited by Santer; Delors; (*Delors Colloquium* 1991, *op cit*, n 1); Commission Communication 1992; Conclusions of Edinburgh Presidency 1992.

[64] *Supra*, n 32.

"it is for the Community to demonstrate the justification for Community action in preference to action taken, or which could be taken, by the Member States to achieve the objectives of the Treaty".

Even though Community objectives are set in *general* terms by the EC Treaty, *specific* Community action must be justified wherever the Community has concurrent competence with Member States.

(2) to control the exercise of power by the Community once the need for action has been established.

This dual function was underlined by the Commission in 1992:

"For more than 40 years the subsidiarity principle has satisfied two requirements: the need for action; and the need to ensure that the means employed are commensurate with the objectives pursued".[65]

To what extent are these functions performed by paragraphs 2 and 3 of Article 3b?

According to paragraph 2 the Community:

"shall take action . . . only if and so far as the objectives of the proposed action cannot be sufficiently achieved by the Member States, by reason of the scale or effects of the proposed action".

Under paragraph 3:

"Any action by the Community shall not go beyond what is necessary to achieve the objectives of this Treaty".

Paragraph 2 embodies the subsidiarity principle, expressed in terms of comparative efficiency as regards *the achievement of objectives*, assessed by reference to the scale or effects of the proposed action.[66] It is thus an *efficiency by better-results* criterion. Although the need for action may be established by reason of the scale OR effects of the proposed action, without expressly requiring that the effects extend beyond national boundaries,[67] it is submitted that the concept of effects must comprise a cross border dimension.

Paragraph 3 lays down a principle of proportionality. According to the well established caselaw of the Court[68] a proportionate action is one which is no more than is appropriate and necessary to achieve its desired goals. It is thus a necessity test, stricter than the test of paragraph 2.

As noted above, the Commission has suggested[69] that *both* paragraphs embody the principle of subsidiarity.

The role and interrelationship of paragraphs 2 and 3 is not immediately clear. It was suggested by the Commission that paragraph 2, described as the "comparative efficiency" test, determined "whether it would be better for action to

---

[65] Ibid.

[66] *Cf* Art 12(2) draft Treaty 1984, *supra* n 18. The Union shall only carry out those *tasks which may be more effectively undertaken* in common than by Member States acting separately, in particular those whose dimensions and effect extends beyond national frontiers'.

[67] *Cf* Art 12(2) draft Treaty cited *supra*, n 66.

[68] *e.g.* Case 170/84 *Bilka Kaufhaus GmbH* v *Weber von Hartz* [1986] ECR 1607.

[69] *Supra*, n 32.

be taken by the Community or Member States".[70] If it is decided that action at Community level will be more effective in achieving a particular Community goal, "the question of intensity of action must then be considered. At this point the principle of proportionality comes into play". This analysis indicates that paragraphs 2 and 3 are cumulative in their effect. Paragraph 2 provides the initial justification for specific action by the Community, on administrative efficiency grounds, determined by reference to the scale or effects of the proposed action: paragraph 3 ensures that the action undertaken does not exceed what is appropriate and necessary to achieve its proposed objectives. The proportionality test thus acts both to control the scope of legislation (avoiding excessively detailed prescription) and to determine the most appropriate (*i.e.* least intrusive) means for its implementation. The Commission suggested that paragraph 3 would apply to control the Community in the exercise of its powers in *all* areas of Community competence, exclusive and non-exclusive.

The Commission's analysis is convincing. It would explain the exclusion in paragraph 2 in respect of areas "falling within the Community's exclusive competence".[71] Clearly, if the Community has exclusive competence, *a fortiori* has already acted, the case for Community action is already established; only its exercise need be controlled. It would also explain why the Commission's analysis of paragraphs 2 and 3 was largely in terms of the ways and means of achieving objectives (*i.e.* the best instrument; binding or non-binding; framework or detailed provision) rather than the need for action itself. Having taken such a broad view of the concept of exclusive community competence there was, in most cases, no need to prove a need for Community action. Moreover, as worded, paragraph 2 appears to be concerned with comparative efficiency *in achieving Community objectives*; unlike Article 12(2) of the draft Treaty of 1984, it does not address the need for action in terms of the scale or effects of the *tasks to be undertaken*.[72] The justification for specific Community objectives appear to be presumed.

This is a serious weakness in paragraph 2. Although the EC Treaty prescribes *general* Community objectives and confers potential competence on Community institutions to act to achieve these objectives, surely the need for *specific* Community action must always be proved. It is not enough simply to control its exercise, under paragraph 3.

It is submitted that if the principle of subsidiarity under Article 3b is adequately to perform its dual function of testing both the need for action and the exercise of Community powers, a three-stage enquiry must be made. First, it is necessary to establish whether the matter in question falls within the Community's exclusive competence. It has been argued that the concept of exclusive competence should be given a restrictive interpretation, preferably confined to areas in which the Community has already acted. If the matter falls outside the Community's exclusive competence it must then be asked, applying paragraph 2,

---

[70] To be assessed in terms of resources and effectiveness of action ('value added test').
[71] See also Conclusions of Edinburgh Presidency 1992 that paragraph 2 'applies only to the extent that the Treaty gives a choice to act'.
[72] *Supra*, n 66.

whether Community action in a particular area will be more effective than action by Member States, in view of the scale or (cross border) effects of the matter in question. This is a relatively weak test. An efficiency test, particularly when expressed in terms of the attainment of (presumed) objectives does not focus on the nature of the *problem* giving rise to the need for Community action. In many areas, particularly in matters pertaining to the single market, in which Community action would achieve "improved coherence", or a more level playing field, the advantage of Community action simply in terms of efficiency will not be hard to establish. Whether the problem is one which the Community *should* address is a different matter. Paragraph 2 should thus be applied in the light of the principle that decisions be taken as closely as possible to the people. Efficiency should be weighed against the need to promote social responsibility.[73]

Having established a justification for action as suggested above, the enquiry moves to the third stage, the application of the proportionality principle, under paragraph 3. Here the proposed action itself must be justified, in terms of content ("intensity")[74] as well as form, as necessary, or no more than is necessary, to achieve its desired objectives. This is a more rigorous test, designed to curb excessive or oppressive legislation.

Such an approach to Article 3b corresponds broadly with guidelines issued by the Commission[75] and the Conclusions of the Edinburgh Presidency.[76] It should not prove excessively onerous. In a number of fields, for example in matters of external policy, particularly Commercial Policy, the need for regulation at Community level is clear; only the exercise of power need be controlled.[77] Likewise where there is consensus that a particular problem needs to be addressed, and clearly spills across national boundaries; or where regulation at national level creates significant barriers to the single market. But, in matters in which the need for action is disputed, and the Community dimension, although it exists, is slender, for example policies "flanking" the single market, particularly those designed to create a level playing field, the need for action is less clear. Although no doubt justifiable on the grounds of pure efficiency, decisions on these matters may be better taken more closely to the people. There is room for the application of a *de minimis* principle here.[78] In many areas the "level" field may require no more than the setting of minimum standards,[79] buttressed by the principle of mutual recognition.[80] It will rarely be necessary for decisions concerning education and welfare, or culture, matters of special concern to States and individuals, with a tenuous Community dimension, to be taken by the

---

[73] See Emiliou's comment that the concept of effectiveness is 'not one of technocratic advantageousness but of balancing effectiveness against other conflicting values' (1991) 17 EL Rev 383.

[74] The Commission's term (see Bull EC 10/92).

[75] *Supra*, n 32.

[76] As to future practices in applying the subsidiarity principle.

[77] The EC institutions are in any case bound to comply with the principle of proportionality, since, as a general principle of law it is part of the unwritten law of the Community; see *Supra*, n 33.

[78] The Commission noted in its 1992 Communication that it is looking into the question of the application of a *de minimis* rule.

[79] As is provided by the TEU in the areas of health and safety (Art 118a EEC) and consumer protection (Art 129a EEC).

[80] The possibility of setting minimum standards and applying the principle of mutual recognition was acknowledged by the Commission in 1992 (Bull EL 10/92, *supra*, n 32).

Community. Such decisions should be taken as closely as possible to the people, as they are in many federations. It may be asked whether it is necessary for the Community to act at all to promote a "European Year of Older People and Solidarity between Generations", or to save Oxleas Wood.[81]

Much support for Community action, both by individuals and States,[82] stems from a desire to achieve particular policy objectives, which, due to a lack of political will, cannot be achieved at home. But, however desirable Community objectives may be, they, like national objectives, can change over time. The individual's capacity to influence policy, subject to the democratic process, is still greater at the level of the State. The subsidiarity principle is concerned not with the achieving of particular objectives, but with responsibility for action. The pursuit of policy should not colour the question of principle, which is whether, and on what basis, *power* should be transferred.

The Role of the Court

Prior to the signing of the TEU there was considerable divergence of view as to whether of the Court of Justice should have a role in interpreting and applying the subsidiarity principle. Since the principle has now been incorporated into the TEU, Article 3b will, on ratification of the Treaty, be part of EC law. Thus it is inevitable that the Court will be asked to interpret the principle or to apply it, either on request for a preliminary ruling from a national court under Article 177[83] or in proceedings for annulment under Article 173.[84] Despite the doubts expressed as to the desirability of the Court interpreting the concept of subsidiarity, on the grounds of its lack of precision and objectivity,[85] or of its being "a political decision which only political institutions can take",[86] it is submitted that the Court is the institution best placed to undertake that task. It is immune from political pressures. It has acted throughout its existence effectively and creatively as a constitutional court.[87] It is accustomed to applying general principles of law, which are often political in nature. It applies these principles with due regard to the respective roles of the Community institutions under the EC Treaty.[88] Precisely because of its lack of precision, subsidiarity, along with proportionality and the elusive concept of exclusive Community competence

---

[81] *Independent*, 26 April 1992; 'Campaign to save Oxleas Wood goes to Europe'.

[82] Pressure groups particularly have sought to exploit the Community's potential.

[83] For interpretation of Art 3b or a declaration on the validity of secondary legislation.

[84] Or under Art 175, 184 or 215(b).

[85] House of Lords Scrutiny Committee, cited by Lord Mackenzie-Stuart, *Delors Colloquium, op cit*, n 1, p 41.

[86] Toth *supra*, n 12; Belgian Memorandum on Institutional Relaunch, Agence Europe, cited by Wilke & Wallace (*supra*, n 8).

[87] See Mancini, 'The Making of a Constitution for Europe' (1989) 26 CML Rev.

[88] It is open to question whether it would be necessary to limit its powers of review to situations of 'grave and manifest disregard' of the limits on the exercise of its powers or 'manifest error of law', as suggested by Emiliou, *supra*, n 3 and Weatherill, *supra*, n 2.

require interpretation and elucidation by a single body such as the Court. Control by the Court is particularly important if decisions on subsidiarity, as well as on the substance of proposed legislation, are taken by qualified majority.[89] Although, as Wilke and Wallace pointed out,[90] it cannot prevent differences of political interpretation, and cannot provide a watertight judicial guarantee that Community powers will be unbridled, it can enunciate principles and settle cases, and can,[91] as it has done in the past, "move with the grain of changing economic and social realities".

Conclusion

If the views expressed above suggest that Article 3b, and the concept of subsidiarity, be interpreted strictly, in the light of the Community's concern to promote the "responsible society", it is not through a desire to halt the Community's progress, still less to reverse the movement towards closer union, but rather in response to a widely acknowledged need to control the inevitable drift to centralization,[92] and to ensure that the original philosophical concept of subsidiarity is not overlooked, despite the lack of its express recognition in Article 3b.[93] Its double presence in the TEU indicate that it was intended to be taken seriously.

Recent and continuing social upheavals throughout the world, including the Community itself, particularly the resurgence of national sentiment, demonstrate the need to respect diversity, sometimes at the expense of efficiency,[94] and to protect and preserve the autonomy of traditional social groups despite, indeed perhaps because of, their increasing economic involvement with, and dependence on, a wider society. This need is reflected in federal systems.[95] It is particularly important at times of economic depression, when individuals are less willing or able to take the "larger" view. Current movements towards greater regional autonomy in Europe reflect a similar movement away from centralism. Thus, particularly in matters closely concerning individuals, if competence is to be transferred to centralised authorities, the transfer must be justified. The burden is on the Community institutions to show that there is a real need for Community action, by reference to the scale or effects of the *problem*,[96] and that the particular action proposed is appropriate and necessary to achieve *specific* Community goals. In many areas Community action will clearly

---

[89] As suggested by the Commission (Bull EC 10/92). Since the qualified majority vote is itself anti-subsidiarity arguably it should only be used where there is a compelling case for action by the Community.

[90] See *supra*, n 3.

[91] Or, as Wilke & Wallace (*supra*, n 8) suggest 'must'.

[92] Lang's 'moving boundary' (1988) NILQ 209; see also Santer on the German experience, *Delors Colloquium, op cit*, n 1, p 21.

[93] Except as an aspect of proportionality.

[94] Acknowledged by J S Mill, Barrington, cited by Wilke & Wallace (see *supra*, n 8) at 11, 14.

[95] In which educational and cultural, health and welfare matters are often reserved for states.

[96] As provided in Art 12(2) of Parliament's draft Treaty, OJ 1984 C77/33.

be justified, even on the most rigorous application of Article 3b. There are sufficient pressures from the world outside, for admission, for association, for trade and aid, and sufficient problems, both inside and outside the Community, in respect of which there is a real and acknowledged need for Community action, and where Community action would clearly be more effective than action by Member States alone. Is it too much to hope that the subsidiarity principle, as well as affording an opportunity to "mediate power distribution" and "defuse political conflict"[97] will provide a new impetus for the Community to re-order its priorities?

JO STEINER

---

[97] Cass, *supra*, n 4.

Chapter 5
Subsidiarity: Panacea or Fig Leaf?[1]

The analytical framework

The influence of federal models can be detected in the Treaty on European Union, notably as regards the (implicit) distinction between exclusive and concurrent competence and the application of the principle of subsidiarity to the latter. Indeed a number of distinguished writers have taken the view that subsidiarity is one of the basic tenets of federalism.[2] It is therefore strange, to say the least, that references to a "federal goal" for the Community had to be dropped at Maastricht in order to ensure acceptance of the new Treaty by the UK Government.[3]

It should be made clear at the outset that there is no consensus as to the exact definition of federalism. It could, nevertheless, be said that federalism refers to a vertical division of political power as opposed to a horizontal division between legislative, executive and judicial arms of government.[4] Lenaerts draws a distinction between *integrative federalism* and *devolutionary federalism*. Whereas the former "... refers to a constitutional order that strives at unity in diversity among previously independent or confederally related component entities", the latter "... refers to a constitutional order that redistributes the powers of a previously unitary State among its component entities."[5] It could be argued that the European Community is moving towards the model of integrative federalism.

Friedrich, widely recognised as a leading authority on federalism, discussing the role of federalism in the nascent European Union concluded that in such "a world of ever widening contacts and interests", federalism should be "recog-

---

[1] See also Toth, 'A legal analysis of subsidiarity', Steiner, 'Subsidiarity under the Maastricht Treaty' in this volume at 37 and 49 respectively.

[2] See for example, Brugmans & Duclos, *Le fédéralisme contemporain: critéres, institutions, perspectives* (1963) 39–45; Heraud, *Les Principes du fédéralisme et la fédération européenne* (1968) 48–51; Brugmans, *La pensée politique du fédéralisme* (1969) 65–81.

[3] See Laursen, 'The Maastricht Treaty: a critical evaluation' in Laursen & Vanhoonacker (eds), *The Intergovernmental Conference on Political Union: Institutional Reforms, New Policies and International Identity of the European Community* (1992) 259.

[4] Carey, 'Federalism: historic questions and contemporary meanings – a defence of political processes, in Earle (ed), *Federalism, Infinite Variety in Theory and Practice* (1968) 43. For different views on federalism see Friedrich, *Man and His Government, an Empirical Theory of Politics* (1963) 585; Riker, *Federalism: Origin, Operation, Significance* (1964) 11; Friedrich, *Constitutional Government and Democracy* (1968) 4th ed, 193.

[5] Lenaerts, 'Constitutionalism and the many faces of federalism', (1990) 38 AJCL, 205–263 at 220.

nised not as a panacea but as a useful instrumentality for good government". Only federalism would allow "the small state and the small political community ... to survive".[6]

Subsidiarity and the future of federalism in Europe[7]

But, if indeed the federal solution to the European political question is to be adopted, what type of federalism is meant? For Anglo-Saxons, the contractual and constitutional model of federalism is the obvious answer to that question. Under this model, constituent Member States, acting as independent and auto-nomous units, initially agree to establish a new level of government and to endow a new, superordinate entity with certain specified powers. The granting of those powers is never clear enough to prevent a need for future elaboration and interpretation. Nevertheless, some attempt is made to allocate powers and to form a binding and enduring contract. There is a consensus that in most such federal arrangements it quickly becomes apparent that only the higher level of government is capable of regulating effectively the many interactions and exter-nalities that result from the independent actions of individuals and State governments.[8]

For many Europeans on the Continent, federalism has a different connota-tion, stemming from the principle of subsidiarity as expressed in Catholic social thought.[9] President Delors, for example, is an ardent supporter of this model of federalism for the European Community.[10] Given the fact that the principle of subsidiarity has been enshrined in the European Community legal order by Articles A(2) and B of the Treaty on European Union and Article 3b(2) of the EC Treaty which were introduced as a result of the Maastricht Agreements of December 1991, if Europe adopts the federal option, this is the most likely approach.

The meaning given to subsidiarity by Delors implies that all actions in social and political life should be performed by the lowest possible unit. In other words, subsidiarity establishes a presumption that the primary responsibility and decision-making competence should rest with the lowest possible level of authority of the political hierarchy.[11] This view suggests a more organic view of society and political life than does the more mechanistic and legalistic approach

---

[6] Friedrich, *Europe: an Emergent Nation?* (1969) 215.

[7] This question is discussed authoritatively by Guy Peters in a seminal article on the politics and institu-tions of the EC, one from which I have drawn liberally for the purposes of this part. See Peters, 'Bureaucratic politics and institutions of the European Communities', in Sbragia (ed), *Europolitics: Institu-tions and Policymaking in the 'new' European Community* (1992) 75 at 109–112.

[8] See Peters, *ibid*, 110. Also Emerson, 'The finances of the European Community: a case study in embry-onic fiscal federalism', In Oates (ed), *The Political Economy of Fiscal Federalism* (1985) 129–169.

[9] Kapteyn, 'Community law and the principle of subsidiarity', *Revue des Affaires Européennes* (1991) 2, 35. See also Heinze (ed), *Neue Subsidiarität: Leitidee für eine zukünftige Sozialpolitik?* (1986).

[10] See Delors, 'The principle of subsidiarity: contribution to the debate', in *Subsidiarity: the Challenge of Change: Proceedings of the Jacques Delors Colloquium* (1991) 7–18.

[11] See Task Force Report on the Environment and the Internal Market, EC Commission, December 1989, x.

of the Anglo-Saxon model.[12] In the context of the Community, this approach would mean that the Community should take action in a particular area only to the extent to which given objectives can be attained more effectively at the Community level than at the level of the individual Member States.[13] That is, Brussels would do as little as possible, leaving most functions to the national, and perhaps especially, subnational[14] governments.[15] It may even mean that as many things as possible would be done by private and voluntary organizations rather than by any form of government.[16] This approach also leaves a wide margin for interpretation, most obviously in determining the "lowest possible" unit best placed to perform a function.

These alternative visions of federalism would have rather different implications. The Anglo-Saxon version would make the nation State central in bargaining over the shape of a future political entity in Europe. In essence the Member States would be bargaining over how much of their "sovereignty" to grant to the European Community in exchange for benefits derived from common policies, the effective operation of the single market, and perhaps direct subsidies for some sectors, such as agriculture and aid for less developed regions. In the Continental conception of federalism, the Nation States are still important, but are only one among many sets of institutions that have a right to participate in the bargaining. The "subsidiarity" approach, therefore, may allow the Community to deal directly with subnational governments, interest groups, and citizens without too much concern for the rights or views of the Member States. It should be stressed though, that the Community is already involved in relationships that circumvent national governments. In this respect, therefore, the acceptance of subsidiarity as the key concept of federalism might only institutionalise and legitimise what is already being done.[17]

The "subsidiarity" approach: Community power v Member State power

It is clear therefore, that subsidiarity constitutes one of the main tenets of federalism. Every federal system is based on a distribution of legislative and administrative powers among the federation and its Member States.[18] The

---

[12] See Delors, *op cit*, n 10, 8–10.

[13] Emiliou, 'Subsidiarity: an effective barrier against 'the enterprises of ambition'?", (1992) 17 EL Rev 383–407 at 406.

[14] The term subnational government in the context of the present discussion refers to both regional and local government, as the case may be, in each Member State.

[15] This approach would seem to give the subnational governments an important role in governing the EC, even though the Court has ruled that it is the responsibility of national governments to make subnational governments conform to EC law; see more recently, Case C-103/88 *Constanzo v Milano* [1989] ECR 1839.

[16] Delors, *op cit*, n 10, 16–18.

[17] See Biancarelli, 'La communauté et les collectives locales', (1988) 48 *Revue Française d'Administration Publique*, 41–55.

[18] See Hailbroner, 'Legal institutional reform of the EEC: what can we learn from federalism theory and practice?' (1991) 46 *Außenwirtschaft*, 485–496 at 492.

Communities have only the powers assigned to them by the Treaties, while all residual powers are left with the Member States. According to that model, the various types of competences can be categorised so that in individual areas either the Community or the Member States enjoy exclusive powers. In other areas, however, the Member States may legislate even if Community powers exist but have not been exercised at all or have been exercised in an incomplete manner or have been exercised in such a way as to authorise the exercise of Community powers by national authorities. This latter category has been described as "concurrent" powers. If the Community exercises a concurrent power, it normally displaces conflicting national legislation (because of the supremacy of Community law). Furthermore, it supersedes the pre-existing legislative powers of the Member States. This effect is described in American constitutional law as "pre emption".[19]

The residual powers of the Member States have no reserved status. The Community may indeed exercise its specific, implied or non-specific powers in the fullest possible way, without running into any inherent limitation set to these powers, as a result of the sovereignty which the Member States retain as subjects of international law. As Lenaerts succinctly put it: "there is simply no nucleus of sovereignty that the Member States can invoke, as such, against the Community".[20] This is equally true even when the Treaty expressly recognises the existence of residual powers for the Member States.[21]

In a federal system, it is not enough to establish areas of federal competence. It is also necessary to determine whether, and to what extent, the conferral of legislative authority on the federation in those areas precludes states from acting. The framers of a constitution may of course indicate, either through general or specific clauses, whether the federal power is exclusive or concurrent and, if concurrent, whether it is plenary or somehow limited in deference to state law. The EC Treaty is mostly silent on these issues.

The Member States ordinarily keep a concurrent power, over the subject-matter entrusted to the Community, to the extent that the latter has not acted upon them.[22] As a rule, the Community powers contain only a potential for their exercise; in the absence of such exercise the Member States may take action, although they may not, in doing so, harm in any way the Community interest.[23]

---

[19] See Bieber, 'On the mutual completion of overlapping legal systems: the case of the European Communities and the national legal orders', (1988) 13 EL Rev 147–158 at 148. Waelbroeck, 'The emergent doctrine of Community pre emption – consent and redelegation' in Sandalow & Stein (ed) *Courts and Free Markets* (1982) Vol II, 548–577. Weatherill, 'Beyond pre emption? Shared competence and constitutional change in the European Community' in this volume at 13.

[20] See Lenaerts, *supra*, n 5 at 220. See Cases 6 & 11/69 *Commission v France* [1969] ECR 523 *per curiam* at 540: 'The exercise of reserved powers cannot ... permit the unilateral adoption of measures prohibited by the Treaty'.

[21] A prominent example is Art 36 EEC. The Court confirmed the above position in, *inter alia*, Case 153/78 *Commission v Germany*, [1979] ECR 2555 *per curiam* at 2564. For a similar line of reasoning see also Case 120/78 *Rewe-Zentral* v *Bundesmonopolverwaltung für Branntwein (Cassis de Dijon)* [1979] ECR 649; Case 148/78 *Pubblico Ministero* v *Ratti* [1979] ECR 1629.

[22] For further discussion see Capotorti, Hilf, Jacobs and Jacque, *The European Union Treaty* (1986) 77 *et seq*; Emiliou, *supra*, n 13, at 391–392.

[23] See the general obligation imposed on the Member States by Art 5(2) EEC.

The mere grant of power to the Community cannot therefore be considered to be an absolute prohibition to the exercise of any power over the same subject by the national authorities. Member States may enact measures and such measures are valid unless they come into conflict with Community legislation. The key question then is whether national measures are in conflict with Community legislation. According to the Court ". . . once the Community has, pursuant to . . . the Treaty, legislated . . . Member States are under an obligation to refrain from taking any measure which might undermine it or create exceptions to it".[24]

The preemption by Community legislation of the concurrent power of the Member States, over the same subject-matter, presents particular difficulties when, in the absence of an actual conflict between Community and national pieces of legislation, the argument is made (usually by the Commission) that the silence of the Community legislator[25] on a specific aspect of an otherwise regulated matter, reflects the intention that this aspect remain beyond any regulation. This would mean that Member State power over it is preempted, just as it is in relation to those aspects which have been regulated by the Community. The prevailing view in the United States is that "silence of Congress" restricts state power but this restriction is reversible by Congress. Nevertheless, in cases where the Congress remains silent, it is up to the courts to interpret this silence.[26]

This is precisely what the Court has done in relation to the Community legislator's silence. In *Amsterdam Bulb* v *Produktschap voor Siergewassen*,[27] the Court ruled, in effect, that the Community legislator's silence meant, indeed, that it was keeping silent. The power of the Dutch authorities therefore to fill lacunae left by Community legislation had not been preempted. The Court took the view that the silence of the Community legislator had no meaning in terms of policy, but simply resulted from the fact that the issue at hand had not been dealt with at the Community level. The opposite conclusion was reached in *Officier van Justitie* v *van den Hazel*[28] when the Court considered the Council Regulation establishing the common organization of the markets in poultry. Here the Court concluded that:

". . . the absence of measures concerning the withdrawal, where necessary, of products from the market does not stem from an omission or from an intention to leave measures of this nature to the appraisal of the Member States but is rather the consequence of a considered choice of economic policy of relying essentially on market forces to attain the desired balance."

---

[24] See Case 111/75 *Officier van Justitie* v *van den Hazel* [1977] ECR 901 at 909 *per curiam*; confirmed in Case 83/78 *Pigs Marketing Board* v *Redmond* [1978] ECR 2347.

[25] The issue of the 'silence of the congress' is very well explored in American constitutional law; see *Bowman* v *Chicago and Northwestern Railway Company*, 125 US 465 (1888); *Leisy* v *Hardin*, 135 US 100 (1890); *Clark Distilling Company* v *Western Maryland Railroad Company*, 242 US 311 (1917). See also Biklè, 'The silence of Congress', (1927) 41 Harv L Rev, 200–224.

[26] See Powell, *The Still Small Voice of the Commerce Clause*, in Proceedings of the National Tax Association, Washington, DC, (1937) '. . . when the Congress keeps silent, it takes an expert to know what it means. But the judges are experts. They say that Congress by keeping silent sometimes means that it is keeping silent and sometimes means that it is speaking.' Cited by Lenaerts, *supra*, n 5 at 225–226.

[27] Case 50/76 [1977] ECR 137. In Case 237/82 *Jongeneel Kaas et al* v *The Netherlands* [1984] ECR 483, silence was understood as failure by the Community to exercise its concurrent powers and thus the continuing existence of national powers.

[28] Case 111/76 [1977] ECR 901 at 909–910 *per curiam*. Silence was understood as exercise of Community's concurrent powers in Case 159/73 *Hannoversche Zucker* v *Hauptzollamt Hannover* [1974] ECR 121.

This judicial interpretation of the legislator's silence was based to a significant extent on an analysis of the *travaux préparatoires* that had led to the adoption of the Regulation in question.

In more exceptional cases, the mere grant of power to the Community entails a complete loss of power for the Member States.[29] Such Community power is known as exclusive, because the Member States are excluded from its concurrent exercise, irrespective of any action or inaction on the part of the Community. The exclusive character of a particular power of the Community is not stated in the Treaties. Bieber considers that:

"... the Community has *exclusive* powers if it can clearly be deduced from the wording of the Treaties that such powers have been conferred upon it or if a provision cannot be properly applied if this were not the case (*e.g.* the setting up of the Common Customs Tariff in accordance with Article 21(2) EEC, provisions concerning the institutional system).[30]

The judicial definition, delineation and protection of the exclusive powers of the Community is a rather complex, and more often than not, politically sensitive task.[31] A great deal of effort and creativity is often needed to balance the conflicting interests of the Community in protecting its exclusive powers, and of a Member State acting in the name of an overriding policy concern that, in its view, cannot await Community legislation. The Court has developed two main techniques as a means of compromising those conflicting interests.

First, legislation enacted by the Community under one of its exclusive powers may contain "a specific authorization by the Community" in favour of the Member States.[32] Secondly, when the Council was unable to reach an urgently needed decision in the area of fish stocks conservation due to political difficulties, the Court rather imaginatively ruled that Member States could act "as trustees of the common interest" under the supervision and with the approval of the Commission.[33] In this way the Court protected, in effect, both the Community's exclusive powers from undue encroachment by the Member States and the preservation of fish stocks.

Generally, the Court's role in the key area of definition and delineation of the

---

[29] Within the framework of the EEC Treaty this is the case with Community powers derived from Art 113 (Common Commercial Policy), see Case 41/76 *Donckerwolcke v Procureur de la République*, [1976] ECR 1921; Opinion 1/75 *Re Local Cost Standard Agreement* [1975] ECR 1355; Opinion 1/78 *Re Natural Rubber Agreement* [1978] ECR 2871. With regard to fisheries conservation measures see Case 804/79 *Commission v United Kingdom* [1981] ECR 1045.

[30] Bieber, *supra*, n 19 at 150 (author's italics). Lenaerts, *supra*, n 5 at 227, argues that: 'The exclusive character of a particular power of the Community ... flows from a judicial appraisal of the intrinsic content of the power under consideration'.

[31] For an authoritative discussion of this issue see Lenaerts, *supra*, n 5 at 228–230.

[32] See Case 41/76 *Donckerwolcke v Procureur de la République*, [1976] ECR 1921 at 1937 *per curiam*. The Court went a step further in Case 174/84 *Bulk Oil (Zug) AG v Sun International Ltd et al* [1986] ECR 559, where it considered the absence of Community regulation of the common commercial policy as 'a specific authorization by the Community' in favour of the Member States to act upon the matter. This decision has been criticised by Kapteyn (currently sitting at the Court) and Verloren van Themaat (an ex Advocate General) as 'less than wholly convincing'; see Kapteyn and Verloren van Themaat (in Gormley (ed)), *Introduction to the Law of the European Communities*, 2nd ed, (1989) 393 and 800.

[33] See Case 804/79 *Commission v United Kingdom* [1981] ECR 1045 at 1075–1076 *per curiam*.

respective Community and national powers has been authoritatively described as follows:

"... the Court of Justice does not pronounce on the division of powers between the Community and the Member States by way of a simple definition of the powers granted to the Community as opposed to those which remain for the Member States. Its jurisprudence should rather be characterised as a *continuum* delineating the *specific powers* of the Community and possibly the *implied powers* linked to them, the *non-specific powers* of the Community and, finally, as a "leftover category", the *residual powers* of the Member States (which in some cases, are voluntarily exercised in common by the latter meeting within the Council on an intergovernmental basis)".[34]

The scope of application of the principle of subsidiarity

One of the main arguments of this article is that the principle of subsidiarity is applicable only in areas where concurrent competence is conferred on the Community. This argument is based on (a) the German paradigm; (b) Article 12(2) of the draft Treaty on European Union of 1984; (c) Article 130r(4) of the EEC Treaty and; finally on the wording of Article 3b(2) EC itself.

The relevance of the German model for the role of national governments in the EC has been pointed out in a seminal article by Scharpf. He argues that advocates of a:

" 'United Europe' had in mind ... a federal system fashioned after the American model. What was created, however, were institutional arrangements corresponding more closely to the tradition of German federalism ... More specifically *Länder* governments have a significant share in the exercise of many of the important functions of federal government. It is in this regard that German federalism is most comparable to the European Community."[35]

Institutional arrangements in the Federal Republic and the Community are sufficiently similar to suggest that some of the difficulties of European integration might be illuminated by reference to some of the problems of German federalism which have been studied more systematically.[36]

The parallelism between EC and German institutions appears to be particularly close in the area of key constitutional concepts and principles. Some of these concepts and principles, which have been the subject of extensive doctrinal discussion and constitutional litigation in Germany, have been transplanted in the Community legal and constitutional order.[37] Subsidiarity clearly belongs to this category.[38]

---

[34] See Lenaerts, *supra*, n 5 at 217–218. Author's italics.

[35] Scharpf, 'The joint-decision trap: lessons from German federalism and European integration', (1988) 66 *Public Administration*, 239–278 at 242–243.

[36] This is not to suggest that there are no significant differences between the EC system and German federalism. In fact, European Community institutions are much weaker in relation to Member States' governments than the German federal government in relation to the *Länder*. For a full discussion of this issue see Scharpf, *ibid* at 243–244.

[37] Many of the most important principles applied by the Court – principles such as *Verhältnismässigkeit* (proportionality), *Rechtssicherheit* (legal certainty) and *Vertrauensschutz* (protection of legitimate expectations)- have been borrowed from German law.

[38] See Emiliou, *supra*, n 13 at 388–391.

The legislative power of the federal government covers all subjects falling within federation's (*Bund*) "exclusive" or "concurrent" authority.[39] The federation's exclusive authority is restricted to areas such as foreign policy, citizenship, customs affairs, postal and telecommunications services and federal railroads.[40] The states may legislate in these fields only to the extent expressly authorised by federal law.[41]

Article 74GG embraces a list of 27 topics on which the federation has concurrent power. These areas include ordinary civil and criminal law, public welfare, most economic matters, and following a series of amendments over the years, subjects such as environmental protection, production of nuclear energy, and promotion of scientific research.

Article 72GG is clearly a specific enunciation of the more general idea of subsidiarity.[42] This provision deals with the concurrent legislative powers of the federation and the *Länder*. According to Article 72GG:

"I. In the field of concurrent legislative competence the *Länder* have the power to legislate as long and insofar as the Federation does not make use of its right to legislate.
II. In this field the Federation will have the right to legislate to the extent that federal legal regulation is needed because:
(1) a matter cannot be effectively regulated by the legislation of individual *Länder*, or
(2) the regulation of a matter by a *Land* might prejudice the interest of other *Länder* or of the people as a whole; or
(3) the maintenance of legal or economic uniformity or living conditions beyond the territory of any one *Land*, necessitates such regulation."

Articles 30[43] and 72GG make clear that in the first instance, all government competence is presumed to lie with the *Länder*, so that there is a relationship of subsidiarity between *Länder* and the Federation.[44] The only criteria by which competence should be transferred to the federal government are whether the *Länder* are able to handle legal competences adequately and administrative obligations effectively despite their regional limitation.[45] The effect of Article 72GG is clear: as soon as the federation decides to legislate, the *Länder* are precluded from further legislative regulation and their existing regulation becomes permanently inoperative to the extent that the federation has "occupied the field".

The draft European Union Treaty,[46] drawn up by the European Parliament in 1984, calling for a radical reform of the Communities, includes several references to the principle of subsidiarity. The preamble to the draft Treaty makes the division of powers between the Union and the Member States subject to the

---

[39] See Arts 70, 72 and 73 GG.
[40] Art 73 GG.
[41] Art 71 GG.
[42] See Hailbroner, *supra*, n 18 at 260–261.
[43] Art 30 GG provides that: 'The exercise of governmental powers and the discharge of governmental functions shall be incumbent on the Lander, in so far as this Basic Law does not otherwise prescribe or permit.'
[44] 'Zwischen Bund und Ländern herrsecht also das Verhältnis der Subsidiarität.' See Isensee, *Subsidiaritätprinzip und Verfassungsrecht* (1968) 225.
[45] Isensee, *ibid* at 227.
[46] OJ 1984 C77/33.

principle of subsidiarity: common institutions will be entrusted "... only with those powers required to complete successfully the tasks they may carry out more satisfactorily than the States acting independently". Reference to subsidiarity was made, expressly or implicitly, in other provisions of the draft as well. Article 12 of the draft Treaty incorporated the principle of subsidiarity as a condition of the exercise of concurrent powers by the Union:

"Where this Treaty confers *concurrent competence*[47] on the Union, the Member States shall continue to act as long as the Union has not legislated. The Union shall only act to carry out those tasks which may be undertaken more effectively in common than by the Member States acting separately, in particular those whose execution requires action by the Union because their dimension or effects extend beyond national frontiers."

Following the pattern established by the German *Grundgesetz*,[48] Article 12 of the draft Treaty draws the distinction between exclusive and concurrent powers.[49] According to the scheme established under Article 12, therefore, the Union will exercise only powers attributed to it exclusively. Under Article 12(2), however, the Union will be able to take action in the field of concurrent powers provided that the criteria established by the principle of subsidiarity are observed.

The Single European Act (1986) introduced the principle of subsidiarity, albeit in a limited field, into the positive law of the Community. Article 130r(4) of the EEC Treaty provides:

"The Community shall take action relating to the environment to the extent to which the objectives referred to in paragraph 1 can be attained better at Community level than at the level of the individual Member States."

Environmental protection is one of the areas where concurrent powers have been conferred on the Community by the Treaty.[50]

According to Article 3b of the EC Treaty:

"The Community shall act within the limits of the powers conferred upon it by this Treaty and of the objectives assigned to it therein.

In the areas which do not fall within its exclusive competence, the Community shall take action, in accordance with the principle of subsidiarity, only if and in so far as the objectives of the proposed action cannot be sufficiently achieved by the Member States and can therefore, by reason of the scale or effects of the proposed action, be better achieved by the Community.

Any action by the Community shall not go beyond what is necessary to achieve the objectives of this Treaty."

Article 3b(1) EC establishes the principle that the Communities will have only the powers assigned to them exclusively or previously exercised by them. By the operation of this provision, all the powers of the Communities are derived from

---

[47] Author's italics.
[48] Arts 71 and 72 GG. See also Commission's proposals during the preparation of the Tindemans report, Bull EC Supp 5/75.
[49] This distinction is not novel to Community law. See *e.g.* Opinion 1/75 [1975] ECR 1355.
[50] See Kapteyn and Verloren van Themaat, *op cit*, n 32, 650–657. See also Hession-Macrory, 'Maastricht and the Environmental Policy of the Community: legal issues of a new Environment Policy' in this volume at 151.

the Treaty, and they are assigned powers (*compétences d'attribution*) while the Member States hold all residual powers. The drafters of this provision obviously took account of the case law of the Court of Justice[51] and recognised, by virtue of the rule of effectiveness (*effet utile*), the existence of implied powers of the Communities to achieve their objectives.[52]

This provision should be read together with Article 235 EEC. This provision gives the Community the power to act, in the absence of specific enabling provisions, in all cases where action is required at the Community level in order to complete the common market. Article 235 EEC was not meant to be a means of expanding Community powers by "the back door", but rather an expression of subsidiary competences in the sense of supporting and complementary functions.[53] The express recognition of the doctrine of "implied powers" in the revised Treaty, however, has the advantage that it introduces a certain element of flexibility in the definition of the powers of the Communities, thus allowing for their broad interpretation.

Article 3b(2) provides that Community action "... in the areas which do not fall within its exclusive jurisdiction ..."[54] is subject to a substantive condition, that is, observance of the principle of subsidiarity. Since the Community enjoys both exclusive and concurrent powers and Article 3b expressly excludes the application of the principle of subsidiarity to exclusive powers one can safely assume that subsidiarity is relevant only in areas where there is concurrent competence. Where exclusive competence has been conferred, the principle of subsidiarity, by definition, does not apply; exclusive competence lies either with the Community or with the Member States. This does not of course rule out the possibility of exclusive Community powers exceptionally being conferred on the Member States and vice versa.[55]

Admittedly though, it is far from clear which areas should be regarded as falling within the exclusive jurisdiction of the Community. The Commission takes the view that an area falls within the exclusive jurisdiction of the Community if the Treaties impose on it an obligation to act because it is regarded as having sole responsibility for the performance of a particular task.[56] The Commission has indicated that the following areas meet the above criterion: the removal of barriers to the free movement of goods, persons, services and capital; the Common Commercial Policy; the general rules on competition; the common organization of agricultural markets; the conservation of fisheries resources; and the essential elements of Transport Policy.[57] Even though this is a

---

[51] See *e.g.* Case 22/70 *Commission v Council (ERTA)* [1971] ECR 263.

[52] In Cases 281, 283–5, 287/85 *Germany v Commission* [1987] ECR 3203, the Court held that whenever a provision of the EEC Treaty confers a specific task on the Commission, that provision must also be regarded as impliedly conferring on the Commission '... the powers which are indispensable in order to carry out that task.'

[53] Gretschmann, 'The subsidiarity principle: who is to do what in an integrated Europe?' in *Subsidiarity: the Challenge of Change: Proceedings of the Delors Colloquium* (1991) 54.

[54] This provision does not refer to legislation but to action by the Community which makes it possible to argue that administrative action is covered as well.

[55] See the editorial comment 'The subsidiarity principle' in (1990) 27 CMLRev 181–184 at 184.

[56] See Communication of the Commission to the Council and the European Parliament, 'The Principle of Subsidiarity', COM Doc SEC(92) 1990, 27 October 1992, 5.

[57] *Ibid* at 7.

substantial area the Commission has made clear that "The demarcation lines of this block of exclusive powers will have to change as European integration progresses".[58]

It is respectfully submitted that the Commission's approach is correct. Subsidiarity should not apply to areas covered by the internal market and some common policies that play a key role in its smooth functioning. In those areas the Member States, by ratifying the Single European Act, have explicitly agreed that the lowest desirable level for deciding and carrying out a policy is that of the Community. A leading commentator, echoing the recommendations of the Sutherland Report,[59] observed that:

"The lack of subsidiarity is the whole point of the single market. The application of 'subsidiarity' in this area would imply a return to inefficient market systems from which Europe is rightly moving away, a return to protectionism and the Europe of non-tariff barrier".[60]

As seen above the Court has taken the view that whenever the Treaty gives the Community a power to enact binding measures, and the Community exercises that power by adopting legislation or entering into an international agreement, that area is regarded as falling within the exclusive competence of the Community.[61] In other words , once the Community has "occupied the field", the original power of the Member States has been transferred to the Community. If the Court were to follow the same line of reasoning with regard to Article 3b, any given area would be regarded as falling within the exclusive jurisdiction of the Community once the Community had occupied the field; consequently subsidiarity would be applicable only when the Community legislated for the first time in a new area.[62]

Since subsidiarity is applicable only in the fields where the Community does not enjoy exclusive competence, this means that the *acquis communautaire* will largely remain unaffected by the application of this principle. Theoretically, at least, Member States will retain all the powers which they are able to exercise more efficiently themselves and must transfer to the Community those powers which they are unable to use effectively. The Community should therefore intervene, in the sphere of concurrent powers, only in a subsidiary capacity and:

"... in accordance with a principle of exact appropriateness whereby each level is granted powers only because these cannot, given their nature and scope, be exercised efficiently and effectively at any other level."[63]

---

[58] *Ibid* at 8.

[59] See Report to the EC Commission by the High Level Group on the Operation of the Internal Market, presided over by Peter Sutherland, 28 October 1992; supp to the *European Report* no 1808, 31 October 1992.

[60] See *The Times*, 30 October 1992.

[61] See Case 22/70 *Commission* v *Council (ERTA)*, [1970] ECR 263, at 275 *per curiam*: '... Community powers exclude the possibility of concurrent powers on the part of the Member States ...'; Opinion 1/75 *Re Local Cost Standard* [1975] ECR 1355 at 1364. Also Case 24/83 *Gewise* v *Mackenzie* [1984] ECR 817 shows that once delegated, power cannot be withdrawn.

[62] See Hartley, 'Constitutional and institutional aspects of the Maastricht Agreement', (1992) 42 ICLQ, 213–237 at 216.

[63] See 'The Principle of Subsidiarity', EP Committee on Institutional Affairs, Rapporteur: Valery Giscard d' Estaing (European Parliament, October 1990). DOC EN\RR\98228.

The role of the political institutions

Subsidiarity was one of the key areas of discussion of the European Council in its Edinburgh Summit in December 1992. A document[64] was adopted in order to ensure the effective application of the principle of subsidiarity by the Community institutions. This document attempts to give a more precise form to subsidiarity and sets out practices and procedures which will require Community institutions to bear subsidiarity in mind at every stage of the legislative process. An inter-institutional agreement aimed at ensuring, that Community institutions at least consider the principle before proposing or enacting legislation is also envisaged.

It is also made clear that the principle of subsidiarity "cannot be regarded as having direct effect".[65] In examining whether a proposal for a Community measure conforms with Article 3b, specific guidelines have also been laid down.[66] These can be summarised as follows:

(1) Is the proposed action within the limits of the powers conferred on the Community by the Treaty and aimed at meeting one or more of the Treaty objectives?
(2) If so, can the objectives of the proposed action not be sufficiently achieved by Member States?
(3) If not, what should be the nature and the intensity of Community action?

These guidelines are somewhat general, but they do help to make the Community institutions question whether they should act even where the Community does have the competence to do so. A key issue here is how the objectives of a proposed measure are to be formulated. According to Hartley:

"In practice, it will almost always be possible to formulate the objectives of the measure in different ways. In defending the measure, the Commission and the Council will argue for a formulation which requires Community action. One can even expect that the preamble and wording of the measure will be drafted so as to facilitate this."[67]

In practical terms, the Commission has indicated that it will be consulting more widely before proposing legislation. It will also be making a more systematic use of consultation documents (Green Papers). In the proposed measure it will justify its conformity with the principle of subsidiarity and, whenever necessary, give details on this issue in the exploratory memorandum accompanying the proposal.

The Council will examine the compliance of every Commission proposal with Article 3b on a regular basis. Where appropriate, reports from both working groups and COREPER will describe how Article 3b has been applied.

The European Parliament will be receiving an annual report from the Commission concerning the application of Article 3b. This report will be discussed

---

[64] See 'Overall Approach to the Application by the Council of the Subsidiarity Principle and Article 3b of the Treaty on European Union', Annex 1 to Part A of the 'Conclusions of the Presidency', European Council in Edinburgh, 11–12 December 1992.
[65] *Ibid* at 4.
[66] *Ibid* at 6–9.
[67] Hartley, *supra*, n 62 at 217.

by the Parliament along with the annual report which the European Council has to submit to the European Parliament, on progress achieved by the Union.[68] In all cases where the co-operation and co-decision procedures are to be applied, the Council will fully inform the European Parliament of its position concerning the observance of Article 3b. The Council will also inform the Parliament if it partially or totally objects to a Commission proposal on the ground that it is contrary to the principle of subsidiarity.

At the political level these procedures may make the Commission more cautious in the measures it proposes and the Council more careful in the measures it enacts. "Perhaps of greater importance [though] is the change in culture within the Community institutions created by having to consider the principle [of subsidiarity] seriously before embarking on new legislation".[69] All three political institutions of the Community will have to take the principle seriously because "interpretation of this principle, as well as review of compliance with it by the Community institutions are subject to control by the Court of Justice".[70]

The role of the European Court

"The true worth of the principle [of subsidiarity] will be known only once some busybody Directive has been challenged in the European Court and the judges have ruled on where Brussels stops and nations are to be left alone."[71]

Presumably, Member States would be able to invoke subsidiarity in their political opposition to various legislative proposals. It remains to be seen, however, whether the principle will operate in practice as a restraint on Community legislation. Among the legal issues bound to arise is the extent to which the European Court will entertain challenges of EC legislation on the ground that the measure concerned has been adopted contrary to the principle of subsidiarity. In other words, to what extent will subsidiarity prove to be a justiciable principle?

Severe doubts have been raised, however, as to whether the European Court is fitted for the task to decide whether the principle of subsidiarity has been breached in a particular case or not. Lord Mackenzie Stuart[72] has complained that:

"The interpretation of subsidiarity is a political issue and not one for the Court of Justice of the European Communities. Maastricht, however, places that responsibility squarely on its shoulders. Worse, ... the definition of subsidiarity contained in the Treaty ... is a rich and prime example of gobbledygook embracing simultaneously two opposed concepts of subsidiarity. To regard the chosen formula as a constitutional safeguard shows great optimism."[73]

[68] See Art D, TEU.
[69] Weatherhill & Beaumont, *EEC Law* (1993) 780.
[70] *Supra*, n 64, Annex to Part A at 4.
[71] See *The Economist*, 11 July 1992; Survey: the European Community, 14.
[72] President of the Court of Justice from 1984 to 1988.
[73] Letter to *The Independent*, 15 June 1992.

Questions such as whether Community action is more effective than action by Member States or whether a task can better be attained at the Community rather than at the national level will inevitably allow the Court to indulge in political considerations (*i.e.* second guessing). This might release the judges from their proper reserve in interfering with decisions on the grounds of policy, or assessment of facts or merits. This will inevitably destroy the credibility of the Court of Justice which, given its jurisprudence, is arguably the Community's most effective institution.

But even if it is accepted that subsidiarity should be justiciable this does not solve the problem of political debate and negotiation. The Treaties and the powers of the Communities have to be adapted to changing political, economic and social circumstances. The history of the Communities shows that the attribution of competences and the interpretation of the Treaties has varied. The Treaties have an evolutionary character; they adapt to changing circumstances. This holds true especially in the grey areas where Community and national powers overlap. Subsidiarity may help to set the boundaries in these grey areas but will not take the political debate away from this problem. For this reason justiciability will not provide a watertight answer in those grey areas between what the Community is entitled to do and what is the province of the national administrations.

Another problem as far as the justiciability of subsidiarity is concerned is the subjective character of the principle in question. This means that the application of subsidiarity is a policy decision which should be left to political bodies democratically answerable for their decisions. Therefore, unless subsidiarity can be formulated in an objective way judicial review will be impossible. But even in this case, judicial review should be of a limited extent and only manifest or grave disregard of the principle would nullify the challenged measures. Thus the Court will have to leave a wide margin of discretion to the decision making institutions.[74]

The experience of the *Bundesverfassungsgericht* (*BVerfGE*) in reviewing the compatibility of federal legislation with Article 72(2)GG is instructive in this respect. According to this constitutional provision, federal legislation must be necessary on three grounds, two of which are roughly equivalent to the "effectiveness" test. Originally the *BVerfGE* interpreted this clause very widely as a non-justiciable guideline for the federal legislator. In the *Federal Amnesty Act* case[75] the Court declined to review the question whether the conditions of Article 72(2)GG were met. It confirmed the view expressed in its previous judgments that the decision as to whether a need for regulation by federal legislation existed was a matter for the "conscientious discretion" of the federal legislator, which by its nature was not justiciable and could therefore not be subject to judicial review. The Court said that the conditions for the exercise of concurrent powers, which were individually specified in Article 72(2)GG, limited the

---

[74] Such views have been adopted by the House of Lords' Select Committee on the European Communities in their '*Report on Economic and Monetary Union and Political Union*', Session 1989–90, 27th Report (1990) at 55.

[75] 2 BVerfGE 213 (1953).

federations's freedom of discretion. This fact, however, did not affect the essentially discretionary nature of the decision. The question as to how far the decision was subject to review by the Court if the federal legislator had mistaken the limits of its discretion or abused it was left open. The Court said that, with regard to the enactment of the contested measure, there was no basis whatsoever for supposing that this discretion had been exceeded or abused. It is clear from this judgment that the *BVerfGE* virtually abandoned control over the conditions under which the federation could exercise its wide-ranging concurrent powers.[76]

In the *Shop-Closing Act* case[77] the Federal Government invoked the "need" to achieve legal or economic unity of living conditions beyond the borders of a single state[78] in order to justify the enactment of the *Ländenschlussgesetz*. The Court held that the federation must be permitted to strive after the degree of uniformity in social life which it felt to be desirable. This was a pre-emptive political decision which the Court had in principle to respect, since it was the task of every legislator, especially in the field of the economy, to shape and determine living conditions. However, the federal legislator had then to consider whether the uniformity of living conditions to which it aspired required it to take action itself. The *BVerfGE* accepted that the maintenance of legal or economic unity and the maintenance of the uniformity of living conditions were legal concepts (which would in principle make them now justiciable), but found them so indeterminate that their closer specification, in itself, went a long way towards deciding whether a federal law was necessary to achieve them. For this reason the Court confined itself to reviewing whether the federal legislator had in principle interpreted the terms correctly and kept within the bounds defined by them.

This time, however, the *BVerfGE* did not content itself with a simple assertion that the federation had not exceeded or abused its discretion. This conclusion was reached only after a detailed consideration of the factors in favour of a need for federal regulation which the federal government had put forward in the oral hearings. The fact that the *Länder* had urged federal action was also considered by the court as evidence that an "effective" regulation by the *Länder* in terms of Article 72(2)(1)GG was not possible.

This judgment represented a doctrinal shift form the idea of the non-justiciability of the terms of Article 72(2)GG. Yet, in practice it did not limit the federation's room for manoeuvre to a considerable extent. In the *Building Law* case,[79] the *BVerfGE* in an *obiter* remarked that Article 72(2)GG was not a general competence clause establishing new federal legislative powers wherever a "need" for uniform regulation could be claimed. Such a "need" was an additional requirement in accordance with Article 72(2)GG, when a federal power had already been accepted in principle on other grounds.[80]

---

[76] This position was subsequently reaffirmed by the BVerfGE in the *North Rhine-Westphalia Salaries* case (4 BVerfGE 114) and the *Platow Amnesty* case (10 BVerfGE 234).

[77] 13 BVerfGE 230 (1961).

[78] Art 72(2)(3) GG.

[79] 3 BVerfGE 407 (1954).

[80] In the 1962 *Federal Waterways* case, 15 BVerfGE 1, the court seemed to have departed from the above, otherwise undisputed, rule. Nevertheless this ruling seems to have been quietly forgotten.

According to Blair:

"The general picture remains one of extreme self-restraint on the part of the Court and willingness to leave almost entirely to the discretion of the Federal Government and Parliament the question of how far they have the right to legislate in the wide field of concurrent powers ... In taking up this stance the Court has had the support of a substantial body of literature, and there is no doubt that it is also supported by some common sense considerations. The Federal Government and Parliament are indeed better placed than a court to exercise the distinctively political judgment as to whether a matter can be effectively regulated by individual *Länder* ..."[81]

On the other hand, the *BVerfGE's* position has drawn some criticism on the ground that the *Länder*, which might at least theoretically all disagree with the federation on the question of a "need" for federal legislation,[82] are left with no remedy (except in quite blatant cases). In this respect the Court's approach disregards a useful instrument given by the Basic Law for controlling an expansionist approach to federal powers.

With subsidiarity now enshrined in Article 3b of the EC Treaty, its interpretation and application is subject to the jurisdiction of the Court of Justice in the same way as that of any other Treaty provision. The emphasis on legal norms and on institutional devices for ensuring that Community action conforms to them expresses a continued preference on the part of the framers of the Treaties for the resolution of political disputes through authoritative judicial decisions rather than by resort to the more informal methods of political accommodation. The establishment of the Court of Justice and its subsequent activity has introduced a new dimension of essentially political decision making into the theory and practice of constitutional adjudication.[83] Fulfilling its task under Article 164 EEC, the Court had to interpret the Treaty and had by necessity to base some of its decisions on explicitly political value judgements even though it has been reluctant to acknowledge this fact.[84]

A sensible course of action for the Court will be to restrict itself to a "marginal review"[85] of subsidiarity. This is the attitude which has been adopted by the Court in examining whether the Council and/or the Commission have kept within the limits of their discretion. In this case the Court examines only

---

[81] Blair, *Federalism and Judicial Review in West Germany* (1981), 83. This view has been expressly confirmed in the *Hesse Salary Adaptation Act* case (34 BVerfGE 9; 1972).

[82] The BVerfGE will not deal with the question of necessity as this is considered to fall within the ambit of legislative discretion. It only examines: (a) whether the legislature has interpreted these grounds properly; (b) whether it has exceeded its powers; and, (c) whether there had been a misuse of powers. See *e.g. the State Liability* case, 61 BVerfGE 149 (1982).

[83] See Jacobs, 'Is the Court of Justice of the European Communities a constitutional court?'; in Curtin & O' Keeffe (eds), *op cit*, n 88 at 25–32; Due, 'A constitutional court for the European Communities', *ibid* at 3–10.

[84] For a detailed discussion of this issue see Rassmussen, *On Law and Policy in the European Community* (1986); Hartley, *The Foundations of European Community Law* (1988), 2nd ed, 49–81; Shapiro, 'The European Court of Justice', in Sbragia (ed), *Euro-Politics* (1991) 123–156; Rassmussen, 'Between self-restraint and activism' (1988) 13 EL Rev 28–38.

[85] Schermers uses the term 'marginal review' in the cases where the Court's review is strictly confined to questions whether the administration remained within the proper bounds and did not uses its authority in a manifestly incorrect manner. See Schermers and Waelbroeck, *Judicial Protection in the European Communities* (1992), 5th ed, paras 313, 437, 601–603.

whether "... the evaluation of the competent authority contains a patent error or constitutes a misuse of powers".[86] Support for this argument may be drawn from the Court's caselaw on the Community institutions' liability for damages in respect of normative acts. Here the Community will incur liability only when "... a sufficiently serious breach of a superior rule of law for the protection of the individual has occurred".[87]

The Court certainly may not be expected to push the extent of its judicial review, as far as subsidiarity is concerned, any further than is absolutely necessary for ensuring and respecting the Rule of Law.[88] It is idle to point out in this connection that an appropriate reasoning of a judgment supporting the Court's findings, in respect of the observance of the principle of subsidiarity, may be a proper guarantee for a judicial review, exercised properly and within reasonable limits. Nevertheless, the authoritative interpretation and application of the principle of subsidiarity by the Court will further enhance its function as the Community's constitutional tribunal.

Conclusions

In the years after the Second World War there was shift, especially in the Federal Republic of Germany,[89] from a socio-philosophical to a legal concept of subsidiarity. Thus the original relationship between the individual, the group and society has been extended to embrace political institutions and authorities. In the latter sense, subsidiarity establishes a presumption in favour of the lower authorities and jurisdictions. That is, certain areas of decision making will not be subject to interference from the central authorities.[90] Thus the centre should exercise only those powers which cannot be discharged by the smaller political units. The reverse of course can be true. That is, the central authority, pointing to the autonomy of the lower level, may transfer some of their responsibilities to the latter.

One of the aspects of the Rule of Law in a democratic state is the separation and division of powers both on the vertical and horizontal axis. The idea behind this is that fragmentation of power will best protect liberty. As a result, executive, legislative and judicial functions, both at national and supranational level, are attached to different organ-groups. It is the functional and institutional interdependence of these organ-groups rather than their independence that prevents any of them from achieving dominance over the others.

Federalism adds an extra safety valve to the system of checks and balances, which shields against abuse of power, protects the freedom of the individual and safeguards justice. Power, attributed to the state by the people, is exercised

---

[86] Case 78/74 *Deuka* v *Einfuhr- und Vorratsstelle für Vorratsstelle für Getreide und Futtermittel* [1975] ECR 421.
[87] This doctrine is known as the 'Schöppenstedt formula'; see Case 5/71 *Zuckerfabrik Schöppenstedt* v *Council* [1971] ECR 975.
[88] See Case 294/83 *Parti Ecologiste 'Les Verts'* v *European Parliament* [1986] ECR 1339 *per curiam* at 1365.
[89] See generally in Stadler, *Subsidiaritätsprinzip und Föderalismus* (1951).
[90] See Gretschmann, *op cit*, n 53, at 48–49.

under separate headings on a horizontal axis – legislative, executive and judicial arms of the state authority – and divided on a vertical axis – local government, state and central government. Separation of powers and the federal state division are closely linked; in the context of competing powers and levels of authority individual rights are best protected. Federalism fosters the model of subsidiarity: that is, as many tasks as possible should be administered by small groups before making the next level responsible for them. In practical terms, this implies that local government should precede state administration, which, in turn, should precede federal government.

Thus subsidiarity can only be fully understood and defined within the context of federalism. Federalism is the most important element of the vertical division of powers.[91] Decentralization and devolution, as expressed by the principle of subsidiarity, are the main constitutional reasons for fostering activities and re-sponsibilities at the federal level. Since all these sources of power are in accordance with the basic principles of the federal constitution,[92] they strengthen its vitality. Thus issues of federalism, subsidiarity and separation of powers are inextricably intertwined. The federal judicial power constitutes an aspect of the separation of powers as well as federalism; the distribution of legislative and executive responsibilities to the federation and the component states is a federal issue as well as part of the horizontal division of powers.[93]

With centralising models firmly rejected by all parties concerned, the model of federalism based on the principle of subsidiarity, as described above, has a strong appeal to most of those who are concerned with the Community's consti-tutional future. Under this model EC institutions are seen as having extensive, but nevertheless restricted, areas of power. The actual implementation of Com-munity policies will fall almost exclusively to the national authorities, which in turn will have *exclusive competence*, in some fields, such as for instance education and culture, police and organization of local government.

In this way, central institutions strong enough to act on behalf of the whole political community can be established, but at the same time the restrictions on their competence for the administration of most of its policies will help to ensure an acceptable level of dispersion of political authority throughout the Com-munity. Properly observed and enforced, the principle of subsidiarity could function as an instrument for the decentralization of political power. Sub-sidiarity is, therefore, essentially a device which will perpetuate into the era of supranational international institutions the particular national characteristics and traditions which are dominant in the sovereign Member States of the Euro-pean Community.

This principle would also serve as a means of maintaining a high degree of administrative decentralization: EC Member States surrendered their preten-sions to pure and undiluted sovereignty, but each retains its own governmental apparatus to administer national legislation and those services which remain in its competence and to implement EC legislation. Yet, distribution of power of

---

[91] Loewenstein, *Political Power and the Governmental Process* (1957) 295 *et seq.*

[92] See Art 28 GG and Art IV para 4 US Constitution.

[93] Doehring, *Staatsrecht der Bundesrepublik Deutschland* (1980) 107 *et seq*; Stein, *Staatsrecht* (1982) 67 *et seq.*

this kind is not simply a mechanical device or an exercise in the division of labour in the Community organization. It places restrictions on the discretion and freedom of manoeuvre of the central authority and inevitably encourages substantial decentralization of political power.

NICHOLAS EMILIOU

Part 3

Citizenship and Fundamental Rights

Chapter 6
Union Citizenship

This article examines the concept of citizenship of the Union established by the Treaty on European Union (TEU).[1]

Background to the TEU provisions

The concept of European citizenship was mentioned from a very early stage in the development of the Communities. The free movement provisions of the EEC Treaty, and in particular those concerning the free movement of workers, were seen as being the first steps in creating "an incipient form of European citizenship".[2] The first concrete steps towards a European citizenship came in 1974 when the Paris Summit established a working group to study the conditions "under which the citizens of the Member States could be given *special rights* as members of the Community".[3] The Tindemans Report on European Union in 1975 advocated granting special rights to nationals of the Member States, consisting of certain civil and political rights, including the right to vote and eligibility for public office.

Subsequent reports followed, such as the European Parliament's Scelba Report.[4] However, as Jessurun d'Oliveira has pointed out, a parlance developed in which reference was made to a citizens' Europe and to European citizens without any clarity about the meaning of these terms.[5] In 1985, the second Addonino Report on 'A People's Europe'[6] dealt with the special rights of Community citizens, from the stance of education, culture, communication

---

[1] See Closa, 'The concept of citizenship in the Treaty on European Union', 29 CML Rev. (1992), 1137–1170; Closa, 'Citizenship of the Union and Nationality of Member States' in this volume at 109; Jessurun D'Oliveira, 'European Citizenship: Its Meaning, Its Potential', forthcoming, to appear in College of Europe/Institut für Europäische Rechtspolitik (eds.), Colloque on the Results of the Intergovernmental conference on Political Union, held 27–29 February 1992 at Bruges (hereinafter referred to as Bruges colloque) and in R Dehousse (ed.), *The European Union Treaty* (1993); O'Keeffe, 'New aspects of the Free Movement of Persons: Towards a European Citizenship', Report for the FIDE Congress, Lisbon, 1992 (FIDE, 1992), 367–391; O'Keeffe, 'Citizenship of the Union', to appear in Demaret (ed), *1993, the Single market and the Free Movement of Persons* (proceedings of the Liège colloque of 26 and 27 June 1992), forthcoming; O'Leary, 'Nationality Law and Community Citizenship: A Tale of Two Uneasy Bedfellows', to appear in vol 12, *Yearbook of European Law*, forthcoming; O'Leary, 'The evolving concept of Community citizenship – from the free movement of persons to Union citizenship', doctoral thesis submitted to the European University Institute, 1993.
[2] Bull EC 11–1968, 5–9.
[3] Bull EC 12–1974, point 111. (Author's italics).
[4] E.P. Working Documents 1977–8, Doc. 346/77, p 10.
[5] Bruges colloque, *op cit.*, n 1.
[6] Reports of the ad hoc Committee on a People's Europe to the European Council, Supplement 7/85 – Bull EC, p.18.

exchanges and the image and identity of the Community. Proposals for conferring special rights on Community nationals considered free movement as one of the keystones of the rights of Community citizens. Following the Commission's proposal for a Directive on the general right of residence irrespective of the exercise of an economic activity,[7] the Commission's guidelines for a Community Policy on Migration[8] stated that the free movement of persons should go beyond a Community employment market and should embrace the concept of European citizenship. The Commission also proposed giving voting rights in local elections to Community nationals in their Member State of residence.[9]

The debate on citizenship gained momentum in the process preceding the intergovernmental conference on the TEU. The Belgian memorandum on institutional relaunch contained elements of what were later to figure in the citizenship debate such as the inclusion of human rights in the Treaties, accession to the European Convention on Human Rights (ECHR), and provisions to allow Community nationals to vote in local and European Parliament elections in their country of residence.[10] However, the first traceable reference to the concept of citizenship was contained in a letter of the Prime Minister of Spain to the President in Office of the Council prior to the Dublin Summit in June 1990.[11] At the heart of this concept were free movement, establishment, access to employment, and the right to vote and stand for election irrespective of the country of origin. The Dublin Summit endorsed the concept of citizenship in principle and asked the Council to examine the question "How will the Union include and extend the notion of Community citizenship carrying with it specific rights (human, political, social, the right of complete free movement and residence etc) for the citizens of the Member States by virtue of these States belonging to the Union?"[12]

The Spanish Government submitted a Memorandum on European Citizenship.[13] It argued that nationals of the Member States were still being treated as no more than privileged foreigners, and it called for a change towards European citizenship. It sought the granting of European citizenship to citizens of Member States, who would have special rights and duties. The memorandum proposed granting (i) full free movement and right of residence, including the right to participate in the political life of the Member State of residence, (ii) specific rights in the areas of health, social affairs, education, culture, the environment, consumer protection (in so far as the Union had or acquired competence in these areas), (iii) assistance and diplomatic protection by other Member States, (iv) petition to the European Parliament and the creation of a European Ombudsman, and (v) other rights to materialise in the future. The Spanish Memorandum had as its basis the notion that the Treaty should define the rights of individuals affected by a transfer of competence to the Union. As

---

[7] OJ 1979, C 207/14.
[8] Supplement 9/85, Bull EC, p. 5.
[9] COM (88) 371 final, 11.7.88.
[10] *Europe documents* No. 1608, 29 March 1990.
[11] *Europe* No. 5252, 11 May 1990, p. 3.
[12] Bull EC 6–1990, Annex I, p. 15.
[13] Towards a European Citizenship, *Europe documents*, No. 1653, 2 October 1990.

regards human rights, whereas the Spanish Memorandum maintained that human rights should be part of the rights of the European citizen, they were considered separately from the citizenship issue. Thus, human rights protection should be extended to all Community residents, irrespective of nationality.

The Commission opinion of 21 October 1990[14] supported the concept of citizenship and made clear that it saw citizenship as a means of counteracting the democratic deficit and strengthening democratic legitimacy. This emphasis was shared by the Danish Government in a Memorandum in which it proposed the right of Community nationals to vote in local elections in the Member State of residence, and the establishment of the Ombudsman.[15]

The European Council at the Rome Summit in December 1990 decided that the concept of citizenship should be examined with a view to creating the Union. It considered that there might be three groups of rights: civic rights such as participation in local and European Parliament elections, social and economic rights, such as freedom of movement and equal treatment, and joint diplomatic protection of Community citizens in third country countries. The Council also decided that the issue of the protection of citizens' rights should be considered, a mandate which was to result in the creation of the office of the Ombudsman. The Council did not consider human rights as part of the citizenship package. Subsequently, the Commission and Parliament rejected this exclusion of human rights from the citizenship proposals.[16] The Commission maintained that citizens should be entitled to invoke the rights guaranteed under the ECHR, to which there should be explicit reference, and recalled the proposal for the Community to accede to the Convention. The European Parliament Rapporteur, Rosy Bindi, considered that citizenship should be based on the expansion of fundamental rights.

The citizenship provisions which were approved by the personal representatives of the Heads of State and Government, at ministerial level, and the Luxembourg European Council and finally inserted in the TEU largely followed the original outline given by the Rome Summit. In particular, they did not contain a reference to human rights, which was separately contained in Article F(2) TEU. The provisions which did emerge had all been raised earlier in the debate on citizenship.

The TEU provisions on citizenship

The preamble to the TEU states that the High Contracting Parties "resolved to establish a citizenship common to nationals of their countries". In Article B, under the heading Common Provisions, one of the objectives of the Union is stated to be "to strengthen the protection of the rights and interests of the

---

[14] Supplement 2/91 – Bull EC.

[15] *Europe*, No. 5353, 19 October 1990.

[16] Union citizenship. Contributions by the Commission to the Intergovernmental Conference, Supplement 2/91 – Bull EC. Bindi Report on Union Citizenship, PE Doc. A 3–0139/91, 23 May 1991.

nationals of its Member States through the introduction of a citizenship of the Union."

The detailed TEU provisions on citizenship are contained in a new Part Two of the EC Treaty (*i.e.* the EEC Treaty as amended by the Maastricht Treaty); the Part is devoted solely to this topic.[17] It has been argued that this location in a separate Part indicates that the citizenship provisions are an essential component of the Treaty,[18] and that it shows that they are implementing measures and not merely declaratory.[19]

Articles 8–8e EC, as inserted by the TEU, contain the provisions on Union citizenship. A citizenship of the Union is established, to be conferred on every person holding the nationality of a Member State. Seven rights are enumerated. The right of free movement and the right of residence are, as they had been throughout the debate on European citizenship, the foundations of Union citizenship. There are also the rights to vote and to stand for election in municipal elections and elections to the European Parliament. There is the right to diplomatic and consular assistance in countries in which a Union citizen's Member State of nationality is not represented. There are two provisions concerning the protection of citizens' rights, the right to petition the European Parliament and to apply to the Ombudsman. Finally, the Treaty provides that this catalogue may be added to or strengthened and provides for a review procedure.

Although Article 8(2) states that Union citizens shall be subject to the duties imposed by "this Treaty", it does not specify such duties. Civic duties differ between the Member States but they include voting obligations, military service, the payment of taxes and contribution to the mandatory social security systems. With the exception of voting rights, the TEU provisions do not appear to lay down duties. Although Article 8e provides for adding to the rights laid down by the citizenship provisions, there is no equivalent provision to add to the duties laid down thereby.

The catalogue of rights contained in the citizenship provisions is limited. A full catalogue of rights might have included social rights such as housing and social welfare, fundamental rights, and stronger political rights. It could also have consolidated rights the basis for which is to be found elsewhere in the Treaty which also imply rights for the citizen, such as those concerning consumers' rights, culture, education and vocational training, working conditions, public health and the environment, as well as the social rights deriving from the Agreement on Social Policy.

The TEU citizenship provisions do not refer to documents of a constitutional character, albeit soft-law, such as the Community Social Charter and the European Social Charter. The Preamble to the Single European Act, by contrast, refers to the "fundamental rights recognised in ... the European Social Charter".

Nationality of the Member States and national citizenship are unaffected by

---

[17] Art 138a EC states that political parties express the political will of the citizens of the Union.
[18] The Bindi report, *supra*, note 16, had argued that they should be in a single Title.
[19] Closa, *supra*, n 1, 1992 CML Rev. 1158.

the citizenship provisions. The TEU does not create a nationality of the Union, but rather a complementary citizenship to citizenship of a Member State. Nationality was described by the International Court of Justice in the *Nottebohm* case,[20] as "a legal bond having as its basis a social fact of attachment, a genuine connection of existence, interests and sentiments, together with the existence of reciprocal rights and duties", and characterises the relationship between a state and an individual externally. Citizenship, on the other hand, implies the rights and duties applicable in the internal legal order, many of which follow from or depend on nationality. The essence of citizenship has been defined as "the constitutional arrangements made for participation by a defined category of individuals in the life of the State".[21] Political rights, pertaining to citizens, may be contrasted with those fundamental rights more generally available within a state to all, irrespective of nationality.

The Union citizenship created by the TEU does not create a new political subject. Political subjects remain associated with notions of nation or people or with citizenship of a state. The rights conferred by the TEU on Union citizens do not equate to the full political rights of the national citizen. In this respect, Union citizenship cannot be likened to national citizenship.

The nationality requirement

The criterion set by Article 8 EC for inclusion within the personal scope of the Treaty provisions on Union citizenship is the possession of the nationality of one of the Member States. This issue is dealt with by Carlos Closa in his contribution to this book,[22] but a few comments will be made here.

Determination of the possession of the nationality of a Member State is the subject of a Declaration on nationality of a Member State attached to the TEU whereby the IGC declares that wherever in the EC Treaty[23] reference is made to the nationals of the Member States, the question whether an individual possesses the nationality of a Member State shall be settled solely by reference to the national law of the Member State concerned. Member States may make declarations as to who are to be considered their nationals for Community purposes.

The purpose of the Declaration is to confirm that, from the point of view of Community Law, it is the Member States which control which of their nationals may enjoy rights under Community Law. This exclusive competence is in line with Article 1 of the Convention on Certain Questions relating to the Conflict of Nationality Laws,[24] and was recently upheld by the Court of Justice in its

---

[20] *Liechtenstein* v *Guatemala*, [1955] I.C.J. 15 at 23.
[21] Evans, 'Nationality law and European integration', 16 EL Rev. 118.
[22] Closa, 'Citizenship of the Union and Nationality of Member States' in this volume 109.
[23] The Declaration refers to the EC Treaty and not to the Union Treaty.
[24] 'It is for each State to determine under its own law who are its nationals'.

judgment in *Micheletti*.[25] Declarations on nationality were made by Germany and the United Kingdom on the occasion of their accession to the Community.

This exclusive competence is rather anomalous. Normally, in Community law concerning the free movement of persons, the Court has been at pains to hold that the concept of, for example, a worker, is a Community concept, which cannot be defined by reference to national law, but rather must be interpreted in the light of Community law, as otherwise it would be subject to unacceptable variations. Nevertheless as regards nationality, possession of which is a *sine qua non* for primary entitlement to fundamental Community rights such as the free movement of persons,[26] the Member States are deemed to have exclusive competence. In *Micheletti*, the Court held that the definition of conditions governing the acquisition and loss of nationality were, according to international law, matters which fell within the competence of each Member State, whose decision must then be respected by the other Member States. However, as Jessurun d'Oliveira points out, this seemingly absolutist view is subject to the statement that the Member State's competence must be exercised in compliance with Community law.[27] He argues that in fact there are no limits on the Member States' discretion in this area, and maintains that the principle of subsidiarity would lead the Community to abstain from laying down guidelines.

Competence as to nationality is jealously guarded by the Member States. They rightly see decisions concerning the acquisition and loss of their nationality as being an essential part of their sovereignty. The nationality provisions concerning Union citizenship respect the exclusive competence of the Member States in this area. Although this may produce anomalies, nevertheless, because of the attitude of the Member States, reinforced by the *Micheletti* judgment, it seems improbable that Community legislation or the caselaw of the Court will alter the competence of the Member States in this domain. If change will come, it will be as a result of the success of the Union and of the internal market, accompanied by an ever-increasing bundle of rights attached to Union citizenship. At that stage, nationality of the Member States may appear increasingly irrelevant in a real union where the focus would be on the relationship between the Union and the citizen, overshadowing that between the citizen and the Member State. That day is far off.

The TEU provisions deny the possibility of extending Union citizenship to third country nationals legally resident in the Community by tying access to Union citizenship to possession of nationality of the Member States. The inclusion of certain groups, defined by nationality, has as its corollary, the exclusion of others.[28] The position of third country nationals is discussed below.

---

[25] Case C-369/90, *MV Micheletti and others* v *Delegaçion del Gobierno en Cantabria* [1992] ECR I-4239. See Jessurun D'Oliveira, annotation of Case C-369/90, *Micheletti*, 30 CML Rev. (1993), 623–638;

[26] Art 48 does not specify that the workers to which it refers must have the nationality of a Member State but it is generally interpreted in this way. In Case 238/83 *Meade* v *Caisse d'Allocations familiales de la Region Parisienne* [1984] ECR 2631 the Court arguably so held. The Treaty articles on freedom of establishment and freedom to provide services on the other hand refer to nationals of the Member States.

[27] See Jessurun d'Oliveira, *supra*, n 25, 634.

[28] Jessurun d'Oliveira, Bruges colloque, *supra*, n 1 .

Free movement and right of residence

The free movement of persons is the cornerstone of the Union citizenship provisions, as it had been throughout the evolution of the concept of European citizenship. Article 8a EC provides for freedom of movement and residence within the territory of the Member States. This is stated to be subject to the limitations and conditions laid down by "this Treaty" and by the measures adopted to give it effect. Presumably the reference to "this Treaty" is a reference to the EEC Treaty as amended by the TEU. In that case, the exceptions to the rights of free movement regarding public policy, public security and public health continue to apply to those already covered under Articles 48–66 of the EC Treaty. Moreover, since Article 8a refers to limitations and conditions, it is clearly envisaged that analogous provisions to the existing exceptions to the free movement of persons may apply. It is likely that such restrictions will be introduced in secondary Community legislation adopted under this heading. However, it is also possible that the wording "this Treaty" could refer to the TEU as a whole, including its intergovernmental part on the third pillar, dealing with Justice and Home Affairs. In that case, it could be argued that limitations on freedom of movement and the right of residence as conferred by the citizenship provisions could arise from measures adopted intergovernmentally.

The right of the free movement of persons was conferred on economic actors by the EEC Treaty.[29] This conferral of economic rights contrasted strongly with the Treaty's failure to extend political rights to the same subjects and the denial of the right of free movement as regards access to employment in the public service. Nevertheless, from a very early stage, as noted above, the free movement provisions, and in particular those concerning the free movement of workers, were associated with the concept of European citizenship.

Apart from the rights of free movement conferred on economic actors by the Treaty, and on their family members by secondary legislation, Directives 90/364–366 have conferred rights of free movement on those who are not or have not been economically active.[30] Derogations are allowed by the Member States on the grounds of public policy, public security and public health.[31] The right is subject to the condition that individuals seeking to rely on the Directives must have enough resources to avoid become a burden on the social security system of the host state, and must possess health insurance.

Article 8a does not confer the rights of free movement and residence on family members of Union citizens who do not possess the nationality of a Member State. Such derived rights are an essential component of the rights of

---

[29] Subsequent caselaw of the Court of Justice has turned on discerning a constitutional character in these provisions, where possible independent of an economic nexus. See O'Keeffe, 'Trends in the free movement of persons within the European Communities', in O'Reilly (ed.), *Human Rights and Constitutional Law, Essays in honour of Brian Walsh* (Round Hall Press, Dublin, 1992), 263–291.

[30] Council Dirs 90/364–366 on the right of residence, on the right of residence for employees and self-employed persons who have ceased their occupational activity and on the right of residence for students, OJ 1990, L 180/26, 28 and 30 respectively.

[31] According to Art 2 (2) of each Directive, Dir 62/221 is applicable.

93

those who enjoy free movement under the EEC Treaty and the residence directives.

The emphasis on freedom of movement as a source of citizenship rights is in fact odd. Although some national constitutions refer to freedom of movement on the national territory for their own nationals or citizens,[32] the right is economic rather than overtly political.

Since Community law covers both the economically active and inactive, the TEU does not appear to have added anything new to the right of free movement and of residence in existing Community law. The Commission itself appears to take this view, maintaining that since economic actors are already covered by the Treaty, and non-economic actors are covered by Directives 90/364–366, no further legislation is necessary, even though the Directives do not cover the poor or those who are on the margins of society. The TEU therefore appears only to consecrate existing Treaty law as regards economic actors, and secondary legislation as regards non-economic actors. It will only be if the legislator uses Article 8a(2) as the basis for further legislation that anything new will be added. Qualified majority voting will be available for legislation involving the free movement of economic actors.[33]

The TEU provisions are built on an assumption that exceptions to the general right of free movement and residence may continue, and do not come to terms with the fact that the single market, based on an area without internal frontiers, will alter the realities of the right to expel or to prevent the entry of an individual from the territory of a Member State. Moreover, Directives 90/364–366 impose conditions for the right of exercise not imposed on economic actors, and their definition of family member is restrictive.[34] The rights of free movement and residence conferred by the TEU citizenship provisions are therefore more limited than might otherwise appear.

Participation in municipal elections

Article 8b(1) confers on citizens of the Union the right to vote and stand for election (active and passive voting rights) at municipal elections in their Member State of residence, under the same conditions as nationals of that

---

[32] *e.g.* Italian Constitution.

[33] Under Art 8a(2), legislation is to be adopted unanimously 'save as otherwise provided by this Treaty'. However, Arts 49, 54(2), 56(2) and 56 EEC on legislative action to implement the rights of freedom of movement conferred by the EEC Treaty have all been amended by the TEU to allow the use of the procedure under Art 189b, including the use of qualified majority voting.

[34] The conditions in Directives 90/364–366 requiring health insurance and adequate means of support in order to prevent one becoming a charge on the State do not apply to those who take advantage of the right of free movement under Art 48: Case 139/85, *Kempf* [1986] ECR 1741. The moment one ceases to fulfil these conditions, the right of residence under the Directives ceases: Art 3 of Dirs 90/364–365; Art 4, Dir 90/366. In addition, the class of family members who may derive rights under the Directives is more limited than in the definition of family members with derived rights of free movement and residence contained in the rules concerning the free movement of persons generally.

state. Implementing measures[35] must be adopted before 31 December 1994, and derogations may be made.[36]

This right is completely new as regards Community law, but like so many of the rights conferred by the TEU, existed in a disparate fashion under national law, and has now been generalised. It is also provided for under the provisions of the Council of Europe Convention of 5 February 1992 on the Participation of Foreigners in Public Life at Local Level which grants passive and active voting rights in local elections to all foreigners who satisfy a residence requirement.[37]

Under national law, only three Member States[38] grant voting rights to all resident Member State nationals, three others allow it on a reciprocal basis or to certain categories,[39] but the other six reserve this by constitutional provision to their own nationals.[40]

The right to vote is the political right *par excellence*. Political participation in society through exercise of the right to vote is generally seen as an inherent right of citizenship pertaining to nationals of the state whereas aliens were excluded from this and from other political activity.[41] Community law did not confer political rights on economic actors, and indeed specifically denied a quasi-political right, the right to serve in the public service exercising the public authority of the State.[42]

Granting local election rights to resident foreigners is desirable from the point of view of integrating the individual in the society in which he/she lives. Local authorities normally control issues which touch the life of the individual directly, such as housing, health, education and public services of all kinds. However, local voting rights are a pale substitute for participation in national parliamentary elections, in direct presidential elections where they exist, and in referenda. These are the votes which most affect the political life of a Member State, and its participation in the process of European integration. The grant of such voting rights would be a far stronger component of Union citizenship, but realistically, at this stage of European integration, it was not to be expected that

---

[35] The Treaty does not state, but presumably legislation will specify the circumstances in which the migrant may also vote in municipal elections in the Member State of nationality (if qualified) if he/she may vote in the country of residence.

[36] Initially considered to be for States like Luxembourg where the right to vote would have posed enormous problems given the very high percentage of resident nationals from other Member States. Foreigners resident in Luxembourg account for 26.3% of the population, and 92.7% are Community nationals: Commission Report on Voting Rights in Local elections for Community Nationals, Supplement 2/86 – Bull EC.

[37] E.T.S. 144.

[38] Ireland, The Netherlands and Denmark.

[39] The United Kingdom gives local voting rights to Irish and Commonwealth citizens; Spain grants them to nationals of foreign countries on a reciprocal basis and Portugal grants nationals of Brazil and the former colonies on a reciprocal basis.

[40] Closa, *supra*, n 1, 1992 CML Rev 1149 states that this challenges the Commission's belief that local elections are not an expression of national sovereignty. For details of voting rights in local elections, see Council of Europe Study of Civic Rights of Nationals of other Member States in Local Public Life, RM-SL (82) 55 Rev (1982), and 'La situazione del diritto di voto alle elezioni comunali degli stati membri della CEE al 1989', (1989) *Affari sociali internazionali*, p 231.

[41] Evans, 'The Political status of aliens in International, Municipal and European Community law' 30 ICLQ (1981) 20. However in Case 36/75, *Rutili*, [1975] ECR 1219 the Court arguably restricted the power of Member States to expel nationals of other Member States for political activity.

[42] Arts 48(4) and 55 EEC.

the Member States would take a step which would go to the heart of sovereignty and national identity, and would have political impact in countries with sizable proportions of Community resident nationals. As it is, the effects of the change in local elections could be substantial.

Active and passive voting rights in local elections were proposed by the Tindemans Report[43] as one of the "special rights" which should be granted to Community citizens. The report based this right (as well as the right of access to public office) on the principle of equal treatment and as being in accordance with the aim of integrating the migrant in the host country. The Scelba and Macciochi[44] reports also emphasised the participation in political life at local level. No specific legal basis in Community law was obvious however for the creation of such political rights and various bases were considered. The Macciochi report considered the Preamble and Articles 2 and 3 EEC before identifying Article 235 EEC.[45] The Addonino report, while supporting active and passive voting rights in local elections, considered that since there was no basis in the EEC Treaty, the matter was one of Member State competence.[46] Although the IGC leading up to the Single European Act had before it a Danish proposal on passive and active voting rights in local elections, it was not adopted.

The Commission's Report on voting rights in local elections for Community nationals in 1986[47] considered that whereas national elections were part of sovereignty, in which migrants should not participate, local elections did not impinge on national sovereignty and should be accessible to foreigners. The Commission considered that the reference to democracy in the Preamble to the SEA showed that this was one of the objectives to be achieved by the Community and that Articles 235 or 236 could serve as a legal basis. In its Report, the Commission also showed the consequences of giving the vote to foreigners, which would alter the pre-existing political balance in the Member States. It also surveyed the constitutional, legal and political obstacles in the Member States to granting the right of vote to foreigners.

In 1988, the Commission presented a draft Directive on voting rights for Community nationals in local elections in their Member State of residence[48] based on Article 235 EEC, which reiterated the notion that voting in local elections did not impinge upon sovereignty. It maintained that councillors elected locally should not be able to vote in choosing parliamentary assemblies, as they do in the case of elections to the Senate in Ireland and France, because, as elections to Parliament touch national sovereignty, they should be reserved to nationals.

The TEU provisions give a clear legal basis for the conferring of local election rights which was previously lacking in Community law. As the French ratification difficulties show, however, they do not solve the difficulties posed by the

---

[43] Tindemans Report on European Union, 'Towards a Europe for Citizens' – Bull EC (8) 1975 II no. 7/8, 12.

[44] Doc 1–121/1983, E.P. Working Documents 1983–4, 29. 4. 1983.

[45] Arts 2, 3c and 235 were variously considered.

[46] Supplement 7/85 – Bull EC, point 2.2.

[47] Supplement 2/86 – Bull EC.

[48] OJ 1988, C 246/3.

constitutional requirements and the internal legal orders of the Member States.[49] The *Conseil Constitutionnel* ruled that the French Constitution had to be amended in order to permit ratification of the TEU in that it conferred on foreign nationals the right to stand for election in local elections.[50] This would involve participation of non-nationals in the election of the Senate, which is elected by an electoral college representative of local councillors. French legislation was subsequently adopted to exclude Union citizens elected to local councils from participating in the process for electing senators. They were also excluded from becoming mayor or deputy mayor, because of concerns that they would then be involved in exercising control over the police power in accordance with French law.

The French legislation is in line with the view of national sovereignty adopted by the Commission's 1988 Report on voting rights in local elections for Community nationals. Exclusions will therefore presumably be permitted in the legislation to be proposed by the Commission to implement Article 8b(1). It is probable that exceptions such as those discussed here will not be classed as derogations (which we would submit is what they are), but rather as being on either side of the demarcation line between the exercise of national sovereignty and legitimate participation in local political life. It is also likely that in accordance with the Commission's 1988 draft Directive, the application of the relevant rules will differ from one state to another even though a lack of uniformity in the Union citizenship rights enjoyed in the Member States is hardly satisfactory.[51]

Article 8b(1) raises two problems. First, it does not define what is meant by municipal elections. This raises the question whether the Council will allow Member States to define what is meant by municipal elections, as the Commission had proposed in the 1988 draft Directive. If this were the case, the scope for diversity would be enormous, and would be another example of the phenomenon mentioned above in relation to citizenship and nationality, in that Community law would permit Member States to determine access to and exercise of Community rights by reference to national law, a practice forbidden by the Court in relation to the free movement of persons. On the other hand, if the Community were to legislate, it is not clear if Community legislation in this area would be compatible with the principle of subsidiarity.

Secondly, it is not clear what are the consequences of an eventual failure by the Council to adopt "detailed arrangements" before 31 December 1994, the deadline set down by Article 8b(1). If the deadline were not met, it would be up to the courts to determine the legal effect to be given to the provision.

A final observation flows from the changes which the grant of local election rights may bring about. As has already been noted, Articles 48(4) and 55 EEC exclude nationals of Member States resident in another Member State from access to the public service and from activities which involve the exercise of

---

[49] Jessurun d'Oliveira, Bruges colloque, *supra*, n 1, maintains that since constitutional changes may be required in a number of countries to allow the entry into force of Art 8b(1), it contradicts Art F(1) which states that Union shall respect the national identities of its Member States.

[50] Decision 92–308 DC, 9 April 1992, *Journal Officiel* 11 April 1992, 5354.

[51] For example, Ireland has an analogous position to France as regards senatorial elections by local councillors and yet there is no exclusion regarding Union citizens elected in local elections.

official authority. Nevertheless, under Article 8b(1), Union citizens resident in a Member State of which they are not nationals may become local councillors responsible for supervising the functioning of the very services from which they are excluded from becoming employed. Under these circumstances it will become progressively difficult to justify the exclusion of Community nationals from the public service with local authorities. The concept of nationality which is at the heart of Articles 48(4) and 55 may face ever-increasing strain.[52]

Participation in elections to the European Parliament

Article 8b(2) grants active and passive voting rights for elections to the European Parliament to Union citizens residing in a Member State of which he/she is not a national. Like the provisions concerning voting rights concerning local elections, it generalises rights which exist in some states.

Article 138(3) EEC envisages direct elections to the Parliament in accordance with a uniform procedure, which has proved impossible to achieve, with the result that the electoral procedure is governed in each Member State in accordance with national provisions.[53] In some Member States, residents who are nationals of other Member States may vote in European Parliament elections,[54] but the right to stand for election is normally, with some exceptions, reserved for nationals of the Member State concerned.[55]

Article 8b(2) EC poses two serious problems. First, it introduces a very tight deadline, 31 December 1993,[56] which would seem impossible to achieve. The consequences of failure to meet the deadline will no doubt be the subject of litigation.[57]

Secondly, Article 8b(2) confuses the issue of competence as regards the legislative initiative for proposals for the uniform electoral procedure to the European Parliament. Under Article 138(3) EEC, such competence belongs to the Parliament, whereas under Article 8b(2) EC, the right of initiative lies with the Commission. Whereas Article 8b(2) states that its provisions are without prejudice to Article 138(3), this is hardly the case as the rights of nationals of a Member State residing in another Member State are a part of the uniform electoral procedure. Moreover, the TEU provision allows for derogations, making the outcome of a uniform procedure more unlikely. Jessurun d'Oliveira rightly points out that it is likely that the Parliament will oppose Commission initiatives in this area as infringing upon its right of initiative.[58]

---

[52] See O'Keeffe, 'Judicial Interpretation of the public service exception in Article 48, paragraph 4 of the EEC Treaty' in Curtin and O'Keeffe (eds.), *Constitutional Adjudication in European Community and National Law* (Butterworths, 1992), 89–106.

[53] Art 7(2) of the Act concerning the election of the representatives of the Assembly, OJ 1976, L 278/1.

[54] Ireland, The Netherlands and Belgium.

[55] The United Kingdom permits Irish nationals to stand for election; Italy permits all Member State nationals.

[56] Curiously this deadline is different from the one provided for local elections, 31 December 1994.

[57] See Jessurun d'Oliveira, Bruges colloque, *supra*, n 1.

[58] Ibid.

Diplomatic and consular protection

According to Article 8c, Union citizens in a third state in which their Member State of nationality is not represented, may receive protection from the diplomatic and consular authorities of any Member State, on the same conditions as the nationals of that state. This is a new feature in Community law. This Union citizenship right mixes elements of the characteristics of nationality and citizenship, as nationality, constituting the link between the individual and the state in public international law, is the principal basis for diplomatic protection, whereas citizenship essentially describes rights within the municipal legal order. The diplomatic and consular protection will be offered by Member States, not by the Community or the Union.

Early steps to give an external dimension to the Community included the Passport Union, but this was largely a failure. Even the introduction of the so-called European passport was misleading as essentially the passports are national passports in every respect bar their design, issued according to a common format which was agreed upon intergovernmentally.[59] The Addonino Report proposed that Member States should co-operate in offering consular assistance in a third country to one another's nationals where a national's Member State was not represented. This possibility already existed under the European Convention on Consular Functions 1967,[60] Article 2(3) of which provides that "any Contracting Party is entitled to entrust the protection of its nationals and the defence of their rights and interests to consular officers of another Contracting Party".

According to Article 8c EC, the Member States are required *to establish* the necessary rules among themselves by 31 December 1993, and *to start* the international negotiations required to secure this diplomatic and consular protection. Thus only a very short deadline is given for agreement between the Member States, and no deadline is given for the negotiations with the third states as the outcome of such negotiations depends on those states as well as on the Member States. Unlike the rights examined until now, those of free movement and residence, and voting rights in local and European Parliament elections, there is no right of initiative for the Commission or any other Community institution as regards diplomatic and consular protection. The procedure envisaged is intergovernmental. In the normal course of events, the agreements made between the Member States themselves and with third states would not be justiciable by the Court of Justice. However, as one is dealing here with a right of Union citizens, conferred by the EC Treaty, the issue could be raised in litigation before the Court, which would then have to decide as to whether it was justiciable.

In order to carry out this protection, the Member States must negotiate with third states. Presumably they will negotiate as a bloc though this is not explicitly required by the Treaty. It might be expected that negotiations among the Member States as regards protection for another's nationals may be easier than

---

[59] OJ 1981 C 241/1.
[60] 11 November 1967, E.T.S. no 61.

with third countries, but this is not altogether certain. The Vienna Convention on Diplomatic Relations 1961[61] does not provide for diplomatic protection of the nationals of other states. The negotiations with third countries may moreover be hampered by the fact that the TEU sets only the requirement of nationality of a Member State to trigger diplomatic and consular protection whereas the *Nottebohm* requirement of a genuine link is disregarded. Such a link between the protecting state and the individual may be constituted, in addition to nationality, by factors such as residence, business interests or family ties. However, in the final analysis, it is likely that the success of the negotiations with third states will depend upon the commitment of the Member States in pursuing negotiations and the importance they attach to them in their dealings with third states.

The diplomatic protection provisions are unlikely to be used excessively. Their importance will be largely on the external level, as third states decide whether to recognise such diplomatic and consular protection. However, from the point of view of the Union citizens who need to avail of this opportunity, it could promote a sense of belonging to the Union. The crossing of nationality barriers inherent in the facility to avail of diplomatic and consular protection of other Member States implies a shared responsibility of all the Member States towards the citizens of the other Member States. This could be a significant blurring of the differences imposed by the possession of the nationality of a Member State.

Right of petition and applications to the Ombudsman

Article 8d EC provides that Union citizens may petition the European Parliament and apply to the Ombudsman.

The right of petition is not new. It was already provided in Articles 128–130 of the Rules of Procedure of the European Parliament. Under Article 138d EC, in addition to Union citizens, any natural or legal person residing or having its registered office in a Member State also has the right of petition on matters which affect him or her directly. However, this is subject to the condition that the matter must come within the fields of activity of the Community. Matters which arise from the Union's activity are not subject to this right. Thus issues falling under intergovernmental co-operation under the second and third pillars are not subject to scrutiny by Parliament's Committee on Petitions (although doubtless Parliament will in any event monitor their impact on individuals).

The right of petition, like that of appeal to the Ombudsman, is shared by Union citizens with third country nationals resident in the Member States. This marks a move away from the granting of "special rights" to Community citizens, which had been the basis of the earlier debates on citizenship, starting with the Paris 1974 Summit, and the Tindemans Report. As the unique nature of Union citizenship rights is "diluted" because they are also conferred on third

---

[61] 8 500 UNTS 95.

country nationals, it will become increasingly difficult to justify denying them that status.

It should be noted that whereas third country nationals must be residents of the Union in order to make a petition or complain to the Ombudsman, it is not apparent that such a requirement is imposed on Union citizens, who may petition or complain even though they live outside the Union.

The Ombudsman provided for in Article 8d and Article 138e EC is an entirely new figure. As with the right of petition, the right to apply to the Ombudsman is not confined to Union citizens, as mentioned above, but is also conferred on any natural or legal person residing or having its registered office in a Member State.

The Ombudsman is allowed to investigate complaints against the Community institutions or bodies. He/she has no remit to investigate complaints against the Union. The Ombudsman may act on own initiative or on complaints from individuals. Unlike the case with petition, there is no requirement that the matter complained of must directly affect the complainant. Complaints may be submitted through members of the European Parliament. Oddly there is no provision for the transmission of complaints by national agencies (including the national equivalent of the Ombudsman in the Member States) or by members of national Parliaments. Presumably, if seised of such complaints, the Ombudsman could investigate them as though acting on own initiative.

Under Article 138e, the Ombudsman may receive complaints only concerning instances of maladministration in the activities of the Community institutions or bodies. No reference is made to maladministration by national bodies acting in pursuance or in violation of Community law, although this is crucial if the Ombudsman is to function as a satisfactory complaints procedure.[62] The logic of the Treaty-makers would seem to be that Article 138e must be read together with Article 138d. The latter article allows a petition to the European Parliament on a matter which comes within the Community's fields of activity and which affects the petitioner directly. This is wider than Article 138e in that it would seem to allow complaints also in relation to the activities of national bodies acting within the sphere of Community competence or in violation of Community law. Nevertheless, the failure to make similar provision as regards the Ombudsman is to be regretted. It is to be hoped that as the office develops, it will acquire such competence.

Article 138e does not refer to the activities of the Union, which would thus seem to be excluded. However, it is possible to argue both sides of the coin: either the article refers only to the activities of the institutions acting as Community institutions, and not as Union institutions, or it could be taken to refer to any act of the institutions, whether acting on behalf of the Community or not, on the basis that according to Article C TEU, the Union has a single institutional framework. The latter interpretation seems less likely.

---

[62] The connection with the national system had been recognised by the Commission as crucial during the course of the Intergovernmental conferences, and it had suggested the creation of an Ombudsman for each Member State. SEC (91) 500.

The Ombudsman appears to be required to investigate all complaints. The lack of a discretionary filtering mechanism may lead to overload on the office.

Dynamic character of Union citizenship

Article 8e EC provides for regular reporting to the European Parliament, the Council and the Economic and Social Committee on the application of the citizenship provisions. The Council is authorised to adopt provisions to strengthen or to add to the existing citizenship rights, which it shall recommend to the Member States for adoption in accordance with their respective constitutional requirements. One of the crucial features of citizenship is apparent here: it is envisaged as a dynamic concept, with the prospect of change being explicitly built into the mechanisms for its future review. The right of legislative initiative lies with the Commission, and the Parliament must be consulted, though its approval is not required. The Council must act unanimously. The final decision lies with the Member States. There is a presumption (which the TEU ratification process may have undermined) that the governments of the Member States, having approved changes at the Council, should be able to win approval for these changes in accordance with their respective constitutional requirements.

The second remarkable feature of the provisions in Article 8e is that the Council may only "strengthen or add to" the citizenship rights laid down in the TEU. It may not diminish them. However, since there is comparatively little that is actually new in the citizenship provisions, this means less than it might have otherwise. The position will change if the catalogue of citizenship rights grows. Article 8e makes no reference to increasing the duties imposed on Union citizens.

The catalogue of rights conferred by the Union Treaty is thus only an intermediate stage in the conferring of new rights on the European citizen. These rights could include social rights such as housing, education, welfare, working conditions, environmental and consumer protection as well as fundamental rights, political rights and unlimited rights of free circulation and residence. As the Union acquires competences, the Union should grant rights to citizens in these areas. Since citizenship should ensure equal treatment, there should be an equal treatment principle of general application, which is currently missing from the TEU provisions. As the Union develops as a political entity, its citizens should be able to participate fully in its political life.

Additional nature of Union citizenship

In addition to its dynamic character, the other key feature of Union citizenship is the fact that it is additional to the nationality and the citizenship of a Member State. These concepts remain untouched by the TEU citizenship provisions.

Oddly, the additional character of Union citizenship is not spelled out in the TEU. However the legislative history makes this clear. It was so suggested in the Spanish Memorandum on citizenship to the IGC, referred to above, was endorsed by the Commission in its submission to the IGC[63] and agreed at the European Council Summit held in Rome in October 1990.[64]

Human rights

The human rights issue is covered in detail elsewhere in this book, and only a couple of points will be made here.[65] Human rights are not as such part of the citizenship package. Instead, there is a statement in Article F.2 that the Union will respect fundamental rights, as guaranteed by the ECHR and as they result from the constitutional traditions common to the Member States, as general principles of Community law. This is a notably entangled provision: the Union is to respect these rights as general principles of Community law, not of the Union. Moreover, since the provision is in Title I of the TEU, it is not subject to the jurisdiction of the Court of Justice.

Article F(2) appears only to confirm the existing caselaw of the Court. Does the provision add anything further? It is suggested that if the conventions adopted on the basis of Article K.3(2)(c) give jurisdiction to the Court of Justice, then Article F.2 could be applied by the Court. Even if competence in the area remained intergovernmental, nevertheless it would have to be exercised in respect of fundamental human rights and the general principles of law, and subject to judicial review. In the case of legislation under the other passerelle provision, Article K9, the Court's existing caselaw on human rights and the general principles of law would in any event apply.

It is to be regretted that the citizenship provisions do not have a human rights component. As Rosy Bindi pointed out in her report to the European Parliament, "it is inconceivable to base citizenship on anything other than the expansion of fundamental rights and freedoms in addition to their recognition and protection."[66]

The TEU citizenship provisions may be compared with the Council of Europe Convention of 5 February 1992 on the Participation of Foreigners in Public Life at Local Level which guarantees to all foreign residents certain basic rights such as the freedoms of expression, assembly and association, as well as active and passive voting rights at local elections. The combination of fundamental rights and political rights in the one package is, it is submitted, a useful precedent.

---

[63] Contribution by the Commission to the intergovernmental conference, SEC (91) 500; Supplement 2/91 – Bull EC.

[64] Bull. EC 1990/10. The United Kingdom reserved its position on this point as on so many others.

[65] See Patrick M Twomey, 'The European Union: Three Pillars without a Human Rights Foundation' in this volume, p 121.

[66] Bindi report, *supra*, n 16, p 12.

Third country nationals

Third country nationals resident in the Union do not come within the personal scope of the Union citizenship provisions. Nevertheless, under other TEU provisions, they are entitled to two of the rights conferred on Union citizens, the right of petition to the European Parliament, and the right to apply to the Ombudsman. The Union Treaty otherwise offers third country nationals little or nothing. It must be admitted with hindsight that if they had been covered by the TEU provisions, the ratification process would probably have foundered in at least one country, if not in others.

The position of third country nationals is nonetheless a Community-wide issue, and needs a Community response. It is not acceptable that 8–9 million people by some estimates, (13 million by others), many of whom live on the margins of society, should be excluded from the rights conferred by Community/Union law. Like nationals of the Member States, their economic activities contribute to the economic success of the Union. They pay taxes and contribute to the social security systems of the Member States in the same way as nationals of the Member States. Their cultural, human and other contributions enrich the societies of the Member States. They are and will continue to be a permanent presence in the Community. They are not "guests", but their integration is hindered by numerous factors, including restrictive nationality and naturalization laws. In some cases, naturalization is not an option due to the consequences it would have in the state of nationality,[67] and in any event, it may be questioned whether it is appropriate to make the acquisition of nationality (and possibly the renunciation of the previous nationality) a *sine qua non* for the enjoyment of rights when this is not required of migrants with the nationality of a Member State, as this would violate the principle of formal equality of treatment, recognised by the general principles of law.

The integration of third country nationals into the Community and the Member States is hindered by a host of other factors, but what concerns us here is their exclusion from those rights which the TEU has conferred on the nationals of the Member States. The generalization of political rights at local and European Parliament levels to Community nationals by the TEU shows that sovereignty is not threatened by the enfranchisement at these levels of non-nationals; the example of the granting of such rights to Community nationals should make it more difficult to justify denying them to third country nationals. The very arguments concerning the integration of foreign residents into the local community which militated in favour of granting these rights to Community nationals, also apply in the case of third country nationals.

Moreover, as Jessurun d'Oliveira points out, it is anomalous that the criterion of residence should be used in the case of voting rights of nationals of Member States resident in another Member State in local and European elections, but not in the case of third country nationals who are also resident.[68]

---

[67] Turkish citizens, for example, lose their right to inherit land in Turkey if they renounce their citizenship.
[68] Bruges colloque, *supra*, n 1.

The Community regulates the life of third country nationals resident in the Member States, but they for their part, are generally excluded from the decision-making procedure, and are not represented at municipal, national or European levels. In so far as they are subjects of Community law, they should not be excluded from the democratic process in the Community.

As noted above, the Council of Europe Convention of 5 February 1992 on the Participation of Foreigners in Public Life at Local Level guarantees to all foreign residents certain basic rights such as the freedoms of expression, assembly and association, and provides that consultative bodies are to be formed at local level to represent foreign residents. It grants the right to vote and to stand for election in local elections to foreign residents after five years residence. This Convention thus gives to third country nationals resident in the Community local election rights similar to those conferred by the Union Treaty. The implementation of the Convention in national law will erode the difference between the third country national and the Union citizen as regards rights in this area, though not as a matter of Community law.

As regards the rights of free movement and residence conferred by the TEU on Union citizens, the case for extending these rights to third country nationals lawfully resident in the Community is even stronger than in the case of political rights. Third country nationals legally resident in a Member State have no right of circulation within the Community, unless they are family members of Community nationals, nationals of EFTA States acceding to the European Economic Area, or their family members,[69] or nationals of other states which have Association Agreements with the Community providing for free movement. Thus, a second or third generation migrant living in one Member State and wishing to go to another may have to apply for a visa if he/she is a national of one of the hundred odd countries whose nationals now require visas to enter a Community Member State. In that process, he/she may be subjected to the most extensive probing administrative inquiries even though he/she may have lived in the Community all of his/her life. Apart from the bureaucratic inconvenience, this can only heighten the sense of exclusion of the third country national. Moreover, since the right of free circulation is already granted to certain third country nationals, it is anomalous to deny it to third country nationals lawfully resident within the Community as a category.[70]

As far as fundamental rights are concerned, they are not part of the citizenship package as such, but in so far as the Union is committed to respecting them, and in so far as they are part of the general principles of Community law, they apply to third country nationals resident in the Community as well as to Union citizens.[71]

Union citizenship could be conferred on third country nationals lawfully resident in the Union. It could be made subject to the satisfaction of certain criteria, modelled on those required in national law. Such criteria could include lawful

[69] Freedom of movement for workers, the self-employed and providers of services is provided by Arts 28–39 of the EEA Agreement. The EFTA countries likely to accede to the Agreement are Austria, Finland, Iceland, Liechtenstein, Norway and Sweden.
[70] See European Parliament Resolution on Migrant workers from third countries, OJ 1990, C 175/180.
[71] Jessurun d'Oliveira, Bruges colloque, *supra*, n 1.

entry and residence, age, employment or other economic activity, good character, loyalty to the aims of the Union, assimilation (language proficiency,
knowledge of the fundamental principles of the Union, attachment to the Union
etc). A qualifying period of residence could be attached, in the same way as
residence periods are required for the acquisition of the nationality of Member
States.

The conferral of Union citizenship on third country nationals resident in the
Community could create problems with their state of nationality. Whereas
Member States have already consented to their nationals acquiring Union
citizenship, this would not be the case for third country nationals. Their states of
nationality may object to the acquisition of Union citizenship by their nationals:
the very title "Union citizen" suggests that it is akin to national citizenship. As
Union citizenship has a complementary character, the laws of the country of
nationality must permit the acquisition of Union citizenship. Third states would
doubtless wish to be satisfied that what was at issue here was not the acquisition
of nationality (there being no such concept as nationality of the Union), but
rather a bundle of rights conferred by supranational law and entitled citizenship, but which did not in fact have a bearing on the national citizenship rights
and duties of the third country nationals. It would therefore be necessary to
conduct negotiations possibly leading to a series of international conventions
after the relationship between the citizenship of the country of nationality and
the citizenship of the Union had been explored and defined. One Union
citizenship right, that of external diplomatic and consular assistance, might give
rise to particular problems.

Conclusion

The importance of the TEU citizenship provisions lies not in their content but
rather in the promise they hold out for the future. The concept is a dynamic
one, capable of being added to or strengthened, but not diminished. The rights
conferred are part of Community law, and as such, capable of being enforced by
the Court of Justice and the national courts. The Court may fashion constitutional guarantees from the citizenship provisions through its caselaw.

The TEU citizenship provisions do not add substantially to Community law.
For the most part, they reiterate existing rights (freedom of movement and
residence, right of petition to Parliament), or generalise rights already existing in
a disparate fashion in the laws of the Member States (active and passive voting
rights in European Parliament and local elections). Of the two new rights
created, one, diplomatic and consular protection, was already envisaged under
the European Convention on Consular Functions 1967. The other new right,
that of application to the Ombudsman, like the right of petition, is shared with
third country nationals and thus is hardly distinctive of the status or condition of
Union citizen. It is striking that active and passive voting rights are given in
respect of local elections and elections to the European Parliament, but not in

respect of national parliamentary elections, referenda or direct presidential elections. Human rights do not feature in the catalogue of rights of the Union citizen, and this catalogue in any event is exiguous. The citizenship provisions do not include a general prohibition on the grounds of nationality.

Union citizenship is available only to nationals of the Member States, and the latter may determine which of their nationals may qualify for the purpose. Family members of Union citizens who do not possess the nationality of a Member State are not covered by the TEU provisions. Nationals of third states legally resident in the Community are excluded. No new political subject has been created: individuals remain nationals of their Member States. The Member States also retain control over future developments in the concept of Union citizenship.

Nevertheless, because of the prospect it offers for the future as a dynamic concept, and because of the possibility that it may bring the Union nearer the individual and assist the democratic process, the establishment of Union citizenship by the Maastricht Treaty is a hopeful first step towards a more complete catalogue of rights, with a wider personal scope.

DAVID O'KEEFFE*

------

* The author directs a project for the ESRC on the free movement of persons and the Single European Market within the context of the ESRC's Single European Market Programme.

Chapter 7
Citizenship of the Union and Nationality of Member States
Introduction

The explicit creation of the citizenship of the Union within the Treaty on European Union has implied the recognition of an extra status for individuals further to the nationality of Member States. Citizenship of the Union implies the harmonization of the conditions of nationals of any given state in a status defined by seven positive rights: freedom of movement and residence, voting rights in the country of residence in local and EP elections, entitlement to diplomatic protection in certain cases, the right of petition and the right to appeal to the Community ombudsman.[1] Citizenship of the Union might have seemed a superfluous category, since the catalogue of rights incorporated by this new concept was implicit anyway in EC law, stemming as they do from the EEC Treaty and the Single European Act. The importance of citizenship, though, lies in the eventual constraints and limitations that it may pose on the concept of nationality. In fact, scholars such as Meehan have concluded that a new multiple citizenship, neither national or cosmopolitan is emerging. This multiple citizenship enables the expression of various identities and the exercise of rights and duties:

"through an increasingly complex configuration of common institutions, states, national and transnational interest groups and voluntary associations, local or provincial authorities, regions and alliances of regions".[2]

Although her thesis has been constructed against Aron's opinion that multinational citizenship is not possible, the latter conceded also that this might become a reality:

"as long as the governments involved are committed to respecting the rights of man and/or citizen without regard for the nationality of the individuals living within the community".[3]

Citizenship may be deemed to be independent from nationality in the specific sense that the enjoyment of certain concrete rights is guaranteed for all the nationals of Member States of the Community regardless of their nationality. However, being a national of a Member State is still the prerequisite for being considered a citizen of the Union.[4] An individual who cannot claim to be a national of a Member State cannot claim to be a citizen of the Union either.

---

[1] For a more detailed explanation on the concept of citizenship, see Closa, "The concept of citizenship in the Treaty on European Union' (1992) 29 CML Rev 1137–1169; and O'Keeffe, "Union Citizenship" – in this volume at 87.
[2] Meehan, "Citizenship and the European Community' (1993) 64 *Political Quarterly* 185.
[3] Aron, "Is multinational citizenship possible?' (1974) 41 *Social Research* 647.
[4] Art 8.1 para 2.

However, he or she may still enjoy citizenship rights. Four aspects that show the subordination of citizenship of the Union to nationality will be discussed: firstly, human rights, which are not a part of the rights of citizenship of the Union as listed by Articles 8 to 8e, are incorporated in EC law and the Union Treaty as result of their common regulation in *national* citizenship. Second, the erosion of the concept of nationality has been prevented, at this stage, by a cautious and restrictive interpretation of citizenship of the Union. Third, the harmonization of the enjoyment of certain rights implied by citizenship of the Union is not, at the moment, matched by a parallel evolution of the civil law of the Member States concerning nationality. Finally, judicial protection of citizens within the Union needs to be supplemented through reference to their status as nationals.

The foundation of citizenship on human rights

The link between the concept of citizenship and human rights seems to be firmly established by constitutional doctrine. Since the 1789 Declaration of the Rights of Man and Citizen, human rights and citizenship have appeared indissolubly linked as the foundation of the constitutional determination of the status of individuals. This domestic dimension appeared to be in contradiction to the external order where the distinction between men and citizens came to be regarded as the critical problem in international relations: as an exclusive moral community, the sovereign state emphasised its freedom to promote its interests without recognising any fundamental obligation regarding the welfare of outsiders.[5] However, the differences between the respective conditions of citizen and alien have been reduced in modern European societies, where constitutional texts commonly contain a catalogue of rights that guarantee basic human rights for nationals and foreigners alike. These are the *fundamental* human rights: they lie at the foundation of the international community backed by a real consensus and are valid under all circumstances, irrespective of time and place, with limited possibility for derogation.[6]

The recognition of the status of citizen, on the other hand, implies a series of rights that establish a given *status of citizenship*. The concept of *status civitatis* or *status of citizenship* has been developed from constitutional doctrine as well as sociological theory. Thus, Jellinek considered the affirmation of subjective public rights as a process with successive stages. Whilst the initial stages appeared linked to the achievement of essential human rights, the notion of citizenship has been built in latter stages mainly by reference to rights with a social and economic content and connected to the development of the welfare state. Similarly, Marshall divided citizenship into three parts which have been developed in a historic sequence: civil (*i.e.* fundamental) rights during the 18th century;

---

[5] Linklater, *Men and citizens in the theory of international relations* (1982) 25.
[6] van Boven, "Distinguishing criteria of human rights', in Vasak (ed) *The international dimensions of human rights* (1982) 43–59.

political rights during the 19th century and social rights during the 20th century.[7] These three groups of rights constitute, in constitutional orders, the fundamental rights or *Grundrechte*. There is no definitive agreement on the concrete rights to be included within a catalogue of fundamental rights; in fact, the doctrine of fundamental rights may be regarded as a particularization of the universal human rights in concrete constitutional situations, *i.e.* human rights plus nascent and disputed rights, certain programmatic social and economic rights as well as collective rights.

In contrast to the universalization of the enjoyment of human rights enshrined by constitutional orders, states still consider that there are certain privileges exclusively attached to the notion of citizen or national. The legitimacy of the sovereign entity's discretionary power to grant different rights to different individuals has not been challenged, although Western European states reserve nowadays only few rights, with a high socio-economic or political content, of which the criterion for their enjoyment is that of being a national. Given this agreement on certain essential rights, differences are caused not only by divergent conceptions of the relationship of the individual with the state, but also by the stage of socio-economic development achieved by a society.

The construction of the concept of citizenship in the TEU has not mirrored this constitutional model, since citizenship has been effectively dissociated from human rights. The catalogue of rights comprised by the citizenship of the union does not include human rights, although mention of these is made in the Common Provisions of the TEU,[8] where the Union is commanded to respect human rights as a general principle of Community law. The belief commonly shared was, though, that the concept of citizenship of the Union *should* be the natural channel for the explicit and positive incorporation of human rights into the Community legal order. Prior to the TEU, human rights featured permanently as one of the constitutive elements in the proposals on citizens' rights or a people's Europe,[9] and the claim was further repeated by most of the submissions to the 1991 intergovernmental conference.[10]

The severing of this link, first postulated by the Spanish contribution to the intergovernmental conference, may be explained by doctrinal as well as practical reasons. Union citizenship has been created and defined as being additional to nationality, which implies that the substantive rights granted are additional to the ones recognised in the respective constitutional orders for nationals. Since human rights are a basic component of the constitutional orders of the 12 Member States, either in a positive sense or as interpretative criteria of the basic rights, it may, therefore, be argued that the legitimating function which inspired the creation of citizenship of the Union might be brought into question because of the absence of human rights from the catalogue of rights. However, it is difficult to accept that the inclusion of a positive catalogue of

---

[7] Jellinek, System der Subjektiven Offentlichen Retchte (1964) *passim*; Marshall, *Citizenship and social class* (1950) 10–18.

[8] Art F.2.

[9] See 'Towards a European citizenship', Bull EC Supp 7/75 and 'A people's Europe', Bull EC Supp 7/85.

[10] See, for instance, 'Union citizenship'. Contribution by the Commission to the intergovernmental Conference SEC (91) 500, and the Interim Report on a Union citizenship PE Doc A 3–0139/91.

rights within the concept of Union citizenship would have afforded a greater protection of human rights for *nationals of Member States* than that guaranteed by national constitutional orders. In fact, there have been cases where constitutional courts have blocked the passage of EC legislation by invoking the defence of constitutionally guaranteed human rights. Thus, the Italian Constitutional Court went so far as to argue that the safeguarding of the principles on the basis of the constitution and, particularly, of fundamental rights, comprised a limit to the transference of competences to the Community.[11] Although the Italian court revised its caselaw in 1984,[12] it reiterated, in 1989, that the Court considered that a provision of Community law might be held to be inapplicable in Italy if it were to infringe fundamental rights.[13]

The defence of constitutionally guaranteed human rights by the German Constitutional Court has been more assertive. Although it acknowledged the protection of human rights afforded by Court of Justice rulings, the German Court held that the Court's caselaw was not enough to compensate for the lack of a Bill of Rights, which should be elaborated with the participation of a Parliament elected by universal suffrage (the ruling was prior to the first direct elections to the European Parliament in 1979).[14] Thus, the inclusion of a exhaustive catalogue of human rights within the concept of Union citizenship would not add significantly to the *status civitatis* of any of the nationals from Member States, whose constitutional texts guarantee human rights. On the other hand, the Court of Justice's judgments defending human rights have been repeatedly referred to the constitutional tradition of Member States. In the *Stauder* case,[15] the Court ruled that respect for fundamental rights is enshrined in the general principles of Community law and protected by the Court. The reasoning was repeated in the ruling of the *Nold* case.[16] However, the Court has preferred to invoke these general principles as an interpretative criteria rather than to identify a precise list of human rights attached to the individuals within the scope of EC law. This seems to reinforce the case put forward above.

The way in which Union citizenship has been designed as being additional to nationality, implies the generalization of certain rights reserved by constitutional orders for their own nationals to all nationals of Member States. Since fundamental human rights are by no means a privilege reserved for nationals in the Member States, there seems to be no solid foundation to the claim for incorporating them into the concept of citizenship of the Union. Human rights have been incorporated as interpretative criteria for EC law through the reference to the status of nationals within their constitutional orders. The reference to the European Convention on Human Rights, as providing interpretative criteria for EC law, adopted by the TEU seems to secure a high level of protec-

---

[11] Case 183/74 *Frontini* v *Ministero delle Finanze* [1974] ECR 372.

[12] Sentenza No 170 del 1984 Granital. See Gaja, 'New developments in a continuing history: the relationship between EC law and Italian law' (1990) 27 CML Rev 83–95.

[13] Decizione No 232 of 21 April 1989. (1989) 72 *Rivista di Diritto Internazionale* 103 *et seq.*

[14] Case 52/71 *Internationale Handelsgesellschaft mbH* v *Einfuhr- und Vorrastelle fur Getreide und Futermittel* [1974] ECR 540.

[15] Case 29/69 *Stauder* v *City of Ulm, Sozialamt* [1969] ECR 419.

[16] Case 4/73 *Nold, Kohlen und Baustoffgrosshanldlung* v *Commission* [1974] ECR 491.

tion for citizens and foreigners alike.[17] A different question is whether some rights included under the notion of citizenship, such as the unqualified freedom of movement, for instance, are, in fact, human rights and whether they should be detached from the notion of citizenship and be applicable to any individual within the Community. Again, this is not a self-evident case; for instance, freedom of movement is explicitly and unconditionally guaranteed only for nationals in certain constitutional orders.[18]

Interpretation of the concept of citizenship of the Union by reference to nationality

The exclusion of the prohibition of discrimination on grounds of nationality included by Article 7 of the Treaty of Rome from the provisions regulating citizenship of the Union, sanctions the belief that exclusive privileges attach to nationality. The emphasis on equal treatment regarding social and civic rights has led to the opinion that "a reconceptualization [of the concept of citizenship] is taking place in which legal status and the content of rights are not determined by nationality alone".[19] This opinion seems to be sustainable as long as the rights referred to are human, social, economic or even certain political rights. In fact, some Member States do not find it incongruous liberally to extend civil and social rights to foreigners in tandem with a very restrictive interpretation of the concept of citizenship.[20] There are two facts that might explain restrictive interpretations of the concept of citizenship. First, certain legal systems have not constructed a conceptual difference between citizenship and nationality (for instance, Italian law on nationality refers exclusively to citizenship. Equally, the British Nationality Act 1981 refers in its wording exclusively to citizenship). The substantiation of this difference allows the generous granting of citizenship rights, without rendering the idea of reserved rights of nationality meaningless. Secondly, citizenship has traditionally been an exclusive condition in certain cases (*i.e.* an individual can be citizen or national of only one country), as is the case with Germany or Denmark.[21]

---

[17] This was the option preferred by some reputed specialists arguing that "even if agreement could be reached on which rights should be put into the catalogue, the rights would become rigidly entrenched and possibly narrowly interpreted". Clapham, 'A human rights policy for the European Community' (1990) 10 YEL 360.

[18] *e.g.* Art 11 Basic Law FRG; Art 44.1 Belgian Constitution; Art 19 Spanish Constitution; Art 16 Italian Constitution.

[19] Meehan, *supra*, n 2 at 179.

[20] Along this line, Aron argued that "A state can without self-contradiction grant aliens the economic and social rights it accords its own citizens and still refuse them political rights'. Aron, *supra*, n 3 at 651.

[21] A similar provision contained in the Netherlands Nationality Act has been recently removed: the applicant possessing a foreign nationality was expected to make every effort to renounce it, unless this cannot reasonably be expected from him. Netherlands Nationality Act 19 December 1984 9.1.b. The UK, France and Italy (Art 11 *Legge sulla cittadinanza*) allow dual citizenship. This is limited in the case of Spain to countries which were part of the Spanish Crown: Latin American, Philippines, Equatorial Guinea plus Portugal, Andorra and to Sephardic Jews (Ley 18/1990 17 diciembre 1990 *Reforma del Código Civil en materia de nacionalidad*). Portugal allows the enjoyment of plurinationality (Decreto-lei n 322/82 *Regulamento da nacionalidade portuguesa*).

Typically, the existence of citizenship of the Union, parallel to Member States' nationality, does not seem to cause excessive *conceptual* problems in some of the Member States with a Roman law tradition. In these states, nationality has come to mean the affiliation of an individual from the point of view of international law, whilst citizenship implies the host of rights domestically attached to that affiliation. Along this line, Soledad García, for instance, distinguishes between the formal and the substantive meanings of citizenship.[22] Formally, citizenship is associated with membership of a political community (state), that is, with nationality. Substantively, it relates to the possession of specific rights and the obligation to comply with certain duties within the state or the political community. As Aron stated, this is rooted in the Hegelian distinction between the member of the civil society (*bürgerliche Gesellschaft*) and the citizen: the first is a private person; the second, thanks to the publicization of the state through universal suffrage, is a participant.[23]

Given their constitutional traditions, the generalization of the enjoyment of certain rights of citizenship poses no insuperable obstacles for Member States. Doctrinal and political problems have appeared in relation to the lack of conceptual distinction between citizenship and nationality, where the question: 'Is it possible to consider the existence of citizenship that does not imply a parallel nationality and/or does not question the nationality of a given Member State?' becomes fully meaningful. Allegedly, this paradox was at the root of the problem raised in Denmark regarding the concept of citizenship of the Union. The solution adopted by the Danish government, after the negative vote in the first referendum, was to attempt to clarify the conceptual differences between the two terms by means of a unilateral Declaration, attached to its instrument of ratification of the TEU. Denmark declares that:

"citizenship of the Union is a political and legal concept entirely different from the concept of citizenship within the meaning of the constitution of the Kingdom of Denmark and the Danish legal system".

The differences between these, *i.e.* citizenship of the Union and nationality, ensue from two elements: the reserve of certain exclusive privileges and the recognition of certain individual rights. Thus, the Declaration states that:

"citizenship of the union in no way in itself gives a national of another Member State the right to obtain Danish citizenship or any of the rights, duties, privileges or advantages that are inherent in Danish citizenship by virtue of Denmark's constitutional, legal and administrative rules".

Accordingly, Denmark interprets citizenship of the Union as the fulfilment of its Treaty obligations, regarding the implementation of the catalogue of rights explicitly listed by the TEU. Obviously, this interpretation neutralises the potential challenge to nationality that may be posed by the current stage of development of the citizenship of the Union. Two Declarations by the European Council have endorsed a similar construction. In its Birmingham Declaration, the European Council made it clear that "citizenship of the Union

---

[22] García, *Europe's fragmented identities and the frontiers of citizenship* (1993) 20.
[23] Aron, *supra*, n 3, 651.

brings our citizens additional rights and protection without in any way taking the place of their national citizenship".[24] In Edinburgh, the European Council repeated that rights and protection granted by the citizenship of the Union do not in any way take the place of national citizenship.[25]

However, the establishment of conceptual differences seems to be more relevant regarding the future development of the *status civitatis*. As has been argued elsewhere,[26] the most important characteristic of the citizenship of the Union is its dynamic character, the capacity progressively to incorporate new rights. The two European Council Declarations have merely recognised the current *status quo* and, in this sense, they do not seem to condition or burden, interpretatively or practically, the future development of the concept, through the extensive use of provisions on Article 8e. Quite different, however, is the line adopted by the Danish Declaration:

"Nothing in the Treaty on European Union implies or foresees an undertaking to create a citizenship of the Union in the sense of citizenship of a nation state. The question of Denmark participating in any such development does, therefore, not arise".[27]

There are solid foundations for these fears; the affirmation of the role of individuals by reference to their rights as citizens will legitimate Community actions and, eventually, the integration process, should this process be understood as the creation of new rights for the citizens of the union. If Article 8e provisions were to be read, for instance, in the light of the reference to the federal goal contained in the wording of the early drafts submitted to the intergovernmental conference, this could establish a clear line of evolution towards a federal citizenship that might call into question the notion of nationality itself.

Accordingly, the most important aspect of the unilateral Danish Declaration lies in the procedural mechanisms introduced to guarantee the control of the application of Article 8e: Council decisions in pursuance of Article 8e may be considered to imply a transfer of sovereignty. In this case, they will require a five-sixths majority of the *Folketing* or a simple majority plus a favourable referendum. Again, the contradictions between a generous and extensive system of citizens' rights and a restrictive view of nationality are revealed by the fact that the procedural guarantee would not be invoked automatically, but only if it is understood that a transfer of sovereignty is involved. The fulfilment of the Treaty obligations derived from the other provisions on citizenship are understood to be within the scope granted by the instrument of ratification.

The Treaty requirements on unanimity and adoption in accordance with the respective constitutional requirements afford a *de facto* similarly discretionary use for any Member State. The difference with these is that Denmark has defined *a priori* its own future interpretation of the concept of citizenship of the Union. Should this procedure be activated and Denmark fail to ratify a decision, this would not imply a loss of the concrete measure, but a failure to bring it to within the EC constitutional framework. The example of the Social Protocol proves

---

[24] Birmingham Declaration – a Community close to its citizens, Bull EC 10–1992 pt I.8, 9.
[25] Bull EC 12–1992 pt I.35 at 25.
[26] Closa, *supra*, n 1.
[27] Bull EC 12–1992 pt I.42 at 26.

that the implementation of certain citizens' rights without the participation of a Member State is possible. However, the creation of a citizenship of the Union with variable geometry does not seem to be an acceptable alternative, since this would imply a derogation of the principle of generalization.

Citizenship and acquisition of nationality: the question of naturalization

The reservations included by the Danish Declaration illustrate that, despite the advances regarding the enjoyment of certain rights implied by the citizenship of the Union, Member States still consider nationality to be a superior privileged status with exclusive rights attached. The enjoyment of this reserved status is protected through the domestic regulations to grant nationality. As an extreme case, for instance, Belgium, which distinguishes between ordinary naturaliz-ation and full naturalization, excludes from the former the exercise of the functions of minister, and the eligibility for legislative chambers and for prov-incial councils;[28] whilst only the Irish Republic among the Member States foresees and explicitly expresses a general system of *reciprocal citizenship rights* with any other country.[29]

The Declaration on Nationality of a Member State, included by the TEU, acknowledges that the granting of nationality is a discretionary power exclu-sively reserved for Member States. Citizenship of the Union may not be a constraint on the Member States' discretionary use of civil law granting nation-ality. The question is whether this conceptual reserve is challenged by undermining the procedural defenses. It has been pointed out that the pro-cedures for becoming a citizen have been made difficult and unattractive because, from the point of view of the host state, naturalization is seen as a matter of national identity and national sovereignty.[30] Since the Treaty on European Union has established co-operation on areas pertaining to internal and external security, the justification on these grounds to operate restrictive naturalization systems seems to be challenged. In fact, recourse to the principle of internal security to restrict some of the rights now embodied by the citizen-ship of the Union (such as freedom of movement and residence) has already been severely curtailed by the Court of Justice.[31] The preservation of national identities seems to be the claim that in reality justifies restrictive regimes.

The question to be elucidated is: 'Do the privileges accorded by citizenship of the Union ease the requirements posed by Member States' legislation on the acquisition of nationality?' Among the several common legal entitlements to qualify for nationality (*ius sanguini, ius soli, etc*), the provisions on citizenship of

---

[28] Art 5 Belgian Constitution. See also n 36, Arts 18 and 19.
[29] Irish Nationality and Citizenship Acts, 1956 and 1986; Nos 23, 1956 and 26, 1986; 26(1).
[30] García, *supra*, n 22 at 21.
[31] Cases 115 & 116/81 *Rezguia Adoui* v *Belgian State and City of Liège* and *Dominique Cornuaille* v *Belgian State* [1982] ECR 1665.

116

the Union directly affect only the most restricted one: *ius loci* or naturalization by residence without the concurrence of any other title.[32] Member States grant the possibility of achieving nationality/citizenship to foreigners who were not born within the national borders provided that they have resided within them during a given period of time. However, nationals from Member States face qualifying periods of residence of various lengths, reflecting particular national circumstances and/or beliefs in the desirable duration of attachment. These are five years in Ireland,[33] the United Kingdom,[34] the Netherlands[35] Belgium[36] and France; six years in Portugal;[37] seven years in Denmark;[38] ten years in Italy,[39] and Spain,[40] and 15 years in Germany.[41] Since the allocation of permits is the traditional restrictive instrument used by states to reduce the chances of claiming naturalization through residence, the consolidation of the right of residence in the provisions regarding citizenship of the TEU can be said to have removed *de iure* and *de facto* these impediments for nationals from EC Member States.

The parallel processes of European integration, the progressive development of citizens rights and finally, the citizenship of the Union, have undoubtedly sanctioned the existence of a community of individuals. However, this community of individuals has not been (as yet) confirmed as a privileged status by the civil law of the Member States. The development of the citizenship right of residence is not matched by a parallel reduction in the periods of residence required to become naturalised. In fact, the granting of particular derogations would not be alien to the traditions of some of the Member States which recognise, instead, the existence of other particular links. Thus, Spain limits to two years the qualifying period for nationals from Latin America, Portugal, Philippines, Equatorial Guinea and for Sephardic Jews. Denmark reduces its qualifying period to two years for nationals from Nordic countries.[42] The acknowledgement of specific Community links between individuals, has been reflected only in Italian legislation: Italy has modified the qualifying period of residence for nationals from a Community Member State to four years. Without denying the importance of the supranational construction of the citizenship of the Union advanced by the TEU, the recognition and sanctioning by domestic civil laws is an essential element for the creation of a meaningful identity associated with citizenship.

---

[32] Obviously, certain nationals from Member States may be included in some of the many cases resulting from combining several entitlements described by national legislation.

[33] Irish Nationality and Citizenship Acts 1956 and 1986, s 15 (c).

[34] British Nationality Act 1981, s 6 (1).

[35] Netherlands Nationality Act 19 December 1984 s 8.1c.

[36] This is the period for ordinary naturalization. Loi du 28 juin 1984 *Code de la nationalité belge*, s 4, Art 19.

[37] Art 15.3(b) Decreto-lei n 322/82 *Regulamento da nacionalidade portuguesa*.

[38] *Cirkulære* 1992–02–06 *om dansk indfødsret ved naturalisation* 2.

[39] Art 9 (e) *Legge sulla nationalità*.

[40] Ley 18/1990 17 diciembre 1990 *Reforma del Código Civil en materia de nacionalidad*.

[41] Provisions for naturalization are not incorporated into the German Nationality Act *Verfassungs- und Verwalungsgesetze*, but in the Aliens Act, *Ausländergesetz* 86.

[42] *Cirkulære* 1992–02–06 *om dansk indfødsret ved naturalisation* 2. Furthermore, seven years of residence in a Nordic country satisfy the requirements of residence in Denmark (for Nordic countries nationals). *Lovbekendtgørelse* 1991–06–17 nr 457 *om dansk indfødsret* 10.A. It is also common to reduce the residence qualifying period for these seeking asylum and refugees; three years in the case of Belgium; five years in the case of Spain and six years in the case of Denmark.

Nationality and citizenship as entitlements for the protection of rights

The subordination of Union citizenship to nationality as regards a full deployment of the rights listed is also illustrated by the non-exclusive judicial protection afforded by the Court of Justice. Certain rights can, at this stage, be protected by invoking the title of citizens of the Union and the Court's jurisdiction. Thus, rights of citizenship as well as human rights may be protected by the Court within the scope of the EC Treaty and EC law. The protection of these rights by the Court extends equally to international law conventions signed by Member States, in pursuance of the objectives included in the provisions on home affairs and judicial co-operation. However, this is limited to the extent that (and only if) these conventions stipulate Court of Justice jurisdiction.[43] The exclusion of the juridical guarantee by the Court may be explained by the fact that the Court might have invoked them progressively to extend its jurisdiction over areas where it has been partially excluded. This would have the effect of reversing the intentions of the Treaty drafters.

However, the Court's entitlement to protect certain other rights of citizenship may not be straight forward. This is the case with the right to diplomatic protection by diplomatic missions (where there is no national one). Given that the implementation has to be effected through traditional instruments of international public law, it is not self-evident that citizens could be protected by the Court of Justice, at least the conventions signed contain an explicit entitlement for the Court. Equally, it seems that the protection of the human rights of citizens of the Union in Union areas other than the two above mentioned above (EC Treaty and Article K.3) will have to be invoked either before domestic courts or the European Court of Human Rights. In both cases, the claim that seems to secure protection for individuals lies not in Union citizenship but in nationality.

Conclusion

The reliance of citizenship of the Union on nationality reflects merely the subordination of the Union to its Member States. The progressive evolution of citizenship of the Union depends on the evolution of the Union itself, but a citizenship that may imply a challenge to nationalities of the Member States is foreseeable only when the responsibilities upon individuals, derived from their belonging to a European Political Union, are perceived as being as justified as those derived from their belonging to respective Member States. Citizenship of the Union, as enshrined in the TEU, in its current stage of development, is

---

[43] Art K.3.

equivalent to a generalization of the principle of non-discrimination on the grounds of nationality, regarding exclusively the group of rights specifically spelled out in the Treaty.

CARLOS CLOSA

Chapter 8

The European Union: three Pillars without a Human Rights Foundation

Introduction

The "transnational state" resulting from the Treaty on European Union (TEU) is, in many respects, the logical successor to the common market of 1958. The new Union was promulgated as a rival to the economic powers of the United States and Japan: an embryonic United States of Europe. The reality, however, is that setbacks to economic and monetary union, the failure to formulate cohesive foreign policies and the revived spectre of nationalism to the East have blunted the optimism of December 1991. It may be that the principal components of the TEU, cohesiveness in terms of monetary and commercial affairs, and to a lesser extent, common foreign and security policies, are effective as the central planks of a federalising Europe. However, in shifting the focus from the nation state, the proponents of integration have underestimated the extent to which enumerated human rights form the constitutional bedrock of a legal order, be it national or transnational.

Without underestimating the impediments to the process of European integration referred to above, this article seeks to highlight how the TEU's failure to deal adequately with human rights issues represents a lost opportunity and a fundamental defect in a Community in the process of expanding towards the Urals. The Treaty endorses and supplements the current approach of incremental development of rights protection under the aegis of the Court of Justice.[1] In so doing, the drafters appear to have felt that this obviated the need for a fundamental reappraisal of human rights protection in the new Europe. The alternative options (which are not necessarily mutually exclusive) of formal affiliation to the Council of Europe's human rights machinery and the drafting of a comprehensive code for the new legal order have, to the detriment of the individual, not been acted upon.

Rights protection: the approach to date

The ambitious nature of the European Political Community aborted in 1953 was mirrored in the human rights provisions of that Community's draft Treaty. The Treaty proposed the incorporation of Section 1 of the European

---

[1] In committing the Union to respect fundamental rights "... as they result from the constitutional traditions common to the Member States. ..." Art F.2 adopts the language of the Court of Justice first enunciated in Case 4/73 *Nold* v *Commission of the European Communities* [1970] ECR 1125.

Convention on Human Rights (hereinafter the ECHR) as well the First Proto-col.[2] In comparison with the Political Community, the other three Communities were less ambitious in scope and the drafters of the Treaty of Rome can hardly have envisaged the extent to which Community law would diversify beyond the field of economic activity. Despite being founded with a backdrop of mass abuse by totalitarian regimes of the civil and political rights on which classical liberal thought focused, the ambit of the three Communities that survived the Political Community provide some explanation for the absence of an explicit catalogue of human rights in the Treaty of Rome.[3] The foundation of the Economic Community pre-dated the incorporation into "rights language", on the United Nations or regional level, of social and economic aspects of society. However, it is no longer the case that:

" . . . the essentially economic character of the Communities . . . makes the possibility of their encroaching upon fundamental human values, such as life, personal liberty, freedom of opinion, conscience etc, very unlikely".[4]

In a paper attached to the 1976 *Report of the Commission on the Protection of Fundamental Rights as Community Law* (see below) Professor Bernhardt was of the view that "[o]f the classical fundamental rights, few seem greatly to be threatened by Community organs". However, he added the qualification that:

"[t]he fact that some fundamental rights are particularly apt to be infringed by Community authority and are therefore to be protected as a matter of priority, should not, however, obscure the fact that numerous other fundamental rights can, if only in exceptional cases, acquire significance under Community law; any catalogue of fundamental rights purporting to be comprehensive would therefore require to be more widely drawn".[5]

In addition to referring to the Charter of the United Nations, the preamble to the Treaty of Rome refers to the objectives of "the constant improvement of living and working conditions" and the pooling of resources "to preserve and strengthen peace and liberty". Though not formulated in "rights language" many of the provisions in the Treaty are concerned with the rights of the individual.[6] Several points must, however, be borne in mind. First, the protections afforded under Community law[7] do not, for the most part (Article 119 of the Treaty of Rome being an exception), inhere in the individual by virtue of his or

---

[2] The first Protocol guarantees protection of property, a right to education and free elections.

[3] As the *travaux préparatoires* of the Treaty of Rome were never published, reasons for the omission of enumerated rights remain a subject of conjecture.

[4] Toth, "The individual and European law", 24 ICLQ (1975) 659, at 667. Similar optimism was expressed by Drzemczewski provided the Member States and Community institutions "remain within the confines of the powers and responsibilities conferred upon them within the ambit of Community law". See *The European Human Rights Convention in Domestic Law* (1983) 251.

[5] See paper "The problems of drawing up a catalogue of fundamental rights for the European Communities", attached to the Report of the Commission on the protection of fundamental rights, 4 February 1976. 5/76-Bull EC Supp.

[6] *E.g.* Arts 2, 7, 48, 51, 52, 57, 117, 118, 119, 123. The Treaty also sets out limitations and exceptions to these rights, *e.g.* Arts 36, 48(3), 55, 223 and 224.

[7] In addition to the application of Treaty provisions even greater concern for the protection of fundamental rights has been evident in secondary Community legislation, particularly since the advent of a directly-elected Parliament in 1979.

her humanity, but flow from one's status as a Community national. Secondly, non-natural persons do not automatically benefit from the protections afforded.[8]

These two qualifications are not rectified by the Treaty on European Union. The discrimination between Member State and third country nationals, which lies at the heart of the EC, is reinforced by the location within the TEU of its only explicit enumeration of rights. By concentrating the rights attendant upon Union Citizenship in Title II, the TEU brings those rights within the jurisdiction of the Court of Justice. In confining its *general* statements on human rights to Title I, which is not subject to review by the Court, the Treaty has failed to make the leap from the protection of fundamental Community rights to concern for human rights proper. The human rights concerns attendant upon a federal Europe are no less, and in terms of vindication of rights, far more, of a concern for the nine million third state nationals living within the Community than for the citizens of the Union.

To the extent that the TEU goes beyond concern for the rights of the citizen, it follows on the precedent set by the Single European Act 1987, in that it stresses the importance of human rights in general and the European Convention for the Protection for Human Rights and Fundamental Freedoms in particular.[9] In line with the Union objective in Article B "to assert its identity on the international scene ...", the signatories "confirm their attachment to the principles of liberty, democracy and respect for human rights and fundamental freedoms and of the rule of law". In addition Article F.2 states:

"The Union shall respect fundamental rights, as guaranteed by the European Convention for the protection of Human Rights and Fundamental Freedoms signed in Rome on 4 November 1950 and as they result from the constitutional traditions common to the Member States, as general principles of Community Law".

The fears of indirect incorporation of the ECHR into the legal orders of the dualist Community Member States (the so-called 'Bill of rights by the backdoor' scenario) are assuaged by the fact that Article F is not enforceable before the Court of Justice. Accordingly, any facilitation of judicial activism in the protection of rights, as an alternative to a code of rights, has been circumvented. For the protection of their rights in the context of the EC and the Union the relevant claimants are obliged to rely on the piece-meal pronunciation that has been the hallmark of fundamental Community rights protection heretofore.

In the absence of a catalogue of rights in the Treaty of Rome on which to base its jurisprudence, the Court of Justice initially proved reluctant to protect fundamental rights other than those explicit in the text of the Treaty. Its

---

[8] See for example Case 374/87 *Orkem*, [1989] ECR 3283 at 3350 *re* natural person's privilege against self-incrimination not being available to a legal person.

[9] The preamble to the SEA sets out the Community Member States' "determination to promote Democracy on the basis of the Fundamental Rights recognized in the constitutions of the Member States, in the Convention for the Protection of Human Rights and the European Social Charter, notably freedom, equality and social justice."

subsequent distillation of a rights jurisprudence from general principles of law, following the conflict with the German and Italian Constitutional Courts, is well documented.[10] The Court's reliance on the *common constitutional principles* of the Member States and subsequently on human rights treaties adhered to by the Member States has culminated in the situation where the Court now feels at liberty to draw upon international human rights law (primarily in the form of the ECHR) without explicitly linking it to the common constitutional traditions.[11] At the core of the Court's protection of Community fundamental rights lies the principle, first enunciated in *Handelsgesellschaft*, that such protection as is afforded must "be ensured within the framework of the Community's structure and objectives".[12] Accordingly, the potential for using the supremacy of Community law and principle of direct effect to provide a level of rights protection beyond that guaranteed by Member States is necessarily restricted.[13]

The extent to which the Court of Justice is prepared to replicate the activist approach that marked its initial incursions into the field of human rights has not gone unquestioned. Weiler has expressed some reservations about a lack of resolve in relation to individual rights on the part of the Court of Justice.[14] This is of particular concern in the context of the loss of review jurisdiction by the Member States. Even more forcefully, the Court has been accused of hijacking the fundamental rights discourse to facilitate its main priority of economic integration, resulting in the devaluation of fundamental rights and the Court's "bringing its own standing into disrepute".[15]

The citizens' rights, set out in Articles 8 to 8e,[16] combine freedoms that have long been at the foundation of the EC (freedom of movement and residence) with rights that take account of more recent changes to the institutional equilibrium of the Community (freedom to vote in and stand for municipal and European Parliament elections, seek redress from the EP and Ombudsman,

---

[10] See generally, Mendelson, "The European Court of Justice and Human Rights" (1981) 1 YEL 125–165, McBride and Neville Brown, "The United Kingdom, the European Community and the European Convention on Human Rights", (1981) 1 YEL 167–205.

[11] Case 136/79 *National Panasonic (UK) Ltd* v *Commission* [1988] ECR 2033. An attempt to argue that this case incorporated the ECHR rights as fundamental principles of Community law thereby making the ECHR part of national law failed before the Scottish Court of Session. See *Kaur* v *Lord Advocate* [1980] 29 CMLR 79.

[12] Case 11/70 *Internationale Handelsgesellschaft mbH* v *Einfuhr-und Vorrasstelle für Getreide und Futtermittel* [1970] ECR 1125. Case 4/73 *Nold* v *Commission of the European Communities* [1974] ECR 491 qualified this, by adding that the objectives of the Treaty could only justify limiting fundamental rights when the substance of the rights was not affected. Nonetheless it is far removed from Justice Frankfurter's concept of judicial elucidation of rights as a "disinterested inquiry pursued in the spirit of science", *Rochin* v *California* 342 US (1952) 165 at 172.

[13] On integration through the Court of Justice's jurisprudence leading to higher standards of fundamental rights protection in Member States' legal orders, in non-Community as well as Community law matters, see Frowein, "Fundamental rights as a vehicle of legal integration in Europe" in Cappelletti, Seccombe, Weiler (eds), *Integration through Law* (1986) Vol 1 Book 3 at 302.

[14] See "Eurocracy and distrust: some questions concerning the role of the European Court of Justice in the protection of fundamental human rights within the legal order of the European Communities", 61 Wash Law Rev (1986) 1103, 1109.

[15] Coppell and O'Neill, "The European Court of Justice: taking rights seriously?", (1992) 12 *Legal Studies* 227–245 at 245.

[16] See O'Keeffe, "Union Citizenship" and Closa, " Citizenship of the Union and Nationality of Member States" in this volume at 87 and 109 respectively.

claim the protection of any Member State's diplomatic or consular authorities when in a third country). The limitations of Articles 8 to 8e, in terms of the ambit of the rights and their beneficiaries, preclude the provisions having any resonance of a Bill of Rights as it is commonly understood.

Another direct reference to human rights in the Treaty lies in the requirement that the justice and home affairs matters enumerated in Article K.1 be dealt with in compliance with the European Convention on Human Rights 1950 and the Refugee Convention 1951. However, the qualification in Article K.2(2), "This Title shall not affect the exercise of the responsibilities incumbent upon Member States with regard to the maintenance of law and order and the safeguarding of internal security", echoes the freedom of action allowed to states under the derogation provisions and margin of appreciation doctrine of the ECHR. However, the provision does so without any accompanying qualifications similar to those in the ECHR and the Strasbourg Court's jurisprudence.[17]

While the use of the expression "responsibilities incumbent upon Member States" might be viewed in the positive light that it recognises the consequences for the rights of the collective when law and order and internal security are threatened, the accompaniment of adequate protection for the individual is a prerequisite for ensuring that concern (or alleged concern) for the collective does not veil the abuse of individual rights. The experience at national level of draconian *special* powers being transplanted into *ordinary* criminal legislation ought to be borne in mind by Community nationals prepared to endorse, without question, protectionist measures under the third pillar of the TEU (Title VI) directed against third country nationals.

It is regrettable that the European Parliament, which of all the Community institutions has been most progressive in the field of human rights, is restricted to a consultative rôle in respect of justice and home affairs.[18] Furthermore, Article K.3(2)(c) precludes judicial review of any conventions on Article K.1 matters drawn up by the Council of Ministers unless such jurisdiction is stipulated. The failure to mandate compulsory jurisdiction of the Court of Justice or at the least put an onus on the high Contracting Parties to *justify* the exclusion of such jurisdiction, in effect, disarms the undertaking in Article K.2.

Accession to the European Convention on Human Rights

The debate regarding the accession of the European Community to the European Convention on Human Rights has run in parallel with the growing realization that the Community's sphere of activities could have repercussions

---

[17] States' freedom to take measures derogating from human rights instruments (see Art 15 ECHR, Art 4 ICCPR) is, in theory at least, strictly marshalled by requirements of proclamation, notification, exceptional threat, proportionality, non-discrimination and the inalienability of certain *fundamental* rights. See generally, Higgins, "Derogations under human rights treaties", (1976–77) 68 BYIL 281; Warbrick, "The protection of human rights in national emergencies", in Dowrick (ed) *Human Rights: Problems, Perspectives and Texts* (1979) 89–106.
[18] Art K.6.

for individual human rights.[19] Although the Community is not formally bound by the terms of the ECHR, the drafters of the Treaty of Rome did envisage close links with the Council of Europe; Article 230 of the Treaty stating "The Community shall establish all appropriate forms of co-operation with the Council of Europe".[20] The Council of Europe likewise has endorsed the creation of links between the two entities. Following a Resolution[21] of the Committee of Ministers, a Liaison Office now operates as a conduit when either body adopts measures on areas of mutual interest.

However, despite current and future co-operation several significant, if not impassable, obstacles block the accession route.[22] The Council of Europe and its major instruments, the ECHR and the European Social Charter, envisage states as members and signatories respectively. It does not countenance the possible involvement of a supranational entity such as the Community. Despite the fact that all the Member States of the Community have ratified the ECHR, recognise the jurisdiction of the Court of Human Rights as compulsory and accept the right of individuals to petition the Commission,[23] the EC itself is not bound by the Convention.[24] Where a Community measure breaches a right protected under the Convention it cannot be challenged directly before the Strasbourg organs. The only possibility of redress lies in an application regarding the Member State's implementation measures.[25] The Strasbourg organs will not entertain applications against the Community institutions. As more powers move to the centre and over a widening sphere of activities this lacuna has obvious human rights implications.

A Memorandum adopted by the Commission on 4 April 1979 was the first formal endorsement of the accession option.[26] Detailing the technical complications attendant upon this possibility, the Memorandum envisaged that it would be followed at some point by the drafting of a separate code of rights for the Community that would take account of economic and social rights not adequately protected by the Council of Europe machinery.

---

[19] There is a strong body of opinion that does not accept that accession would provide any greater rights protection, in real terms, than is currently the case under the Court of Justice jurisprudence. See House of Lords Select Committee on the European Communities, 71st Report, 1979–80, HL 362.

[20] There are also some precedents for Council of Europe instruments being open for Community ratification. The Community is a party to the European Agreement on the Exchange of Tissue-typing Reagents and the Convention on the Conservation of European Wildlife and Natural Habitats with the option of ratifying the European Convention for the Protection of Animals kept for Farming Purposes and the European Convention for the Protection of Animals for Slaughter.

[21] Resolution (74)13 of 6 May 1974.

[22] See Generally, Neville Brown and McBride, "Observations on the proposed accession by the European Community to the European Convention on Human Rights" (1981) 29 AJCL 691–705 and Schermers, "The Communities under the European Convention on Human Rights" (1978) LIEI 1–8.

[23] Recognition of the compulsory jurisdiction of the Court of Human Rights, Arts 48 and 46 of the ECHR. Recognition of individual right to petition, Art 25(1).

[24] See Application No 8030/70 *Confédération Française Démocratique du Travail* v *European Communities* [1979] 25 CMLR 229, where an alleged violation of the ECHR by the Council of Ministers was declared inadmissible *ratione personae*, under Art 48 of the Convention.

[25] *i.e.* where the right asserted does not come within the "general principles" of Community law thereby precluding a challenge to the Community measure before the Court of Justice under Art 173 or Art 175 EC.

[26] 2/79 Bull EC Supp. See Economides and Weiler, "Accession of the Communities to the European Convention on Human Rights: Commission Memorandum" (1979) 42 MLR 683–695.

126

More significant than the technical difficulties involved in accession is the question of the case load that would arise were actions against Community measures to be entertained, particularly in the light of increasing Community competencies and powers. As it is, the current work-rate of the Strasbourg Commission, sitting for 16 session weeks in 1992, is proving inadequate for the then 26 Council of Europe States.[27] One of the means of filtering out claims arising under the ECHR is the requirement that applicants first exhaust all local remedies as a precondition of admissibility and this presents a fundamental complication for Community involvement in the ECHR mechanism. Much attention has focused on the symbolic value of accession, but obliging claimants to undertake the circuitous route from national courts to Strasbourg via Luxembourg would sit uncomfortably with the Court of Human Rights' jurisprudence regarding expeditious justice and the guarantee in Article 6.1 of the ECHR of "a hearing within a reasonable time".

In the context of an enlarging Community, two significant advantages accruing from accession have been noted. First, the formal linking of the Community and the Council of Europe was perceived as a means by which the Community's concern with human rights could be stressed to aspiring Member States emerging from the shadow totalitarian regimes. This concern arose in the past with the enlargement of the Community to include Greece, Spain and Portugal following their return to democratic government.[28] Following the Copenhagen Summit in June of this year this concern arises again, to varying degrees, with the likelihood of Poland, Hungary, the Czech Republic, Slovakia, Rumania and Bulgaria applying for membership of the Community. It is a legitimate concern that in too many cases the desire to gain access to the fortified Community market is not accompanied by a willingness to embrace the Rule of Law ethos subscribed to by the current Member States. Ratification of the ECHR by the Community would ensure more uniform and effective application of the Convention in the East European states.[29] Secondly, by combining membership of the Community with the incorporation of the ECHR, the fledgling constitutional rights of Europe's newest democracies would be concretized and supplemented. This uniformity would minimise the possibility of conflict between the Court of Justice and legal orders that retain vestiges of the socialist legal tradition.

It is hardly surprising that a certain amount of jealousy with regard to the protection of human rights is evident in the interaction between the Council of

---

[27] The Commission disposed of 1,725 applications in 1992. But 2,465 were still pending at the end of the year, 57% of which had not received a first examination. For cases ultimately decided by the Court the average period between application and resolution currently stands at five years. This is before the accession of 13 East European and former Soviet states, currently with or awaiting Special Guest Status. Assuming that these states accept the right of individual petition and recognise the compulsory jurisdiction of the Court of Human Rights (and considerable informal pressure is being exerted on new members to do so), the Commission's chambers system adopted in 1990 will require further revision.

[28] See Neville Brown and McBride, *supra*, n 10 at 174.

[29] Some delay is evident in the ratification of the ECHR by East European states *e.g.* Hungary and Poland ratified the Convention two years after becoming members of the Council of Europe. Of greater concern is the fact that Poland has not accepted the right of individual petition or the compulsory jurisdiction of the Court of Human Rights.

Europe, Conference on Security and Co-operation in Europe and the European Community. This may well be a factor in the accession debate. The President of the European Court of Human Rights, Rolv Ryssdal, has observed that:

"[a]ccession of the Community to the Convention is surely the right way. It would not only serve to fill the conspicuous gap in the Community's legal order in that the Community is not subject to the Convention's control mechanism, but would also be the surest way to avoid the separate development of two different European standards of human rights protection, in an area where common standards are essential."[30]

As the EC and Union acquire ever-increasing powers over greater areas of human activity, the possibility of different standards evolving and coming into conflict becomes more real, and as regards the Court of Justice, there is some force in the view that:

" ... le contrôle de sa jurisprudence par les organes de Strasbourg, inconcevable tant qu'il s'agissait de juridictions internationales distinctes, chacune avec une compétence sectorielle, pourrait être perçu aujourd'hui comme un signe de maturité et une consécration de son rôle de cour suprême d'une Communauté quasi-étatique".[31]

A Bill of Rights for the Union?

Perhaps the most significant aspect of the "lost opportunity" is the fact that, in the creation of the Union, the Maastricht deliberations neglected to consider codification of the political, social, economic, cultural and environmental rights the people within the remit of the Union might seek to assert in the decades ahead. That the progenitors of such a catalogue, the French *Déclaration des Droits de l'Homme et du Citoyen* and the American Bill of Rights, were drawn up in the context of post-revolution nation states ought not necessarily preclude such an instrument for a supra-state entity undergoing a modern revolution.

The case in favour of such a code focuses on the merits of legal certainty, whereby individuals can assert their basic rights and be aware of the corresponding duties and limitations. The current piece-meal development of Community rights before the Court of Justice does not meet these criteria. However, a Community code will not provide a magical panacea clarifying all rights issues.[32] First, no code of rights can (nor should seek to) be exclusive; as a substantial body of rights will always remain unenumerated until a specific

---

[30] Winston Churchill lecture delivered at the Academy of European Law, Collected Courses of the Academy of European Law, 1991, "The Protection of Human Rights in Europe", Vol 1 Book 2, 1 at 31.

[31] Mancini et Di Bucci, "Le Développement des Droits Fondamentaux en tant que partie du Droit Communautaire", Collected Courses of the Academy of European Law 1990, *Community Law*, Vol 1 Book 1, 51.

[32] See generally, Gaete, "Postmodernism and human rights: some insidious questions" [1991] 2 *Law and Critique* 149–170. For the case against the necessity of such a Code in the Community context, see Clapham's excellent article, "A Human Rights Policy for the European Community", (1990) 10 YEL 309–366 at 361.

claim or societal development results in concrete formulation.[33] Secondly, and even more fundamental, is the objection that the focus on enumerated rights serves only to distract individuals from engaging in a more fundamental questioning of power distribution in society. These points do not defeat the case for a code of rights, but highlight how the effectiveness of such a code is linked with issues such as institutional accountability, the democratic deficit and the doctrine of subsidiarity. An effective Community code of rights would provide an important framework within which a new rights discourse could take place. By encapsulating the nature of the legal order which it underpins, a code would create an integrationist *culture* of rights currently lacking at the Community level.

Judge Lenaerts' suggested "Concentric circles" model[34] represents one possibility for making the transition from the protection of fundamental Community rights to the protection of human rights. This involves taking the ECHR rights as the nucleus for a Community code within increasing circles encompassing the rights elucidated by the Court of Justice from the *general principles* of Community law, citizenship rights and so-called "aspirational" rights respectively. The Commission's doubts in 1976,[35] in relation to the necessity of such a catalogue, are now outweighed by the more "political quality" of the Community and its growing encroachment into the lives of individuals.

One of the principal advantages presented by the drawing up of a new code lies in the opportunity to take account of the advances in the concept of *rights* since the ECHR was signed in 1950. The Council of Europe's Social Charter, which came into force in 1965, marked an advance in terms of rights recognition and a break from the classical liberal approach. The Council of Europe's commitment to economic and social rights has been strengthened in that matters relating to the Charter are no longer dealt with by a separate body, but are now handled in conjunction with ECHR issues by a single Directorate of Human Rights. Nonetheless, the distinction between *fundamental* economic and social rights in the Charter and civil and political rights in the ECHR remains evident from the means of enforcement. Compliance with the provisions of the Charter is ensured by monitoring by the Council of Europe and reports from governments of Contracting States,[36] employee's and employer's associations. Although governments are required to submit reports every two years, there is no judicial enforcement mechanism.

A first step at the EC level towards taking account of second, if not third, generation rights, is evident in the European Parliament's Resolution of 12 April 1989 and Declaration of Fundamental Rights and Freedoms.[37] In addition to the traditional civil and political rights, the Declaration enumerates rights in relation to occupation, working conditions, collective action, social welfare,

---

[33] *E.g.* the ninth amendment to the US Constitution provides that "The enumeration in the Constitution, of certain rights, shall not be construed to deny or disparage others retained by the people."

[34] "Fundamental rights to be included in a Community catalogue", (1991) 16 EL Rev 367 at 376.

[35] See Report of the Commission of 4 February 1976 submitted to the European Parliament and Council, *supra*, n 5 (Bull EC Supp 5/76).

[36] All the EC Member States, apart from Portugal and Luxembourg, have ratified the Charter.

[37] OJ 1989 C120/51.

education and the abolition of the death penalty.[38] The arguments against such a formulation are wide-ranging if not particularly new. Apart from the legal objections of Member States with dualist legal orders, Denmark, Ireland and the United Kingdom, the economic consequences and indeterminacy of such a programme arouse strong opposition. The threat to political sovereignty was also a particular concern, as was the Weberian notion of increased legalization of political issues and ethics.

Several of the criticisms of the Declaration in a rather scathing *Common Market Law Review* editorial[39] were valid in the context of the Declaration, but fail to persuade against the idea of a code in principle. Whether or not the European Union takes the form of a "super-state" is irrelevant to arguments on the necessity for a catalogue of rights. The fact that an entity with powers affecting the most fundamental rights of the individual is not properly accountable under the present legal order should be the sole concern. Similarly, the editorial's argument that a Community catalogue necessarily involves the denigration of the ECHR and the encroachment in matters adequately dealt with by the Council of Europe and the CSCE is flawed.[40] The affixing of protocols to the ECHR and its interpretation as a "living instrument" by the Strasbourg Court is itself recognition that the spread of human activity coming within the scope of human rights law is not static. Securing states' compliance with international legal norms in relation to first generation rights is but the first step towards formulating second and third generation rights. As Cappelletti has observed: "... to exclude social rights from a modern Bill of Rights, is to stop history at the time of laissez-faire ...".[41]

Following the Parliament's Declaration, 11 of the Member States adopted the Community Charter on the Fundamental Rights of Workers on 9 December 1989.[42] While drawing inspiration from the Council of Europe's Social Charter

---

[38] Arts 12, 13, 14, 15, 16 and 22 respectively. These guarantees are, however, adopted in the form of *fundamental* as opposed to *human* rights and are guaranteed variously to *everyone, European* and *Community citizens*. Despite increased concern at a Community level, the Declaration failed to formulate environment and consumer protection as *rights* (third generation rights), opting instead for the politically safe formulation of Art 24: "1. The following shall form an integral part of Community policy: – the preservation, protection and improvement of the quality of the environment, – the protection of consumers and users against the risks of damage to their health and safety and against unfair commercial transactions. 2. The Community institutions shall be required to adopt all the measures necessary for the attainment of these objectives."

[39] Editorial comments (1989) 26 CML Rev 589–593.

[40] The safeguarding of human rights is a central concern for the North American and European States in the CSCE. Its Charter of Paris for a new Europe specifically affirms the individual's right, without discrimination, to freedom of thought, conscience and religion or belief; freedom of expression; freedom of association and peaceful assembly; freedom of movement; freedom from arbitrary arrest or detention; freedom from torture or other cruel, inhuman or degrading treatment or punishment; to know and act upon ones rights; to participate in free and fair elections; to fair and public trial if charged with an offence; to own property alone or in association and to exercise individual enterprise; to enjoy ones economic, social and cultural rights. Without an enforcement mechanism the CSCE is restricted to educational and promotional means, the defects of which are evident from the recent expulsion of its human rights monitors from the former Yugoslavia.

[41] "The future of legal education: a comparative perspective" (1992) 8 SAJHR 1 at 10.

[42] Despite the purely declaratory nature of the Charter the UK Government declined to become a party to it.

the former document's 12 rights are restricted in their application to Community nationals and depend upon legislative action for their implementation.

Rather than simply listing, in general terms, respect for human rights and the protection of minorities as prerequisites for Community membership, the Community's expansion would be facilitated by the existence of a complete (in the sense that such catalogues can ever be complete) statement of the rights protected at the Community level. This observation applies equally to *negative* rights and to *programmatic* rights that may not meet traditional notions of enforceability. Obviously, a code requires a mechanism for the vindication of the rights therein. By requiring applicants to opt for one route of redress, the parallel existence of two European mechanisms protecting human rights presents no greater difficulties than exist at present with the regional and universal systems. Instead it might be argued that the sharing of the burden would be to the advantage of Community and non-Community nationals. A Community court responsible for human rights issues could still rely, where relevant, on the long-established jurisprudence of the Strasbourg organs; while applying the Community catalogue in areas under-developed at the Council of Europe level.

In addition to reducing the workload of the Strasbourg organs, a greater Community involvement in human rights issues would bolster the means of enforcement. The response of the Council of Europe to breaches of human rights culminates with the unsatisfactory option of expulsion from the Council of Europe.

As with the rejection of Turkey's application for membership in 1989, the freezing of the "Association" status of the Greek Regime of the Colonels (after the latter had withdrawn from the Council of Europe) and more recently in the case of Rumania, the denial of access to the economic benefits of *Fortress Europe* has proved to be more potent in bringing recalcitrant states into line than the means available to the Council of Europe.

Conclusion

To date the fears expressed regarding Member States' loss of sovereignty in a federal Europe have not been couched in terms of concern for individual rights. The undertaking in Article A, that the Union will take decisions "as closely as possible to the Citizen", is to be commended, but on its own is insufficient. Without an explicit formulation of the rights that can be asserted in relation to that decision-making there is no real guarantee of institutional accountability. The instruments and bodies of the Council of Europe provide a starting point, but the end goal should be a complete Code of rights. Without such a code, the fact that:

"Maastricht has been sold to a skeptical citizenry with *promises*[43] of greater reward and further rights and privileges as citizens of a federalising Europe ..."[44]

may well prove to be the real stumbling block to the process of integration.[45]

PATRICK M TWOMEY

---

[43] Author's italics.

[44] Brenner, "EC: confidence lost" (1993) 91 *Foreign Affairs* 24–43 at 28.

[45] The accession debate has gained new momentum in the context of a reforming Council of Europe. Addressing the Vienna Summit of the COE in October, EC Commissioner Haas van der Broek said that the Commission was of the view that the entry into force of the TEU should allow the EC to join the Council of Europe and he spoke in favour of the Community's accession to the ECHR.

Part 4

Economic and Monetary Union

Chapter 9
Legal and Institutional Issues affecting Economic and Monetary Union[1]
Introduction

In the image called up by a former President of the Commission of the European Communities[2] economic union and monetary union are the left boot and right boot for Europe to wear in its advance towards the ever-closer union of the peoples of Europe. If you tie the two boots together you will not make fast progress, no matter that the boots are three-league boots. Nevertheless, the Delors Committee (1989) did not hesitate to fuse the two ideas. In the words of that committee's report, "the creation of an economic and monetary union must be viewed as a single process".[3]

This article considers how closely the Maastricht Treaty has linked the two ideas. It examines the legal expression which the Treaty gives to the two concepts. It looks especially at the legal and institutional form imparted to the notion of monetary union. Since economic union remains relatively inchoate in its institutional aspect, the legal analysis of the economic arrangements will be brief. In both spheres the article measures the Treaty provisions against the yardstick of the rule of law, and considers the risk that the advances in economic union will be inadequate to match the constraints imposed by monetary union. Finally, it considers the nature of the UK's relationship to EMU and the effect of the "opt-out".

Provisions for Economic and Monetary Union

Objectives and timetable of EMU

The Treaty[4] conceives EMU as an instrument of the growth and development of the economy of Europe. The Delors Committee saw it as a process, not a goal, and envisaged three essential economic elements in the process: a strengthening of Community structural and regional policies by the increase of

---

[1] The views expressed in this article are those of the author and do not necessarily represent the views of the European Investment Bank. Unless otherwise specified, all references in this paper to Articles are to Articles of the Treaty of Rome, as most recently amended by the Treaty of Maastricht.
[2] Jenkins, *European Diaries* (1989) 23: also Jenkins, *A Life at the Centre* (1991) 463.
[3] *Report on Economic and Monetary union in the Community* (1989), para 39 (the "Delors Report"). The majority of the members of the Committee were governors of central banks of the Member States.
[4] Art 2 EEC, as amended by Art G.2 TEU.

funds; the tying of funds to measurement of progress on specific targets; and a laying down of Community rules for national budget deficits.[5] The process, which started in 1957, has advanced slowly. The Maastricht Treaty, since it deals in detail only with the third of the three elements foreseen by the Delors Committee, is but a step in the process.

In contrast to the economic sphere, for monetary union the Treaty sets a very fast timetable: by 1 January 1994[6] stage two, the convergence period, will begin. Before the end of 1996,[7] the Council must decide whether enough Member States meet the criteria for replacing their own currencies by the common single currency, *i.e.* the so-called convergence criteria, in order to permit the launch of stage three, *i.e.* the final single-currency stage and the adoption of the ECU, on 1 January 1997.

By 1 January 1999[8] stage three must start in respect of the national currencies which meet the convergence criteria. After that date the Member States without a derogation should "rapidly" withdraw their own currencies and adopt the ECU as the single currency.[9] Other Member States will be granted a derogation from the essential provisions regarding stage three, until such time as they meet the criteria.

The linking of monetary with economic union reflects the policy aims of the German government and the Bundesbank. It reflects the economic belief, most strongly held in Germany,[10] that a monetary union cannot function without prior economic convergence. It is not a view which is shared in France. One French view was expressed succinctly by former Prime Minister Rocard as follows: "*C'est de ce genre d'archaïsme, entrave à la croissance, que la monnaie unique, enfin, nous débarrassera*".[11] In other words, once the common currency is established, France may reflate on the back of the strong ECU.[12]

Economic union

The concrete advances towards economic union, as introduced by the Treaty, are twofold, namely the adoption of a common policy of price stability and the beginnings of an enforceable common policy on controlling national fiscal deficits.

Price stability

Price stability has over recent years assumed an increasing priority among the economic goals of Western governments. It is an objective to which British

---

[5] Delors Report, para 59.   [6] Art 109e(1).   [7] Art 109j(3).
[8] Art 109j(4).   [9] Art 109l(4).
[10] This belief is known as the "economic" or "coronation" theory, in that it views monetary union as the culmination and prize for a process of economic convergence. The opposite belief, namely the "monetarist" or "institutionalist" theory, stresses the power of monetary union to bring about economic convergence.
[11] Translation: "The single currency would finally rid us of this kind of archaic impediment to growth", *Le Monde*, 24 April 1992.
[12] The conflict of viewpoint has been often described. See, for instance, Gros and Thygesen, *European Monetary Integration: From the European Monetary System to European Monetary Union* (1992) 386 (referred to below as Gros & Thygesen).

governments feel able to adhere. For the Germans it is a legal imperative and an aim to which public opinion is strongly attached.[13]

This objective has not been translated into legal terms. The European Central Bank (ECB), which will be established at the start of stage three, will have the primary duty to translate the objective into monetary targets and to work towards their achievement. The absence from the Maastricht Treaty of any recital of motives for the setting of this objective will not facilitate the interpretative task of the European Court of Justice, if ever the Court should be called to decide on the lawfulness under Article 173 of measures taken by the ECB.[14] On a practical level the Treaty gives the ECB discretion to interpret the objective reasonably. The emphasis should logically be on producer input prices rather than retail prices, since the aim of the policy is, principally, to maintain the competitiveness of EEC manufacturers and thereby sustain the rate of growth and employment. However, on balance the choice may fall on the consumer price index.[15] Since, in a period of more or less constant prices, retail prices and producer prices could well move in opposite directions, and since national price trends could diverge, the ECB will have to make political choices.[16]

Excessive budget deficits

The second economic goal of reducing and containing excessive budget deficits is a weaker version of the goal set by the Delors Committee.[17] So long as over 98% of public revenue in the Community is controlled by national governments, some fiscal discipline may be required in the common interest.[18] It is therefore provided that "Member States shall avoid excessive government deficits".[19]

The Member States' compliance with this obligation will be monitored by the Commission. The Commission will in particular examine two indices, namely, (a) the ratio of actual or planned government deficit to gross domestic product; and (b) the ratio of government debt to gross domestic product. It will study the present value and likely trend of these indices and, subject to a limited discretion, will report to the Council any instance where in respect of any Member State the value of the first ratio exceeds a reference value of 3% or the value of the second ratio exceeds a level of 60%.[20]

---

[13] The Bundesbank by the Bundesbank Act of 1957 is under a duty to safeguard the value of the currency (Gros & Thygesen, *op cit*, n 12 at 406).

[14] The preamble to the Maastricht Treaty recites that the Member States are "resolved . . . to establish . . . a single and stable currency". This aim is not the same as price stability and no guide to policy.

[15] See Gros & Thygesen, *op cit*, n 12 at 2 415.

[16] Whereas the Bundesbank's basic goal of a stable currency is single-valued and in principle achievable though instruments of monetary policy, the objectives of the ECB are multi-valued and not necessarily responsive to the instruments which the ECB will possess. Consequently, the ECB's role will be more difficult and more sensitive.

[17] Para 33 of the Committee's report. See also Report to the Council and Commission concerning the realization by stages of economic and monetary union in the Community (OJ 1970 C136/1) (the Werner Report), s VII.

[18] Economic opinion is divided on the point.

[19] Art 104c(1).

[20] See Protocol on the excessive deficit procedure, annexed to the Maastricht Treaty (OJ 1992, C224/120).

The Council may make recommendations to the offending Member State for curing the deficit. If the offending Member State fails to adopt the recommendations, the Council may on its own initiative, apparently without further advice from the Commission, impose sanctions.[21] Perhaps for the first time, the Council has taken the power significantly to penalise a Member State for failure to perform a Community obligation. The probable publicity[22] attendant on such an action may be the most severe of the penalties.

Common policies

Apart from these two concrete measures of economic policy, the Maastricht Treaty restates, with some reinforcement, two economic obligations which the Single European Act already imposes on each Member State. These obligations are:

(1) to treat its economic policy as a matter of common concern and to co-ordinate policy within the Council;[23] and

(2) to treat its exchange rate policy as a matter of common interest.[24]

These obligations do not advance economic union to any great extent, since they lack any sanction.

Monetary union

In contrast to the economic front, a fundamental advance is made towards monetary union. The most extensive definition of monetary union, which is that advanced by F.A. Mann,[25] is a system which comprises the following indispensable ingredients:

– a central bank as lender of last resort;
– a single currency and a single legal tender;
– pooled monetary reserve assets and pooled external monetary liabilities;
– a single body determining the interest rate and the volume of domestic money.[26]

The chief features of EMU which correspond to Mann's test are a central bank, a single currency and a single monetary policy-making body. Certain of Mann's ingredients are partially missing: the central bank will not necessarily be a lender of last resort; national central banks will retain certain reserve assets;

---

[21] Art 104c(11).

[22] While the Treaty states that the Council may make its recommendations public (Art 104c(8)), it does not so state in regard to the imposition of sanctions. Publicity is nevertheless to be expected.

[23] Art 103(1). *Cf* former Art 102a and Art 105, providing for cooperation to ensure convergence of economic and monetary policies and for coordination, and the former Art 103 on conjunctural policies, whose efficacy is now doubted (Commission, *op cit*, n 77).

[24] Art 109m(1); see the former Art 107(1).

[25] Mann, *The Legal Aspect of Money* (1992) 5th ed, 508.

[26] Compare the weaker definition in the Delors Report, *op cit*, n 3 at para 22: "a monetary union constitutes a currency area in which policies are managed with a view to attaining common macroeconomic objectives". A mere *de facto* alignment of currencies, as prevailed between Ireland and the UK, is not a monetary union even in this looser sense. The distinction between types of union is not always clearly drawn (see *e.g.* Verloren van Themaat, (1991) 28 CML Rev 291 at 300).

external liabilities will not be pooled; and the volume of domestic money may be affected by the exercise of external monetary powers retained by the Council and the Member States. We briefly study these omissions.

Lender of last resort

This role is not considered by the Maastricht Treaty. This role goes with prudential supervision of banks. No specific task of prudential supervision has been conferred upon the ECB, but the possibility has been created by Article 105(6).

Reserve assets

The ECB will progressively acquire up to 50 billion ECU's of foreign reserves from the national central banks,[27] but for technical and operational reasons part of the reserves will stay with those banks.

External liabilities

Member States are understandably unwilling to pool their liabilities. Indeed, the Community and the Member States are explicitly prohibited from guaranteeing or otherwise supporting other Member States' commitments.[28] The states may, however, provide credits to each other, in a crisis, under the mutual assistance provisions of Article 109h(2) and the Commission may in times of crisis make loans to Member States under powers granted by the Council under Articles 109h (formerly 108) and 235.[29]

External relations

Finally, the union will be imperfect so long as national central banks, whether or not following guidelines laid down by the Council under Article 109(2), are free to intervene on the foreign exchanges for political reasons, and so long as its members maintain individual monetary rights and obligations under international law pursuant to Article 109(5).

ECB and monetary policy-making

In the third stage of the union, monetary policy will be entrusted to the ECB.[30] In the second stage, which is to commence on 1 January 1994, Member States retain their own right to make and implement monetary policy. Since 1971, this

---

[27] Art 30 of ECB Statute.

[28] Art 104b. This provision was introduced at the suggestion of the British government. It seems to have been accepted without demur.

[29] See, for instance, Council Regulation (EEC) 1969/88 (OJ 1988 L178/1). Compare the Bank of the United States, established in 1791 by the US Treasury. Private subscriptions to its capital were paid mainly by the transfer of a specific issue of US Treasury bonds. The Bank lent considerable sums to the union. It issued its own notes in parallel with state banks (see, for example, Hepburn, *A History of the Currency of the United States* (1915) 74 *et seq.* For an instructive account of 19th century German monetary union, see Holtfrerich in de Cecco and Giovannini (eds), *A Central Bank for Europe?* (1989), 216.

[30] Art 105(2). This provision does not of itself make it clear that the ECB has sole responsibility but Art 3a(2), referring to a "single monetary policy", taken with Art 14(3) of the Statute of the ECB, subordinating the NCBs to the ECB, makes that clear.

right has been qualified by the duty, and practice, of co-ordination which has exercised notably through the European Monetary Co-operation Fund.[31]

From the start of the second phase, there will be established a European Monetary Institute, which will "strengthen the co-ordination of the monetary policies of the Member States, with the aim of ensuring price stability".[32] The lack of powers of the EMI has been criticised.[33] The refusal to transfer policy-making powers to this institution reflects the principle, to which the Bundesbank is strongly attached,[34] of the "indivisibility" of monetary policy. When the EMI is dissolved upon the commencement of stage three, the ECB will take over the EMI's continuing tasks[35] while assuming its own far larger powers. The ECB will be the head of a European System of Central Banks (ESCB)[36] comprising the national central banks (NCBs) and the ECB itself.[37] The capital of the ECB will be held by the NCB's. The ECB's consolidated accounts will be published and independent audits will be required of the NCB's.[38]

The ECB's Governing Council, comprising governors of the NCBs and the members of the Executive Board, will determine the policy of the Bank. The Council will recommend the choice of President, Vice-President and other members of the Executive Board of the ECB[39] and will define the forms and limits for the instruments of monetary policy.[40] The ECB will be independent, but accountable. It will report annually on its activities and monetary policy to the European Parliament, the Council, the Commission and the European Council.[41]

Convergence criteria

The entry into stage three is automatic for the currencies of Member States which fulfil the so-called convergence criteria; three of the criteria are relative and one is absolute; the three relative criteria relate to movement of prices, interest rate convergence and maintenance of the currency's exchange value over the previous two years.[42] The fourth criterion is that the current government budget deficit and aggregate debt shall meet the tests laid down by Article 104c, as described at page 137 above. Whereas, by the precise working of the definitions, at least three countries will at any time satisfy the first two criteria, few now meet the third criterion and, as for the fourth, only Luxembourg now

---

[31] See Baer and Padoa-Schioppa, "The Werner Report revisited", appendix to the Delors Report, *op cit*, n 3, 56.

[32] Art 109f(2).

[33] *E.g.* Gros & Thygesen, *op cit*, 360–363. See also Kenen, *EMU after Maastricht* (1992) 72.

[34] See Pöhl, 'On the further development of the European Monetary System', appendix to Delors Report, *op cit*, n 3, 146–147.

[35] Art 109l(2).

[36] Which will not itself have legal personality, partly in order to avoid assuming NCBs' debts.

[37] Arts 4a and 106.

[38] With regard to the ECB the role of the Court of Auditors is limited to examining its operational efficiency (Art 27(2) ECB Statute).

[39] Art 109a(2).

[40] Art 106l(6).

[41] Art 109b(3).

[42] Art 109j(2) and the Protocol on the convergence criteria referred to in Art 109j (OJ 1992, C224/121).

fulfils it.[43] The criteria are indicative and are neither binding nor comprehensive. The Council retains considerable discretion on the application of the criteria.

Respect for rule of law

A test of EMU is to examine its respect for the rule of law. For the purpose of this examination we will consider the rule of law to embrace the concepts of the separation of powers, parliamentary control, equality between states and between persons, judicial control and natural justice.

Separation of powers

The simplistic concept of total separation of the functions of the legislature, the judiciary and the executive has not been accepted without qualification even by those whose names are most closely associated with it.[44] Nevertheless, the confusion of functions in EMU, as envisaged by the Maastricht Treaty, calls for comment.

The Council exercises the power to legislate for the following purposes among others:

- adoption of rules governing the powers of the ECB;[45]
- amendment to certain provisions of the Statute of the ECB;[46]
- adoption of rules permitting the ECB to impose obligations on "third parties";[47]
- adoption of "detailed rules and definitions" for the application of the Protocol on the excessive deficit procedure[48] and of provisions to replace that Protocol;[49]
- adoption of provisions to replace the Protocol on the convergence criteria referred to in Article 109.[50]

Furthermore, the Council has been granted certain judicial or quasi-judicial powers over Member States, notably:

- to decide whether an excessive deficit exists;[51]
- to decide, if a Member State fails to comply with the Council's recommendations with regard to an excessive deficit, to impose upon it penalties, including fines and obligatory deposits;[52]
- to decide whether a Member State shall have a derogation from entry into

---

[43] *Economist*, 3 July 1993.
[44] See Aristotle, *Politics*, Book IV, Chap 14, and Montesquieu, *L'Esprit des Lois*, Book XI.
[45] Art 106(6).
[46] Art 106(5).
[47] Art 20 of the Statute of the ECB, annexed to the Maastricht Treaty.
[48] Art 104c(14).
[49] Ibid.
[50] Art 6 of that Protocol.
[51] Art 104c(6).
[52] Art 104c(11).

the third stage of monetary union[53] and whether to abrogate such a derogation.[54]

In exercising these powers the Council acts by a qualified majority.[55] These powers are essentially political, although couched in the language of objectivity.

The executive roles of the Council are numerous and fundamental and, like the judicial roles, essentially political. Briefly, they include the fixing of the exchange rates at the start of the third stage,[56] the appointment of the members of the Executive Board of the ECB, the conclusion of agreements for an exchange rate system for the ECU in relation to non-EEC currencies,[57] the formulation of "general orientations for exchange rate policy",[58] the authorization of protective economic measures by Member States[59] and the recommendation of measures to remedy a Member State's excessive deficit.[60]

This concentration of economic powers in the Council is seen by the French authorities as a necessary counterweight to German insistence on the independence of the ECB.[61] However, this concentration of powers, which is not offset by any direct accountability to any democratic body, creates its own imbalance. The Council, representing the states in the Community system,[62] does not derive its legitimacy from the popular will.[63] Its legitimacy is hardly sufficient for the wide political discretion now entrusted to it in the economic and monetary sphere. Distrust of the Council is already manifest, for example, in the terms of the *Bundestag*'s consent to German ratification of the Maastricht Treaty.[64] A lasting authority could derive only from a political union administered by common institutions under democratic control.

Parliamentary control

The powers of the European Parliament are inadequate to exercise control over the actions and decisions of the Council, since the Parliament may not initiate any measure within the field of monetary policy and since it has no blocking

---

[53] Art 109k(1).
[54] Art 109k(2).
[55] Except that a simple majority is sufficient for action under Art 104c(11) (Art 148(1)).
[56] Art 109l(4).
[57] Art 109(1); in case such a worldwide system should ever be re-established.
[58] Art 109(2).
[59] Art 109i.
[60] Art 104c(7).
[61] See Guigou, "La place et le rôle de l'autorité économique dans l'Union Européenne" (1992) 19 *ECU*, 36–37, expressing the French government's position. The role of the Commission is correspondingly reduced.
[62] See Pescatore, "L'executif communautaire: justification du quadripartisme institué par les traités de Paris et de Rome" (1978) *Cahiers de droit européen* 387 at 392–394. Whereas the Treaty of Rome gave legislative and executive power to the Council (Id 394), the Maastricht Treaty confers upon it quasi-judicial powers.
[63] Especially as the Council's debates are governed by a duty of confidentiality (see Louis, "L'Union Economique et Monétaire" (1992) *Cahiers de droit européen* 251 at 304).
[64] "The Bundestag will oppose any attempt to evade the stability criteria that were agreed at Maastricht ... the move to Stage Three of EMU also requires an assessment from the German Bundestag". Resolution of the Bundestag of 2 December 1992, as quoted in *Frankfurter Allgemeine Zeitung* of 3 December 1992.

power, other than on amendments to the technical provisions of the Statute of the ECB[65] and on the conferring on the ECB of tasks in relation to policy on prudential supervision of credit institutions.[66]

On most matters the Parliament has, at best, a right to be consulted. However, over a range of issues, including exchange rate policy and international monetary relations, the Parliament has not even a right to be informed. Likewise, in the economic sphere Parliament's role is severely limited.

It is not surprising that the Maastricht Treaty, drawn up by, and on behalf of, national governments, should allocate power to the Council, the paramount intergovernmental institution. This has created the notorious "democratic deficit". Means to achieve a better balance of power should be studied in advance of the intergovernmental conference scheduled to take place by the end of 1996.[67] The EMU provisions pay scant regard to the goal, stated in Article A of the Maastricht Treaty, of creating "an ever closer union of the peoples of Europe, in which decisions are taken as close as possible to the citizen".

Equality between states and equality between persons

An essential feature of monetary union, as envisaged in the Treaty, is the uniformity across the Community of the interest rates imposed by the ECB through its market and credit operations, carried out under Article 18 of its Statute. By contrast, there is no express obligation of uniformity in the application of minimum reserve requirements or in the use of other instruments of monetary control under Article 19 of the ECB Statute. Even in the absence of an express obligation it is doubtful whether the Council, in laying down the scope of those instruments, could permit the ECB to discriminate explicitly between credit institutions of different Member States participating in stage three. Nevertheless, uniformity of treatment may well result in non-uniform effects, since differences in banking structure, level of corporate and private debt, taxation of interest payments and use by the banking system,[68] as well as differences in economic activity and employment, are likely to persist. These differences will determine the local effect of the common policies practised by the ECB. The resultant inequalities may lead to popular resentment and opportunistic populist rhetoric. They might also infringe the principle of non-discrimination laid down by the Court of Justice.[69]

Judicial control

Decisions of the Council in relation to EMU are, in general, subject to judicial control by the Court of Justice pursuant to Article 173 of the Treaty. The ECB within its fields of competence may bring or defend actions or proceedings before the Court under Article 175.

---

[65] Art 106(5).

[66] Art 105(6).

[67] Art 2, Maastricht Treaty.

[68] See, for a brief discussion, Alleron, (1990) *De Pecunia* 339 *et seq.*

[69] "Discrimination in substance may consist not only in treating similar situations differently but also in treating different situations identically." Case 13/63, *Italian Republic* v *Commission* [1963] ECR 165 at 166. See generally Schwarze, *European Administrative Law* (1992), 1st English ed, 571 *et seq.*

The power of judicial control is weakened by the vagueness of some basic concepts, in particular the ECB's primary goal of price stability.[70] The scope for challenge to an act of the ECB is as slight as the discretion accorded to that body is wide. For example, so long as the ECB interprets the concept of price stability reasonably, it will be difficult to allege that the ECB has wrongly defined its objectives and is abusing its powers. It will be even harder to assert that the means adopted by the ECB (*e.g.* under Art 19.1 of its Statute) are disproportionate to the objective. The ECB will have no express duty to state its objectives.[71] If it does state them, it will naturally be inclined to express them in wide terms. It is doubtful whether a Member State or individual, even one who might be especially affected by the action of the ECB, would have an effective judicial remedy.

The extent of the delegated discretionary power given to the ECB is all the more remarkable in that it is virtually irreversible. To reverse the transfer of power would require an amendment of the Treaty, to be ratified with the consent of the legislatures of all Member States.

Natural justice

The Maastricht Treaty does not directly infringe the principle of natural justice. Nevertheless, it creates anomalous breaches of the rule against being judge in one's own cause and pays insufficient heed to the principle of the rights of defence.

In the economic sphere, when the Council passes judgement on the excessive deficit of a Member State under Article 104c, that Member State may vote, and its vote will count in the calculation of the qualified majority required for the decision.[72] The same is true in relation to the assessment of the criteria for commencement of the third stage under Article 109j(4) and to the grant or abrogation of a derogation, under Article 109k, from the duty to enter the third stage.[73]

Where administrative measures are contemplated by the Council against a

---

[70] Which is the result of compromise (see Professor Jochimsen's speech at Nuffield College, Oxford, reported in (1993) *BIS Review* No 42 of 12 March 1993). For an eloquent justification of price stability and an implicit definition of the corresponding policy goal, see the speech of Dr Tietmeyer at St. Edmund's College, Cambridge, reported in (1992) *BIS Review* No 234 of 7 December 1992.

[71] The Council, acting under Article 19.2 of the ECB Statute, ought to require the ECB to give reasons for its regulatory actions, for the same motives as those which inspired Art 190 of the Treaty of Rome, requiring the Council and Commission to state reasons for their acts.

[72] This pattern of voting is also objectionable because it gives, on the determination of a matter of judgement not of balance of interest, an advantage to the four largest Member States. Each of these has, under Art 148 of the Treaty, 10 out of 76 votes in the Council. Since 54 votes will normally secure a majority, 23 negative votes will block a decision.

[73] Contrast the approach expected both of the Monetary Committee and its ultimate successor in stage three, the Economic and Financial Committee, to be set up respectively by Arts 109c(1) and (2). The task of these Committees is to contribute to the work of the Council on some but not all of its monetary and economic responsibilities. The members of these Committees, whether nominated by a Member State, the Commission or the ECB, should express their own opinions, not those of the authorities which appoint them. It is doubtful that they will: "Article 109c of the Treaty bears embarrassing witness to the successful effort of unelected and yet not independent officials to constitutionalise their position of power" in the view of Smit & Herzog, *The Law of the European Economic Community* (1982–1992), 3–630.17.

non-conforming Member State under Article 104c, or by the ECB against a national central bank, under Article 35(6) of the ECB Statute,[74] reasonable provision is made for hearing the party concerned. There is, however, no provision to permit states or individuals to show that they might be affected in a discriminatory manner by any act of general application.

Risks of EMU

Among the risks which the Community takes in aiming for monetary union are the risks arising from the impact of the two forms of union on each other. The chief such risk is that, following the adoption of monetary union, a Member State will suffer a country-specific economic shock which it will be unable to treat by national fiscal means. The risk will be compounded by the lack of an appropriate fiscal instrument within the Community budget.

Successive reports to the Commission have stressed the need for a common fiscal policy to compensate for the Member States' loss of the instrument of exchange rate adjustment and the curtailment of their right to run a budget deficit.[75] This opinion is shared by others. The former Bundesbank governor stated in 1989 that "a substantial transfer of authority will be necessary in the fiscal field" (leaving open whether this would include an increased central budget).[76] The Commission seems to hold that greater central fiscal powers are not needed,[77] but is not consistent in this view.[78]

It has been said that the power of the capital markets is sufficient to permit a state to address its crisis. However, if the Member State concerned has an excessive budget deficit, its access to the capital markets will depend on the approval of the Council under Article 104c. Moreover, the Member State will be entitled neither to raise funds from its national bank[79] nor, of course, to monetise its debt by causing an issue of bank notes.[80]

---

[74] Thus recognising the principle of "*audi alteram partem*". However, the state is given no formal right to comment on the sanctions which may be imposed upon it under Art 104c(11).

[75] See Delors Report, para 29, Werner Report, 13 and 14 and Report on the Role of Public Finance in European Integration (Commission pub ref II/10/77 E) (the MacDougall Report) 12: "If only because the Community budget is so relatively very small ... in present circumstances monetary union is impracticable."

[76] Pöhl, appendix to Delors Report, *op cit*, n 3, 136.

[77] In its publication, "One market, one money", (1990) 44 *European Economy* 11, the Commission states that such shocks may be countered by adjusting real labour costs and by budgetary policies at national and Community level.

[78] The Commission also points out the constraints (*op cit*, n 77): real wages are rigid (*ibid* at 149–151), fine-tuning by national budgets is ineffectual (*ibid* at 103) and the Community budget is too small to have any impact (*ibid* at 101). The Commission seems to waver; on the one hand, "fiscal discipline is ... a vital component of EMU" (*ibid* at 100) but, on the other hand, "a high degree of fiscal autonomy" is potentially desirable (*ibid* at 169).

[79] Art 104.

[80] Art 105a. The ECSB could technically support a national government by selectively buying its paper on the secondary capital market. This function is not among the basic tasks given to ECSB by Art 105(2) but the ECSB has a broad duty to support general economic policies within the Community (Art 105(1)). This duty might extend to saving those policies from a disturbance in one Member State.

The optimists may be right. Nevertheless the Community took an unnecessary risk in failing to provide a mechanism for fiscal transfers to a Member State suffering from a special economic shock. The Delors Committee identified the need but, under political pressure, the need was ignored.[81]

The UK opt-out

The scope of the UK's potential exemption from monetary union is wide, but far from complete. The United Kingdom assumes certain obligations under EMU and acquires certain rights. It may also retain certain other rights. The United Kingdom has assumed the following obligations:

- to accept under Article 2 the common goal of price stability;
- to accept the obligation under Article 102a to conduct its economic policy with a view to contributing to the achievement of the objectives of the Community, as defined in Article 2; and to treat its economic policy as a matter of common concern under Article 103; and
- to continue to accept, likewise, that its foreign exchange policy is a matter of common interest under Article 109m.

The United Kingdom retains the right:

- to run excessive budget deficits within the meaning of Article 104c;
- to fund government operations through the Bank of England through the so-called *Ways and Means* facility, notwithstanding Article 104;[82] and
- to retain the power to give directions to the Bank of England, in the public interest, under section 4 of the Bank of England Act 1946, notwithstanding Article 108 of the Treaty.

Even if it opts out, the United Kingdom has acquired certain common rights, in particular:

- to participate, rather asymmetrically, in the vote of the Council as to whether the conditions for the launch of the third stage are met,[83] or whether a Member State is entitled to a derogation from participation in the third stage;[84]
- to receive "mutual" assistance under Article 109h, in case it is in difficulties as regards its balance of payments, and to take necessary protective measures in the case of a sudden crisis in the balance of payments, within the meaning of Article 109i;

---

[81] See Gros & Thygesen, *op cit*, n 12, 480.
[82] Para 11 of the Protocol on certain provisions relating to the UK (OJ 1992 C224/123) (the "UK Protocol"). Nevertheless, by Art 104a the UK is forbidden from giving itself or any public body privileged access to the capital markets.
[83] Art 109j(2) and (3).
[84] Art 109k(1).

- to participate in the General Council of the ECB, established under Article 45 of the Statute of ECB;[85]
- to participate in the Monetary Committee and Economic and Financial Committee set up under Article 109c in order to advise the Council and the Commission;
- to vote on financial matters requiring a unanimous Council decision, *e.g.* under Article 109k(6) changing the convergence criteria or under Article 105(6), conferring upon the ECB specific tasks concerning policies relating to prudential supervision of credit institutions.

Exemption comes at a cost. The ESCB, while supporting the general economic policies of the Community under Article 105(1), would not be obliged, if the United Kingdom were to opt out, to have regard to the effect of its policy on the United Kingdom; nor would the United Kingdom participate in the external monetary affairs of the Community.[86]

It is noteworthy to compare the UK opt-out to the present position of Denmark and Germany. Denmark, by a Declaration made at the Edinburgh summit of December 1992, announced that it was exercising its right not to take part in the third stage of EMU. Germany has no such right. Nevertheless, the *Bundestag* has stipulated that Germany's move to the third stage should depend on its own assessment of the attainment or failure of the conditions laid down for that stage. This stipulation, which the German Constitutional Court has upheld as an essential constitutional safeguard, may put the German government in conflict with its obligations under Community law.

Conclusion

There are defects of conception and of expression in the EMU provisions of the Treaty of Maastricht. The defects may flow from national administrations' wish to protect their prerogatives and from a fear that public opinion will not accept economic reality. The Treaty reflects too precisely the prevailing economic wisdom. The Treaty is vague on important concepts, but excessively precise on administrative procedures. Finally, the Treaty fails fully to respect the principle of the rule of law or, indeed, its own precept that decisions be taken close to the people. In short, the means for attaining economic and monetary union, and the powers of the institutions to administer it, are imperfectly devised. How well the structure of EMU, which bring's undoubted benefits, will withstand the pull of divergent economic forces and the pressure of speculative interests, remains to be seen.

D R R DUNNETT

---

[85] This body contributes to the advisory functions of the ECB to the preparation of the third stage of EMU.

[86] Para 5 of the UK Protocol, *supra*, n 82.

Part 5

Environment

Chapter 10

Maastricht and the Environmental Policy of the Community: Legal Issues of a New Environment Policy[1]

Maastricht tends to compound rather than resolve difficulties inherent in designing a comprehensive and consistent Community policy concerning the environment. The first problem is one of definition. Environment does not describe a discrete area of action in the manner of the many other Community policies. The ends which it pursues are various and inchoate.[2] Nearly all policies might be said to have environmental impacts and environmentally motivated action might be said to encompass the operation of all policies.[3] The problem has been demonstrated repeatedly in institutional battles over the correct legal basis for measures with an environmental purpose. Certain environmental objectives can only be attained through the medium of other policy areas, trade, agriculture and other areas of action and the legal bases for measures in these areas may provide an attractive alternative to Article 130s of the EEC Treaty for procedural and other reasons.

This first problem leads logically to the second which is the task of reconciling the goals of environmental protection with the fundamental objectives of Community policy which are primarily economic. Several years before the Single European Act introduced provisions to the EEC Treaty expressly relating to the environment, the European Court of Justice found environmental protection to be a matter of general interest which the Community will protect even in the face of more traditional interests such as economic integration and free movement.[4] The extent to which this general interest modifies or prevails over other principles of the Treaty remains fluid.

The third problem is one of competence or justification. Prior to the 1987 amendments the Community generally relied on Articles 100 or 235 (or both) as legal bases for environmental legislation. Article 100 on the assumption that environmental measures would effect the functioning of the market in most cases; and Article 235 on the basis of a generous interpretation of the Com-

---

[1] This article is derived from work undertaken for a research project funded by the European Commission (DG XII) entitled 'Designing European institutions for climatic change' co-ordinated by the Centre for Economic and Social Research on Global Environment (CSERGE), University of East Anglia.
[2] The policy is inchoate in the sense that its objective is not fixed according to a final, if theoretical, outcome such as the single market, but instead a high standard of environment protection.
[3] Reg 1872/84 of 28 June 1984 (OJ 1984 L176) defines environment as 'the combination of elements whose complex interrelationships make up the settings, the surroundings and the conditions of life of the individual and of society as they are felt'.
[4] Case 240/83 *Disposal of Waste Oil* [1985] ECR 532 and Case 302/86 [1988] ECR 4607.

munity task set out in Article 2. Community action was justified positively in terms of necessity (to achieve the objectives of the Treaty) and negatively in terms of avoidance of effects on the internal market. Article 100, and since 1987, Article 100a have remained important to environment policy despite the adoption of explicit environmental provisions under Article 130s SEA, measures adopted under these Articles might be said to fall within the exclusive competence of the Community with only limited opportunity of derogation.[5]

Article 130s maintains some of the characteristics of the residual Article 235 in that action must still be justified not on grounds of necessity in achieving a discrete objective of the Community, (the achievement of the single market), but because they contribute[6] to the pursuit of far more broadly drawn objectives. The Community remains on firmer political ground justifying harmonization measures, as it does in justifying trade and competition regulation, which have the distinctive final objective of the functioning of the market rather than the vaguer standard of a high level of environment protection.

In the current political climate the development of national legal initiatives in the field of environmental protection is pervasive and dynamic, and the constraints, or from another perspective, the opportunities, offered by the Community dimension rest upon a legal base of some complexity. From both the structure of the existing Treaty and existing caselaw of the European Court a number of general principles concerning national and Community competence can be derived as follows.[7]

National environmental measures

Environmental measures at this level;

- are, (in the absence of Community legislation[8]), permissible under Article 30[9] subject to certain conditions laid out in the *Danish Bottles*[10] and *Wallonia*[11] cases;
- may be maintained (though not introduced[12]) as a derogation from Community harmonization measures adopted under Article 100a, provided they do not operate as arbitrary discrimination or a disguised restriction on trade between the Member States;

---

[5] Case 92/79 *Commission* v *Italy* [1980] ECR 1155 confirmed Art 100 as a proper basis for environment measures.

[6] The extent of the Community contribution is limited by subsidiarity. See Nollkaemper, 'The European Community and international environmental co-operation: legal aspects of external Community powers' (1987) 2 LIEI, 55–91 on the relationship between subsidiarity and necessity.

[7] Kramer, 'Community environment law – towards a systematic approach' (1991) 11 YEL 151 at 163–165.

[8] *Denkavit* [1988] ECR 2982.

[9] See also Cases 120/78 *Cassis de Dijon* [1979] ECR 649–665, 54/85 *Maleic Hydrazine* [1986] ECR 1067–1080 and 94/83 *Pesticide on Apples* [1984] ECR 3263–3281.

[10] Case C-302/86 *Danish Bottles* [1989] 1 CMLR 619 and 631.

[11] Case 2/90 *Commission* v *Belgium* [1993] CMLR 365.

[12] Kramer, *Focus on European Environmental Law* (Sweet and Maxwell 1992) 76–79.

- may be maintained and introduced despite the existence of a Community measure adopted under Article 130t SEA provided they are compatible with the Treaty;
- may not conflict with and are preempted by Community measures in other policy spheres, (though legislation may provide for additional legislation or allow complementary national regulation[13]);
- may not be adopted at all within the sphere of Article 113 (Common Commercial Policy)[14] or Article 102 of the Act of Accession (Marine Fisheries Conservation)[15] unless authorised by legislation.[16]

Community environmental measures

Environmental measures at the Community level;

- may be adopted under Article 130s as minimum standard provisions by virtue of Article 130t, provided the objectives of environment policy are better attained at Community level than at the level of the individual Member States (Article 130r(4));
- may be adopted under Article 100a as approximation measures with the aim of progressively establishing the single market provided they have as their object the establishment and functioning of the internal market;[17]
- may be adopted under other Articles 113, 75, or 43[18] with other objects by virtue of which no stricter standard is permissible *per se*[19] (though individual measures may provide that more stringent standards may be adopted and Community rules may allow a degree of administrative amendment if the Community fails to take action).

Maastricht represents a redraft of the Treaty of Rome in a holistic manner taking account of environmental concerns at the core of the Community purposes, by a restructuring of the fundamental task in Article 2 and the raising of environment to the status of a policy in Articles 3 and 130r. By altering the basis of all the Community policies and directing them towards the pursuit of "sustainable growth" rather than "a continuous and balanced expansion" Article 2 represents the most fundamental greening of the Treaty.[20] Simultaneously, the requirement that environmental considerations be a component of

---

[13] For application of the rule of conflict/ exhaustion see Temple Lang, *infra* at 189–194 and Cases 40/69 *Bollman*, 16/83 *Prantl* [1984] ECR 1299, 47 & 48/83 *Poultry* [1984] ECR 1721, 148/85 *Forest* [1986] ECR 3449 and *Gourmetterie van de Burg* 169/89 [1990] ECR 2143 (an environment measure under Art 235).

[14] Case 104/81 *Kupfeberg* [1982] ECR 3641–3671.

[15] Case 804/79 *Commission* v *United Kingdom* [1980] ECR 1045–1080.

[16] Case 370/88 *Marshall* [1990] ECR 4071.

[17] The scope of Art 100a for environment measures has been the subject of much dispute: *Commission* v *Council: Waste Directive Case* judgment of 17 March 1993, Case 300/89 *Commission* v *Council: Titanium Dioxide Case* [1991] ECR 2867.

[18] Case 62/88 *Greece* v *Council: Chernobyl Case* [1990] ECR 1527.

[19] See Kramer, *op cit* n 7 at 167–168.

[20] Wilkinson ' Maastricht and the environment : the implications for the EC's Environment Policy of the Treaty on European Union' (1992) 4 *Journal of Environmental Law* No 2, 221.

other policies is strengthened to a requirement that environment policy be integrated into the definition and implementation of other policies.

On a more procedural level and in an effort to increase the efficacy of Article 130r qualified majority voting is introduced, subject to important exceptions. The role of the European Parliament is enhanced by the introduction of the co-decision procedure in respect of general action programmes and co-operation in other areas of majority voting. Several amendments are made in an attempt to create a political equivalence between Articles 100a and 130r though important differences remain. The Community's external competence is underlined by the addition of a fourth objective to the new policy and Parliament's role in the adoption of certain agreements enhanced and extended in a fundamental redraft of Article 228.

The Community task and sustainable growth

There is a general broadening of the purposes of the Treaty of Rome in Articles 2 and 3. Article 2 as amended provides that:

"the Community shall have as its task ... by establishing a common market and an economic and monetary union and by implementing the common policies and activities referred to in Articles 3 and 3a, to promote throughout the Community a harmonious and balanced development of Economic activities, *sustainable* and non inflationary growth *respecting the environment* ...."

Article 3(k) includes, for the purposes set out in Article 2, amongst the Community's activities "a policy in the sphere of the environment." In one sense this is so much unfinished business. The express introduction of the environment into the Treaty under the Single European Act involved no alteration of Article 2 or 3 as it might have done.[21] The meaning of sustainable growth, (and the Treaty studiously avoids the more familiar concept of sustainable development), is uncertain and its definition is unlikely to give a sufficiently precise standard for judicial intervention where conflicts between interests arise or a co-ordinated implementation of policy is demanded. Perhaps the best that can be said is that it represents an attempt to achieve one of the recommendations of the Brundtland Report concerning the merging of environment and economics in decision-making.[22]

Article 2, cannot on its own be considered a sufficient legal basis for review of the legality of Community policies, though its wording in the past has supported a broad interpretation of Article 235. Yet, it provides a strong mandate for the equal status of environmental policy within the operation of economic policies and support for the obligation to integrate. It confirms the jurisprudence of the Court which has ruled environmental concerns to be a matter of general

---

[21] A revision of the Community task has long been on the agenda: see Evidence to House of Lords Select Committee on EC Environmental Problems and the EEC, 27 July 1979; and Wilkinson 'Greening the Treaty' Institute of European Environmental Policy Pamphlet, October 1990.

[22] *Our Common Future* : Report of the World Commission on the Environment 1987, Chap 2 'Towards Sustainable Development' (OUP 1987).

Community interest, which may modify the operation of other Community interests including the free movement of goods.

Obligation of integration

Article 130r(2) currently provides that environmental protection requirements shall be a component of the Community's other policies. Maastricht upgrades this to a more positive obligation; that environmental protection requirements must be integrated into the definition and implementation of other Community policies. The legal status of the integration requirement can be questioned. The provision could be read as providing a mandate for the Court of Justice to review the whole range of Community measures for their environmental credibility. If measures which fail to meet the integration criterion could be found invalid the Community legal order would bolster environment requirements by the introduction of superior obligations providing a counterbalance to the economic market principles. The difficulty is that in applying the principles of environmental protection the Court would almost inevitably involve itself in complex economic and social questions to which it may feel itself ill-suited.[23]

What is meant by "environmental protection requirements" is not defined. Requirements in this context may be interpreted as being limited to the objectives of existing Community secondary legislation in the environmental sphere, but the definition could be extended to include more general policy goals contained in the Action Programmes, or indeed the principles derived from the objectives of Article 130r(1) or the principles listed in Article 130r(2). Whatever requirements may be, Community law insists that they be integrated. It may be open to the Court to annul where it is clear that the Council and/or the Commission has not considered these requirements or not provided adequately for their integration into the definition and implementation of individual policy measures. In other cases, (perhaps the great majority of cases where legislative choices are necessary), formal integration by legislation and administrative action may be required. The effect of the Single European Act integration provision is already demonstrated on the policy front. The Commission has produced several papers on Environment and Energy,[24] Sustainable Transport,[25] Agriculture and Trade Policy in an attempt to meet the requirements of the first part of the obligation.[26]

The Maastricht integration requirements are not confined to the development of policies, but now expressly refer to "implementation" as well. This may prove a more demanding and controversial obligation. In particular, there is concern that the massive expansion of transfer of funds to the less developed regions of the Community may be used to promote projects which degrade the

---

[23] See Berlin 'Interaction between lawmaker and the judiciary within the EC' (1992/2) LIEI, 17 at 41 and 42 on the difficulties of balancing interests supported by the Treaty scheme.

[24] COM (89)369 of 8 February 1990.

[25] COM (92) 46 final of 20 February 1992 'Sustainable Mobility'.

[26] See also 'Towards Sustainability' The Fifth Action Programme which identifies five priority areas: industry, energy, transport, agriculture and tourism.

environment. The legal controls on the spending of funds, the system of pro-gramme approval, and the ability of the Commission to police them effectively can be called into question. A case currently pending before the Court, based on a requirement within the Structural Funds Regulation, may provide an illustra-tion of the issues raised by a claim that integration obligations may be formally justiciable.[27]

Other principles of environmental action

After Maastricht, Article 130r(2) specifies in common with Article 100a(4) that Community policy shall aim at a high level of protection. Article 130r(2) also prescribes principles of environmental action upon which the policy shall be based. These principles are novel, as no other Community policy is governed by equivalent principles of action. The principles are of general application, but as they form only the basis of Community legislative action they are probably not justiciable. Nevertheless, Article 130r(2), in common with the integration requirement, assumes that Community action will be taken in accordance with the principles prescribed. It is not inconceivable therefore that the principles should also be relevant at least to the review of discretionary decisions.[28]

Prior to Maastricht three general principles were contained in the Treaty: preventative action should be taken, damage should, as a priority, be rectified at source and the polluter should pay. To these Maastricht adds the precautionary principle which states[29] that it is not sufficient that the cause or derivation of environmental damage must be proved before action is taken, but only that the risk attached is sufficient to require proof that no environmental damage will result from a failure to take action.[30] As the precautionary principle has rele-vance to liability and evidence principles there may here be the germ of a justi-fication for provisions providing for strict liability or an alteration of the rules of evidence in environmental liability and licensing cases.[31]

Another of the principles, that environmental damage should as a priority be rectified at source, was invoked by the European Court in the recent *Wallonian Waste* case[32] where the Court held that local measures restricting the import of waste from other regions or Member States were a justifiable exception to Article 30. The principle was used not simply to support an environmental

---

[27] Case C-407/92 *An Taisce* v *Commission*.

[28] See Kramer, *Focus on European Environmental Law* on the polluter pays principle, 252.

[29] Principle 15 of the Rio Declaration 1992. In order to protect the environment, the precautionary approach shall be widely applied by states according to their capabilities. Where there are threats of serious or irreversible damage, lack of full scientific certainty shall not be used as a reason for postponing cost-effective measures to prevent environmental degradation.

[30] See generally 'The precautionary principle in British Environment Policy,' Nigel Haigh IEEP Paper, March 1993.

[31] In the absence of Community legislation and a clear legal basis for measures harmonising procedural rules the Court of Justice has in a series of decisions laid down certain *minima* on the basis of Art 5 and a principle of effectiveness. See Curtin, 'The decentralised enforcement of Community law rights: judicial snakes and ladders', in Curtin and O'Keeffe (eds), *Constitutional Adjudication and National Law* (Butterworths 1992) at 48 and 49.

[32] Case 2/90 *Commission* v *Belgium: Wallonia Waste Case* [1993] CMLR 365.

mandatory requirement, but to justify a measure that would otherwise be discriminatory.

"It follows that having regard to the differences between waste produced in one place and that in another and its connection with the place where it is produced, the contested measures cannot be considered discriminatory."[33]

There is, however, a difference between the application of such principles to validate unilateral action by a Member State and their use as a criterion for review of the contents of Community legislation. The effect of the principle on the validity of the Hazardous Waste Directive 84/631, which authorises inter-state movements of hazardous waste was not expressly considered in the *Wallonian* case, although provisions of the Directive were considered relevant to the resolution of at least part of the case. Any question that the Directive itself might be contrary to the rectification at source principle was not raised.

A measure which flies in the face of these general principles could conceivably be invalid. But one assumes that both the Court and the Commission will take care to ensure that reference is made to these principles in the preamble to legislation or in background policy documents, and in these circumstances, it is doubtful whether the Court would be prepared to look behind such statements, to question the validity of legislation. Their main impact is likely to be gravitational, providing a basis and direction for the interpretation of Community law, especially where ambiguities exist.

Article 130s and the nature of the environmental interest

The present framework of Article 130r specifies three objectives of Community environmental action: to preserve, protect and improve the quality of the environment, to contribute towards the protection of human health, and, to ensure a prudent and rational utilization of natural resources. Given such broad objectives there is very little which does not fall within the scope of environmental action. But, with the upgrading of action to the status of policy the limitations of Community competence in the area are emphasised. Article 130r, as amended, reads as follows:

"Community policy on the environment shall *contribute to the pursuit of the following objectives*:
– preserving, protecting and improving the quality of the environment
– protecting human health
– prudent and rational utilization of natural resources
– *promoting measures at international level to deal with regional or worldwide environmental problems*."[34]

Community policy now *contributes* to the pursuit of these objectives where before Community action had these objectives. The change reflects the concurrent nature of Community powers in the area and the (only) partial delegation of power. The extent of the Community contribution is probably defined with

---

[33] *Ibid* at para 36.
[34] Author's italics.

reference to the subsidiarity criterion and the requirements of Article 130t which allows Member States to adopt more stringent measures not incompatible with the Treaty. Both of these requirements have been present in environment policy at least since 1987 on creation of Article 130r.

Three general points on the nature of the Community interest may be made. First, the integration requirement itself extends the Community's interest to the environmental impacts of all existing policies. Secondly, insofar as environment has an independent basis for action, it extends to the global environment by virtue of the new fourth objective of environment policy and is not limited to the territory of the member states. Thirdly, the three traditional objectives of environment policy are extremely broad ranging in any event.

The limitations on the policy are that it is a contribution to the pursuit of these objectives, and the Treaty does not posit that the Community shall itself fulfill the objectives. The contribution requirement is more concretely defined in two areas, namely minimum standards and subsidiarity.

International Action

The new fourth objective of environment policy is uncontroversial.[35] The Heads of State and Government dedicated themselves to establishing a leading role for the Community in international environmental issues at the Dublin Summit of 1987. It reinforces the notion that the environment knows no political boundaries and confirms the independent nature of the Community's external power. This latter point is important as the Community previously had to rely on the existence of internal measures to justify external competence in application of the *ERTA* principle. The fourth objective strengthens the argument that the Community's interest is general and is unrelated to any functional relationship with internal problems or measures.

Yet, the provision of an objective which confirms the validity of a Community role in the development of action to deal with global environmental problems, which by definition the Community alone cannot solve, lies uncomfortably with the Treaty definition of subsidiarity.

The Member States have again made a Declaration on the effect of Article 130r(5) on the principles of the *ERTA* case, which defines the scope of implied external powers and the circumstances under which they might be deemed exclusive. The Declaration reads:

"The conference considers that the provisions of Article 130r(5), second subparagraph do not affect the principles resulting from the judgement handed down by the Court of Justice in the *ERTA* case."

---

[35] Through participation and ratification, individual Conventions are part of Community law and may be directly effective, but are not as a rule enforced by the Commission (Kramer 'The implementation of Community Environment law' *German Yearbook of International Law* (1991) 431).

On two counts the principles deriving from the *ERTA* case[36] appear to have no relevance to Article 130r or any part of Article 130r-t for that matter. First, even were the *ERTA* principles[37] confined to the area of external relations[38] they relate to the scope and quality of *implied* external relations powers, while Article 130r(5) creates an express power to conclude treaties in co-operation with the Member States. Secondly, the recent *ILO* case,[40] in an application of *ERTA* principles to a policy which provides for minimum standards measures only, found that these minimum standards measures did not create exclusive competence in the external sphere. Member States were entitled to participate in international treaties which fell within the subject matter of minimum standards measures and negotiate stricter standards. The *ERTA* case is merely an application of the superiority of European law and the *Simmenthal* case,[39] outside the area of Common Commercial Policy and Marine Fisheries Conservation Policies which are governed by separate, but consistent principles. The consequences, therefore, relate to internal matters as well. It has a continuing relevance insofar as *ERTA* provides that Member States are preempted from adopting measures which interfere in the operation or scope of existing Community measures, measures which in the case of Article 130r-t require no more than that lower standards may not be adopted.

If, according to *ILO*, the ability of the Member States to adopt more stringent standards not incompatible with the Treaty in the areas of social policy means it is not exclusive; neither then, can environment policy, which is subjected to almost similar requirements, be considered exclusive.[41]

Maastricht amends the text of Article 130t by requiring in common with the existing requirements of Article 100a the reporting of new measures to the Commission. This may not make much practical difference as the effects of Directive 83/189 are such that measures other than in the field of nature protection must be reported in any event.[42] In *ILO* the Court ruled[43] that Article 100 and 100a Directives did entail exclusive competence as they did not allow more stringent measures. The Directive in question, 67/548, was adopted under Article 100 and amended by two Directives adopted under Article 100 and 100a respectively. The Court did not rule on the effects of Article 100a(4): those minimum standards measures found not to create exclusive competence were found to do so by reason of the terms of Article 118a(3), (which has no reporting requirement, even post Maastricht), or by reason of the express terms of the Directive.[44] It may yet be possible to argue that where the Treaty authorises

---

[36] Case 22/70 *Commission* v *Council* [1971] ECR 263.

[37] For an examination of these principles see Temple Lang 'The *ERTA* judgment and the Court's caselaw on competence and conflict' (1987) *YEL* 183.

[38] This is not the case as the Court does not draw a distinction between external and internal powers at least in respect of competences which are exclusive by reason of a Treaty article as opposed to secondary legislation.

[39] Case 106/77 [1978] ECR 629.

[40] Opinion 2/91, judgment of 19 March 1993, not yet reported.

[41] Nollkaemper at 84 and also for pre-SEA commentary Koers, 'The participation of the European Community in a new Law of the Sea Convention' (1979) 73 AJIL and Mastellone (1981) 30 ICLQ 104–117, Leenen (1984) 10 LIEI 93.

[42] Kramer, *op cit*, n 7 at 172 *et seq*.

[43] *Supra*, n 40 at para 22.

[44] *Ibid* at para 21.

more stringent standards by the Member States, but subject to an obligation of prior report, the Community reserves for itself sufficient interest in the area of prospective legislation to preempt unilateral action. This would particularly be the case if the consequences of a failure to report as required by a *Treaty Article* was invalidity.[45]

The new stringent measures under Article 130t must be reported to allow the Commission to test their compatibility with the Treaty, and arguably the Community maintains a sufficient interest to prevent unilateral action by the Member States, at least insofar as international action is concerned. Member States themselves may challenge an authorization or refusal of authorization, by the Commission, in the Court. Article 100a measures which do not expressly authorise more stringent standards probably do create areas of exclusive competence as Article 100a(4) authorises, at best, only the maintenance of existing standards.

Subsidiarity, legislative competence and levels of action[46]

Subsidiarity was implicit in the First Environmental Action Programme[47] of 1972 and in the environmental sphere was given Treaty recognition in 1987 under Article 130r(4) of the Treaty. It has operated without apparent problem, and certainly without legal action, within a system based on unanimous voting. Under Maastricht, though, the requirement is removed and remolded in a new Article 3b. It applies to the environment policy at least insofar as that policy is not exclusive. The application of the principle to areas of qualified majority voting may lead to judicial challenge to the actions of the majority, by the minority utilising the principle. In this context the importance of its legal meaning and applicability crystallises. A further question concerning the subsidiarity principle remains unanswered as yet; is it purely applicable to future measures or does it also apply to measures already adopted? Once a measure is adopted and has presumably passed the test, can it later be subject to review on the grounds that the circumstances of its adoption have changed? The two month time limit for actions to annul under Article 173 may provide the answer, at least with respect to challenges by Member States.

Subsidiarity does not apply to areas of exclusive competence, and a key question therefore concerns the extent of exclusive competence in the environmental field. The Treaty prescribes the following allocation of competences:[48]

---

[45] Case 380/87 *Enichem* v *Balsamo* [1989] ECR 2491, a failure to report measures under Reg 442/75 did not result in invalidity.

[46] See Toth, 'A legal analysis of subsidiarity', Steiner, 'Susbsidiarity under the Maastricht Treaty' and Emiliou, 'Subsidiarity: panacea or fig leaf?'; in this volume 37, 49 and 65 respectively.

[47] OJ 1973 C12.

[48] See generally Temple Lang, *supra*, n 37, Cross, 'Preemption of Member State law in the EEC: a framework for analysis' (1992) 29 CML Rev 447–472, Weatherill, 'Beyond preemption? Shared competence and constitutional change in the European Community' in this volume, 13.

– exclusive competences based on Treaty interpretation where the text confirms that the Community is the appropriate and only permissible actor.

On one view, exclusive competence is confined to competences which are exclusive by reason not of the adoption of Community measures, but by reason of the Treaty article creating them. These core competences, the Common Commercial Policy and Marine Fisheries Conservation, the only areas declared by the Court to be exclusive in this respect, are not subject to subsidiarity. The effect of this view is to allow retrospective analysis of measures adopted within the so called concurrent competences including the environment. In these cases, and possibly in the case of internal market and monetary competences, the Treaty framework operates on the assumption that certain policy areas require common and uniform regulation which can encompass no unilateral action which may undermine this requirement. Where this is established in the Treaty itself, by means of a positive duty to act or a statement of uniform principle, the Treaty creates exclusive policies.[49] Insofar as environmental measures are adopted under these bases (such as Marine Fisheries Conservation) subsidiarity does not apply:

– Where Treaty confirms that the Community level can be the appropriate level of action creating potential competence, (or sometimes concurrent competences), the exercise of which create areas of exclusivity in the *ERTA* sense.

Areas not declared to be exclusive by reason of interpretation of the Treaty are in a curious exclusivity twilight. They may indeed be exclusive in respect of some elements, in the same manner as the Common Commercial Policy, but caselaw suggests that the model of legislative preemption rather than full exclusivity applies. Free movement is a directly effective and mandatory principle and probably does create an area of exclusive competence, even if Articles 100a and 30–36 encompass the ability to take legislative action derogating from the absolute principle. The conditions of derogation concern questions of the scope, rather than of the quality, of the policy obligations imposed. It is likely that measures adopted within the internal market framework are exclusive also, subject to the ruling of the European Court concerning the minimum standards regulations under Article 100 in the *ILO* case.

Agricultural and other sectoral policies, insofar as they are governed by the free market provisions, are exclusive, though Member States may legislate in the absence of a market regulation by secondary legislation. As legislation in the area is extensive, agriculture may be considered exclusive by reason of occupation of the field in the sense that no further national measures, which do not interfere with the operation or scope of the existing body of Community measures, are possible. It is difficult to see how subsidiarity can apply in the context of environment measures adopted under the Common Agricultural Policy.

Concurrent policies which do not prescribe uniformity in application are in an even more fraught position. Where no Community legislation yet exists,

---

[49] SEC (92) 1990. The Commission defines exclusive powers as those including, as a functional element, an obligation to act.

unilateral national measures may modify free market principles, provided they support a mandatory requirement and are neither discriminatory nor dispro-portionate. If the Community has legislated, similar conditions apply in respect of more stringent standards, and only less stringent policies are formally pro-hibited. Subsidiarity as defined in Article 3b applies to this area of concurrent power.

Assuming that the subsidiarity principle applies to a particular field of en-vironmental policy, one must then consider the nature of the requirements of the doctrine, and the extent to which these might be justiciable. It is a *sine qua non* of Community action that it has legal competence to act, on something which is defined by its objectives. Subsidiarity requires that the Community shall act only if the objectives of proposed action cannot be sufficiently achieved by the Member States, and they cannot be so achieved if it appears by reason of their scale or effects that the Community is the better level of action. Applying this test to the environment is not easy, since environmental issues are a tangled web of local, regional, and global problems which sometimes require concerted action to be applied to very small scale activities, and with the Community finding itself at the intermediate level, between global and national. In this context three fundamental types of environmental problem can be identified:

(1) The global or regional environmental problems which have trans-boundary effect in respect of other states or global commons and are defined by the range of effects of particular substances;
(2) The shared local problems which though not global or regional in effect, *per se*, benefit from a sharing of information and resources and are solved by the application of common principles (*e.g.* water supply and treatment);
(3) Problems which affect, what can be described as, the common heritage of mankind or (from an internal perspective the common heritage of Europe), concepts which are determined largely by subjective definition.

When it comes to applying the subsidiarity test to such areas of policy, there are two distinct approaches. The first treats the test as a rule of legislative com-petences, dividing up competences between the levels appropriate to the formulation of policy. The second approach can be described as administrative subsidiarity which requires that the legislative policy should be applied by authorities and individuals closest to the required level of action.[50] The former creates a rule of much greater influence than the latter as Community policy is for the most part executed by the Member States in any event. In the case of environment policy the extensive use of Directives accommodates administra-tive subsidiarity by prescribing principles to be applied nationally, though experience demonstrates the inherent difficulties, concerning effective enforce-ment, when legislative and implementing functions are separated to this extent.[51]

[50] The Commission favours an administrative approach to subsidiarity. See SEC 92 (1990) which states that subsidiarity governs the exercise of powers not their attribution.
[51] Snyder, 'The effectiveness of European Community law: institutions, processes, tools and techniques' (1993) Modern Law Review 19 and Macrory 'The enforcement of Community environmental laws: some critical issues' (1992) 29 CML Rev 347–369.

Neither the Member States nor the Community can on their own undertake the whole range of activities which is required and may be required in the future. In terms of defining a basis for Community action the subsidiarity principle, which recognises the need for differentiation of functions, but provides only a limited guideline as to how this may be determined, can only with difficulty be applied to international action. If the principle can be sensibly applied to the external competence of the Community, it must devolve to the Community only those issues the Community can deal with more effectively. Almost by definition, global and regional issues which predominate in external relations are not of their nature dealt with most effectively at the Community level, save insofar as the Community is coextensive with the region involved. Equally the Member States have an interest, but cannot, on their own, deal with issues they have found necessary to subject to international agreement. While the fourth objective of Community environmental policy, post-Maastricht, does not give the Community an exclusive competence at the international level, it does temper the operation of subsidiarity to the extent that it positively identifies an area in which the Community can and should contribute. It may be that the Community, being closer to the appropriate level of action concerning global problems, is always the appropriate actor under Article 3b. International action may be pursued more effectively by the Community insofar as its economic power and environmental expertise and internal competences can be utilised in achieving agreement and ensuring the implementation of agreed policies.

Procedural amendments to the legislative scheme

The new legislative scheme incorporates three significant changes:

(1) the move to more extensive majority voting;
(2) an increased role for the Parliament – the co-operation procedure introduced under the Single European Act is adopted for certain measures and the new co-decision procedure for others; and
(3) an attempt to resolve the disparities between Articles 100a and 130s – the adoption of qualified majority voting in Article 130s (though not the new co-decision procedure for Article 100a) and the addition of several requirements which applied to Article 100a, but did not apply to Article 130s.

Aspects of these changes will be considered in the following sections.

Action programmes

Community environmental legislation is unusual in that it is systematic, being developed on the basis of successive Action Programmes adopted by Council

Resolution. In practice, though, many of the provisions in such Programmes are vague, and may be substantially added to in annual programmes of measures adopted within the Commission.[52] Maastricht provides that general action programmes must be adopted by the new co-decision procedure which effectively gives the European Parliament a right of veto. The Council is obliged to adopt the measures necessary for the implementation of these programmes. The Action Programme is therefore a norm which now galvanises the Council to adopt measures in its implementation, and a legal challenge against the Council for failure to take necessary measures becomes a possibility under Article 170.

The typical format of the Action Programme has been to assign levels for action at Community, national, and local scale, a practical application of subsidiarity. Given the binding nature of such Programmes in the future, subsidiarity may now be defined by such Programmes, but the continuance of the format may be called into question. If it were to continue, there is a question as to whether Member States, by failing to adopt measures pursuant to the programme, may be in breach of Community obligations. However, where the Member States are designated the appropriate level for action, subsidiarity would suggest the contrary.

Prior to Maastricht, environmental policy has been dominated by unanimous voting with the possibility of qualified majority voting only where this has been agreed in the Council (it has not exercised this discretionary power since 1987). The TEU considerably complicates matters and a major concern must be that the complex division of subject matters adopted will force the institutions into further debilitating argument.

Unanimous voting

The Treaty maintains the pre-Maastricht system of Unanimous Voting in the following areas:

- provisions primarily of a fiscal nature;
- measures concerning town and country planning, land use with the exception of waste management and measures of a general nature, and management of water resources;
- measures significantly affecting a Member States choice between different energy sources and the general structure of its energy supply.

The general limits of these three areas are difficult to ascertain, leaving much room for interpretation, judicial or otherwise. A brief glance at the Community's existing environmental legislation illustrates that a large number of measures may fall within the descriptions above, but the boundaries are unclear. Two examples of existing areas of Community law can be used for illustration. Is the requirement of public access to environmental information a measure of "a general nature"? Is environmental assessment of project proposals a measure concerning town and country planning, where in some countries (such as the UK and Ireland) assessment procedures have been incorporated into national

---

[52] Kramer, *supra* n 12, 136–137.

town and country planning controls, whiles others (such as Germany) have focussed their application into pollution licensing controls?

Relationship between Article 100 and Article 130s

The Commission's preference for Article 100a, since the adoption of the Single European Act, has now been undermined by the adoption of majority voting under Article 130s. A new political balance is created since Parliament will have an incentive to claim Article 100a as a basis for action where a measure other than an Action Programme is proposed. If it can possibly be characterised as a trade measure, the Article 100a procedure effectively enables Parliament to veto any action. Given certain disadvantages of the co-decision procedure, the Commission may well, contrary to past experience, have a preference for Article 130s over Article 100a. Given Parliament's current activist stance, Article 100a may remain attractive as providing considerable leverage to the shared interests of both institutions. Parliament has its right to enforce its prerogatives, before the Court of Justice, confirmed in the new text of Article 173.[53] The triangular relationship imposed by the co-decision procedure is fundamentally different from previous procedures, and will be an incentive to further disputes on the legal bases of proposed measures.

Procedural amendments and international action

Article 228 has not been amended since the Treaty came into force, and therefore takes no account of the development of external competences, since the *ERTA* case, including the inception of an express environmental competence in the Single European Act. The article was intended as a complement to the title governing the Common Commercial Policy, where the methods of controlling the Commission's negotiating role and the provision of negotiating mandates are laid down. The TEU attempts a wholesale recasting of Article 228 to deal comprehensively with the issues of external policy and prescribes a voting system and parliamentary involvement in the procedures. The Commission retains its role as representative of the Community and negotiator of international agreements. The Council has the final role in approving the agreement negotiated, must authorise the negotiations, and may grant a mandate subject to conditions and the advice of expert committees. The European Parliament is given the formal authority to refuse to assent to certain categories of agreement.

The legal position with regard to mandates for external negotiations was not clear in the area of Environmental Policy until the adoption of the TEU. The practice has been to obtain a mandate prior to the substantive negotiations of any treaty.[54] Other agreements or discussions, not intended to lead to international commitments, have not, in the Commission's view, required mandates. In this regard the provisions of the Treaty authorising the Community to deal

---

[53] Case 70/88 *Parliament* v *Council* [1990] ECR 2041.
[54] See Kramer, *supra*, n 7 at 165.

with other international organizations allow the Commission to pursue diplomatic contacts without reference to the Council.[55]

Maastricht may maintain this, but the mandate becomes essential to all negotiations under Article 228 and can only be adopted by the same voting mechanism as would be required for Community legislation on the same area. As there are large and diffuse areas of unanimous voting, unanimity may remain the rule in obtaining such a mandate. The assessment of the appropriate voting mechanism may be difficult, in the circumstances prior to the initiation of any negotiations, and it may be the case that the Commission will need re-approval of its mandate should discussions lead into areas covered by unanimity.

Article 113 provides for special committees to assist the Commission in the negotiation of international agreements in the trade area. Given the difficulty in attaining unanimous agreement mandates and the revision of negotiating Directives these committees may maintain a good deal of power in interpreting the mandate and Directives. It is not unknown for the Commission to be criticised for the outcome of negotiations as is demonstrated by the continuing French criticism of the Commission's Agriculture agreement with the United States under GATT. The Ozone Layer Convention itself required that the Commission referred back to the Council on several occasions, for a reinterpretation and finally an amendment of its mandate to negotiate, before agreement could be reached.[56] As general mandates are now possible in respect of the processes of institutions set up under individual conventions, including amendment, it may be expected that similar controversies to those that arise over the *Comitology* cases will arise in this area as the mandates may prescribe a committee procedure to regulate the exercise by the Commission of its mandate.[57]

If it is difficult to assign an internal measure to a particular category and voting system prescribed by Article 130s, the difficulties of assigning a voting system to an international agreement are compounded by requiring the decision be made prior to a process of negotiation. Where the agreement has multiple purposes of equal value the *Titanium Dioxide* case[58] might suggest that the most democratic of the systems ought to be adopted. The *Physical Protection* case, Ruling 1/78[59], stated that it was the centre of gravity of the proposed treaty which mattered when determining whether it fell within a particular Treaty provision.

Article 228 now provides for the voting mechanisms to be adopted. The Council concludes these agreements by qualified majority on a proposal from the Commission save when "the agreement covers a field for which unanimity is required for the adoption of internal rules".

The significant change to the system is that Parliament's role in the approval of agreements is confirmed, though it has had such a role, in respect of important agreements, by political agreement since the Stuttgart Declaration of 1983:

---

[55] Art 229: the power to maintain appropriate relations with organs of the United Nations.

[56] Jachtenfuchs, 'The European Community and the protection of the ozone layer' (1990) 28 JCMS 261.

[57] Art 228(4): a generalised mandate was proposed by the Commission in respect of three Regional Seas Conventions but was not adopted, COM (86) 5673 final of 2 December 1986.

[58] Case 300/89 *Commission* v *Council*, 11 June 1991.

[59] Ruling 1/78 [1978] ECR 2151 at 2178 not to be confused with Opinion 1/78 *Re Natural Rubber Agreement*.

Article 228(3) provides that the Council shall conclude agreements outside the Common Commercial Policy only after consulting the European Parliament including cases where the agreement covers a field for which co-decision or co-operation procedures are required for the adoption of internal rules. Parliament's opinion may be made subject to a time limit after the expiry of which the Council may conclude the agreement without an opinion. Agreements establishing "a specific institutional framework by organizing co-operation procedures, agreements having important budgetary implications for the Community and agreements entailing the amendment of an act adopted under the co-decision procedure" shall be concluded after the assent of the European Parliament has been obtained. In these cases Parliament may "agree upon a time limit for the assent".

In the area of environment protection only general action programmes and approximation measures will be the subject of the co-decision procedure. If an agreement departs from the action programme it is arguable that the action programme has been amended, though as Programmes are presently rather generalised political statements, this is unlikely to occur.

Conclusion

The development of a vigorous programme of Community environmental policy, together with the agreement of over three hundred individual items of legislation since the early 1980's, has been a remarkable achievement. The impact of Community environmental laws on domestic policies has been profound in many cases, and on the international stage, where the significance and scale of multilateral environmental agreements has dramatically increased in recent years, the Community has carved out a distinctive and often powerful role for itself. The Single European Act 1987 created an explicit legal place for Community environmental policy, and it is already clear that the European Court has embarked on a more substantive contribution to the development of appropriate underlying legal principles in this field. Maastricht strengthens and deepens the role of environmental policy at Community level, placing it at the heart of the Community's role and purpose. Ironically though, the complexities and ambiguities which characterise the legal provisions devised to secure this political achievement may ultimately prove a constraint rather than an opportunity.

MARTIN HESSION
RICHARD MACRORY

Part 6

Institutional Changes

Chapter 11
Institutional and Decision-Making Changes[1]

This article examines the changes to the *formal* institutions and the methods of decision-making.[2]

The European Council and the Council of Ministers

In looking first at the changes to the institutions envisaged in the Maastricht Treaty, I will start at the top, with the European Council. This was originally a creation of the Single European Act (Art 2), but is now the pediment of the structure of the Union (Art D of the TEU). There are obvious similarities with the Council of Ministers and I would like to spend a little time contrasting the two. Unlike the Council of Ministers, the European Council includes in its membership the President of the Commission. Member States are represented by their Heads of State or Government.

The Council of Ministers is constituted under Article 146 of the Treaty of Rome. That is being amended to specify that representatives of Member States are to be at ministerial level, as opposed to Heads of State or Government. The President of the Commission is not a member, although in practice he, or she or a representative of the Commission, will normally attend, with no voting powers. At first glance, there appears to be a clear distinction, therefore, between the European Council and the Council of Ministers. But it is possible for much the same participants to sit either as the Council or as the European Council. It happens already. So long as the President of the Commission, if present, is accorded no voting rights and so long as Heads of State or Government can be regarded as "Ministers", it can continue to be the case in the Union.

What then is the difference between the two types of meeting? Meetings of the Council of Ministers are meetings in terms of the Treaty of Rome and can conclude acts of the Council for the purpose of that Treaty. The European Council has no formal involvement in legislation under the present Treaty of Rome, nor will this change with the new Treaty. It does, however, have a function under both Treaties as a guiding body. Consequently, the European Council can sit, and can continue to sit, as a body recognised by the Treaty. It

---

[1] Crown Copyright 1993. Reproduced by permission of the Controller of HMSO. This article consists of the text as delivered at the Conference, "Unresolved legal issues of the Maastricht Treaty" on 5 March 1993. The views expressed are those of the author and do not necessarily represent the views of the UK Government.

[2] The article does not deal with *informal* institutions, such as the Committee of the Regions or the European Central Bank. For the latter, see Dunnett, 'Legal and institutional issues affecting Economic and Monetary Union' in this volume 135.

can also sit, however, in the field of political co-operation (EPC) at present or intergovernmental co-operation in future. The same meeting can therefore switch from being a Community organization to being an international conference and back again.

However, some articles in the chapter on transition to economic and monetary union have a further variant. These are articles of the Treaty of Rome and therefore references to "the Council" are to the Council of Ministers, yet, they refer to "the Council, meeting in the composition of the Heads of State or Government". This appears to recognise that representatives at ministerial level (as required by the amended Art 146) can actually be Heads of State or Government. Note that these references to the Council in that particular composition do not include the President of the Commission. (See Arts 109j(2)–(4) and 109k(2) TEU).

This confirms that "Heads of State or Government" can be regarded as "Ministers". Why then does the amendment to Article 146 specify ministers? The intention behind it was partly to allow regional ministers from some countries to sit on Council and partly to prevent officials from acting as representatives in place of ministers. The amendment to Article 146 continues to the effect that the Ministers are to be authorised to commit their governments at meetings of the Council. The reason for this is clearer when considering the position of regional ministers, that is, they can attend as ministers but they cannot avoid decisions on the ground that they have to refer back for instructions.

A new Article 151 now brings the existence of COREPER into the body of the Treaty of Rome. The same article goes further than the Merger Treaty, however, to introduce the General Secretariat to the Council. Both these bodies have been in existence (and very useful existence) for some time.[3] The change is one of recognition. This is something which occurs in various places in the Maastricht Treaty, where it gives Treaty recognition to bodies or practices which have already been in existence.

The Commission

The main changes to the Commission, as an institution, are found in the amended Article 158 and relate to the appointment and tenure of the Commissioners. The term of office (beyond 1995) is increased from four years to five. Whereas before it was left solely to the Member States, by common accord, to appoint the Commissioners, the amendments will require the Member States first to consult the Parliament in nominating the President and then consult that nominee in nominating the other Commissioners. The entire package of nominations is then subject to approval by the Parliament.

It is worth noting that the terms of office in both the Commission and the Parliament are intended to be co-terminous. The independence of the Commission is preserved in Article 157(2).

---

[3] See Eaton, 'Common foreign and security policy' in this volume 215.

Most of the detailed provisions about the constitution of the Commission that were set out in the Merger Treaty are now written into the Treaty of Rome. It is perhaps worth noting that a significant amount of what appear to be changes brought about by the Maastricht Treaty are in fact a tidying-up exercise, writing into the Treaty of Rome provisions of the Merger Treaty.

The Court[4]

First, there are changes to the Court of First Instance. The main change is to give greater flexibility to its jurisdiction. It started with competition cases and staff cases. Any extension of the jurisdiction was a matter of a Treaty amendment. The United Kingdom has in fact been struggling to assist the Court in such an extension but has encountered significant opposition from some Member States.[4a]

The significant change, therefore, is that an extension of jurisdiction can now be made under the new Treaty powers. The new Article 168a gives to the Council power to determine the classes of action or proceedings which may be heard and determined by the Court of First Instance. The exclusion of Article 177 references continues but the previous exclusion of actions brought by Member States or institutions is removed; these actions are now possible if the Council so determines. The Council may so determine only at the request of the Court of Justice and it has to consult the Parliament and the Commission. The determination requires unanimity.

The enforcement provisions of Article 171 are being strengthened. If a Member State has been found to be in breach of its obligation but has failed to comply with the Court's judgment, the Commission may issue a reasoned opinion on that failure and, after a specified time, take that Member State back to Court. The Court then has power to impose a fine on the Member State. This provision was put forward at the suggestion of the United Kingdom in order to improve compliance with the Court's judgments and, ultimately, with Community obligations generally. It was done in the days before the *Francovich*[5] judgment in which the Court opened up the possibility of damages being awarded against Member States who are in breach of their obligations. Recidivism at a national level may be a very expensive business in future.

Detailed amendments have been made to many of the other articles dealing with the Court, primarily as a result of increased involvement of the Parliament in the decision-making process. These amendments cover both the situations of a new involvement of the Parliament in decisions affecting the Court and in awarding the Court power to review acts arising from greater involvement in the Parliament. To some extent, the changes are a codification of caselaw, incorporating some decisions relating to the Parliament. The Court has already

---

[4] See Robinson, "The Court of Justice after Maastricht" in this volume 179.
[4a] On 8 June 1993, the extension of jurisdiction was finally agreed by the Council.
[5] Cases C-6/90 & 9/90 *Francovich and Bonofaci* [1991] ECR I-5357.

ruled in 1987 that binding acts of the Parliament may be challenged under Article 173 EEC. In 1989, it ruled that the Parliament could itself bring an action for annulment when its prerogatives were in issue, such as its right to be consulted on legislation. These amendments to Article 173 codify these decisions.

The changes relating to the Court are not nearly as extensive as the amount of print in the Treaty suggests. For example, Article 177 is amended only to the extent that the Court may rule on acts of the European Central Bank, in addition to those of the institutions, yet the entire article is reprinted. Although the changes are fewer than may appear, they are still significant.

The Court of Auditors

At first sight, there are entirely new and extensive provisions on the Court of Auditors. In fact, Articles 188a–e are the former Articles 206 and 206a of the Treaty of Rome, with few changes. The changes flow from the fact that the Court of Auditors is now formally classed, in Article 4, as one of the institutions of the Community, necessitating detailed amendments which change references to the institutions to references to the *other* institutions. There is a new power for it to provide the Parliament and the Council with a statement of assurance as to the legality and regularity of accounts. This was a UK proposal which tightens up accounting practice and should help to prevent fraud on the Community budget.

The Parliament[6]

The greatest institutional and decision-making changes relate to the European Parliament. They are perhaps best encapsulated in the amendment to Article 137. The reference to the "advisory and supervisory" powers of the Parliament is now simply to "the powers" of the Parliament. It is now seeing quite a growth in its powers. I recall being told many years ago by Professor J D B Mitchell that the Parliament should not be given much in the way of powers: what was important was for the Parliament to earn them first. Powers fought for and won are usually more extensive and are then more effectively used. He saw institutional change as the result of tensions between institutions, each flexing their muscles as they grew. It is as interesting to observe the development of rudimentary powers as to observe the use of clear powers. Some of the new powers are, in fact, Treaty recognition of powers which have existed under the Parliament's own Rules of Procedure, such as Committees of Inquiry: looking at these, one can see both how these are powers which have been won, but also which have

---

[6] See Bradley, "Better rusty than missin"?: the institutional reforms of the Maastricht Treaty and the European Parliament' in this volume 193.

been only partially granted, in that the actual procedures and powers of these committees have still to be negotiated by the institutions.

Since 1957, the Parliament's growth has been slow but it has made effective use of such powers as it had. The power to sack the entire Commission (Art 144) is a rather blunt weapon which has never been used in itself, but its existence must have given the Parliament some influence. It gained power over the budget, a vital source of power and developed effectively. Direct elections increased its legitimacy and hence its authority. The effect of this change was to alter the standing of the Parliament, rather than to give it specific powers, but it was arguably the institution's most important development. For example, the attitude of the Court in assessing constitutional balance amongst the institutions appears to have been strongly influenced by this factor. Finally came the "co-operation procedure" under the Single European Act, giving the Parliament greater influence in the passage of legislation: this was a more concrete recognition of the growing importance of the Parliament.

Specific powers are granted in Articles 138b–e TEU. Article 138b appears to give a quasi right of initiative to the Parliament, a role enjoyed almost exclusively by the Commission (apart from the Court's power to suggest changes in the jurisdiction of the Court of First Instance). In fact, it is no more than the Council's power under Article 152 EEC since there is no compulsion on the Commission to comply with the Parliament's request. It is unlikely that the Parliament will sack the entire Commission if it fails to come up with proposals for legislation at the Parliament's request.

The Parliament has been given a power in Article 138c to set up Committees of Inquiry, to investigate contraventions of or maladministration in the implementation of Community law. As mentioned earlier, this is a power which it already has under its Rules of Procedure. This is not, however, necessarily another example of simple recognition in the Treaty of what has gone before. These new Committees of Inquiry will almost certainly be different from their predecessors. Their powers are yet to be fixed (detailed provisions on the right of inquiry are to be determined by common accord of the Parliament, Commission and Council)[7] and therefore it is too early to say how effective they are likely to be. It is important to note the reference to a "right of inquiry" as an indicator of what powers Parliament may be competent to grant to the committees. We shall have to wait and see whether the Parliament will push for something akin to UK Select Committees or whether the Council and Commission will try to restrict them. It is the sort of arena that would have interested Professor Mitchell.

Inquiries by the Committees can be instigated only at the request of a quarter of the Members of the Parliament. Any citizen of, or resident in, the Union may, however, petition Parliament under Article 138d on a wide range of matters, but the Treaty makes no provision for any follow-up to that petition. It is questionable whether it adds much, since there is nothing to stop anyone writing to as many MEP's as he wishes: what it does do is make it easier on the

---

[7] Art 138c TEU.

individual to address his concern to the whole Parliament. However, he already has this power, again under the Parliament's Rules of Procedure, therefore this change is probably one for the "recognition" category.

Finally in this section on Parliament's more specialised powers is Article 138e which makes provision for Parliament to appoint an Ombudsman. This provision makes an interesting contrast with the two preceding it. Individuals may complain to the Ombudsman, as well as to Parliament, and the Ombudsman has authority to investigate such complaints. Again we will have to wait to see what powers of investigation will be granted to him by the Parliament, after consulting the Commission and obtaining the approval of the Council (on a qualified majority).

Taken with the measure mentioned earlier, under Article 171 EEC to permit the Court to fine Member States who are in breach, these articles represent the first real attempt, since the original Treaty, to extend the means of enforcement of Community law at Treaty level. Until now, the emphasis has been on powers to promote more legislation, rather than making more effective the legislation already produced. Whether these new enforcement measures will be as effective as measures taken by the Court in its jurisprudence remains to be seen. The principles of direct effect, consistent interpretation and damages are already effective methods in giving effect to Community obligations, despite the failure or refusal of the Member State.

New decision-making procedures

The real advance for the Parliament, however, is not in the specific new powers granted to it in Article 138a–e. It lies in the wholly new procedures for enacting Community legislation which now give significant power to the Parliament, including a limited power to block legislation.

Article 148 remains unamended. That means that the rules for qualified majority voting remain. Article 149 EEC is repealed, but it appears again as Article 189a and c TEU. The provisions relating to the passage of legislation have been moved to the part of the Treaty dealing with legislation, the primary one being of course Article 189 which sets out the concepts of Regulations, Directives and other instruments. The procedures to be adopted in framing these instruments are now contained in the new Articles 189a–c.

Article 189a retains two general propositions from the former Article 149. It reaffirms the general rule requiring unanimity for an act constituting an amendment to a Commission proposal. This is in itself a subtle provision in that it not only strengthens the power of individual Member States, but at the same time strengthens the Commission's right of initiative. The new article also retains the Commission's power to alter its proposals at any time before the Council acts. This again confirms the Commission's right of initiative, although there is an interesting question as to how far a proposal can be taken before it can be withdrawn.

The remainder of Article 149 sets out what is known as the co-operation procedure: this is now repeated without change as Article 189c. The new procedure – sometimes called, inaccurately, the co-decision procedure, but also called the negative assent procedure – is set out at Article 189b. It is inaccurate to refer to co-decision since the Parliament's power is a negative one: it cannot force the Council to adopt a measure that the Council does not want. Parliament can only block the measure.

Before commenting on the new negative assent procedure, it would be helpful to look at the present relationship between the Council and the Parliament. There are many provisions which require the Council to *consult* the Parliament, but with no procedures set out for doing so, or obligation on the Council to act on the Parliament's views.

At the other extreme, the Parliament is required to *assent* to any new accession or association treaties under Articles 237 and 238. The Parliament also has the power to reject the budget under Article 203. Between these extremes lie a form of conciliation procedure and the co-operation procedure itself. In the area of budget negotiations, there are complex procedures set out in Article 203, which give the Parliament two opportunities to modify the draft budget. This is a detailed procedure for consultation which approaches an attempt at a *conciliation* procedure between the two institutions. (Art 203 survives unamended.)

The *co-operation* procedure was introduced by Article 6 of the Single European Act of 1986 and applied to specific provisions. It still remains in Article 189c, but it no longer applies to many of the articles to which it was applied by the SEA. It applies to Articles 6, 75, 103(5), 104a, 104b, 105a, 118a, 125, 127, 129d, 130e, 130s and 130w. Both the co-operation procedure and the new negative assent procedure apply in Articles 129d and 130s, in different areas. The new negative assent procedure applies to Articles 49, 54(2), 56(2), 57, 100a, 126, 128, 129, 129a, 129d, 130i and 130s.

The new procedure has elements of all the previous procedures outlined earlier. Obviously, it involves consultation. It is built largely on the co-operation procedure. It has a formal conciliation procedure. Finally, it involves a power for the Parliament to block legislation. The Parliament is allowed to amend the Council's common position. If the Council does not accept the amendments, a Conciliation Committee is set up. It consists of representatives of all the Member States and an equal number of Members of the Parliament. The Commission can take part in the proceedings but has no vote: it has a remit to promote a reconciliation. The Committee has six weeks to agree a joint text. If it is agreed, both institutions then have six weeks to approve it. If no joint text is agreed by the Conciliation Committee, the Council confirms within six weeks its common position text, with or without Parliament's amendments: if the Parliament rejects that version within the following six weeks, the proposed act falls.

The position is further complicated by three other factors. First, there are many opportunities in the procedure for voting, either by the Council or by the Parliament, or by their representatives in the Conciliation Committee. Some votes require unanimity, some absolute majority and some qualified majority. It should be noted that votes which approve amendments made by the Parliament may be taken by qualified majority, but unanimity is required in respect of votes on amendments on which the Commission has delivered a negative opinion. Again, the Commission's right of initiative is acknowledged. Generally speaking, it is made easier to vote for what will advance the legislation than for what will block it. An added twist is that some TEU articles (such as Art 128(5) on culture) provide for changes in the method of voting, when acts are proposed with these articles as a legal base, the change being to require unanimity on the part of the Council.

Secondly, the time limits may be altered. Thirdly, there is provision in Article 189b(8) to permit the scope of the procedure to be widened by an Intergovernmental Conference and the Commission is obliged to report to the Council before 1996 with such proposals.

As a postscript to the new co-operation procedure, the new Article 228 on external treaties requires the Parliament's assent to any external agreements which entail amending an Act adopted under the negative assent procedure.

DONALD MACRAE

Chapter 12

The Court of Justice after Maastricht

The Treaty on European Union has made no radical institutional changes to the Court of Justice. This is not to suggest that the Treaty has not left in its wake unresolved legal issues concerning the Court. In particular, it will be suggested in this article that the fundamental failure of the Treaty to review the Communities' institutional legal order threatens the continued high esteem in which the Court of Justice, the Court of First Instance and the Community legal order are held.

The Treaty's alterations to the Court of Justice have, significantly, addressed the allocation of jurisdiction between the two courts and the use of Chambers. These may alleviate some of the pressure to which the Court has been subjected due to the dramatically increasing case-load,[1] which has contributed to the increasing and unacceptable delays in the duration of proceedings.[2] However, these and other amendments have also created new problems. The changes made to the Court of Justice by the Treaty on European Union are considered in the first section of the article.

The Treaty on European Union has posed a plethora of problems for the Court of Justice. The nature of the Union, the increasingly political nature of the Court's jurisdiction, the Social Protocol, imminent enlargement of the Communities and, in particular, the principle of subsidiarity potentially challenge the existing *acquis communautaire* and the character of the Court of Justice. The Treaty on European Union has created, to a limited degree, a federal Europe. The Communities' institutional legal order has not, however, been fundamentally amended to meet these challenges. The problems thus created will be considered in the second section of this article.

Treaty Amendments

This section of the article attempts to pinpoint the changes made to the Court of Justice by the Treaty on European Union in relation to each of the three Treaties establishing the European Communities and those provisions creating the Union. The majority of the changes reflect the Court's jurisprudence, the consolidation of Merger Treaty provisions and amendments arising from changes to other institutions, notably the European Parliament and the European Central Bank. Only the provisions relating to the Court of First Instance

---

[1] Cases pending before the Court of Justice: 1989 – 504, 1990 – 583, 1991 – 639, 1992 – 736.
[2] Average duration of Art 177 references, in months: 1989 – 16.6, 1990 – 17.4, 1991 – 18.2, 1992 – 18.8.

and the use of Chambers stand out as attempts to face the Court's *current* problems.

The drafters of the Treaty on European Union incorporated several provisions of the Merger Treaty into the three Treaties. Article 154 EC[3] enables the Council to determine the salaries of the President, Judges and Advocates General by qualified majority, a power contained in identical terms in Article 6 of the Merger Treaty. Similarly, the powers of the Council and the Commission to apply to the Court for the compulsory retirement of a Commission member, or the deprivation of his or her right to a pension or other benefits, were contained in Articles 10 and 13 of the Merger Treaty and have been incorporated as Articles 157 and 160 EC.[4]

The consolidation of these institutional provisions continued with the inclusion of a separate section in the institutional chapter of the EC Treaty concerning the Court of Auditors. This process of "house ordering" is a welcome development. However, anomalies in other fields, particularly concerning transitional periods, have survived these consolidating efforts. The revision of Article 168a EC,[5] in relation to the Court of First Instance, recognises the establishment of that Court by the Council in 1989[6] and appears merely to update the text accordingly. For example, references to the ability of the Council to attach a court to the Court of Justice have been replaced by statements that "a Court of First Instance shall be attached ...". However, within these minor amendments to Article 168a is a more far reaching change.

Article 168a EEC specified that the Court of First Instance "shall not be competent to hear and determine actions brought by Member States or by Community institutions or questions referred for a preliminary ruling under Article 177." The amended article denies jurisdiction merely in relation to preliminary ruling under Article 177. Article 168a EC therefore allows the Council to transfer actions brought by Member States or Community institutions to the Court of First Instance. This develops and increases the role of the Court of First Instance beyond Article 168a EEC, the potential of which had been almost exhausted by the recent transfer of jurisdiction (Council Dec 93/350). This Decision gives the Court of First Instance jurisdiction "in actions brought by natural or legal persons pursuant to the second paragraph of Article 173, the third paragraph of Article 175 and Articles 178 and 181 of the EEC Treaty".[7] Article 168a EC enables the Council to deny Member States and the institutions, acting as plaintiffs, an automatic audience before the highest Community court, the Court of Justice, including Article 169, 170 and 171 actions.

It would appear unlikely, however, that the Council would take steps towards such a fundamental re-alignment of jurisdiction in relation to the Member

---

[3] Art 29 ECSC, Art 123 EAEC.

[4] Arts 9 and 12a ECSC, Arts 126(2) and 129 EAEC.

[5] Art 32d ECSC, Art 140a EAEC.

[6] The Court of First Instance was established by Council Dec 88/591/ECSC, EEC, EAEC (OJ 1988 L319/1) (corrected version published in OJ 1989 C251/1) and the Decision of the President of the Court of Justice (OJ 1989 L317/48).

[7] Art 1 of Council Dec 93/350/ECSC, EEC, EAEC (OJ 1993 L144/21) which amends Art 3(1) of Council Dec 88/591/ECSC, EEC, EAEC (OJ 1989 C215/1). The Decision took effect on 1 August 1993 by virtue of Art 3.

States and institutions prior to the 1996 Intergovernmental Conference. This proposition is based not only upon the difficulty in securing the required unanimity in the Council, as demonstrated by the 20-month delay in the adoption of the recent (partially incomplete[8]) transfer of jurisdiction, but also upon the lack of a strategic design for the institutional structure of the Community legal order.

The further use of Chambers of the Court may encounter similar political difficulties. The third paragraph of Article 165 EEC requires the Court of Justice to sit in plenary session when hearing actions brought before it by a Member State, a Community institution and certain preliminary references brought under Article 177 EEC.[9] Member States and Community institutions therefore have a right, as plaintiffs, to be heard by a plenum. In addition, the Court may not assign a case to a Chamber, including Article 177 references, if a Member State or an institution is a "party to the proceedings" and requests a plenary session.[10]

The exhaustive text of Article 165 EC in relation to plenary sessions states: "The Court of Justice shall sit in plenary session when a Member State or a Community institution that is a party to the proceedings so requests." This amendment enables the Court to make further use of Chambers. The Member States and the Community institutions have lost their automatic right as plaintiffs to be heard by a plenary session. The Court may therefore consider all cases at the level which it considers most appropriate, subject only to the right to request a plenum which the Treaty has established. However, in the absence of such a request, a Member State may appear, for example, as a defendant in an Article 169 action before a Chamber of three judges. The combined effect of Article 168a and 165 EC will allow this result before the Court of First Instance. This would represent a striking political departure from the present procedure, by which Member States and the institutions have an unconditional right to be heard by a plenum of the highest Community court.

The introduction of a burden on the Member States and the institutions to request a plenum finds echoes in the establishment of a written only procedure by the amended Rules of Procedure. Article 104(4) of those Rules, for example, allows the Court to dispense with the oral hearing in preliminary rulings, provided none of those persons eligible to make submissions has asked to present oral argument. The reversal of the procedural burden focuses the parties' attention on the need for a particular configuration of the Court and the oral hearing. The Treaty amendment to Article 165 will enable the Court to rationalise further its use of judicial time. Cases may be allocated to Chambers on their merits rather than the status of particular parties. This represents a further step away from the notion of the Court as an arbiter between international actors.

---

[8] Art 3 defers the application of Council Dec 93/350, *supra*, to anti-dumping and anti-subsidy cases until a future date.

[9] Those preliminary references to which the Rules of Procedure deny jurisdiction to Chambers. The Rules of Procedure confer the relevant jurisdiction in *all* Art 177 references.

[10] Art 95(2) of the Rules of Procedure of the Court of Justice of the European Communities of 19 June 1991 (OJ 1991 L176/7).

European Parliament[11]

Several amendments to the institutional balance between the European Parliament and the Court were necessitated by the creation of the Parliament's Committee of Inquiry and Ombudsman and the recognition of the Court's jurisprudence. Article 138c EC[12] precludes the Committee of Inquiry from investigating alleged contraventions or maladministration in the implementation of Community law where the alleged facts are subject to legal proceedings. The *sub judice* exception extends to any proceedings, at a national or Community level. The Courts' *judicial* role is specifically put beyond the remit of the Ombudsman by Article 138e(1).[13] However, this would appear to enable the Ombudsman to examine the *administrative* role of the Members of the Court. The administration of the translation, library and research and documentation divisions, amongst others, of the Court may potentially be investigated, although their present operations have been designed by, and for the benefit of, the Members of the Court. It would, of course, eventually fall to the Court of Justice to decide whether the Ombudsman could investigate matters such as delays in translation by interpreting whether a particular process falls within the exception available to the Courts "acting in their judicial role".

The Court of Justice may dismiss the Ombudsman, should the European Parliament request it to do so, if he no longer fulfils the conditions required for the performance of his duties or if he is guilty of serious misconduct.[14]

The Treaty on European Union has combined limited increases in the powers of the European Parliament with an acceptance of the Court's constitutional jurisprudence in this field. Article 173 EC[15] therefore accepts that acts of the Parliament which are intended to produced legal effects *vis-à-vis* third parties are reviewable,[16] and the Parliament may bring actions for annulment for the purpose of protecting its prerogatives.[17] The European Parliament has similarly been added to the first paragraph of Article 175 EC so that its wrongful failure to act may be challenged before the Court of Justice. The Court held, in the *Transport* case,[18] that the Parliament may bring an action for a failure to act as one of the "other institutions of the Community" in the first paragraph of Article 175 EEC. These changes do no more than recognise the jurisprudence of the Court which has been based on the rule of law and the institutional balance established by the Treaties. They are cosmetic to the extent that they have not addressed some of the unresolved institutional questions in the judicial review of Community acts. The jurisprudence in relation to the Court of Auditors,[19] for example, has not

---

[11] See Bradley, 'Better rusting than missin'?: the institutional reforms of the Maastricht treaty and the European Parliament' in this volume 193.

[12] Art 20b ECSC, Art 107b EAEC.

[13] Art 20d(1) ECSC, Art 107d(1) EAEC.

[14] Art 138e(2) EC, Art 20d(2) ECSC, Art 107d(2) EAEC. As a matter of drafting, the Court may 'dismiss' the Ombudsman and 'compulsory retire' a Commissioner, although the situations in which the Court of Justice may take these actions are identical.

[15] Art 33 ECSC, Art 146 EAEC.

[16] Case 294/83 *Les Verts* v *European Parliament* [1986] ECR 1339.

[17] Case C-70/88 *European Parliament* v *Council ('Chernobyl')* [1990] ECR I-2041.

[18] Case 13/83 *European Parliament* v *Council ('Transport')* [1985] ECR 1513.

[19] Joined Cases 193 & 194/87 *Maurissen and others* v *Court of Auditors* [1989] ECR 1045.

been consolidated, even though the provisions in relation to that institution have been extensively house ordered.

European Central Bank[20]

Several of the substantial amendments to the Treaties concerning the European Central Bank affect also the Court of Justice.[21] The ECB is established by Article 4a EC. It may enact legislation, impose fines, submit opinions and be consulted within its field of operation.[22] It is not, however, a "Community institution" within the definition in Article 4 EC. It was therefore imperative that the status of its acts was clarified and that those persons affected by those acts should have recourse to legal protection. The jurisdiction of the Court of Justice has been specifically extended in order to provide such protection within the Community legal order.

First, Article 177 (b) has been amended in order that the Court of Justice may give preliminary rulings on the validity and interpretation of acts of the ECB.

Secondly, the judicial review jurisdiction of the Court has been extended with regard to the ECB.[23] The Court of Justice may review the legality of "acts of the ECB" under Article 173 EC and a fourth sub-paragraph was added to Article 175 EEC to allow the ECB to bring, and be subject to, actions for failure to act. The inclusion of the additional paragraph in Article 175 EEC is sufficiently clear to enable the Court to ensure judicial protection without recourse to purposive interpretation, as was necessary for the European Parliament. The ECB has been restricted, however, in the same way as the European Parliament, to bringing actions for annulment only for the purpose of the protection of its prerogatives. To complete the incorporation of the ECB into the judicial review framework, its regulations may be challenged by a plea of illegality under Article 184 EC and it must take all necessary measures to comply with judgments of the Court.[24]

Thirdly, Article 36(2) of the Statute of the European System of Central Banks and of the European Central Bank provides that the Court of Justice shall have jurisdiction in staff disputes with the ECB. Article 179 EC does not specify the institutions over which the Court of Justice shall have such jurisdiction. The Court has however interpreted Article 179 widely to encompass those institutions established and with a legal personality conferred by the Treaties. The ECB has an identical legal existence under the Treaties to the European Investment Bank, whose staff disputes were held admissible before the Court of Justice.[25] The Court will have jurisdiction in these circumstances and it is envisaged that the Court of First Instance will hear ECB staff cases.[26]

---

[20] See Dunnett, 'Legal and institutional issues affecting Economic and Monetary Union' in this volume 135.

[21] The ECB is to exercise its full powers from the start of the third stage of economic and monetary union (Art 109l(1) EC). During the second stage references to the ECB are interchangeable with the European Monetary Institute (Art 109f(9)).

[22] See Title VI EC, particularly Arts 105, 105a, 106 and 108a.

[23] See Art 35 of the Statute of the European System of Central Banks and of the European Central Bank.

[24] Art 176 EC.

[25] Case 110/75 *Mills* v *European Investment Bank* [1976] ECR 995.

[26] See the Declaration to the Treaty on European Union on Disputes between the ECB and the EMI and their Servants.

Lastly, Article 180(d) EC attributes the ECB with judicial "guardian" powers, equivalent to those of the Commission.[27] The Council of the ECB may bring actions against national central banks before the Court of Justice for their failure to fulfil obligations under the Treaty or the Statute of the ESCB. The Court's jurisdiction has been increased to hear these cases. Four brief observations appear pertinent.

First, the Court of First Instance would not have jurisdiction under Council Decision 93/350 to hear actions brought by the ECB under Article 180(d) EC. Jurisdiction could however be transferred under Article 168a EC. The Court of First Instance will, of course, be competent to hear cases brought against the ECB by natural or legal persons within its judicial review jurisdiction.

The second observation relates to the status of the ECB, either as a plaintiff or as a defendant, before the Court. As discussed above, only Member States and Community institutions may request a plenary session of the Court. As has been seen, the ECB will be considered as an institution for the purposes of staff cases. However, it is not beyond doubt that the ECB is a "Community institution" for the purpose of requesting a plenary session. Article 107 EC, in particular, indicates that the principle of independence from the Community institutions and the Member States underpins the ECB and the national central banks. There is no caselaw on applications made by institutions which fall outside Article 4 EEC. However, as defendants, all such institutions have been heard by Chambers. The status of national central banks as "Member States" is similarly unclear. Although they would almost certainly fall within the extensive definition in *Foster* v *British Gas plc*,[28] it will be necessary for the Court to determine whether such a test is applicable for the procedural purpose of Article 165 EC. Member States are likely to consider central banks able to request plenary sessions, due to the political and economic importance of those bodies. A narrower interpretation would deny the right to request a plenary session. The latter interpretation would avoid unnecessary inefficiencies in the Court's procedure. A case could be assigned to a plenum or a Chamber as appropriate, without extraneous considerations requiring the use of a plenary session.

Thirdly, a national central bank which is found to have failed to fulfil its obligations may not necessarily be in a legal position to implement the judgment. Non-implementation of the judgment by the national central bank would breach the last sentence of Article 180(d) EC and the Member State may have breached Article 5 EC.

Fourthly, although the jurisdiction of the Court has been excluded from government deficit matters by Article 104c(10) EC, the variety of means by which all economic and monetary policy may be achieved would require the Court to determine increasingly sensitive political and sovereignty issues.

The status of the parties in Article 180(d) proceedings is significantly different from that of the parties to the analogous Article 169 actions. These differences are likely to raise problematic procedural and substantive questions. The

---

[27] See Art 35(6) of the Statute of the European System of Central Banks and of the European Central Bank. The ECB does not have power to bring Art 171 EC proceedings.

[28] Case C-188/89 [1990] 2 CMLR 833.

Court's case-load in the economic and monetary field will also inevitably touch upon sensitive sovereignty issues, a feature echoed in the financial liability of Member States and the principle of subsidiarity. Various academics and Member States have criticised the Court's purposive interpretation of the letter and spirit of the Treaties, particularly in expanding the ability of individuals to vindicate Community rights at a local level.[29] Article L TEU and the "*Barber*" Protocol also demonstrate a degree of scepticism in the Court.[30] However, these sentiments should be juxtaposed with the amendments to the Treaties which endow the Court with jurisdiction in increasingly sensitive areas. The ability of the Court of Justice to fine Member States and to determine the level of attribution of powers is a potential example of tension. The Court will be required to operate in a role for which it was not created in its present form.

Financial responsibility of Member States

Professor Deirdre Curtin commented in 1992 that, "European Union . . . will lack any force if it is based upon rules that impose neither obligations nor sanctions upon Member States in their relations with one another or with individuals."[31] The Court established the principle of the liability of the Member State in damages for loss suffered by an individual which is attributable to the failure of the Member State to implement a directive in the *Francovich* case.[32] The principle is the subject of several cases pending before national courts and the Court of Justice, including the latest in the *Factortame* litigation.[33]

The Treaty on European Union has provided further means of coercing Member States, at the institutional level, into fulfilling their Treaty obligations. Article 171 EC[34] entitles the Commission to bring a Member State before the Court of Justice, having followed an administrative procedure akin to that of Article 169, for a failure to comply with a previous judgment of the Court. The Commission may specify a lump sum or penalty payment, in its submissions to the Court, which it considers appropriate in the circumstances. The Court may impose a lump sum or periodic penalty payment. The imposition of a financial penalty for the failure to comply with a judgment of the Court is a marked departure from the creation of the Community legal order based solely upon political and legal co-operation. It does however reflect a political commitment

---

[29] See, for example, the debate concerning the potential development of 'horizontal direct effect of directives' in Case C-91/92 *Dori* v *Recreb*, pending before the Court.

[30] Art L limits the Court's jurisdiction to the three treaties establishing the European Communities, the third subparagraph of Art K.3(2)(c) and the Final Provisions.

[31] Curtin, 'The decentralised enforcement of Community law rights: judicial snakes and ladders' in *Constitutional Adjudication in European Community and National Law* (1992) Curtin and O'Keeffe (eds) at 33.

[32] Cases C-6/90 & 9/90 *Francovich and Bonofaci* [1991] ECR I-5357.

[33] Case C-48/93 *R* v *Secretary of State for Transport, ex parte Factortame*, OJ 1993 C94/13, pending before the Court. In the national courts, see, for example, *The Independent*, 8 June 1993, which reported that a Harley Street rheumatologist, Dr Anthony Goldstein, has issued a writ seeking to recover £1m in damages from the UK Government for its failure to implement properly the 1975 Medical Directive (OJ 1975 L167/1).

[34] Art 143 EAEC.

to the "fundamental task [of the Court of Justice] of ensuring uniform interpretation"[35] and application of Community law.

Although it is not possible to predict the Court's application of Article 171 EC, it must be noted that there is no financial limit contained in the article. The Court may be guided by the Commission's submissions on this issue, but is not bound by them. The political overtones of a second Commission action are increased by the availability of financial penalties. This in turn accentuates the delicacy of the Court's setting of the penalty, which must be contrasted with a review of a penalty imposed upon the Member State by a political institution. However, in the light of the priority placed upon the judicial protection of individuals in the Court's existing jurisdiction and the mounting fines upheld in competition cases, the Court may apply the provision with vigour. Indeed, a Declaration to the Treaty on European Union stresses the need for "effectiveness and rigour" in the implementation of Community law.[36] The Court has, for example, stated in relation to "an appropriate system of sanctions" contained in the Equal Treatment Directive that the "sanction be such as to guarantee real and effective judicial protection" and have "a real deterrent effect".[37] The principle of proportionality, a general principle of Community law in the jurisprudence and now enshrined in the third paragraph of Article 3b EC, will apply to the financial penalty. The principle will require that the "punishment fits the crime". However, there is little or no guidance, other than the submissions of the parties, to assist the Court in the striking of the balance. In the light of the novelty of the Article 171(2) EC concept to Community law and the different methods by which this and *Francovich* actions are brought before the Court, it will be noted with interest whether the use of penalties will encourage compliance with Community law more effectively than actions for quantifiable damages brought by vigilant individuals before national courts.

Subsidiarity[38]

The Court of Justice is accustomed to acting as a constitutional court in the resolution of institutional conflicts arising from the "Constitutional Charter" of the Treaties based upon the rule of law. The recent caselaw on the legal base of environmental legislation is a clear example. The Single European Act introduced an environmental policy into the Communities as Articles 130s-t EEC. The Council was empowered by Article 130s to legislate in this field, acting *unanimously* after *consulting* the European Parliament. However, the Commission considered that certain "environmental" measures, in particular those relating

---

[35] First recital to Dec 93/591, *supra*.
[36] See the Declaration on the Uniform Interpretation of Community law.
[37] Case 14/83 *Von Colson and Kamann* [1984] ECR 1891 at para 18 referring to Art 6 of Directive 76/207 (OJ 1976 L39/40).
[38] See Toth, 'A legal analysis of subsidiarity'; Steiner, 'Subsidiarity under the Maastricht Treaty'; Emiliou, 'Subsidiarity: panacea or fig leaf?' in this volume at 37, 49 and 65 respectively.

to waste ("goods" within the meaning of the EEC Treaty[39]), concerned the establishment and functioning of the internal market and should therefore have been based upon Article 100a EEC. This later article requires a *qualified majority* in the Council and the *co-operation* of the European Parliament. The debate therefore had significant institutional and democratic importance. The Court of Justice has been required to consider the relationship between Articles 100a and 130s in two recent cases.

In the *Titanium Dioxide* case,[40] the Court considered that where the measure had dual aims of environmental protection and the elimination of disparities in the conditions of competition, it was necessary to establish the legislation's "centre of gravity" by reference to its aim and content. Through an analysis of the aim and content of the Directive, rather than the institution's conviction as to the objective pursued, the Court held that Article 100a should have been the legal base. The Directive was duly annulled. The Commission more recently challenged the legal basis of the Council's amendments to a waste Directive, relying upon these successful arguments, in *Commission* v *Council*.[41] However, the Court held that the object of the Directive was environmental protection, and the effects upon competition were merely ancillary to these aims. Article 130s was therefore the correct legal base.

This brief excursion into the judicial review of environmental legislation highlights the difficulties facing the Court of Justice. Adjudication between what would appear to be tightly drafted articles of the Treaty has been achieved by establishing the aim and content of legislation. In addition, both of these articles aim to act at the Community level for the benefit of the environment and, to varying degrees, the internal market. This legal situation must be contrasted with potential applications for judicial review of Community legislation for the infringement of the principle of subsidiarity which, by virtue of its inclusion in the Treaty as Article 3b EC rather than in the preamble,[42] constitutes a general principle of Community law.

The principle of subsidiarity has been described as "national precedence",[43] a "best level" test,[44] "an anti-competitive arrangement among executive branches",[45] "an elementary principle of good government"[46] and "a principle of social organisation developed to be used in combination with other principles of collective and individual action".[47] Any definition of "subsidiarity" will therefore include an ideological underpinning. It serves for the

[39] Case C-2/90 *Commission* v *Belgium* [1992] ECR-I 4431 at para 28.
[40] Case C-300/89 *Commission* v *Council* [1991] ECR-I 2867.
[41] Case C-155/91 *Commission (supported by the European Parliament)* v *Council*, judgment of 17 March 1993, not yet reported.
[42] See the inclusion of the principle of subsidiarity in the ninth recital to the Draft Treaty on European Union; Capotorti, Hilf, Jacobs, Jacqué *The European Union Treaty* (1986), Clarendon Press.
[43] Major, speech to the Conservative Group for Europe, 22 April 1993.
[44] Brittan, 'Institutional Developments of the European Community' (1992) *Public Law*, 567–579 at 574.
[45] Allot, 'Europe after Maastricht: Interim Report', First Report from the Foreign Affairs Committee, HC 205, 1992–93, Ev at 51.
[46] MacKenzie-Stuart, 'Assessment of the views expressed and introduction to a panel discussion' in *Subsidiarity: the Challenge of Change* (1991), European Institute of Public Administration at 38.
[47] Wilke and Wallace, *Subsidiarity: Approaches to Power-Sharing in the European Community* (1990) at 11.

purposes of this article merely to cite the second paragraph of Article 3b as a working definition of the inherently imprecise principle:

"In areas which do not fall within its exclusive competence, the Community shall take action, in accordance with the principle of subsidiarity, only if and in so far as the objectives of the proposed action cannot be sufficiently achieved by the Member States and can therefore, by reason of the scale or effects of the proposed action, be better achieved by the Community."

Whilst it is clear therefore that all parties accept the binding nature of Article 3b EC, their purposes for such acceptance are markedly different. The political motivations range the *Länder*'s fear of the extension of Community responsibility into areas within their exclusive competence under the *Grundgesetz*, through the UK's desire to preserve "sovereignty" at a national level to the introduction of subsidiarity as an acceptance of federalism. Article 3b has enabled national politicians to claim that the Treaty of European Union, and Community law, will serve their requirements. Clearly, the uniformity of interpretation which will arise from the Court of Justice's jurisprudence on the principle will not enable the expectations of all the Member States to be met. Professor Curtin's statement that "subsidiarity is presented in terms capable of papering over any number of cracks and crevices in the structure of the Maastricht Treaty"[48] reflects the difference between the political and legal implications of the principle.

The Treaty on European Union has increased the use of qualified majority voting in the Council. This follows the precedent set by the Single European Act. The combination of varying political perceptions of the principle of subsidiarity and the increase in qualified majority voting is likely to result in litigation. Member States who argued, unsuccessfully, within the Council that the Community should not act on a particular matter may challenge the adopted legislation before the Court on the principle of subsidiarity. The Court of Justice will, seemingly inevitably, be drawn into political dispute resolution which has arisen within one institution, rather than between institutions. This may be regarded as the first significant difference from the Court's existing constitutional jurisprudence.

Secondly, the Court of Justice has determined the majority of its constitutional cases on the interpretation of the aim and content of the particular legislative act, as seen above, the text and spirit of the Treaties and the general principles of law. Challenges by Member States to enacted legislation on the principle of subsidiarity will not, however, seek to annul legislation on the determination of the aim and content of the measure itself, but upon the question whether those aims should be pursued at a Community level at all. Put another way, should those aims exist at all at the Community level within Community legislation?

The way a particular act is phrased will suggest that the Community is indeed both competent in that area and should enact legislation. The adopted act must state the reasons for its adoption. These will have been drafted in order to give

---

[48] Curtin, *The Irish Times*, 16 October 1992 at 16.

effect to the wishes of the majority. The reasons for Community action will therefore be stated on the face of the act. The arguments of the dissenting voices will not appear. The content and aim of the act is therefore unlikely to assist the Court. The Court would consider the Treaty provisions upon which basis the act was adopted. Unless the act is *ultra vires*, the provision will provide jurisdiction for the Community to act, albeit concurrently with Member States. This is unlikely to provide guidance for the level of action. Similarly, the spirit of the Treaty has been interpreted, to date, as integrating action at a Community level in the pursuit of an "ever closer union among the peoples of Europe". The existing *acquis communautaire* and the drafting of the disputed act are unlikely to assist the Court. The applicants would, however, argue that the Community should not have acted at all. The general principle of subsidiarity will require the Court to "step back" from the particular act and the existing *acquis communautaire* to consider the level at which the measure should have been adopted. This is an almost unprecedented task, which requires the Court to place constraints upon its methods of interpretation and to consider arguments based on a general principle against an adopted act and the spirit of the Treaty itself.

In addition to the *ERTA* case,[49] the following joined cases give some guidance, by analogy, to the detachment from the text and the Treaty which will be required to determine questions of subsidiarity. *European Parliament* v *Council and Commission*[50] concerned the granting of aid to Bangladesh following a cyclone which devastated the country on the night of 29 to 30 April 1991. A decision was taken to grant ECU 60 million aid, to be administered by the Commission, at a working lunch of the national Foreign Ministers and a Member of the Commission during a two day General Affairs Council meeting. The decision was announced by a press release. The European Parliament presented a series of arguments to establish that the decision taken by "the Member States meeting in Council" was in reality a decision of the Council. It sought to annul the decision and its implementation as infringing its budgetary prerogatives contained in the Treaty and the Financial Regulation. The Council and the Commission argued that the contested act was not adopted by the Council, but by the Member States. The decision could not therefore be the subject of annulment proceedings before the Court. The admissibility point therefore turned upon the identity of the enacting institution, rather than the effects of the disputed act, which has been subject to extensive jurisprudence.

Advocate General Jacobs considered that the Court of Justice could examine the content and effects of an act and the question of exclusive Community jurisdiction to determine whether, "although ostensibly enacted as an act of the Member States meeting in Council, it is in reality an act of the Council."[51] This approach, based upon the objectives of Article 164 EEC and the rule of law, seems justified. Member States could otherwise avoid the jurisdiction of the

---

[49] Case 22/70 *ERTA: Commission* v *Council* [1971] ECR 263.
[50] Joined Cases C-181/91 & C-248/91 *European Parliament* v *Council and Commission*, judgment of 30 June 1993, not yet published, see *Weekly Proceedings* No 21/93. Opinion of Advocate General Jacobs, 16 December 1992.
[51] *Ibid* at para 20.

Court of Justice by merely naming an act a decision of the 12. The Court of Justice dismissed the Parliament's applications as inadmissible. It held that the Representatives of the Member States were not acting as Members of the Council and that consequently the disputed acts were not subject to the supervisory jurisdiction of the Court. However, the Court, following Advocate General Jacobs, confirmed that it may verify the true author of an act, having regard to its content and *all circumstances in which the act was adopted*.[51a] The description of an act as a "decision of the Member States" is not therefore sufficient of itself to deny judicial review. This may have significant consequences in the substantive overlap between the EC Treaty and the Justice and Home Affairs pillar of the Treaty on European Union. The case demonstrates how the Court of Justice might "step back" from the disputed act to determine, in this case, who in reality entered into the act, and in the case of subsidiarity, whether the act should have been adopted.

The Court of Justice, having "stepped back" and heard the essentially political arguments of the aggrieved Council minority Member State in the hypothetical case in question, must consider the detail of Article 3b to determine the case. This may be considered the third challenge for the Court. It is not within the scope of this article to consider the application of the principle in minute detail. However, one illuminating example will be briefly addressed. Sir Leon Brittan has commented that "the Merger Regulation provides an excellent example of how subsidiarity can be put into practice."[52] However, the requirement that the Commission and the Council must consider the quantitative thresholds for concentrations to be of a Community dimension in the Merger Regulation by the end of 1993[53] also provides a clear example of the difficulties which may be encountered in litigation. The thresholds represent a clear line of demarcation between Member States and the Community.

The first problem would be the applicability of the principle. Article 3b applies in areas which do not already fall within the exclusive competence of the Community, the "occupied field". Professor Hartley has interpreted this as meaning that "subsidiarity would be applicable only when the Community legislated for the first time in a new field."[54] The Commission has suggested lowering the quantitative thresholds, which would result in an increased number of mergers of a Community dimension. It is not clear whether the extended area of competence would constitute an area outside the exclusive jurisdiction of the Community.

[51a] Contrast the Court's analysis of the *aim* and content of the environmental legislation described above.

[52] Brittan, 'Subsidiarity in the constitution of the European Community', Robert Schuman Lecture, European University Institute (Florence), 11 June 1992, see *Agence Europe Documents*, 18 June 1992, No 1786 at 4.

[53] Art 1(3) of Merger Control Regulation 4064/89 (OJ 1989 L395/1). Since writing, the Commission recommended to the Council that it make no formal changes for risk of "jeopardising the existing consensus and commitment built up round the Regulation" (Com (93) 385). However, the domain remains a pertinent example of the issues raised, particularly as the Commission considers there is a strong case for the reduction of thresholds and proposes to reconsider the matter prior to 1996.

[54] Hartley, *supra* n 45, Ev at 48, and 'Constitutional and institutional aspects of the Maastricht Treaty' (1993) 42 ICLQ 213–237 at 216.

Secondly, the tests of "effectiveness" and "necessity" are both included in Article 3b. However, the effectiveness and necessity of Community merger control are essentially different if considered from the perspective of the Community, the United Kingdom or Germany (which have sophisticated national procedures) and the Netherlands (which has no formal procedures).

The third aspect of the variation of the thresholds is the differing administrative and policy considerations within the Commission. The Commission must weigh the goal of the decentralised application of competition law[55] and the initially high setting of the thresholds which have not caught all mergers with a significant Community dimension.

The example of the Merger Regulation thresholds illuminates the political and policy concerns which must be considered in the proposal and adoption of the Council decision by qualified majority. Commissioner Karel Van Miert has recently confirmed the importance attached to the principle of subsidiarity in this matter.[56] As has been seen, however, the matter might fall outside the legal definition contained in Article 3b. If applicable, it would expose the Court of Justice to significant policy choices. The example therefore underlines the importance of the principle at an administrative and policy level, and the vulnerability of the Court of Justice's jurisprudence to criticism on the ground of political motivation. The Court of Justice, whose jurisprudence has developed great respect throughout the Member States, appears to have been exposed to a principle which potentially undermines its integrity and confers upon it a role for which, institutionally, it has not been prepared by the Treaty on European Union.

Conclusion

As has been seen, the Treaty on European Union has reformed the Court of Justice in a way which tackles some of its current problems, as well as creating fresh anomalies. However, whilst Member States, the institutions and Article 177 references maintain preferential positions, the increased jurisdiction of the Court of First Instance and the use of Chambers will not tackle, at a philosophical level, the role of the Court of Justice in the Union. The application of the principle of subsidiarity by the Court of Justice has been described as an "unenviable task" by a former President of the Court.[57] Similarly, its introduction into Community law has been described as a "dangerous" development.[58]

The role of the Court and the principle of subsidiarity have been brought together on a number of occasions. Valéry Giscard d'Estaing's proposal for the

---

[55] See Commission Notice to national courts on the application of Articles 85 and 86, COM(92) 593 and the *22nd Report on Competition Policy*, COM(93) 162 final, at paras 120, 121.

[56] Van Miert, 'Analysis and guidelines on Competition Policy', speech to the Royal Institute of International Affairs (London), 11 May 1993, see *Agence Europe Documents*, 15 May 1993, No 1834 at 7.

[57] MacKenzie-Stuart, *The Times*, 15 June 1992.

[58] Kapteyn, 'Community law and the principle of subsidiarity', (1991) RAE 35–43 at 42.

insertion of the principle of subsidiarity into the EEC Treaty, for example, contained a separate amendment which specifically reflected the Court's new role and provided for a procedure similar to the French *conseil constitutionel*.[59] Subsidiarity is, primarily, a federal principle which requires the necessary administrative mechanisms for implementation and a judicial system designed to complement the political task it engenders. It is therefore a matter of urgency that consideration should be given to the *fundamental* reform of the Communities' institutional legal order with a view to the 1996 Intergovernmental Conference.

Prior to the Intergovernmental Conference, and the rocky road to ratification which will no doubt lie thereafter, the Court of Justice and, potentially, the Court of First Instance must consider the principle of subsidiarity within the existing institutional framework, as amended by the Treaty on European Union. However, the ability of the Court of Justice to respond to innovative, intricate and unpredictable problems has always been, to date, both ingenious and convincing.

WILLIAM ROBINSON

---

[59] European Parliament Session Document, Report of the Committee on Institutional Affairs on the principle of subsidiarity, 31 October 1990, EN\RR\98228. See also, European Policy Forum, *Protocol on the Application of Subsidiarity in the European Community* (1992), London, para (v) of the draft Protocol.

Chapter 13

"Better Rusty Than Missin'"[1]? : Institutional reforms of the Maastricht Treaty and the European Parliament

Introduction

Ensuring popular participation in the functioning of the Communities through the intermediary of the European Parliament has not always been a priority issue for the authors of the Treaties, though the Court considered it relevant in proclaiming the EEC to be founded on a "new legal order" in 1963.[2] The Community's aspiration to embody and uphold the democratic values of its Member States received a first, somewhat ambivalent, recognition in the text of the Treaties in the preamble of the Single European Act. In the third recital, the Member States signalled their shared determination "to promote democracy on the basis of fundamental rights ... notably freedom, equality and social justice". The drafting of this provision is somewhat opaque; whatever the Community may have done in pursuit of these last three objectives, there is surely more to democracy than respect for fundamental rights, and indeed, more to fundamental rights than the promotion of democracy. The preamble also dubbed the European Parliament "an indispensable means of expression" for "the democratic peoples of Europe", though omitting specifically to attribute it a role in promoting democratic decision-making in the Community, as if the Member States were wary of too close an identification between the institution and the objective.

The authors of the Treaty of European Union (TEU) had no such qualms; having affirmed their "attachment to the principles of liberty, democracy, and respect for human rights and fundamental freedoms and the rule of law",[3] the Member States expressed their desire "to enhance further the democratic and

---

[1] Groucho Marx, *A Day at the Races*, on throwing his watch into a basin before performing an operation.
[2] Case 26/62 *Van Gend en Loos* [1963] ECR 1 at 12; in the *Isoglucose* cases, the Court described the consultation of Parliament as the reflection, at Community level, of 'the fundamental democratic principle that the peoples should take part in the exercise of power through the intermediary of a representative assembly': Cases 138 & 139/79 *Roquette Frères* and *Maizena v Council* [1980] ECR 3333 and 3393, at 3360 and 3424, respectively. For simplicity, only the EEC will henceforth be considered.
[3] As respect for human rights could arguably be considered an essential element of the rule of law, the authors of the TEU missed the opportunity of coining a pithy slogan to rival the 'life, liberty and the pursuit of happiness' of the 1776 Declaration of Independence.

efficient functioning of the institutions so as to enable them better to carry out, within a single institutional framework, the tasks entrusted to them". That this ringing declaration might be seen as begging the question of whether, and to what extent, the institutional structures of the Community can already be deemed "democratic" will not be considered here; but these preambular sentiments provide the background to the institutional reforms of the TEU as regards the European Parliament. For reasons of space, only those concerning the revision of the legislative procedures, the participation of Parliament in proceedings before the Court of Justice, Parliament's supervisory powers and electoral provisions will be considered.[4]

Decision-making procedures

Foremost amongst the TEU reforms which directly affect Parliament are those concerning legislative procedures. These are of three orders, *viz* the establishment of a new "negative assent" procedure, widely and not wholly accurately described as the "co-decision procedure",[5] the upgrading[6] of parliamentary participation, generally from consultation to co-operation, for decision-making in certain areas, and the conferral of consultation and information rights in new areas of Community or Union jurisdiction. Parliament may also request the Commission to take legislative initiatives.

The negative assent procedure

In essence, the procedure of Article 189b consists in the co-operation procedure with the addition of the following features:

– on second reading, Parliament may by an absolute majority "indicate" to the Council that it intends to reject the common position. The Council may at this point convene the Conciliation Committee (see below) in order "to explain further its position"; should Parliament confirm its rejection, the proposal fails;
– where Parliament proposes amendments to the common position by an absolute majority, the Council must either amend[7] the proposed act accordingly

---

[4] The question of Parliament's role in Social Protocol matters is not examined here, being just one part of the general procedural morass created by this instrument. Equally, though a significant political power, parliamentary approval of the Commission under Art 158(2), does not appear to pose major legal problems.
[5] The procedure is referred to by its EC Treaty article throughout, to placate British opposition to the notion that the Council should share legislative power with the European Parliament in these areas, rather than as a recognition of the unequal positions of the Council and Parliament.
[6] In one case, Parliament's participation has been downgraded; see below.
[7] As those of Parliament's second reading amendments of which the Commission approves are no longer incorporated into a re-examined proposal, the Council would be expected to consider these individually; a positive qualified majority vote in favour would be required for their adoption, rather than, as at present, a unanimous vote to exclude them. Jacobs et al predict a falling off in the take-up rate of such amendments (*The European Parliament*, (2nd ed) Longman 1992, 192), though this may be offset by Parliament's greater leverage through its powers to block the adoption of the measure as a last resort.

or convene the Conciliation Committee, comprising "members of the Council or their representatives and an equal number of representatives of the European Parliament,"[8] with a view to reaching agreement on a joint text;

- the joint text, if adopted by a qualified majority of the Council and a majority of the parliamentary delegation, is submitted to Parliament and Council, and becomes law only if both institutions approve it, by an absolute majority and a qualified majority, respectively;[9]
- in the absence of a joint text, the Council may confirm its common position; this becomes law unless Parliament rejects it by an absolute majority, in which case no legislative act is adopted.

The whole procedure after the adoption of the Council's common position is subject to fixed deadlines: three months each for the second reading of Parliament and the Council and for the convocation of the Conciliation Committee, and six weeks each for agreement on the joint text, for approval thereof, for confirmation of the common position and, as the case may be, for parliamentary rejection of such confirmation. Though clearly intended to encourage dialogue between the Council and Parliament, with a view to achieving mutually acceptable compromises, the imposition of a unanimity vote in Council for the application of this procedure in two areas rather jeopardises the achievement of that aim.[10]

The negative assent procedure will apply for the adoption of measures in the following areas:

- free movement of workers, freedom of establishment, freedom to provide services, and internal market measures under Article 100a;[11]
- "incentive measures" in the fields of education, cultural policy and public health;[12]
- "specific action" supporting and supplementing national policies on consumer protection;[13]
- "guidelines" on the objectives, priorities and broad lines of measures concerning trans-European infrastructure networks;[14]
- a multi-annual framework programme on research and technological development, and general action programmes on environmental protection.[15]

The Article 189b procedure thus applies for the adoption of legislation properly so called, as opposed to policy orientations and incentive measures, only in the areas of the free movement of workers, establishment, cross-border services

---

[8] This will allow systematic direct contacts, for the first time, between MEPs and COREPER.

[9] The voting requirement may prove more problematic for Parliament than for the Council; in the latter case, the Council is being asked to ratify a text negotiated either by COREPER or the Council itself, while Parliament must find an absolute majority to approve a text which only a handful of members, albeit authoritative on the issue, will even have seen.

[10] Arts 128 (culture) and 130i(1) (research, multiannual framework programme); see also the *Titanium dioxide* judgment, where the Court rejected the combination of a unanimity requirement and the co-operation procedure, as undermining the 'very purpose' of the latter, being 'to increase the involvement of the European Parliament in the legislative process of the Community' [1991] ECR I-2867 at 2900.

[11] Arts 48, 54, 56(2), 57, 66, and 100a.

[12] The first indent of Arts 126(4), 128(5) and 129(4).

[13] Art 129a(2).

[14] Art 129d.

[15] Arts 130i(1) and 130s(3).

and the internal market generally. As the principal legislative measures in each of these areas should, like the TEU itself, have been operational by 1 January 1993, the negative assent procedure was only intended to apply for the adoption of supplementary, ancillary and amending legislation, *prima facie* measures of secondary importance. The material scope of the negative assent procedure will in practice depend on the extent to which the Community has failed to create an internal market, as defined in Article 13 of the Single European Act, by the time the TEU comes into force.[16]

Extension of the assent and co-operation procedures

The assent procedure, which has heretofore only been applied for the adoption of association agreements, including protocols to existing agreements, will henceforth cover decisional acts in the following areas:[17]

- measures to facilitate the exercise of citizenship rights;
- amendments to certain articles concerning the European Central Bank;
- Council provisions on the uniform electoral procedure for elections to the European Parliament;
- rules defining the tasks, priority objectives and organization of the Structural Funds, and the setting up of a Cohesion Fund (for environmental and certain transport infrastructure projects);
- association agreements and other international agreements which establish a specific institutional framework, which have important budgetary implications or which amend an act adopted under the negative assent procedure;
- accession of new Member States to the Union.

Whereas an absolute majority of the component members of Parliament was required for assent to association and accession agreements under Articles 237 and 238 of the EEC Treaty as amended by the Single Act, such a majority will only be required henceforth for provisions on the uniform electoral procedure and accession. This latter modification may be considered the correction of an anomaly, whereby in practice a minority of fewer than 100 members has been able to block Parliament's assent to association agreements and protocols.[18] Though Article N TEU did not accord Parliament the right of veto over future constitutional amendments it had requested, Parliament has indicated on a number of occasions that it will use its power of assent to future accessions to ensure any "widening" of the Community/Union will be accompanied by an acceptable form of "deepening".[19]

The co-operation procedure, referred to throughout as "the procedure referred to in Article 189c", will replace simple consultation in the areas of

---

[16] Some indication of the likely scope of application of the negative assent procedure may be gleaned from the Commission's Programme 1993–94, and its 1993 legislative programme (OJ 1993 C125).

[17] Arts 8a, 105(6), 106(5), 130d, 138(3) and 228(3) of the EC Treaty, and Art O of the TEU, respectively.

[18] The total number of members participating in 'Single Act votes' in a given week rarely exceeds 350, while 260 (or slightly fewer, depending on the number of vacancies) favourable votes are required for assent.

[19] 16 December 1992 (OJ 1993 C21/106).

transport (except for particularly sensitive measures), implementation of the Social Fund, and most environmental protection measures.[20] Co-operation will also apply for measures on vocational training policy – Article 128 EEC did not even provide for consultation of Parliament – on development co-operation policy, and on the interoperability and financing of trans-European networks,[21] as well as for four categories of measures within the EMU framework.[22] In the case of specific research programmes for the implementation of the framework programme (Art 130i(4)), Parliament's role has been downgraded from co-operation to consultation, the avatar of a Council-Parliament dispute on the funding for such programmes.[23]

New rights of consultation and information

Apart from the extension of the consultation procedure to three areas where parliamentary participation was not required heretofore,[24] and to most types of international agreements to which the Community is party,[25] the consultation procedure will apply for the adoption of measures in the following new areas of Community/Union competence:[26]

- citizenship matters (right to vote in municipal and European Parliament elections; additional and improved citizenship rights);
- visa policy;
- specific measures to support Member State action on industrial policy;
- specific measures on economic and social cohesion outside the structural funds;
- within the framework of the Community's environmental policy, fiscal provisions, land use and town planning, and measures affecting national energy policy;
- consultation on the "main aspects and the basic choices" of the common foreign and security policy and Union activities in the fields of justice and home affairs.

Parliament will be regularly informed, presumably after the event rather than before a decision is taken as in consultation, on the conduct of the Union's foreign and security policy, and on co-operation on home affairs and justice,

---

[20] Arts 75, 125, and 130s(1).

[21] Arts 127, 130w, and 129d.

[22] Arts 103(5), 104a, 104b(2) and 105a(2).

[23] See Elizalde, 'Legal aspects of Community policy on Research and Technological Development' (1992) 29 CML Rev 309.

[24] Art 75(3) (particularly sensitive transport measures), Art 94 (State aids) and Art 100 (approximation of laws; before the TEU, parliamentary consultation was only required if the harmonizing directive would involve the amendment of national legislation, though in practice Parliament was consulted on all Directives based on Art 100).

[25] Excepting Commercial Policy Agreements and those for which Parliament's assent is required (Art 228(3)). Where consultation applies, the Council may lay down a time-limit for Parliament's opinion 'according to the urgency of the matter'; the question of principle as to whether the absence of Parliament's opinion on a matter deemed urgent by the Council prevents adoption of the relevant legislation is currently before the Court (Case C-65/93 *Parliament* v *Council*, OJ 1993 C105/9).

[26] Arts 8b, 8e, 100c, 130(3), 130b, 3rd indent, 130s(2), J.7 and K.6.

and the Presidency of the Council "shall ensure that [its] views are duly taken into consideration"; furthermore, it may put questions and submit recommendations to the Council, and is obliged to hold an annual debate, on each of these matters. These parliamentary prerogatives will not enjoy the judicial protection they receive under the EC Treaty regime, by virtue of Article L TEU.

The consultation procedure also applies generally for EMU decisions, though Parliament is only informed of Council measures[27] concerning capital movements to and from third countries, guidelines for national economic policies, financial assistance to a Member State in difficulties, sanctions against a Member State for failure to comply with deficit reduction measures, the adoption, adjustment or abandonment of the ECU central rates, and the composition of the Economic and Financial Committee. This right to information will benefit from judicial protection; given the relative novelty of the concept, an interinstitutional agreement defining the practical aspects of its application could provide a useful means of avoiding possible future conflict.

Legislative initiative

Article 152 EEC has long recognised that the Council may request the Commission to submit to it "any appropriate proposals", though it is not clear if and when the Commission is bound by such requests.[28] The absence from the Treaties of any such equivalent facility for Parliament has not prevented it from adopting resolutions calling upon the Commission to propose legislation, or even drafting legislative texts for the Commmission's consideration.[29] In its amendments to the EEC Treaty of November 1990,[30] Parliament had asked for the right to initiate legislation in cases where the Commission either failed to respond within six months to, or rejected, a specific request adopted by a majority of Members of Parliament to introduce a proposal; Parliament's proposal would in such circumstances have served as its first reading. The second paragraph of Article 138b, which could be seen as a rather truncated response to Parliament's suggested amendment, recognises that "acting by a majority of its members, [Parliament] may request the Commission to submit any appropriate proposal on matters on which it considers that a Community act is required for the purpose of implementing this Treaty". This new provision does not indicate that the Commission is in any way obliged to comply with Parliament's request, nor grant Parliament a right of initiative if the Commission does not, though Parliament welcomed it as such in April 1992.[31] On the other hand, the requirement that Parliament act by a majority of its members, if it is not to be deemed

---

[27] Arts 73g(2), 103(2), 103a(2), 104c(11), 109(1) and 109c(3); Parliament would also be informed of the results of multilateral surveillance, and on the activities of the ESCB (Arts 103(4) and 109b(3)).

[28] The opposing views are set out in Lenaerts, commentary on Art 152, in Constantinesco *et al*, *Traité instituant la CEE – Commentaire article par article*, (1992) 901–904.

[29] Lasalle, 'L'initiative parlementaire dans la procédure normative communautaire', (1971) 7 CDE 127. Such ready-made legislative texts emanating from Parliament are in fact rather rare; for one example in the relatively recent past, see the 'draft proposal for a Directive' on atypical forms of employment it adopted on 10 July 1990 (OJ 1990 C231/32).

[30] OJ 1990 C 324/219.

[31] OJ 1992 C 125/84.

legally superfluous, does appear to recognise that any such resolution would enjoy a particular, if rather undefined, status.

Participation of Parliament in proceedings before the Court of Justice

The story of the evolution of Parliament's standing in institutional proceedings before the Court is well-known, and can now be recounted as an important aspect of the development of a "Community based on the rule of law", in which "neither its Member States nor its institutions can avoid a review of the question whether the measures adopted by them are in conformity with the basic constitutional charter, the Treaty",[32] despite the absence in Article 173 EEC of any mention of Parliament, either as a potential defendant or applicant. In *Les Verts* and *Chernobyl*, the Court first extended the reach of the annulment action under the EEC Treaty to embrace acts of Parliament, and then devised a limited common law right of action for Parliament to defend its prerogatives in the decision-making process.[33] The TEU seeks in effect to enshrine these judicial pronouncements in the Treaty itself, though the wisdom of such a course is open to doubt; at the same time, the TEU fails to address the question of parliamentary participation in two other types of proceeding before the Court.

Action for annulment

Article 173 EEC has been modified in three respects of concern to the European Parliament:

Acts adopted in accordance with the "negative assent" procedure

"[Acts] adopted jointly by the European Parliament and the Council", in accordance with Article 189b, are open to review under the normal conditions of Article 173 for review of Council and Commission acts. Even this seemingly anodyne provision is not without its problematic aspects, apart from the practical difficulties which may arise from the presentation, by two institutions rarely on the same side of a legal dispute, of a joint defence to the Court. The most anomalous case would arise where, in the absence of a joint text approved by the Conciliation Committee, the Council were to confirm its common position, in accordance with Article 189b(6), and Parliament were to fail either to act within the necessary six weeks, or, more likely in practice, to muster the necessary majority to reject the Council's reconfirmed common position. Parliament

---

[32] Case 294/83 *Parti écologiste 'Les Verts' v European Parliament* [1986] ECR 1339, 1365; for further references, see, for example, Bradley, 'The variable evolution of the standing of the European Parliament in proceedings before the Court of Justice' (1989) 8 YEL 27–57 and 'Sense and Sensibility: *Parliament v Council* continued' (1991) 16 EL Rev 245–57.

[33] Case 294/83, cited preceding footnote, and Case C-70/88 *European Parliament v Council* (admissibility) [1990] ECR I-2041.

could, in such circumstances, find itself defending before the Court a text to which a majority, albeit a less-than-absolute majority, of its members are hostile.

Annulment actions against the European Parliament

A further addition to the first paragraph of Article 173 would bring within its scope "acts of the European Parliament intended to produce legal effects *vis-à-vis* third parties". The qualifying expression "intended to produce legal effects *vis-à-vis* third parties" has been extracted verbatim from the Court's judgment in *Les Verts*[34] which indeed established the principle of judicial review of acts of Parliament under the EEC Treaty.[35] The same expression appears in a number of subsequent judgments in annulment actions against Parliament; one might therefore be forgiven for concluding that it constitutes the correct criterion for the admissibility of such actions.

This does not appear to be the case. In its orders declaring inadmissible the actions by the *Group of the European Right* and *Blot and the National Front*,[36] the Court had first referred to its finding in *Les Verts*, before holding that measures which relate only to the internal organization of Parliament's work could not be the subject of a challenge under Article 173 EEC; in neither case did the Court clearly indicate whether this conclusion was based on the nature of the contested measure, or the (lack of) capacity of the third party applicant. The matter was settled, at least for the time being, in the Court's judgment of 23 March 1993 in the case of *Weber* v *European Parliament*;[37] the Court based its finding on admissibility exclusively on the nature of the measure, eschewing any reference to the attributes of the applicant, arguably not a third party.[38] Recalling its case-law on the complete system of judicial protection, the Court held that only two categories of acts of Parliament could escape such review: those which produce no legal effects, and those which only produce legal effects within Parliament and which can be reviewed under procedures laid down in its Rules of Procedure.[39] The Court also thereby avoided the inherent ambiguity of a criterion apparently based on the intention of the institution which adopted the act.[40]

The wording of the revised Article 173 EEC will, at the very least, cast doubt upon the criteria for admissibility of annulment actions against Parliament as they arise from this caselaw. It will be open to Parliament to argue that the TEU expressly excludes from review acts which do not affect the legal situation of third parties, and that it is incumbent upon the applicant to prove Parliament's

---

[34] Case 294/83, *supra*, n 32 at 1366.

[35] Art 38 ECSC provides an express, but limited, annulment action against acts of the European Parliament: Case 230/81 *Luxembourg* v *European Parliament* [1983] ECR 255.

[36] Case 78/85 [1986] ECR 1753; Case C-68/90 [1990] ECR I-2101.

[37] Case C-314/91, not yet reported in ECR.

[38] Advocate General Van Gerven expressly stated that the 'third party' criterion was not a necessary condition of admissibility: opinion of 13 January 1993, para 6, p 5, typed version.

[39] The Court thereby adopted as its own the criteria Parliament had itself suggested in a resolution on its position in annulment actions adopted on 9 October 1986, in the aftermath of '*Les Verts*' (OJ 1986 C283/85).

[40] Van Gerven, *op cit*, 3.

(subjective) intention, rather than (objective) effect. The Court would presumably, in such circumstances, consider germane the fact that the Member States rejected Parliament's own proposal to the intergovernmental conference on political union on this point, which would have entrusted the Court with the duty to delimit the scope of such actions,[41] as it does for those against the Council and the Commission.

Annulment actions by the European Parliament

In *Chernobyl*, the Court held that "an action for annulment brought by the Parliament against an act of the Council or the Commission is admissible provided that the action seeks only to safeguard its prerogatives and that it is founded only on submissions alleging their infringement".[42] The third indent of the amended Article 173 would similarly restrict the scope of Parliament's annulment proceedings to "actions ... brought for the purpose of protecting [its] prerogatives"; though this wording does not expressly restrict the submissions on which Parliament may rely, a submission based on a ground other than one relating to the protection of Parliament's prerogatives might be held to fall outside the permitted purpose of the action.

In restricting Parliament's right of action to the defence of its own prerogatives in *Chernobyl*, the Court was attempting to reconcile, on the one hand, its own duty to ensure the provisions of the Treaty concerning the institutional balance are respected, and on the other, the strictures of Articles 4 and 173 EEC as then drafted. It did not establish as a general principle that parliamentary standing in legal proceedings should be thus limited, but rather that the Treaty as it then stood did not permit any more, or indeed less, extensive role in annulment proceedings for the European Parliament. From the point of view of the rule of law, the *Chernobyl* solution may be considered the minimum necessary consistent with the Treaty, but not the optimum solution which could be imagined, and indeed it does give rise to certain practical disadvantages and anomalies in principle.

Should Parliament consider a particular proposed measure to be outwith the competences of the Community, or that the appropriate legal basis is one providing for a lesser degree of parliamentary participation than that chosen by the Council, it would be unable to pursue this view in annulment proceedings against the measure adopted, notwithstanding any *prima facie* illegality. Neither of these scenarios is taken from the realm of political science fiction; in 1991 and 1992, Parliament's legal affairs committee, responsible for both legal basis matters and Parliament's participation in Court actions, so concluded after examining Commission proposals concerning, respectively, moist oral snuff and liability for defective services.[43] Parliament would be equally legally helpless where it considers that a measure, or certain provisions thereof, fails to respect the human rights or fundamental freedoms of the citizens and voters it repre-

---

[41] OJ 1990 C324/232.
[42] Case C-70/88 *European Parliament* v *Council* [1990] ECR I-2041 at 2073.
[43] See, respectively, Bradley 'Legal developments in the European Parliament' (1992) 11 YEL 383 at 394–395, and EP Doc A3–0420/92.

sents. In such controversial cases, which would hardly be everyday occurrences, the question would, in all probability, end up before the Court at some stage, though not for a number of years; the net effect of the restriction on Parliament's right of action would simply be to prolong the ensuing legal uncertainty. One final inconvenience of this solution arises from the Court's judgment of 17 March 1993 in the *Waste Directive* case, where it was held that submissions of an intervening party which are motivated by considerations completely different from those of the principal parties are inadmissible.[44] This means, in effect, that parties intervening in annulment actions commenced by Parliament will be prevented from presenting arguments unless these concern the protection of Parliament's prerogatives.

The restriction is also open to criticism on grounds of principle. On the one hand, as the House of Lords Select Committee on the European Communities observed "[the] time has come to dispel any impression that the Parliament is a junior partner amongst Community institutions";[45] to that end their Lordships supported the extension of Article 173, without restriction to protection of prerogatives, while voicing their, eminently reasonable, expectation that this power would not be used with any great frequency. Why should the interest of the directly elected Parliament in respect for the rule of law be less worthy of judicial protection than that of the Council, which is responsible for most of the institutional violations thereof? On the other hand, neither institutional nor non-institutional applicants are similarly limited in the scope of their annulment actions against Parliament; the Council does not need to show that any budgetary decision it attacks violates its prerogatives, as distinct from the relevant Treaty provisions, while, if the contested act is not within the *Weber* exceptions,[45a] any ground of illegality a natural or legal person wishes to plead against Parliament is fair game.

It is difficult to discern the motivation behind such a procedural encumbrance. The Member States can hardly have been influenced by the "floodgates of litigation" argument proffered in some quarters as one of the raisons d'être of the *Comitology* ruling;[46] the two annulment actions introduced by Parliament from *Chernobyl* to the signing of the TEU constitute little more than a trickle, and in any case each was held by the Court to be well founded.[47] Even the ten or so such actions initiated since February 1992 fall well short of a politically motivated flood, and most of these either raise novel points of law or seek to put an end to long outstanding disagreements between the institutions which the political processes have been unable to resolve. One other possible motivation, suggested by a rumour current in Community circles in the early part of 1991,

---

[44] The Court refused to examine parliamentary submissions on the grounds that these '*tendent à l'annulation de l'article 18 de la directive pour des motifs tout à fait étrangers à ceux invoqués par la Commission*' (judgment, para 24, Case C-155/91 *Commission v Council*, not yet reported in ECR).

[45] 27th Report, 1989–90, *Economic and Monetary Union and Political Union*, Vol 1, para 151, p 51.

[45a] See p 199 above.

[46] Case 302/87 *European Parliament v Council* [1988] ECR 5615 and see, for example, Weiler 'Pride and Prejudice – *Parliament v Council*' (1989) 14 EL Rev 334 at 345.

[47] Cases C-65/90 and C-295/90 *European Parliament v Council*, scheduled to be reported at [1992] ECR I-4593 and 4193, respectively.

was that the amendment to Article 173 EEC was designed to prevent the Court in any way developing or enlarging the scope of the *Chernobyl* criteria, particularly in the two cases then pending before the Court, lest the Council be called upon to defend the legality of its acts more frequently. In the absence of clear evidence to support this suggestion, it would be quite unjustified to impute such ignoble motives to the authors of the TEU.

Action for illegal failure to act

The revised version of Article 175 EEC opens up the possibility, on which the Court has not yet had occasion to rule, that either the other institutional actors, or natural or legal persons, may bring an action for illegal failure to act against Parliament.[48] The original drafting of Article 175, which on its face excluded such a possibility, did not deter two members of Parliament and a British political party from initiating separate proceedings under this article in 1991 and 1992, though the former two actions were withdrawn, and the Court did not proceed to judgment on the third.[49] For obvious reasons, the Council has to date not felt any need to consider Article 175 proceedings against Parliament, preferring simply to ignore the absence of Parliament's legislative opinion, should this not be available.[50] The extension of the assent procedure in the TEU increases the likelihood of future Article 175 proceedings against Parliament, though it is not clear under what circumstances the withholding of assent could be considered a violation of the Treaty, when the raison d'être of this procedure is to give Parliament a right of veto based on political considerations.

Reforms omitted

Though conscious of the need to reform the jurisdictional provisions of the Treaty as regards Parliament, the Member States omitted, whether through negligence or design, to modify two other jurisdictional provisions where Parliament should, logically, have been given a role. Of these, the more surprising is Parliament's exclusion from the list of possible applicants for an opinion of the Court on the compatibility with the Treaty of a projected international agreement in the revised version of Article 228, which restricts such a facility to the Council, the Commission or a Member State.[51] Under Article 107 of the

---

[48] This possibility was suggested in 1987, on the basis of a pre-*Comitology* reading of *Les Verts*; Bradley, 'Maintaining the balance' (1987) 24 CML Rev 41–64 at 49. In his opinion of 24 March 1993 in *The Liberal Democrats* cited at n 49 below, Advocate General Darmon concluded that such an action was in principle admissible against Parliament under Art 175 in its unamended form.

[49] Cases C-257 & 258/91 *Schlee* and *Grund* v *European Parliament*, withdrawn, OJ 1992 C322/13, and C-41/92 *The Liberal Democrats* v *European Parliament*, order of 10 June 1993, not yet reported in ECR.

[50] A recent example of such Council behaviour is currently before the Court of Justice (Case C-65/93 *European Parliament* v *Council*, OJ 1993 C105/9).

[51] In its proposals to the IGCs, Parliament had expressly advocated its own inclusion, though its amendment, somewhat mysteriously, would have excluded the Commission from the list of possible applicants (OJ 1990 C 324/237).

Court's Rules of Procedure, Parliament is not even informed as of right of the presentation of such a request, though Article 21 of the Statute does permit the Court to invite Parliament to provide it with "information", including its views as to the legality of the agreement.[52]

That the exclusion of Parliament from this procedure is anomalous is illustrated by Opinion 1/91 on the first EEA Agreement. Though in the result it chose not to, the Court could have examined the provisions of the Agreement governing the decision-making process, of obvious and direct concern to Parliament.[53] Furthermore, once it had entered into force, the Agreement would become "an integral part of the Community legal order" binding on the institutions, as the Court itself noted.[54] Most importantly, were Parliament to take to their logical conclusion any doubts it harboured on the legality of the Agreement, it would have only the limited but drastic alternative of refusing its assent. Though the Court declined a request from Parliament to present its views on the first EEA agreement, it has so invited Parliament in respect of both requests submitted in 1992; pending a revision of Article 107 of its Rules, the Court has undertaken systematically to inform Parliament of any future requests.[55]

A similar problem arises in relation to preliminary rulings under Article 177 EC. Though this procedure applies both to acts of Parliament alone, and those adopted jointly with the Council, Parliament is still not systematically informed of the submission of such requests in accordance with Article 20 of the ECJ Statute. The Court has on occasion in the past relied on Article 21 of its Statute to palliate this procedural anomaly, in cases where Parliament was the principal institution concerned.[56] Though creative, the Court's use of this provision is far from satisfactory,[57] as illustrated recently in the *Raulin* case, which in effect decided the principal point at issue in Parliament's annulment action on the students' residence Directive;[57a] of the parties and interveners, Parliament alone was given no opportunity to present its views in the preliminary ruling proceedings. Though such an amendment could still be proposed by the Court under the second subparagraph of Article 188 EEC, the ICG was particularly well placed to evaluate its utility.[58]

---

[52] See the discussion of preliminary rulings below.

[53] Parliament had in 1991 adopted a series of resolutions on the EEA agreement then under discussion, including one of 14 June expressing reservations on the proposed institutional arrangements (OJ 1991 C 183/366).

[54] Opinion, para 37, p 12.

[55] OJ 1992 C 136/1 and 8; the undertaking is contained in a letter from the President of the Court to the President of Parliament of 28 April 1993.

[56] See, in particular, Case 208/80 *Lord Bruce of Donington* [1981] ECR 2205, where Parliament's agents were able to present argument, both in writing and orally, on the extent of its autonomy as this arises from Arts 5 and 142 EEC.

[57] Bradley, 'Variable evolution', *op cit*, n 32 at 29–32 and 53.

[57a] Respectively, Cases C-357/89 [1992] ECR I-1027 and C-295/90 [1992] 3 CMLR 281.

[58] For the sake of fairness, Parliament has consistently omitted to propose this reform to the Court in the years since the SEA came into force; see, however, the Rothley report of 6 July 1993, EP Doc A3–0288/93.

Supervisory powers: inquiry committees, petitions and the Ombudsman

Inquiry committees

The facility for Parliament to establish committees of inquiry to investigate specific matters was introduced into its Rules of Procedure in 1981, as part of the general revision following the first direct elections.[59] Under the former Rule 109(3), provided the other procedural conditions are met, a motion by one quarter of the members of Parliament was sufficient for such a committee to be set up, which thus served as a protection of the rights of the political minority.[60] Though it is difficult to generalise on the basis of the handful of inquiry committees which have been established, it may be considered a relatively useful means of reacting to public concern on topical issues of Community-wide importance: thus transport and the treatment of toxic and radioactive wastes, the rise of racism and xenophobia, the use of growth-promoting hormones in meat production, and drug trafficking and organised criminality have all been investigated by past inquiry committees of the European Parliament. The possibility for Parliament to follow up its findings on these matters is, of course, doubly circumscribed, by the limitations on Community action in general, and those on its own powers of initiative.

The new Article 138c EC elevates the possibility of setting up inquiry committees to a Treaty prerogative, though no longer one enjoyed by the minority, the lineaments of which will be set out in an interinstitutional agreement between Parliament, the Council, and the Commission. Under this provision, Parliament may set up temporary inquiry committees:

"to investigate . . . alleged contraventions or maladministration in the implementation of Community law, except where the alleged facts are being examined before a court and while the case is still subject to legal proceedings".

The terms of reference thus defined are largely identical to those contained in Rule 109(3) of Parliament's Rules of Procedure, with the addition of a *sub judice* exception; though Rule 109(3) further extended to "instances of maladministration with respect to Community responsibilities", such a fine distinction may in practice have only a limited effect. Rule 109(3) also provided that such committees enjoyed only a transitory existence, being required to conclude their work within nine months. The import of the qualification in Article 138c, that Parliament may only set up such committees "[i]n the course of its duties", will require to be assessed in the light of Parliament's "inherent right . . . to discuss any question concerning the Communities, [and] to adopt resolutions on such questions".[61]

---

[59] 26 March 1981, OJ 1981 C90/76.
[60] Jacqué *et al*, *Le Parlement Europeen* (1984) at 103.
[61] Case 230/81 *Luxembourg* v *European Parliament* [1983] ECR 255 at 287.

In December 1992, Parliament submitted a "Draft Common Accord [on] the procedures for exercising the right of inquiry"[62] to the other two institutions concerned. Apart from a number of provisions which rightly belong in Parliament's Rules, the draft agreement would require Community and national authorities to make "any information required and any relevant dossier" available to the committee; officials and other persons employed by the authorities in question would be "automatically authorised to give evidence or testify to the committee", which would also be entitled to have access to "any document deemed useful" for its work, excepting those containing information legally classified as secret. Refusal to provide documents requested, failure to appear, false testimony and the suborning of witnesses would all be deemed offences punishable as if they been committed before a national court.[63] The *sub judice* rule is interpreted as precluding the setting up of an inquiry committee "where the matter in question is identical to a case being examined by a court of law until legal proceedings have finished"; where an investigation is already under way, it would fall to Parliament to decide to cease the investigation if legal proceedings are initiated, such decision being in turn open to review by the Court of Justice.[64]

In the debate on the draft agreement, the Council representative was at pains to proffer no comment on its substantive provisions, emphasising instead that the European Parliament's inquiry committees should complement those of the national parliaments,[65] though these latter have in the past generally shown little interest in the implementation of Community law. Sir Leon Brittan, for the Commission, was marginally more candid, admitting that "some of the provisions proposed ... might cause problems", though without specifying which.[66] Parliament's desire to lay down far-reaching obligations on the Commission and the relevant national authorities responsible for the application of Community law to co-operate with its committees reflects past difficulties in this regard, particularly in the course of its investigation of the Transnuklear scandal in 1988.[67]

Petitions

The practice of Parliament's examining and, where appropriate, acting on petitions submitted to it predates the EEC by some years,[68] and the relevant rule of procedure is said to have constituted one of the first uses, in a legal text, of the

---

[62] OJ 1993 C 21/148.

[63] This provision was based on Art 27 of the ECJ Statute.

[64] In *Group of the European Right* v *European Parliament*, the Court found that, as Parliament's inquiry committees have 'only investigative powers', a decision to set up such a committee concerned only Parliament's internal organization, and could not produce legal effects *vis-à-vis* third parties: [1986] ECR 1753 at 1757. It remains to be seen to what extent this will remain good law after the adoption of the interinstitutional agreement foreseen by Art 138c.

[65] Garel Jones, EP Debates, 16 December 1993, Ann OJ 3–425/156.

[66] *Ibid* at 157.

[67] Schmid report, EP Doc A2–120/88, and Hancher, '1992 and accountability gaps: the Transnuklear scandal: a case study in European regulation' (1990) 53 MLR 669.

[68] Surrel has traced the right to petition the European Parliament to 1953 ('Le 'droit de pétition' au Parlement européen', (1990) 335 RMC, 219–234 at 220).

expression "citizen of the European Community".[67] The practice was dignified by the conclusion of an interinstitutional agreement in 1989.[68] Article 138d now enshrines the right of petition in the Treaty, which is also mentioned amongst the provisions on "Citizenship of the Union", at Article 8d EC. The right of petition is accorded to both citizens and "any natural or legal person residing or having his registered office in a Member State", and may be exercised individually or collectively. In this respect, the drafting of Article 138d is a marked improvement on that of Parliament's Rule 128(1) as it stood at the time of the conclusion of the TEU.[69]

If Article 138d extends the right of petition *ratione personae*, it seeks to limit its material scope to matters which not only come within "the Community's fields of activity", as at present, but which directly affect the petitioner. Such a restriction, which appears to treat the petition to Parliament as an adjunct to the means of judicial recourse available under the Treaty, completely distorts its function; one can only assume the authors of the TEU omitted the requirement of "individual concern" found in Article 173 EEC in order to allow collective petitions. In practice, individuals and groups petition the European Parliament primarily to complain of matters which do not, or not necessarily, affect them "directly" in any meaningful sense of the word.

A useful indication of the matters of most concern to petitioners may be gleaned from the list of mass petitions published periodically in Parliament's minutes.[70] Petition No 280/91, for example, which attracted no less than 2,522,261 signatures, concerned the testing of cosmetics on animals; such a petition would no longer be admissible under Article 138d in the absence of "direct effect", unless the authors of the TEU expected the animals themselves to get up a petition, yet the matter is clearly within the scope of activities of the Communities.[71] Other matters of concern raised by recent mass petitions include environmental protection, arms control, conscientious objection, the Gulf war, the Yugoslav crisis, and summertime: does it fall to Parliament to check that all, some, or at least one of the petitioners is directed affected by these matters?

The European Ombudsman

Stridently rejected by Parliament in June 1991,[74] at the behest of the committee on petitions, which presumably felt under threat from such an

---

[69] Vacca, 'Il fondamento giuridico delle petizioni al Parlamento europeo' (1986) 26 *Rivista di Diritto Europeo* 3–12 at 4. In the *Erasmus* case, the Court of Justice recognised the legimacy of pursuing 'the achievement of a people's Europe' (*sic*) as one of the 'general objectives of the Community' (Case 242/87 *Commission* v *Council* [1989] ECR 1425 at 1456).

[70] OJ 1989 C 120/43 and 90.

[71] On its face, this only admitted petitions from Community citizens, though Parliament had already decided, in its Human Rights Declaration of 12 April 1989, that this right should be open to all without restriction (OJ 1989 C120/56); Rule 128 was eventually amended to bring it in line with Art 138d in January 1993 (OJ 1993 C 42/121).

[72] See, for example, the committee statement of 16 January 1992 (OJ 1992 C39/115) reporting on mass petitions in the middle six months of 1991; the same concerns tend to repeat from one statement to the next.

[73] The question completely dominated Parliament's February 1992 debate on a proposed directive harmonizing national provisions on cosmetic products (OJ Ann No 3–414/43–50).

institution, the creation of the office of the European Ombudsman was hailed as a "reinforce[ment] of the safeguarding of the rights of the citizens of the Union" by Parliament in December 1992.[72] Article 138e, unlike the two preceding articles, is based neither on Parliament's rules nor on any pre-existing interinstitutional agreement or arrangement, and as such constitutes one of the genuinely novel features of the TEU.[73] The Ombudsman is to be appointed by the European Parliament for each legislature, and may be dismissed, at Parliament's request, under the same conditions as obtain for the compulsory retirement of a member of the Commission; the conditions governing his independence in office are also similar to those of Commissioners. Parliament is charged with laying down "the regulations and general conditions governing the performance of the Ombudsman's duties", after consulting the Commission and with the approval of the Council acting by a qualified majority; this gives Parliament considerably more leeway, at least as regards provisions on investigating Commission maladministration, than the equivalent provisions regarding such investigations by an inquiry committee, which latter require Commission approval.

The remit of the Ombudsman is a cross between that of the petitions committee and that of the inquiry committee, in that he may receive complaints of maladministration by Community institutions or bodies (excepting the Court of Justice and Court of First Instance acting in a judicial capacity) from the same categories of persons who may submit petitions. Except where the matter is *sub judice*, the Ombudsman must conduct an inquiry into the complaint, referring it, if well-founded, to the institution/body concerned for comments; the procedure is closed by an Ombudsman's report to the European Parliament and the institution concerned, and a communication to the complainant. As with the draft inquiry committee agreement, Parliament took the initiative in December 1992 of proposing a draft statute for the Ombudsman,[74] though an interinstitutional conference in June 1993 failed to reach agreement on the extent of a confidentiality reserve.[75]

Electoral Provisions

At the same time as it was granted a power of veto over the content of any future Council decision on a uniform electoral procedure (Art 138(3)), a certain onus was put on Parliament to expedite its deliberations on the necessary proposals. The new Article 8b(2) EC could even be said to pre-empt these, to the extent that it determines the baseline rules for the right to vote and to stand for

---

[74] OJ 1991 C183/448.

[75] Resolution of 17 December 1992 on the regulations and general conditions governing the performance of the European Ombusdsman's duties (OJ 1993 C21/141).

[76] Gosalbo Bono's claim that the idea originated in the Commission's proposals to the IGC on political union gives rather too much credit to the institution he serves ('Maastricht et les citoyens: le Médiateur européen', (1993) 64 Rev Fr Admin Publique 639–649 at 639); Surrel cites a parliamentary question which made this same proposal as long ago as 1974 (*op cit* n 68, 222).

[77] OJ 1993 C21/141.

[78] *Europe* No 5996 (ns) 9 June 1993, 12.

election to the European Parliament in 1994, fixes a deadline (31 December 1993) for the adoption of detailed arrangements to give effect to these rights for the next elections, and expressly allows "derogations where warranted by problems specific to a Member State".

That Parliament has so far been unable to come forward with a comprehensive proposal for a uniform electoral procedure, in the one area of the Treaties where it has enjoyed the right of initiative since the establishment of the EEC, is common knowledge, and indeed inspired the Article 175 proceedings instituted in 1992 by the British Liberal Democrats.[79] In its 1982 "Draft Act adopting certain provisions relating to a uniform electoral procedure",[80] whose current status is a matter of dispute,[81] Parliament proposed that its members be elected by proportional representation in multi-member constituencies, each returning between three and 15 members, with the distribution of seats according to the d'Hondt system. Derogations from these basic principles were permitted "to take account of special geographical or ethnic factors recognised by the [written or unwritten] constitution of a Member State", though this would not allow a Member State to avoid its provisions generally. Under the Draft Act, the right to vote in European Parliament elections was dependent on nationality, rather than residence as under Article 8b(2), though long-term residents were to be granted the right to stand for election (though not to vote) in their Member State of residence. The 1982 proposal did not deal with such matters as conditions of eligibility, nomination requirements, national thresholds, incompatibilities or the resolution of electoral disputes. A follow-up proposal, adopted with the positive votes of less than half the committee responsible in 1985, was never examined in plenary.[82]

Galvanised into action by the Luxembourg Draft Union Treaty of 18 June 1991, which contained a provision very similar to Article 8b(2) TEU, Parliament adopted "guidelines" on the draft uniform electoral procedure in October 1991.[83] These adopt a step-by-step approach, and recognise that "the concept of uniformity does not require a completely identical and uniform electoral procedure in all Member States but a harmonization of the main elements", in line with previous parliamentary initiatives in this area.[84] The resolution maintains proportional representation as the basic requirement, with the possibility

---

[79] Case C-41/92 *The Liberal Democrats* v *European Parliament*, Order of 10 June 1993, not yet published in ECR; the Court decided not to proceed to judgment, as the applicants recognised that Parliament had fulfilled its obligations under Art 138(3) in adopting the March 1993 guidelines.

[80] OJ 1982 C87/61; the Fifth Report, 1982–83 Session, of the House of Lords Select Committee on the European Communities provides a useful examination of Parliament's proposals.

[81] In answering Written Question No 2358/91, the Council expressed the view that the 1982 proposal, on which it had failed to agree in 1983, was out of date, and that 'for the time being it does not consider any proposal to have been submitted to it' (OJ 1992 C78/44). Parliament, on the other hand, considers the 1982 proposals to be still pending, with their provisions being periodically supplemented and/or replaced by further resolutions.

[82] EP Doc A2–1/85. In a resolution adopted in July 1988, Parliament called upon the Member States to prohibit the dual mandate in the national parliament and the European Parliament, though recommending the establishment of strong links with national and regional assemblies (OJ 1988 C235/131).

[83] OJ 1991 C280/141.

[84] This majority view was rejected by Parliament's legal affairs committee in both 1982 and 1985 (EP Docs 1–988/81 B-C, 26 *et seq*, and A 2–1/85 18 *et seq*), though not in 1991 (EP Doc A3–0152/91).

of a national system to distribute supernumerary votes between constituencies for a proportion of seats; the right to vote and to stand for election would be granted to Community nationals in their Member State of residence, subject to a one-year minimum period of prior residence. Further guidelines followed in March 1993.[82] These provide for voting based on lists drawn up for the whole territory of the Member State, or for regions or multi-member constituencies; in Member States using single-member constituencies, a maximum of two-thirds of the seats may be decided on a first past the post basis, the remainder to be distributed on the basis of lists in order to ensure proportionality, which is to be assessed on the national, rather than the constituency, level. Member States using lists may opt for either one or more preferential votes, and may institute a minimum threshold for the distribution of seats, though this may not be less than 3%, nor greater than 5%. As in the 1982 Draft Act, derogations to take account of regional features must not violate the principle of proportional representation.

By the Fifteenth Declaration annexed to the Final Act signed at Maastricht, the Member States agreed to examine the question of the number of members of the European Parliament and, though for rather different reasons, that of the number of Commissioners, "no later than . . . the end of 1992". Parliament took the opportunity in June 1992 to propose what is intended to be an "objective and permanent scheme . . . reflect[ing] the need for Parliament to be able to operate efficiently and . . . for a direct relationship between voters and Members".[86] The resolution seeks to take account of both demographic changes since 1976, primarily German unification,[87] though without reducing the current allocation of seats to any Member State, and the state of institutional development of the Community, which is said not yet to require universal proportional representation. The new scheme, which increases the number of seats of all but the three smallest Member States, is set to remain in force until Parliament reaches 700 Members; the increases range from 18 (Germany), to one (Belgium, Greece and Portugal), and would bring the total complement to 567. Parliament's proposal was accepted unamended by the European Council meeting in Edinburgh, formally adopted by the Council on 1 February 1993,[88] and recommended to the Member States as an amendment to the 1976 Act.

Article 138a, which, unusually for the EC Treaties, appears to be purely declaratory in character, recognises political parties at European level as "important as a factor for integration within the Union" and for "expressing the political will of [its] citizens". The Council has already indicated its view that this article "is not in itself a legal basis for Council action in this area" but a matter for the political forces in the Member States.[89]

---

[85] OJ 1993 C115/121.

[86] 10 June (OJ 1992 C176/72); Parliament also proposed a seat allocation for six candidate states 'on which the Commission had not delivered a negative opinion'.

[87] Eighteen observers, nominated by the *Bundestag* at Parliament's invitation to represent the *Länder* of the former German Democratic Republic, had been participating in the Parliament's activities since March 1991 (OJ 1991 C106/3), though without the right to vote or stand for office.

[88] OJ 1993 L33/15.

[89] Written Question No 1210/92 by Mr Vandemeulebroucke (OJ 1993 C40/22); this article, proposed by the President of Parliament, was included amongst the Citizenship provisions as Art 8c in the version of the TEU agreed in December 1991, before being moved to Art 138a.

Conclusions

Of the institutional reforms considered above, those defining new and extended supervisory powers for the European Parliament, apart from the restriction *ratione materiae* on the right of petition, may be deemed to contribute most positively to the declared objectives of the Treaty on European Union. Properly exercised, these should assist the citizen in the pursuit of his Treaty-given rights, and improve the general level of respect for Community law, though in the long run the Court's decision in *Francovich* may prove to be more significant than the entire TEU in this regard.[87] The new provisions on electoral procedure, in themselves unexceptionable, have already proved, even before coming into force, a useful spur both to Parliament action and Member State acceptance of the necessity to reach a decision in this highly sensitive area. Each of these reforms can safely be considered a step in the right direction.

The same cannot be said with any conviction of the revision of the jurisdictional clauses. At best, these display a lack of courage and/or imagination, in simply writing into the Treaty the solutions reached by the Court of Justice at a given point of time on the basis of institutional necessity and the limited jurisdictional clauses of the EEC Treaty in its original form; at worst, they reflect an anti-Parliament bias,[88] in according Parliament, alone amongst the institutional actors of the Community, a restricted access to the judicial process. In either case, the tactic has proved itself inconvenient and short-sighted, as the caselaw of the Court has in the meantime evolved, in line with the needs of the Community of law, leaving the new provisions an embarrassing source of legal uncertainty.

It is hard to garner much enthusiasm for the reforms in the area of legislative procedure either. As a result, there will be no less than six different procedures for the adoption of primary legislation involving the European Parliament, being assent (two variants), negative assent (two variants), co-operation, and consultation, with a variety of other decision-making procedures excluding Parliament. It is also true to a certain extent that the degree of Parliament's participation is inversely proportional to the importance of the matter under discussion; negative assent for guidelines and action programmes, consultation on agricultural legislation. The Court has already had occasion to comment on the absence of coherent criteria in the choice of the degree of parliamentary participation in Community decision-making;[89] in a document which purports to create a European Union, this attachment to unnecessary procedural distinctions is elevated to an art form.

The provisions of the TEU on legislative procedure signally fail to tackle two of the most urgent and important institutional questions facing the Community/Union. In the first place, they exacerbate, rather than reduce, the

---

[90] Joined Cases C-6 & 9/90, judgment of 19 November 1991, due to be published at [1991] ECR I-5357.
[91] One influential commentator did not hesitate to qualify the Council's attitude in the *Comitology* case as 'prejudice'; Weiler, 'Pride and Prejudice – *Parliament* v *Council*' (1990) 14 EL Rev 334.
[92] Case 242/87 'Erasmus', *Commission* v *Council* [1989] ECR 1425 at 1453.

existing diffusion of political responsibility for the adoption of legislation between the Member States in Council, the Commission and Parliament, and add to the present opacity of the decision-making process. As a matter of principle, if an issue is legislative in character, then the elected representatives of the peoples should have a decisive, or co-decisive, say in its regulation.

Perhaps more important in terms of public acceptance of a European Union with extensive powers to regulate societal activity, and impinge upon the life of the citizen, the TEU ignores the problem of the accountability of the Council, which will retain the primary decisional power, even in those few cases where Parliament enjoys a veto. Though ministers may, theoretically, be considered indirectly accountable to their national parliaments, the Council as a body is politically accountable to no one. If it is not to be thought that the authors of the TEU, ministers and national officials, were seeking merely to transfer governmental powers from the ambit of national parliamentary scrutiny, the institutional reforms at least display a peculiar lack of vision as to how a well-functioning political entity should operate, and the proper role the parliamentary branch of government should play in such a system. In the words of Chief Justice Marshall, "[in] considering this question, we must never forget that it is *a constitution* we are expounding".[93]

KIERAN ST CLAIR BRADLEY[94]

---

[93] *McCulloch* v *Maryland*, 4 Wheat 316, (1819) 407.

[94] The views expressed are those of the Author and do not necessarily represent the views of the European Parliament.

Part 7

Common Foreign and Security Policy

Chapter 14
Common Foreign and Security Policy[1]

Introduction

It is obvious from the complex structure of the Treaty on European Union that legal issues and problems will arise. But seen from the standpoint of the government and particularly the Foreign Office, the UK intention is to make the Treaty work and to operate on the presumption that others share that aim. Put in more legal language the basic principle is *pacta sunt servanda*, *i.e.* "every Treaty in force is binding upon the parties to it and must be performed by them in good faith".[2] We may see some potential problems in the Treaty, gaps in the scheme, ambiguities or even contradictions. But, with a will, these things can all be overcome.

Anyway, history shows that predicting problem areas in EC Treaties is a very uncertain business. Immediately after the negotiation of the Single European Act it was thought that Article 100a(4) would cause major problems and lead to much caselaw but, so far, this has not been the case.[3] On the other hand, few in 1957 would have anticipated some of the legal issues which later arose from the Treaty of Rome, still less, perhaps, the way they were decided.

The Common Foreign and Security Policy (commonly abbreviated to CFSP), in particular, is an area where we should not expect legal problems. There are two main reasons for this, stated below.

History

Like European Political Co-operation (EPC) before it, the Common Foreign and Security Policy is largely a *codification of existing practice*. Political co-operation among the EC Member States has more or less continuously evolved over more than 20 years. EPC had been going at least, since the Luxembourg Report of 1970 (*i.e.* 15 years) before the Single European Act (SEA) first put it in Treaty form in Article 30.

The steps in the evolution until then were marked by successive reports and conclusions of European Councils, in Luxembourg in 1970, Copenhagen in 1973, London in 1981, and finally the Stuttgart Solemn Declaration of 1983. None of these were Treaty documents. But, by the time the SEA Article 30 came to be written in 1985, there was a substantial history and practice which, basically, it codified.

---

[1] Crown Copyright 1993. Reproduced by permission of the Controller of HMSO. The views expressed are those of the author, and do not necessarily represent the views of the UK Government.
[2] Vienna Convention on the Law of Treaties, Art 26.
[3] Case C-41/93, *France* v *Commission*, is the first such case to reach the Court of Justice.

Since 1985 European Political Co-operation has continued to develop. There are very many common positions already agreed. Some, *e.g.* on the Middle East, have stood for years. The concept of joint action is newly codified in CFSP. But, in reality the Member States already act jointly on many issues, and some of these actions fit the joint action criteria, *e.g.* some action on the former Yugoslavia. The Political Committee (PoCo), composed of the political directors of the Foreign Offices of each Member State and a Commission representative and performing a similar function to that of COREPER under the Community Treaties, has taken on an increasingly active role. There is co-ordination on many more subjects. Working Groups on a variety of issues *e.g.* geographical (Africa, Asia, etc) UN, Disarmament, human rights, non-proliferation, Consular, Public International Law – have proliferated. Co-ordination, on the spot, at international conferences and in international organizations is the norm. And Member States treat themselves as though bound by common positions even though that is not formally what the SEA requires. As an example of the level of activity, during the UK Presidency, 35 démarches on human rights in third countries were made in the name of the Community and its Member States.

So though the CFSP articles are a very important new Treaty basis for political co-operation, the changes, in terms of procedure, are less significant than they may appear. The changes, in terms of scope, are, however, significant.

Legal character

Like EPC, CFSP remains intergovernmental in character rather than coming within the EC Treaty structure. Its products will not be instruments of Community law in the sense of Article 189, nor even Member State conventions as in Title VI (Article K.3), but common positions and joint action.

The role of the Commission as watchdog and enforcer[4] is absent, as is the jurisdiction of the Court of Justice.[5] So, inherently the mechanisms for pursuing *legal* routes to problem-solving are absent and other routes of a more traditional kind are likely to be taken. I will return to this later.

If, for these reasons of history and legal character, it is right to anticipate fewer legal problems in the implementation of the Common Foreign and Security Policy than may arise elsewhere in the Treaty, that does not lessen the legal interest.

Analysis[6]

Before making a comparison between the CFSP and EPC, and discussing some legal issues of interest, a brief survey of the CFSP provisions is instructive.

Article J.1 sets out the basic obligation on the Union and its Member States: "to define and implement common foreign and security policy, governed by the provisions of this Title and covering all areas of foreign and security policy".

---

[4] Art 155 EC.

[5] Art L TEU.

[6] See also Cremona, "The Common Foreign and Security Policy of the European Union and the External Relations Powers of the European Community", in this volume, 247.

There follow very broad objectives, and a statement of the two ways in which those objectives are to be pursued, through co-operation under Article J.2 and joint action under Article J.3. This is a new distinction. Although joint action is mentioned in EPC,[7] it is mentioned as an aspect of co-operation rather than a distinct concept. Article J.1(4) contains a broad general obligation on the Member States, phrased both positively and negatively, to support the CFSP and refrain from undermining it:

"They shall refrain from any action which is contrary to the interests of the Union or likely to impair its effectiveness as a cohesive force in international relations".

It is "for the Council to ensure that these principles are complied with".

Article J.2 is basically EPC-style co-operation, the product of which is common positions. But, unlike EPC, it is cast in mandatory form: "Member States *shall* inform and consult one another", and "whenever it deems necessary the Council *shall* define a common position".[8] The decision whether to define a common position is by unanimity, "The Council shall act unanimously, except for procedural questions and in the case referred to in Article J.3(2)".[9] Any common position adopted is to be upheld in international conferences and organizations (the special case of the UN Security Council is dealt with in Art J.5).

Article J.3 sets out the new procedure on joint actions. It is for the Council to decide, on the basis of guidelines from the European Council, that a matter should be the subject of a joint action. This again is by unanimity.[10] It will, also by unanimity, set out the specific scope, general and specific objectives, and, if necessary, duration, means, procedures and conditions for implementation. Implementation may be by qualified majority voting but the decision on that must itself be taken by unanimity. The Member States are then committed to follow the joint action in the conduct of their national foreign policy: Paragraph 4 says "joint actions shall commit the Member States in the positions they adopt and in the conduct of their activity". This should prevent the effectiveness and coherence of agreed positions being undermined by sudden unilateral action by an individual Member State. But there are safeguards: Article J.3(6) provides for Member States to act nationally in cases of urgency, provided they have regard to the general objectives of the joint action and inform partners immediately afterwards. There is also provision for review, if circumstances change,[11] and for adoption of special solutions for particular Member States that have major difficulties in implementing a joint action.[12]

Article J.4 is about defence and security. The reference to defence is one of the important differences between CFSP and EPC. The latter was basically about foreign and security policy, (Art 30.6), but not defence. All questions of security of the Union are included in the CFSP as are "the eventual framing of a

---

[7] Arts 30.2(c) and 3(c) SEA.
[8] Author's italics.
[9] Art J.8(2) TEU.
[10] *Ibid.*
[11] Art J.3(3) TEU.
[12] Art J.3(7) TEU.

common defence policy which might in time lead to a common defence". These words were much fought over. Some wanted to go further, faster; others were dubious about including defence at all. The compromise is that it is there but a long way off. Any common defence policy, and a common defence would of course require the consent of all Member States.

By Article J.4(2) it is the WEU that will be responsible for elaborating and implementing decisions and actions of the Union which have defence implications. The WEU aspects and its role are fleshed out in two declarations of those Member States who were at the time also Members of WEU, which were adopted by the Maastricht Conference and are set out in its Final Act. States that are Members of the Union are invited to become members of the WEU.

Joint action will *not* be available for issues having defence, as opposed to purely security, implications[13] (*e.g.* co-operation in disarmament conferences). There are two important provisos: first, the CFSP must be compatible with the NATO Treaty and respect the position of particular Member States in relation to that Treaty. This second point was included primarily for Ireland, which is the sole Member State not a Member of NATO, but also covers the special French position in NATO. Secondly, bilateral co-operation in the framework of WEU and NATO is not excluded – this would include, *e.g.* the European Corps (composed of French, German and, now Belgian Units). This article is subject to specific review in the 1996 Inter-Governmental Conference (but, in fact, under Art J.10 the whole of Title V will be reviewed then).

Article J.5 is about representation. The basic rule remains that the Presidency (not, as in EC external policy, the Commission) represents the Union and *in principle* will present the Union's positions in international organisations and international conferences. But, Article J.5(4) includes an important exception for conferences where not all Member States are represented. In that case those that are represented must keep the others informed. This is also to be the case in the specific example of the United Nations Security Council. Permanent members of the UNSC (who are not named) undertake to ensure the defence of the positions and interests of the Union, but "without prejudice to their responsibilities under the provisions of the UN Charter". This is an important and specific proviso (see below).

Article J.6 provides for co-operation among diplomatic and consular missions of Member States and Commission delegations in third countries and international conferences. There may even (though the article does not require this) be joint missions or missions sharing facilities; some are already planned, *e.g.* at Abuja in Nigeria and in some of the Republics of the former Soviet Union.

Article J.7 provides for consultation with the European Parliament on the main aspects and basic choices of the CFSP and for regular information to the EP on the development of the policy. Questions may be asked of the Council and recommendations given to it and the EP is to hold an annual debate on progress in implementing CFSP.

Article J.8 is about institutional procedures. The *European Council* defines the principles and gives general guidelines.

---

[13] Art J.4(3) TEU.

The *Council of Ministers* takes the decisions defining and implementing CFSP and ensuring consistency of the Union's action, *i.e.* across the board of the Community Pillar and CFSP. The voting rule is unanimity except for procedural questions and where it is (unanimously) decided under Article J.3(2) to allow qualified majority voting. Any Member State or the Commission has the right of initiative. The main official body serving the Council on CFSP matters is the Political Committee (PoCo); both in providing input and in monitoring implementation, but the position of COREPER as the normal channel of preparation of Council business is safeguarded.

Article J.9 gives the position of the Commission; it is the same as in EPC, *i.e.* it is "fully associated" with the work carried out in CFSP.

Article J.10 is a general review clause. All Title V will be reviewed in 1996, not just Article J.4.

Article J.11 applies to CFSP many of the Treaty of Rome's "nuts and bolts" articles on the composition and procedures of the institutions – a change required because of the participation of the European Community institutions. But articles related to EC powers (*e.g.* Art 155) are omitted. As for the budget, *administrative* expenditure is charged on the Community budget, – see also Article 199 EC as amended at Maastricht. As for *operational* expenditure, it may be charged either, on the Community budget or to the Member States in accordance with a key to be decided. This reflects practice: the cost of the monitors in Yugoslavia was divided on a key based on GDP, with the Commission paying for its monitors.

Declarations

I have already mentioned the WEU Declarations. There are four others relevant to CFSP. First, on voting: where unanimity is required, Member States will try to avoid preventing adoption if a qualified majority exists. This reflects the existing practice of striving towards consensus. Secondly, the division of work between COREPER and PoCo and the Secretariat's arrangements are for later examination. Thirdly, the use of languages is to be in accordance with the rules of the European Communities and there are specific agreements on COREU communications and texts for the European Council, the Council of Ministers and for publication. The precise application of these rules, in practice, to the rather different working methods of the CFSP will probably be one of the harder issues on which to reach agreement. Lastly, there is a Declaration on Dependent Territories (see below).

Comparison with the EPC

The main differences are:

(1) *A strengthened commitment to common positions*. Contrast Article J.2 "Member States shall ensure that their national positions conform to the common positions" with Article 30.2(b) SEA. "The determination of common positions shall

constitute a point of reference for the policies of the High Contracting Parties." Similarly contrast Article J.1(4) "Member States shall support CFSP and shall refrain from action impairing its effectiveness" (reminiscent of Art 5 EC) with Article 30 SEA "The High Contracting Parties shall endeavour to avoid impairing . . . ."

(2) *Full coverage of security issues* and provision for the eventual framing of a common defence policy which might in time lead to a common defence.

(3) *Strengthening of the co-operation procedure* to include development of the concept of joint action and the procedure for defining which issues are to be subject to joint action and how that will be implemented.

(4) *Moving from High Contracting Parties language to using the EC institutions.* The Commission, European Parliament and European Council played a role before: but the Council's involvement as the main executive body is an important change – a part of the single institutional structure which links the pillared structure of Maastricht.

From the legal point of view the most obvious and significant change is from the language of *endeavour*, in EPC, to the language of *obligation*, in CFSP. In practice this may not be so significant. Member States have regarded themselves as committed by common positions. And it remains the case that nothing will fall either under co-operation (common position) or joint action unless unanimously agreed.

Legal Issues

Single institutional structure: what will it mean?

Articles C and E of the Opening Provisions set out the concept of the single institutional structure which applies throughout the Treaty on the Union. But it is made clear by Article E that the institutions operate by different rules in the Community Treaties on the one hand and the intergovernmental sections on the other:

"The European Parliament, the Council, the Commission and the Court of Justice shall exercise their powers under the conditions and for the purposes provided for, *on the one hand*, by the provisions of the Treaties establishing the European Communities and of the subsequent Treaties and Acts modifying and supplementing them and, *on the other hand*, by the *other* provisions of this Treaty".[14]

The "other provisions" are primarily those of Titles V and VI.

Role of institutions

The Commission is "fully associated" with CFSP[15] as it was with EPC.[16] That does not make it a full participant on an equal basis with the Member States,

---

[14] Author's italics.
[15] Art J.9 TEU.
[16] Art 30.3(b) SEA.

nor the sole executive. The main point is to ensure consistency with the Community action, where the Commission *is* the executive. The Commission also now has an explicit, but shared, right of initiative; but no watchdog role. The European Parliament too has a very similar role as it had in EPC, *i.e.* consultative. As for the European Council (which is *not* a Community institution), its position is now spelled out, but in practice, is the same as in the EPC, *i.e.* the source of general guidelines.

The main change is the involvement of the Council in the executive role performed in EPC solely by the Member States as such. It will, however, not operate as it does under the EC Treaties, and in particular will not adopt legislation. Again the main purpose is to ensure consistency between action under CFSP and under the Community Treaties. A by-product will be an increasing role for the Council Secretariat, into which the existing EPC Secretariat will be subsumed as a special autonomous division under the Secretary General, but reporting to the Presidency. In practical terms this will be an important development. For example, the intention is that the small existing EPC Secretariat should be expanded to a full complement directorate staff of 24. In most cases they would, as now, be seconded diplomats. But obviously the scale of operations and the expertise available will change substantially. (See below on *legal advice*).

Enforcement

The jurisdiction of the Court of Justice over the Treaty on Union is set out in Article L. It gives the Court no jurisdiction over Title V. It is important to note that this is not new, as the same basic exclusion of jurisdiction over intergovernmental action is contained in the SEA.[17] But the Court *does* have jurisdiction over all the final provisions, Articles L-S, which include Article M.[18] Article M safeguards the European Community Treaties and the Acts amending them from being affected by any part of the Maastricht Treaty other than Titles II, III and IV. So Title V, the CFSP Title, cannot affect the Community Treaties, and if any attempt is made under Title V to do so, *that* can be taken to the Court. The *effect* is that the Court can and must police the borderline between the Community pillar and CFSP. Thus, if the Council were to purport to adopt a joint action on GATT, making the Presidency the representative in the GATT, the Commission could take that to the Court. But matters internal to the CFSP are outside the Court of Justice's jurisdiction, so, for example, no Member State can be sued for failure to abide by a common position. The basic method of enforcement in the CFSP is political pressure – J.1(4) "The Council shall ensure these principles are complied with".[19] What about a situation where a CFSP decision was relevant to an EC measure – *e.g.* under Article 228a? My expectation would be that the Court would take the CFSP act as a given (like a matter

---

[17] Art 31 SEA.
[18] Comparable to Art 32 SEA.
[19] Art J.1(4) TEU.

of foreign law) and proceed to use it as necessary to resolve the Community sanctions measure, but *without* ruling on the validity, or any other aspect of the CFSP act.

Is CFSP justiciable in the International Court of Justice?

In theory, at least, the answer is "Yes" (provided the other conditions for the ICJ to have jurisdiction were fulfilled).

Title V creates Treaty obligations binding in international law but not Community law, outside the jurisdiction of the ECJ. But it is difficult to see a situation where Member States were taking one another to the ICJ over CFSP breaches and the Union could still be said to be functioning, in any real sense. Those asking this question seem to equate justiciability before a particular tribunal with binding character. The two are distinct. We are all familiar with the situation where a Treaty creates binding obligations, but it would be difficult to get a dispute in front of a Tribunal. It seems unlikely that Title V will give rise to cases in the ICJ.

Interface with EC

The basic rule is *consistency*, see Articles A and C. Article 228a is designed to clear up a long-standing problem; how the Community and its Member States are to give effect to sanctions, which pursue political ends by economic means. Present practice is based upon the Regulation on chemical precursors.[20] The effect was to require consensus for its adoption, not the qualified majority the Article 113 base would suggest. It was always in doubt what the Court would make of that *ad hoc* arrangement. Article 228a clarifies the position and provides a specific power for Community action (by qualified majority) to give effect to common positions or joint action agreed (by unanimity) in CFSP. As a result, Article 113 will no longer need to be used in such circumstances.

UNSC: position of permanent members

I have already outlined this position in relation to Article J.5. The obligation on the Members of the Security council who are also Members of the Community is to "concert", *i.e.* among themselves, and "to keep the other Member States fully informed". In both respects this is already the practice. The Permanent Members are also to ensure, in the execution of their functions, the defence of the positions and interests of the Union. This too reflects practice: throughout the history of EPC since the Single European Act, I am not aware of any occasion where the United Kingdom has not, in the Security Council, followed and upheld common positions of the Twelve where such existed. The interesting *caveat* is that this obligation is "without prejudice to the responsibilities of the

---

[20] Reg 428/89 (OJ 1989 L50/1).

Permanent Members under the provisions of the UN Charter". For obvious reasons I would not want to put any precise limits on the meaning of this proviso. But at least one important responsibility under the Charter is that in Article 24, where the UN Members confer on the Security Council primary responsibility for the maintenance of international peace and security "in order to ensure prompt and effective action by the United Nations". It is conceivable that there might be insufficient time to go back for a further CFSP decision if the requirement for prompt and effective action demanded a departure from a common position to accommodate the views of the other UNSC members and get action moving. In such a situation UN considerations would prevail over the European ones. This corresponds, in any case, to the position under Article 103 of the UN Charter. However, this is likely to be a very unusual situation. The important and interesting thing is that the exception was agreed in the text of the Treaty.

Declaration on Dependent Territories

This Declaration is expressed to apply generally, not only to CFSP, but the latter is probably one of its most likely applications. It is based upon a Joint Declaration of the Council, the Commission and those Member States with Dependent Territory interests. The Joint Declaration was agreed in 1989, to settle issues which had arisen in relation to voting rules at international conferences, where a Member State with Dependent Territories to represent might find that the interests of those dependencies conflicted with those of the Community. The classic instance, that the Declaration was designed to deal with, arises under the Washington Convention on Endangered Species, where some Dependent Territories have interests which may differ from those of the metropolitan state or the Community as a whole, *e.g.* in relation to species indigenous to them and which they might wish to continue to farm. A special procedure was agreed in that Declaration so that the Member States concerned could continue, in such exceptional cases, to represent the interests of their dependencies.

A similar idea was followed in the current Maastricht Declaration. If, in exceptional circumstances, divergences arise between the interests of the Union and those of overseas countries and territories, and efforts to find a solution fail, the Conference agreed that the Member State concerned may act separately in the interests of the country concerned without this affecting the Community's interests. The sort of case where this might conceivably occur would be where there was a common policy towards China, and Hong Kong's interests differed.

This is not a likely situation, but if it happened, then the Declaration would apply. It is of some interest that the definition of the dependencies concerned is so framed that it does not cover the UK's European dependencies, the Channel Islands and the Isle of Man and Gibraltar. This is because the prospect of such European territories having interests significantly divergent from those of the United Kingdom, so as to justify exceptional treatment by this means, was considered remote.

Denmark and defence

Defence was one of the major issues in the first Danish Referendum campaign in 1992 and it was apparent that misconceptions about the obligations undertaken (that it would lead to conscription into a European army, etc) played a fairly large part in the "No" vote. This was therefore one of the issues which the Danish Government wanted to resolve. The solution, at Edinburgh, in the Decision of the Member States reached at the European Council (which is a binding international Agreement) was to emphasise that the responsibility for implementing the defence aspects of CFSP fell on WEU, at which Denmark is an Observer, but not a member, (though of course, it is a staunch member of NATO). The section in the Decision on Defence Policy accordingly records that Denmark "does not participate in the elaboration and implementation of decisions and actions of the Union which have defence implications, but will not prevent development of closer co-operation between Member States in this area". The effect of this is to emphasise the effective exclusion of Denmark *already* from the implementation of any defence policy by the terms of the Treaty *as it stands*. But that is a very important matter domestically and it was of the utmost importance to the Danish Government that the other Member States concurred in, and endorsed, their view of the situation.

Does the Union have legal personality?

The Union will be *sui generis*. It is not like any other organization. It can best be described as an association of Member States which, for certain purposes and in certain ways described in the Treaty, act in common. It acts through its components, namely the Community on the one hand and the Member States acting inter-governmentally under CFSP and co-operation on justice and home affairs on the other.

The main reasons for concluding that the Union does not enjoy legal personality are:

(1) There is no provision in the Treaty on European Union similar to Article 210 of the Treaty of Rome, which expressly says that the Community shall have legal personality.

(2) Various functions that you would expect the Union to exercise, if it did have such personality, are in fact exercised by the Community, *e.g.* all the provisions on concluding external treaties are in the Community Treaty and provide for the Community to conclude such Treaties. There are no such powers given to the Union, in CFSP or elsewhere. Similarly, citizenship is in the Community section.

(3) The evidence of the (unpublished) *travaux préparatoires*: there was a clear intention during negotiations *not* to confer legal personality. The question was raised, and the Dutch Presidency said firmly that the Union would not have legal personality. They were supported by the Director General of the Council Legal Service. The Director General of the Commission Legal Service has taken the same view in evidence to the European Parliament.

Legal advice to the Political Committee

Recent events have increasingly shown the need for speedy and expert advice for PoCo and for Ministers. As EPC has grown in its scope and breadth of activities, inevitably issues of international law arise – a prime example is that of the recognition of states, following the break up of the Soviet Union and Yugoslavia. There are various existing sources of advice on public international law within the EPC structure. There is an Ad Hoc Working Group on Public International Law, which at the moment meets relatively infrequently, but at a very senior level. There will of course also be the legal advisers to the various Foreign Offices from whom the Political Directors come, and no doubt the Commission Legal Service will advise the Commission representative. And, in the future when the Council Secretariat is involved, the Council Legal Service will be another and very valuable source of legal advice. Just how these various sources are to be articulated is a matter for further discussion. But it is an important question and one to which the United Kingdom is encouraging the Member States, meeting in Political Co-operation, to address their minds.

Conclusion

Like so much of the Treaty, the CFSP creates a procedural framework within which specific substantive issues can be treated. At this stage one can only say how the provisions came to be the way they are and how they were intended to operate. It remains to be seen if the developing practice bears out that intention. But I continue to hope and believe that *legal* problems (as opposed to political and practical ones) should be relatively rare.

M R EATON

Chapter 15

Foreign and Security Policy and the Implementation of the Requirement of "Consistency" under the Treaty on European Union

Despite the fact that by virtue of Article C of the Treaty on European Union (hereafter: TEU) the Union is served by a single institutional framework, a "dual" system of international relations continues to exist, consisting in part of the "supranational" European Community framework and in part of the co-operation on a still largely intergovernmental basis under the provisions concerning the Common Foreign and Security Policy (hereafter CFSP).[1] Apart from that, the Member States continue to be present individually on the international plane. Since decision-making is getting more complex, it is hardly surprising that "consistency" is made into a guiding principle governing the relations between the various actors concerned.

In this article some of the legal issues which may arise in connection with the requirement of consistency will be discussed, in particular the role of the institutions in bringing it about. First, the possible scope of the foreign and security policy envisaged by the TEU will be examined. Secondly, the significance of the requirement of consistency will be investigated. Thirdly, an idea will be given of the role of the institutions in the achievement of this requirement.

Since these questions will be considered primarily from a legal viewpoint, this raises the preliminary issue as to which legal provisions may be relevant. The legal framework of the Union's Common Foreign and Security Policy is determined in the first place by the 12 articles (J-J.11) contained in Title V of the TEU, interpreted as the case may be in the light of the Declarations adopted by the Intergovernmental Conference and contained in its Final Act. These include Declaration No 27 on voting in the field of the CFSP, Declaration No 28 on practical arrangements in the field of the CFSP, Declaration No 29 on the use of languages and Declaration No 30 on Western European

---

[1] *Cf* Curtin, 'The constitutional structure of the Union: a Europe of bits and pieces' (1993) 30 CML Rev 17–69; Everling, 'Reflections on the structure of the European Union (1992) 29 CML Rev 1053–1077; Remacle, *La politique étrangère européenne: de Maastricht à la Yougoslavie*, Bruxelles (1992) at 20.

Union (WEU).[2] The European Council Decision concerning "certain problems raised by Denmark on the Treaty on European Union" is equally of interest since it declares the Danish "opt-out" of the defence implications of the CFSP to conform with the TEU.[3]

Titles II to IV and VI of the Treaty on European Union, relating to the Community framework and co-operation in the fields of Justice and Home Affairs do not as such apply to the CFSP, but they can be drawn upon where appropriate to establish the relationships among the three "pillars" of the Union.

Obviously, Title I (Common Provisions) and Title VII (Final Provisions) apply to the CFSP as well as to the Community framework and Justice and Home Affairs. It can be taken from the Final Provisions that the provisions of the Single European Act which relate to "European co-operation in the sphere of foreign policy" are repealed (Art P). European Political Co-operation (EPC) therefore ceases to exist.

The various "Reports"[4] which enshrine customary procedures set up to ensure the practical working of EPC subsist. However, they are not formal legal instruments like the TEU or its protocols, and unlike the Declarations mentioned above they cannot be drawn upon to interpret the TEU, because they are not referred to in the Final Act of the Intergovernmental Conference. The same is true for decisions and "Reports" adopted by the European Council after the Intergovernmental Conference, notably also at the Summit of Lisbon.[5]

The scope of the CFSP

The material scope of the CFSP is generously but vaguely described in Article J.1(1) TEU as "covering all areas of foreign and security policy". Article J.4(1) adds to this that it "shall include all questions related to the security of the Union, including the eventual framing of a common defence policy, which might in time lead to a common defence". As to what is to be understood by the notion of Foreign Policy, the TEU is silent.

The matter would be of relatively little importance if the objective of co-operation were merely the holding of voluntary exchanges of views, without the possibility of giving rise to further binding commitments. However, the co-operation in the field goes further than that. Under the Maastricht Treaty the Union and its Member States are to define and implement a CFSP which the Member States undertake to support "actively and unreservedly" (Arts J.1(1) and J.1(4)).

---

[2] In this Declaration the Conference notes two declarations by the Members of the Western European Union (Belgium, Germany, Spain, France, Italy, Luxembourg, the Netherlands, Portugal and the UK) on the role of the Western European Union and its relations with the European Union and NATO and on the accession of other Members of the European Union to the WEU.
[3] Edinburgh European Council, Bull EC 12–1992, pts I.37 and I.41.
[4] In particular the Luxembourg (1970), Copenhagen (1973) and London (1981) Reports and the Stuttgart (1983) Declaration, but also the Ministerial Declaration on the Practical Application of Certain Aspects of Title III of the Single European Act, which is intended to supplement them. Bull EPC, Doc 86/090.
[5] See below, n 24.

Not only have the Member States committed themselves to inform and consult one another within the Council on any matter of foreign and security policy of general interest (Art J.2).[6] So too the Council can define common positions to which national policies must conform (Art J.2(2)). In addition, such common positions must be upheld by Member States in international organizations in which they participate (Art J.2(3)).

Furthermore, in those areas in which the Member States have "important interests in common" (Art J.1(3)) the Council may decide that a matter of foreign and security policy should be the subject of "joint action". It is provided that "joint actions[7] shall commit the Member States in the positions they adopt and in the conduct of their activity" (Art J.3(4)). More so than common positions, joint actions impose a strict discipline[8] on the Member States, and in this context the Council may decide that certain decisions may be taken by majority (Art J.3).

Common positions and the decision to proceed by common action, in addition to containing political statements, might for example envisage the sending of observer missions or diplomats, the institutionalization of political dialogue with third countries, the use of economic instruments (financial aid, economic sanctions) for foreign policy aims,[9] the breaking off of diplomatic and other relations, and so on.[10] It is not provided which form common positions and decisions to proceed by common action might take, but one would assume that the Council would normally use a Declaration or other statement, and possibly a *sui generis* decision. Regulations and Directives in particular are reserved to the Community framework and should be used only to the extent that competence under the Community Treaties exists. Whether the Council will insist on a clear separation between Title V and Titles II-IV TEU cannot be predicted at this stage. If so, the Council would enact two different measures whenever both Community and CFSP competence is involved, for example in case of economic sanctions against third states. If not, it might sometimes adopt a comprehensive measure of a hybrid nature.

Foreign Policy

In determining what foreign policy is, obviously, traditional practices applying in the Member States will be of relevance. However, it is worth noting that the practices of the different Member States may vary, and also that the scope of a

---

[6] *Cf* Art J.5(4) TEU: 'common interest'.

[7] The term is used metaphorically and refers here to the decision to proceed by joint action.

[8] One difference between a decision to proceed by joint action and a common position may be that the former is a plan of action agreed in advance, whereas the latter is an *ad hoc* agreement in an area of Member State freedom subject to mutual information and co-operation only. Another difference is possibly, that a decision to proceed by joint action can not be implemented by non-action, whereas common positions can. Because as a rule a common position would not require positive action to be taken, conformity with a common position can also be obtained through non-action by a Member State. However, it can be taken from Art 228a ECT (*i.e.* EC Treaty as amended by TEU) that common positions can also provide for 'action' to be taken.

[9] The use of Community instruments is of course subject to the Community Treaties. But see the wording of Art 228a ECT quoted below, text accompanying n 43.

[10] Whether they might envisage the sending of a military task force depends on the future development of security policy. See below, under 'Security'.

"European" foreign policy need not be conceived as the equivalent of a national foreign policy. What foreign policy meant for co-operation purposes has in practice always been determined by (formal or informal) agreement or if one prefers, by compromise. The Maastricht Treaty brings no change in this respect. Unlike the Commission's proposals to the Intergovernmental Conference,[11] the TEU does not prescribe any fields in which a common policy is to emerge. Article J.1(3) provides that "joint action shall be *gradually implemented*", thereby suggesting a contained but continuous evolution. But this is confined to areas where the Member States have "important interests in common"; however vague that expression may be, it recognises the possibility of a given interest being of more importance to some Member States than to others. Consequently, where for instance a Member State enjoys special relations with certain parts of the world, it may well maintain its policies, the aim being to co-ordinate national action and to subject it to the requirement of political co-operation as set out in Article J.2 rather than to replace it by a unitary approach.

This being said, the political statements relating to a variety of foreign policy issues such as East-West relations, the Arab-Israeli conflict, human rights in the world, the situation in southern Africa and so forth, which have emanated from the EPC framework in accordance with the "customary procedures",[12] can be taken as examples of an emerging "European" foreign policy.

Furthermore, there have been statements, especially in form of replies to questions from the European Parliament, from which it can be taken that certain matters are not to be subject to common positions. To take a random example, when a parliamentary question was put about alleged telephone tapping (in the UK) of the Anti-Apartheid Group, it was stated on behalf of the Foreign Ministers that such a matter "does not come within the province of European political co-operation".[13] The often used phrase "does not come within the province of EPC" – or any other equivalent expression – means not merely that the subject has not been discussed in the framework of EPC, but rather that it comes outside its scope altogether. Although for the purpose of the Members of Parliament the result is the same (nothing is being done), the exclusion of a matter from the scope of EPC comes down to an at least half-way deliberate agreement, not to take a common position with regard to the matters at issue.

The same attitude was taken, for instance, with regard to a question concerning the free movement of nationals of Member States within the Community.[14]

---

[11] The Commission's proposal was, to consider a certain number of matters in the field of security (which were also included in the *Liste d'Asolo* adopted by the second Rome European Council) as vital interests with regard to which the Council, acting by majority, had to formulate the principles of a common policy. This included the control of armaments, disarmament and related questions, security questions related to the CSCE or debated in the UN, including peace-keeping operations, economic and technological co-operation and co-ordination of policy on arms exports and non-proliferation. In addition, an arms research and production policy was proposed. Art 13(1), Contributions by the Commission to the Intergovernmental Conference, Bull EC Supp 2/91 at 91.

[12] See *supra*, n 4.

[13] Bull EPC, Doc 85/142.

[14] Bull EPC, Doc 85/126.

Security in Northern Ireland is "outside the field of competence" of EPC.[15] Refugee status in the Community for Cypriots who fled from Northern Cyprus has "nothing to do" with EPC.[16] Finally, especially after it was agreed that European political co-operation could cover both political[17] and economic[18] aspects of security, it was frequently stated on behalf of the Foreign Ministers meeting in Political Co-operation that the military aspects of security were "outside the scope of European political co-operation".[19] As we shall see more in detail below, such a categorical exclusion would no longer be permitted under the TEU.

There are many more examples of statements concerning the scope of co-operation, since the Members of the European Parliament, undoubtedly led by other concerns, do not seem to care much for the subtleties of the scope of "European co-operation in the field of foreign policy". The patterns which emerge from the answers of the Foreign Ministers to the multifarious questions suggest that the criteria for excluding a matter from the scope of action of EPC can be of a substantive, geographical and instrumental nature. For example, a straightforward substantive criterion would apply with regard to military matters. A geographical or "third country" criterion would be used in order to exclude from political co-operation matters which concern only the relations between the Member States, although the Foreign Ministers have not always acted consistently in this respect.[20] Finally, one may detect the use of an instrumental criterion in those cases where EPC cannot act because it lacks the required instruments, such as the conclusion of a treaty, to which EPC is not empowered, or the imposition of economic sanctions which are governed by the EEC Treaty.[21] In the latter context it is worth noting that there is no scope for something like a "Community criterion": the fact that the Community also has powers in a particular field does not by itself prevent the Foreign Ministers from adopting a common standpoint.[22]

Taking into account that such delimiting statements emanate from the Member States in a field of their own sovereignty, one may assume that in principle they are fully retractable.[23] In other words, the notion of (common) foreign policy can be re-defined in accordance with the need for co-operation, and/or action under Title V of the TEU. The Maastricht Treaty, rather than specifying areas in which co-operation is required, refers generally to "any matter ... of general interest" (Art J.2) and any matter "of common interest" (Art

---

[15] Bull EPC, Doc 90/458.

[16] Bull EPC, Doc 85/176.

[17] This was first agreed in the London (1981) Report.

[18] This was agreed in the Stuttgart (1983) Declaration.

[19] *E.g.* Bull EPC, Doc 85/106. *Cf* Doc 90/079: military aspects of security 'do not come in the purview of European political cooperation'.

[20] See below under Justice and Home Affairs.

[21] *Cf* Bull EPC, Doc 90/159: 'levels of aid to be provided under the Community budget (to Eastern Europe and Latin America) are not a matter for political co-operation'.

[22] See also, *e.g.* Bull EPC, Docs 90/092 and 90/235. *Cf* Doc 89/289.

[23] It is to be noted that the fifth subpara of the first para of Art B ('maintain in full the *acquis communautaire* and build on it') does not seem to be applicable here. That expression is used to refer to the Treaties and the body of Community legislation adopted within their framework, and embodies the idea that newly acceding states will in principle be required to accept all those provisions *in integrum*.

J.5(4)). Similarly, the "gradual implementation" of joint action is left to the Council acting on the basis of guidelines provided by the European Council. The latter has already defined certain areas "open to joint action",[24] but how they will be implemented in practice remains to be seen.

Security

According to Article J.4(1) the CFSP shall include "security of the Union, including the eventual framing of a common defence policy, which might in time lead to a common defence". This is new, as it overcomes the artificial and unworkable distinction hitherto made between political and economic aspects of security on the one hand and military aspects of security on the other.[25] But it is not a truly decisive advance, since the phraseology has all the aspects of a compromise: the "eventual" framing of a common defence policy has a prospective character and in time it "might" lead to a common defence.[26] No great steps forward can therefore be expected to be taken in the near future.

It is worth noting in this context that the safeguard clause in Article J.4(4), laying down the respect for the specific character of the security and defence policy of certain Member States and for the obligations of certain Member States under NATO, may in fact already prohibit the framing of a common policy. The reference to the "specific character of the security and defence policy of certain Member States" would cater not only for the military (*i.e.* "hard security") neutrality pursued by the Irish Government[27] but also for the interests of candidate Member States like Austria, Sweden and Finland who equally have a neutral status. Such a status, if maintained, might well present an obstacle to a real defence policy of the Union.

In the short term this will not present major practical problems, since decisions and actions which have defence implications are a matter for the WEU. According to Article J.4(2) the Union is limited merely to requesting the WEU "to elaborate and implement decisions and actions" of the Union which have defence implications. At least until the expiry of the WEU Treaty in 1998 the WEU remains an organization separate from the European Union, and whether after that date it will become an integral part of the Union rather than just an integral part of its development (Art J.4(2)) is unlikely at this stage. To at least one scholar the continuation of the present separation of tasks would seem to present itself as a viable option in the case of the accession to the Union by further neutral states.[28]

---

[24] Report to the European Council in Lisbon on the likely development of the CFSP with a view to identifying areas open to joint action *vis-à-vis* particular countries or groups of countries. Bull EC 6/92 at 18–22.

[25] *Cf* Art 6(a) para 1 of the Single European Act.

[26] The formula was inserted essentially as a compromise between the advocates of a common defence (notably France) and those who wished to limit the competence of the Union to a common defence policy (in particular the UK).

[27] On this matter there is an, as yet, unpublished EUI conference paper by Patrick Keating, Trinity College, Dublin, entitled 'Ireland and Common Security: Stretching the Limits of Commitment'. (Conference of the European University Institute on 'The Community and the Member States and Foreign Policy: Coming Together or Drifting Apart?' Florence, 1–3 July 1993.)

[28] Regelsberger, 'Gemeinsame Aussen- und Sicherheitspolitik nach Maastricht – Minimalreformen in neuer Entwicklungsperspektive', (1992) 15 *Integration*, 83–93 at 88.

Should fusion between the WEU and the Union be the aim, one would probably have to convince the Irish Government to give up the whole of its neutrality and, by reference to the integration of WEU, make alliance a virtual requirement for accession. Surely, the alternative whereby neutral candidates for accession would be allowed (in accordance with Article O) to negotiate an opt-out as regards defence matters, would not fit easily with the objective of the Union under Article B paragraph 1 to "assert its identity on the international plane, in particular through the implementation of a common foreign and security policy including the eventual framing of a common defence policy, which might in time lead to a common defence".

Meanwhile, that is until such time when co-operation in defence policy implies also membership of WEU, the inclusion of military aspects of security introduced by the TEU and the framing of a common defence policy are merely matters of endeavour.[29] As regards the co-operation between Member States on political and economic aspects of security, the matter is possibly different. It can be taken from Article J.4(3) that if such aspects are not being dealt with by WEU, the procedures set out in Article J.3 for joint action may be used. In case of need, co-operation among Member States of the Union in the context of peace-keeping operations or operations under Chapter VII of the UN Charter might well take place, but this would be agreed in the framework of WEU rather than the Union, with non-Members of WEU possibly participating on an *ad hoc* basis.

Matters governed also by the other pillars of the Union

Although the CFSP is regulated in a separate Title, material overlaps exist between CFSP and co-operation on Justice and Home Affairs (JHA) as well as between CFSP and Community competence.

Like the CFSP, JHA is governed by a separate Title (Title VI, Art K), which suggests that it is in principle excluded from the field of CFSP. Thus, the creation of a separate form of intergovernmental co-operation should put an end to the practice which had emerged under the Single European Act whereby matters such as judicial co-operation, which do not in the first place concern relations with third states, were being dealt with by the Foreign Ministers. The international conventions concerning the transfer of sentenced persons,[30] the prohibition of double jeopardy[31] and the abolition of the legalization of documents between the Member States[32] are examples where matters of judicial co-operation were discussed and decided in the framework of EPC. Although the EPC structure and procedures undoubtedly presented a practical forum for

---

[29] *Cf* Stein, 'Gemeinsame europäische Aussen-, Sicherheits- und Verteidigungspolitik?', (1992) 43 *Politische Studien*, 66–81 at 80–81.

[30] Agreement on the Application, Among the Member States of the European Community, of the Council of Europe Convention on the Transfer of Sentenced Persons. Brussels, 25 May 1987. Bull EPC, Doc 87/232.

[31] Convention Between the Member States of the European Community on Double Jeopardy. Brussels, 25 May 1987. Bull EPC, Doc 87/231.

[32] Convention Abolishing the Legalization of Documents Between the Member States of the European Community. Brussels, 25 May 1987. Bull EPC, Doc 87/233.

discussion and framework for such co-operation, the matter is atypical as compared with the overall field of activity of EPC and its inclusion in this framework raises problems of transparency and co-ordination.[33]

Whereas the exclusion of JHA from the CFSP is therefore an improvement, nevertheless one is led to believe that the distinction between the second and the third pillar is not watertight.[34] For example, just as human rights in third countries are the subject of Political Co-operation whereas human rights in Member States are not, the CFSP might cover matters such as asylum policy or drug traffic prevention whenever policies of third countries are involved while the internal aspects come under JHA. Similarly, foreign policy aspects of terrorist threats could be dealt with under Title V[35] but not internal matters to fight them.

Yet the clearest example of overlap between the pillars is where CFSP requires the use of economic instruments which come within the competence of the Community. In such a case both action in the Community framework and under Title V would seem justified. As regards action by individual Member States, it is well known that this would be allowed only to the extent that it is compatible with the principle of exclusivity under Community law (See further below, under 'Organizational consistency', at 236).

The significance of the requirement of "consistency"

If one considers the possibility of overlaps between the pillars, and also the presence of the individual Member States on the international plane, it is not surprising that consistency is made into a guiding principle of the TEU. Three articles of the TEU are devoted to it:[36] Article A, third paragraph provides that:

"The task [[of the Union] shall be to organize, in a manner demonstrating *consistency* and solidarity, relations between the Member States and between their peoples."

Article C adds to this that:

"The Union shall be served by a single institutional framework which shall ensure the *consistency* and the continuity of the activities .... The Union shall in particular ensure the *consistency* of its external activities as a whole in the context of its external relations, security, economic and development policies. The Council and the Commission shall be responsible for ensuring such *consistency*. They shall ensure the implementation of these policies, each in accordance with its respective powers."

Within Title V, Article J.8(3) provides:

"The Council shall take the decisions necessary for defining and implementing the common foreign and security policy on the basis of the general guidelines adopted by the European Council. It shall ensure the unity, *consistency* and effectiveness of action by the Union."

---

[33] See further Nuttall, *European Political Cooperation* (1992) at 298.

[34] *Cf* Report of the Committee on Foreign Affairs and Security on Shaping the European Community's Common Foreign Policy. PE 201.471/fin, 23 October 1992.

[35] *Cf* Bull EPC, Doc 90/215: 'Foreign policy aspects of terrorist threats are dealt with in European political cooperation.'

[36] Author's italics.

As can be taken from these provisions (in particular Arts C and J.8(3)), the TEU is concerned most of all with material consistency: measures and actions taken must not conflict with one another. They must be compatible and ideally, they must be mutually reinforcing. The responsibility for ensuring such consistency is incumbent on the Council as far as the CFSP is concerned. The Commission also has a responsibility "in accordance with its ... powers". It should further be noted that, while Article C seems to govern consistency between the different pillars, Article J.8(3) may be deemed to regulate also inconsistency between action by the Union and action by the Member States. In so far as this aspect cannot be brought under the notion of consistency, it would in any case come under the requirement of "effectiveness" which is also contained in that article.

By comparison, the concept in the third paragraph of Article A would appear to be a more general requirement of consistency. Although this may well encompass the principle of material consistency set out above, it refers primarily to the manner in which relations are organised. This could entail for instance that measures must not be taken at will now in one structure and now in another decisional structure but as far as possible on the basis of a rational division of powers between institutions. In addition, Article A covers not only external but also "internal" activities. The kind of consistency referred to in Article A will hereafter be called "organizational consistency".

Material consistency

Apart from institutional arrangements which are important for the prevention of inconsistency and which will be considered below, the TEU contains several substantive provisions dealing more specifically with ruling out material inconsistency. They all concern the relations between the CFSP and action by the Member States.

Thus, it is provided that "Member States shall ensure that their national policies conform to the common positions" (Art J.2(2)). Member States "shall uphold the common positions in international organizations and in international conferences" (Art J.2(3)). "Joint actions shall commit the Member States in the positions they adopt and in the conduct of their activity" (Art J.3(4)).

There are also provisions which anticipate inconsistency by taking it into account before the Council takes a decision: "Should there be any major difficulties in implementing a joint action, a Member State shall refer them to the Council, which shall discuss them and seek appropriate solutions .... ." (Art J.3(7)). The common defence policy of the Union "shall respect the obligations of certain Member States under the North Atlantic Treaty and be compatible with the common security and defence policy established within that framework" (Art J.4(4)). These clauses may well be effective as regards the ruling out of material inconsistency, but, as set out in Section 1 above, possibly only at the cost of preventing the emergence of a common policy altogether.

Furthermore, "co-operation between two or more Member States on a bilateral level, in the framework of WEU and the Atlantic Alliance, . . . [should] not run counter to or impede that provided for in this Title" (Art J.4(5)). No sanctions have been provided for these and other obligations.

Perhaps the most interesting provision in this context is Article J.1(4), according to which "Member States shall support the Union's external and security policy actively and unreservedly. They shall refrain from any action which is contrary to the interests of the Union or likely to impair its effectiveness as a cohesive force in international relations . . . ." The reference to active and unreserved support for the Union's policy seems to exclude any direct control of the action of the Foreign Ministers by the national parliaments. From a democratic standpoint this may be difficult to accept, the more so as long as a democratic deficit exists on the European level (see below European Parliament, at 242).

The above provisions all concern the relations with the Member States. Nowhere is it provided that decisions in the framework of the Community shall be binding as regards decisions in the framework of the CFSP, or the reverse. Similarly, the relationship between decisions taken in the framework of JHA and activities in the field of CFSP is not explicitly regulated.

Organizational consistency

The TEU does not provide for organizational consistency. Overlaps may occur between the sphere of action under the different pillars, and also the remaining freedom of the Member States is not altogether clear.

It is necessary, therefore, to consider two principles which might bring about more clarity in the organization of the activities by ruling out activity by some of the actors involved: subsidiarity and exclusivity. Special contributions in this book are devoted to both principles and only the most pertinent aspects need to be discussed here.[37]

Subsidiarity, the principle according to which the Community shall act only if, and to the extent that, the objectives pursued cannot be as adequately attained by action of the Member States, could be based on the second paragraph of Article B: "The objectives of the Union shall be achieved . . . respecting the principle of subsidiarity as defined in Article 3b of the Treaty establishing the European Community". Title V of the Maastricht Treaty, unlike Title VI, does not contain an explicit reference to the principle.[38]

On a close reading of Article 3b of the ECT,[39] it appears first of all that the

---

[37] Toth, 'A legal analysis of subsidiarity', Steiner, 'Subsidiarity under the Maastricht Treaty', Emiliou, 'Subsidiarity: panacea or fig leaf?', Cremona, 'The common foreign and security policy of the European Union and the external relations powers of the EC' in the volume, 37, 49, 65, 247 respectively.

[38] In the context of JHA, Art K.3(2) TEU provides: 'The Council may . . . (b) adopt joint action in so far as the objectives of the Union can be attained better by joint action than by the Member States acting individually on account of the scale or effects of the action envisaged. . .'.

[39] Art 3b ECT provides: 'The Community shall act within the limits of the powers conferred upon it by this Treaty and of the objectives assigned to it therein.

In areas which do not fall within its exclusive competence, the Community shall take action, in accordance with the principle of subsidiarity, only if and in so far as the objectives of the proposed action principle of subsidiarity is intended to govern the relations between the Community and its Member States. Therefore, it cannot, *prima facie*, be used in relations between the pillars. Secondly, it is convenient to distinguish between a political relevance of the principle and its character as a justiciable concept. As regards the former, one can perhaps only be grateful that the Intergovernmental Conference did not include the principle in Title V, where it would seem out of place. In the sensitive area of foreign affairs, political discussions about effectiveness as a means of dividing power should be avoided.

As regards the justiciability of the principle, it should be noted that Article 3b ECT lays down certain criteria against which Community legislation can be marginally tested by the Court of Justice.[39] The question of the Court's jurisdiction, which is determining in this respect, will be examined further below.

What about the principle of exclusivity? There are basically two ways in which this principle may become relevant: first, in relations between the Community and the Member States, and secondly, in order to distinguish the position of the Council in the Community framework from that under Title V. In neither case it is clear which institution is to ensure that the principle is respected.

In accordance with the caselaw of the Court of Justice, the principle of exclusivity prevents the Member States from enacting legislation or entering into international agreements, *e.g.* on matters of the Common Commercial Policy or on fields where the Community has acted internally: only the Community can do so on the basis of its explicit or implied powers in the field of the Community's sphere of action. Because the TEU does not provide for the conclusion of international treaties by the Council in the framework of CFSP[41] the Member States would for the time being have to undertake treaty obligations on foreign policy matters themselves, for instance on the basis of a recommendation by the Council. If such commitments interfere with an exclusive power of the Community both the Council and the Member States might be in breach of an obligation under the Community Treaties.

Secondly, it is a corollary of the principle of exclusivity that whenever it is necessary to use trade policy instruments (such as economic sanctions) to achieve foreign policy objectives, the procedures prescribed for the Community framework have to be applied. In the past this problem tended to be resolved by "simultaneous" action by the Community and the Member States: thus, the

---

cannot be sufficiently achieved by the Member States and can therefore, by reason of the scale or effects of the proposed action, be better achieved by the Community.

Any action by the Community shall not go beyond what is necessary to achieve the objectives of this Treaty.'

[40] Thus, the Court of Justice could invalidate a Community act which does not deal with the question of subsidiarity in its statement of reasons.

[41] *Cf* the contributions by the Commission to the Intergovernmental Conference, Bull EC Supp 2/91 at 94, Art Y25, where it is proposed that the Council should be able to conclude international agreements also in the field of CFSP.

Member States would reach an agreement on the political aspects in Political Co-operation and trade measures would be established in the Community framework. The concentration of the decision-making power in the Council may perhaps bring along greater efficiency in this respect, but again, no greater clarity as to the organizational division of tasks.

The role of the institutions

The TEU mentions the Council and, in secondary place, the Commission as having responsibility for ensuring consistency. However, since the relations within the Union are of a growing complexity, one may doubt whether it is realistic to assume that they could achieve this task alone. Rather, the co-operation of all the institutions and also of the Member States is important in order to avoid frictions.

European Council

The European Council, composed of Heads of State or Government and the President of the Commission and assisted by the Ministers of Foreign Affairs and another Member of the Commission, defines the principles and general guidelines for the CFSP (Art J.8(1)). The European Council has no specific responsibility for ensuring consistency in the definition and implementation of the policies, but *de facto* its role will be extremely important, because it acts as the supreme director of the activities pursued under the different pillars. In terms of Article D, the European Council provides the Union with the impetus for its development and defines the general policy guidelines thereof. In addition, the requirement in the same article to inform the European Parliament is of some importance as a basis for a sound inter-institutional dialogue.[42]

Council

By virtue of the TEU, CFSP is officially brought within the ambit of the Council. This is more than just an affirmation of the practice of the Foreign Ministers discussing EPC matters at the occasion of their monthly General Affairs Council, since the Council can now decide in its capacity as Council, and the custom of meeting in the capital of the country of Presidency rather than in Brussels or Luxembourg is also disposed of. Only the informal Gymnich-type meetings may still be held in other places.[43]

The habit of meeting in the framework of the European institutions will

---

[42] On European Parliament, see below p 242–244.

[43] Regelsberger, *supra*, n 28 at 90. Gymnich-type meetings are meetings between the Foreign Ministers held over the weekend once during each Presidency. Arranged in an informal setting in the country of Presidency, they are called after Schloss Gymnich near Bonn where in 1974 the first such meeting took place. Because the proceedings are informal, no decisions are taken and no official record is made. See further Nuttall, *supra*, n 33 at 15.

stimulate co-operation between the Member States. Within the Council the Member States inform one another on matters of foreign and security policy (Art J.2(1)). The Council defines common positions (Art J.2(2)) and decides joint action (Art J.3(1)). Furthermore, the Council adopts practical arrangements in connection with the WEU (Art J.4(2)). More generally, the Council takes the decisions for defining and implementing the CFSP on the basis of guidelines from the European Council (Art J.8(2)). The Council can act swiftly, at least in theory: it is provided that the Presidency can convene an extraordinary session at the request of the Commission or a Member State (Art J.8(4)).

The concentration of the decision-making power in one single institution also furthers consistency between the pillars. In order to be consistent, it would seem, the Council only has to take non-conflicting decisions under the different Titles of the TEU. Yet because this does not come about automatically, inter-institutional collaboration will be required.

What would happen, for instance, if the Council decided under Title V on the desirability of applying economic sanctions and the Commission, acting in the Community framework, refused to introduce the necessary proposals to bring them about? This matter is governed by Article 228a ECT:

"Where it is provided, in a common position or in a joint action adopted according to the provisions of the Treaty on European Union relating to the common foreign and security policy, for an action by the Community to interrupt or to reduce, in part or completely, economic relations with one or more third countries, the Council shall take the necessary urgent measures. The Council shall act by a qualified majority on a proposal from the Commission."[44]

Although the text of the article would suggest that the Commission would be under an obligation to submit such a proposal, this cannot be pursued upto the point where the Commission's exclusive right of initiative in the field of the Common Commercial Policy is reduced to a mere formality. Since such a situation would in fact amount to a political deadlock, it must be avoided in an early stage. In particular, full advantage must be taken from the association of the Commission with foreign policy activity.

Problems of this type will not arise in the relations between Title V and Title VI, because unlike under the ECT, the Commission does not have an exclusive right of initiative under Title VI (Art K.3(2)).

Finally, there are no provisions on the Ministerial composition of the Council. Within the Community framework, the composition of the Council changes according to the subject involved. If this principle is applied to the CFSP the Council would be composed most often by the Ministers of Foreign Affairs,[45] but other compositions and maybe even "joint Councils" are not prohibited by the Treaty.[46]

---

[44] *Cf* Art 73g ECT.

[45] Regelsberger, *supra*, n 28 at 90.

[46] This would of course challenge the customary practices, *supra*, n 4, and it could re-open an old battle between Foreign and other Ministries. See George, *Politics and Policy in the European Community*, 2nd ed (1991) at 221.

Preparatory institutions

At the level "below" the Council no merger is prescribed by the TEU. Both the Committee of Permanent Representatives (COREPER) and the Political Committee continue to exist. By virtue of Article 151 ECT (Art 30 ECSC, Art 121 EAEC) COREPER is responsible for the preparation of the work of the Council. This would include the drafting of the Agenda and the co-ordination of the Council's working groups. Within the Community, COREPER's role has always been important because it is the institution where agreements are worked out on matters to be decided by the Council. The Political Committee, composed of Political Directors, at present fulfils a similar role in the context of EPC. The TEU provides with regard to this Committee that it monitors the international situation, contributes to the definition of policies by delivering opinions to the Council and surveys the implementation of the policies (Art J.8(5)).

The division of work between the two committees was not agreed at the Intergovernmental Conference, but a Declaration[47] provides for "practical arrangements" to be taken both with respect to this matter and with respect to the merger between the Secretariat of EPC and the General Secretariat of the Council. According to the same Declaration the relations between the Commission and the latter would also be dealt with. As regards the two Committees, it is possible that they will hold joint sessions or their Presidents will meet together with a representative of the Commission.

The General Affairs Council is at present considering the consequences to be drawn from the TEU as regards the work of all the committees provided by the Treaties (including also, for example, the Co-ordinating Committee provided for by Article K.4), the organization of the General Secretariat and the functioning of the Council itself. Obviously, the fusion of the Committees as well as the Secretariats (and the working groups, where appropriate) would have the advantage of organizational simplicity and transparency. However, since a fusion of COREPER and the Political Committee is not envisaged by the TEU, it remains to be seen to what extent these Committees will be involved in the decision-making in the context of CFSP. The European Parliament denounces the current division of responsibilities as being detrimental to the transparency required in the relations between the Council and Parliament.[48]

Commission

Title V does not specifically charge the Commission with responsibility for ensuring consistency of external relations activity, but it follows from Article C that the Commission has a responsibility of its own "in accordance with its ... powers".

According to Article J.9, the Commission is "fully associated" with the work carried out in the CFSP field. This is not new, as in practice the Commission

---

[47] Declaration No 30 attached to the Final Act.

[48] *Cf* Report of the Committee on Foreign Affairs and Security on Shaping the European Community's Common Foreign Policy. PE 201.471/fin, 23 October 1992.

has been associated with EPC ever since the London (1981) Report.[49] There are many ways in which the Commission takes part in matters of foreign policy. In particular, officials of the Secretariat-General's Directorate entitled "Inter-governmental co-operation between Member States, including European political co-operation" represent the Commission in the various EPC bodies below the ministerial level (Political Directors, working groups, EPC Secretariat). In addition, the Commission interacts effectively with the European Parliament on matters of Foreign Affairs. Commissioners take part in Parliament's debates and Commission representatives attend meetings of the pertinent parliamentary committees.[50]

The role of the Commission has always been influential in EPC for several reasons. It was able to fulfil a co-ordinating role between the Council and the EPC meetings, which were not only held at different places, but also attended by different people. Since initially there was no EPC Secretariat, the Commission could secure continuity, and this in a better way than the rotating country of Presidency. Not only had the Commission a valuable, standing body of expertise, it was also in a better position to spot overlaps and, if necessary, to guide a meeting away from making decisions that were incompatible with those already made elsewhere.

In recent years the Commission has played an important role in the relations with Eastern Europe, which is natural because the ex-Communist countries depend on institutionalised relations with the Community for their economic development and the Community has a clear interest in the stabilization of the region. Although the so-called "Europe Agreements" fall squarely within Community competence, the objectives of co-operation are most likely to be successful if the foreign policies of the Member States are like-minded. Thus, the Commission encouraged common standpoints in this area by seeking support for Community policy.

According to the TEU, the Commission is associated with the tasks of the Presidency when it represents the Union, in particular in international organizations and international conferences, and it is associated in the tasks of the "Troika" (Art J.5). The Commission delegations in third countries and international conferences co-operate with the diplomatic and consular missions of the Member States. In international organizations the representatives of the Commission and the Member States also collaborate (Art J.6). Yet the fact that it is the Presidency who represents the Union on matters of CFSP is likely to meet with criticism, not least because, in view of the representative functions of the Commission under the Community Treaties, the division of competence will not always be clear.

The most powerful tool of the Commission is its newly created formal right of

---

[49] See generally Nuttall, 'Where the Commission comes in', in: Pijpers, Regelsberger, Wessels (eds), *European Political Cooperation in the 1980s: a Common Foreign Policy for Western Europe,* (1988) 104–117.
[50] For instance, since January 1993 the new Commissioner for CFSP attends meetings of the Committee on Foreign Affairs and Security. Other Commission representatives attend the Committee on External Economic Relations and the Committee on Development and Co-operation.

initiative with regard to matters of CFSP, which it shares with the Member States (Art J.8(3)). It may also request the Presidency to convene an extraordinary meeting of the Council.

In order to cope with the increasingly demanding tasks incumbent on it, the Commission, in anticipation of a growing co-operation in matters of foreign affairs, has embarked on significant changes in its organization. Thus, Mr Hans van den Broek is the first Commissioner charged specifically and exclusively with CFSP, and a new Directorate-General has recently been created to deal specifically with the matters concerned (DG IA, Common Foreign and Security Policy). It is this new infrastructure which will have to make sure that the Commission makes most of its right of initiative and which will play an important role of achieving consistent and effective policies.

European Parliament

The powers of the European Parliament fall short of what that organ itself had wanted to obtain in the field of foreign and security policy. Parliament had wanted to approve the "important interests in common" that would be defined by the European Council. It had wanted to be associated with the definition of the common foreign and security policy, monitor its application, and dispose of a right of veto over the use of force.[51]

Participation by European Parliament under Title V is mainly regulated in two provisions: directly in Article J.7 and indirectly in Article J.11.

By virtue of Article J.7 the European Parliament is to be "consulted" by the Presidency on "the main aspects and basic choices of the common foreign and security policy". Both the Presidency and the Commission must keep Parliament regularly informed of the development of the foreign and security policy. Parliament may ask questions of the Council or make recommendations to it. It shall hold an annual debate on progress in implementing the CFSP.

Article J.11(1) declares applicable (a.o.) the provision in Article 140 ECT which states that the Commission is to reply to questions by the European Parliament or its Members. This can be taken to mean that the Commission should respond to such questions even if they deal purely with matters of foreign policy. The Council is heard in accordance with the conditions laid down in its rules of procedure (Art 140, paragraph 4 ECT).

Some detailed responsibilities of the Presidency have been laid down in the Ministerial Decision on the practical application of certain aspects of Title III of the Single European Act.[52] These include the presentation of the programme and balance speeches in Parliament, the sending to Parliament of a "written communication on progress",[53] taking part at ministerial level in Parliament's foreign policy debate, the holding of quarterly colloquy with the Political Affairs

---

[51] See EP Resolution of 10 October 1991 on the Intergovernmental Conference on Political Union. OJ 1991 C280/148.
[52] Bull EPC, Doc 86/090.
[53] For an example of such a 'communication' see *Report on European Union*, Bull EPC, Doc 88/499.

Committee[54] to discuss recent developments and transmitting, "as soon as possible", declarations adopted. In addition, Parliament is entitled, if it so requests, to comments on its resolutions. Finally, special information sessions may be arranged between the Ministers and the responsible committees of Parliament.

By virtue of Article D TEU the European Council is to submit to the European Parliament a report after each of its meetings as well as a yearly progress report.

There are therefore several mechanisms in place for the information of Parliament. It is hoped that they will be used timely and effectively, not merely out of respect for Parliament, but also because it can serve the requirements of unity and consistency.

Obviously, all parties involved will have an interest in informing Parliament, especially if matters are at stake in which Parliament has a powerful say. In particular, the conclusion of certain international agreements[55] by the Community is subject to Parliament's assent (Article 228(3) paragraph 2 ECT), and under Article O the European Parliament can prevent the adoption of a Council act relating to the application for membership of the Union by other European States. Parliament's powers with regard to these matters should therefore give it some leverage in its relations with the Commission and the Council. Furthermore, Parliament can exercise its power of the purse, in particular through its influence over non-compulsory expenditure of the Community. This would exclude aid programmes which the Community already engaged under international agreements, but it would include new commitments as well as programmes such as PHARE and TACIS, which equally have foreign policy implications.[56] More dramatic measures concerning the entire budget or the adoption of a motion of no-confidence or censure against the Commission would equally exist, but they are obviously to be used with caution.

There is, however, no formal requirement to consult Parliament before taking a decision in the field of the CFSP, and *a fortiori*, no right of co-decision. Similarly, under the ECT Parliament's powers are not comprehensive. It does not have to be consulted before the conclusion of trade agreements, nor in case of economic sanctions under Article 228a. Finally, Parliament has no powers over the WEU Council or over preparatory institutions like the Political Committee.

The most powerful tool which Parliament has at its disposal is its power to make recommendations. These are non-binding acts addressed to the Council and/or the Commission, notably in form of Resolutions. Careful use of this

---

[54] Since 1992 the Committee on Foreign Affairs and Security.

[55] These include association agreements, cooperation agreements containing special institutional provisions and treaties having important budgetary implications or entailing amendments to decisions taken under the codecision procedure.

[56] Moreover, Art J.11 TEU provides in its second para that the administrative expenditure relating to the CFSP and, if the Council decides so by unanimity, the operational expenditure to which its implementation gives rise, will be charged to the budget of the European Community. This might represent another source of influence for Parliament. However, it is not clear whether the expenses concerned would be classified as compulsory or not. On this question generally see Jacobs, Corbett and Schackleton, *The European Parliament*, 2nd ed (1992) at 213 *et seq.*

instrument would enhance the impact of its opinions. Because of its relative weakness as a legislature, the European Parliament occasionally adopts exaggerated foreign policy resolutions which in turn reinforce the Council's reluctance to involve Parliament more.[57] To further a judicious use of recommendations, Parliament should establish in its Rules of Procedure that resolutions containing recommendations under Article J.7 be adopted by specified majorities and that their drafting is in principle reserved to a Parliamentary Committee.

Court of Justice

By virtue of Article L the powers of the Court of Justice of the European Communities are in principle limited to Titles II to IV and VII. The application of the provisions of the Community Treaties concerning the (exercise of the) Court's powers to the Final Provisions and to Article K.3(2)(c) is equally assured. The Court of Justice can therefore not rule on the Common Provisions, and also Titles V and VI are in principle excluded from its jurisdiction. Nevertheless, it would seem permissible for the Court of Justice to decide matters with foreign policy implications whenever a provision from one of the Community Treaties (as amended) is at issue.

First of all, the Court of Justice is to ensure that "in the interpretation and application of this Treaty the law is observed" (Art 164 ECT). In the spirit of this article the Court of Justice is used to referring to international treaties to which Member States are parties, not in order to enforce them, but, where they are relevant, to assess the meaning of Community law the enforcement and uniform interpretation it is to ensure. It may be considered unlikely that Article L is intended to amend this power, also because, if the Court of Justice cannot interpret Community law in the light of Title V, it would not be in a position to reconcile the meaning of Community law with those provisions and consequently, it could only act as the unconditional defender of the Community pillar irrespective of any conflicting provision in the titles relating to the second and third pillars of the Union. It would seem that Article L is inspired on the one hand by the necessity to include an explicit grant of powers as regards the third subparagraph of Article K.3(2)(c) and the Final Provisions and on the other hand by the desire to prevent the coming into being of a body of "Union Law" – as opposed to Community law – by judicial activism on the part of the European Court of Justice. Therefore, it is suggested, the article should be interpreted to mean merely that the Court of Justice cannot directly enforce or interpret the Common Provision or Titles V and VI. There is no compelling reason why it should be interpreted as restricting also the existing jurisdiction of the Court under the Community Treaties.

Secondly, Article M provides that:

---

[57] Dinan, 'European Political Cooperation', in: Hurwitz and Lequesne (eds), *The State of the European Community. Policies, Institutions and Debates in the Transition Years*, (1991) 403–421 at 405.

"Subject to the provisions amending the [Treaties establishing the European Communities] and to these final provisions, nothing in this Treaty shall affect the Treaties establishing the European Communities or the subsequent Treaties and Acts modifying or supplementing them".

It can be taken from Article M that the Court of Justice could pronounce on acts of the Council taken in application of Title V, but by virtue of Article L only when the Community Treaties are concerned. If the Council's act is based on a decision by the European Council, also that decision can be incidentally scrutinised.[58]

Thirdly, the Court of Justice may of course consider the consistency of foreign policy measures of the Member States with the ECT.

It remains to be seen how such a matter could come before the Court. One of the issues which the Court of Justice could be required to tackle is, whether Articles 228a and 79g ECT relating to economic sanctions would curtail the autonomy of the Commission. This matter can scarcely be raised in a plea against the Commission for failure to act, since under Article 175 ECT the Court could be involved only if the Commission fails to define its position. Yet, another possibility would be that the Commission institutes an action for annulment against a decision of the Council based on Title V. At first sight, such an act cannot be annulled, since it is not subject to the jurisdiction of the Court of Justice. Nevertheless, such actions have a chance of success, for instance when a Council decision based on Title V is cast in words which would suggest that economic sanctions are imminent rather than merely a possibility. In such a case the Commission could argue that the measure could only be taken in the Community framework and would suffer from a wrong choice of legal basis. Article 228a ECT would then have to be interpreted as well.

Moreover, as argued before, in some circumstances the Council might want to adopt a "hybrid" act based both on Article 113 ECT and Article J.2(2) or J.3 TEU, without a separate decision under Title V, and also this might be subject to scrutiny by the Court of Justice.

Another issue could be the interpretation of Article 228(3) sub-paragraph 2: what are "important budgetary implications" (or any other of the criteria) establishing Parliament's right of assent to the conclusion of an international treaty? This question could be raised by Parliament in an action for the annulment of the Council act concerned under the third paragraph of Article 173 ECT. The fact that such an action is only for the protection of Parliament's prerogative powers means that Parliament cannot contest the act concerned on substantive issues, such as the adequacy or otherwise of the protection of Human Rights.

Further questions which the Court of Justice may perhaps be asked to settle at some stage are: the compatibility with Community law of a decision of the Council to charge certain expenditure relating to the implementation of Title V to the Community budget,[59] and the applicability of subsidiarity in the relations between Community acts and Title V acts.

---

[58] See Everling, *supra*, n 1 at 1063.
[59] See *supra*, n 54.

On the whole it is submitted that the jurisdiction of the Court of Justice is not as restricted as it may seem at first sight. In any case it covers questions as to the compatibility with Community law of CFSP measures of the Council, including their choice of legal basis. A further extension of the Court's jurisdiction would occur should the Council make use of hybrid acts, covering both matters governed by Title V as well as matters governed by the Community Treaties. Such acts would be subject to the Court's jurisdiction in much the same way as mixed agreements are: *prima facie*, they are dealt with as acts of the Community under the Community Treaties. It is doubtful whether the jurisdiction of the Court of Justice could be stretched still further. A most intriguing question in need of further study is whether the Court of Justice, as constitutional court of the Community, would be willing to interpret Article L TEU in the light of a mandatory requirement such as the "foundations of the Community", which it seems to use as a determining factor and perhaps to attribute a higher legal status in the interpretation of Treaty provisions and positive rules of law.[60] On this basis Article L might for instance be found not to cover situations where a Council decision under Title V interferes with the human rights of Community citizens, or even more generally, the Court might exercise its personal jurisdiction over the Council for the protection of private individuals. Obviously, this matter reaches far beyond the question of consistency and therefore cannot be dealt with in this framework.

Conclusion

Consistency is more difficult to bring about to the extent that relations between the actors involved are getting more complex. Although, as we saw, the institutions are in the process of adapting to the new tasks which lay ahead, the TEU raises challenging questions the solution of which rests on the shoulders of politicians and lawyers alike.

NANETTE NEUWAHL[61]

---

[60] Curtin, *supra*, n 1 at 64.

[61] The author is grateful to Jörg Monar (College of Europe) and Malcolm G Ross (University of Leicester) for their helpful comments.

Chapter 16

The Common Foreign and Security Policy of the European Union and the External Relations Powers of the European Community

Introduction

The coming into force of the Treaty on European Union will, it is generally agreed, bring a new complexity to issues relating to the competence of the European Community and the proper legal base for Community (or Union) action. In particular, substantial legal questions remain concerning the relationship between, and respective competences of, the constituent elements of the Union. In this article I will touch on some of the questions raised by the relationship between the Common Foreign and Security Policy of the Union (CFSP) and the external relations powers of the European Community, in particular its economic relations and common commercial policy.

The European Union Treaty (TEU) provides for the Union to be served by a single institutional framework: a common foundational structure for the three pillars of the Union,[1] to reconstruct the metaphor. The TEU goes on to imply that this single framework is to consist of, on the one hand the European Council (Art D TEU), and on the other, the European Parliament, the Council, the Commission and the Court of Justice (Art E TEU). Already the distinction between the two elements of the single framework is apparent; this becomes even clearer when one takes account of the expressly political function given to the European Council[2] and the different decision-making processes within the three pillars. As Professor Demaret points out[3] the methodology of the institutions within the two new pillars (Common Foreign and Security Policy and Justice and Home Affairs) is essentially intergovernmental, in comparison with

---

[1] Art C European Union Treaty (TEU). Metaphors for the European Union abound, but one refers to the Union as a temple, with three pillars: the European Community, the Common Foreign and Security Policy and Co-operation in Justice and Home Affairs. The unifying conception is so undefined as to leave much scope for architectural speculation.

[2] Art D TEU para 1 states: "The European Council shall provide the Union with the necessary impetus for its development and shall define the general political guidelines thereof."

[3] "The Treaty Framework" in this volume p 3.

the supra-national aspects of the European Community (such as majority voting and the role of the European Parliament and European Court of Justice).

The TEU uses the rhetoric of a "single institutional framework" in an attempt to bolt together the old and the new, to ensure, in the words of Article C, consistency and continuity between the activities of the Union and the development of (or "building upon") the *acquis communautaire*. The resulting tensions between these two very different methodologies will impose stresses on the Community's legal order, in particular on the autonomy of its institutional decision-making and internal balance of power.

The Union Treaty acknowledges the particular importance of consistency in the external field, and responsibility for ensuring this is given to the Council and Commission.[4] It is clearly desirable that the "international identity" of the Union[5] should not be compromised by confusion over responsibility for policy formation and execution, between the Common Foreign and Security Policy and (for example) the common commercial policy of the European Community. Even if the face the Union presents to the outside world is consistent (by no means a certain proposition), the inter-institutional conflicts which have become a feature of the external relations of the European Community are likely to increase as the legal base and competency questions become more complicated.

It is not even absolutely clear from the Treaty which institution(s) has competence to decide such questions; where it is a matter of the borderline between the Common Foreign and Security Policy and the European Community's powers, Article M TEU implies that the European Court of Justice will have jurisdiction.[6] However, where the scope of the CFSP *vis à vis* the Member States themselves is in question (for example, questions over Article J.4(4) TEU; or over the Danish defence opt-out) this is clearly outside the jurisdiction of the European Court.[7] Responsibility in the first instance would presumably lie with the Council of Ministers, both under the provisions of Article C TEU mentioned already, and also under Article J.1(4), which gives the Council the duty to ensure the loyalty and mutual solidarity of the Member States in their support of the Union's external and security policy. In the last resort, the impetus-providing role of the European Council[8] may enable it to break any deadlock. It is striking that both these possibilities point to an essentially political decision, by political institutions, rather than one based

---

[4] Art C TEU para 2 provides: "The Union shall in particular ensure the consistency of its external activities as a whole in the context of its external relations, security, economic and development policies. The Council and Commission shall be responsible for ensuring such consistency. They shall ensure the implemetation of these policies, each in accordance with its respective powers."

[5] Art B TEU states as one of the objectives of the Union, "to assert its identity on the international scene . . .".

[6] Art M TEU protects the EEC Treaty (and other Community Treaties) from the effects of the TEU itself, except in respect of express amendments, and this provision is itself subject to the jurisdiction of the European Court of Justice (Art L TEU). The Court therefore appears to have the jurisdiction to police the borderline (see Eaton, "Common Foreign and Security Policy" in this volume 215) by ruling on the scope of the Community's powers.

[7] Under Art L TEU the Court has no jurisdiction over Art J TEU.

[8] Art D TEU; *supra*, n 2.

on legal concepts of competence and institutional balance such as we expect from the Court of Justice. Again the intergovernmental nature of the CFSP pillar is emphasized.

In what follows, a brief outline of the European Community's external relations powers and of the scope of the CFSP, stressing issues of competence, will lead into an examination of possible areas of overlap and the implications of these for the Community legal order.

European Community's external relations powers

In addition to expressly granted external powers, for example in the implementation of the common commercial policy (Art 113 EEC), or the power to conclude Association Agreements (Art 238 EEC), the Community has been held to possess whatever external powers are necessary in order to implement an internal policy effectively (the so-called doctrine of parallelism, expounded by the Court of Justice in *Commission* v *Council (ERTA)*[9]). In addition, external powers even under the common commercial policy may extend beyond the fields expressly mentioned in Article 113 to cover new aspects of commercial policy reflecting changing conditions in world trade,[10] such as trade in services, for example.

The dynamic character of the Community's external powers is important in this context because it indicates that the boundary between the powers of the Community, the Union and the Member States will need continual re-definition. The extension of the Community's powers in the cultural field, for example, under Article 128 EEC as amended by the TEU may include the growth of a parallel external competence (see Art 128(3)EEC) which would in turn have an impact on the foreign policy of the Union, with its commitment to safeguarding the common values of the Union (Art J.1(2) TEU). A similar point can be made in relation to the protection of fundamental human rights, which is taking on a political dimension in the European Community context,[11] and which also appears in Article F TEU, raising questions as to participation in relevant treaties such as the European Convention on Human Rights and Fundamental Freedoms.

The dynamic nature of the Community's powers has another implication: insofar as those powers are exclusive, their extension into new areas or new aspects of existing fields of activity will exclude the Member States. It has been clear since 1975 that the Community's powers in implementing the common commercial policy are exclusive, in the sense that the Member States do not possess concurrent powers.[12] In other areas, the exclusivity of the Community's

---

[9] Case 22/70 [1971] ECR 263.

[10] See Opinion 1/78 (*re the Natural Rubber Agreement*) [1978] ECR 2871; Case 45/86, *Commission* v *Council* [1987] ECR 1493.

[11] See Art 8 EEC as amended by the TEU; see O'Keeffe, "Union Citizenship", in this volume 87.

[12] See Opinion 1/75 (*re OECD Understanding on a Local Cost Standard*) [1975] ECR 1355; and Case 41/76, *Donckerwolcke* v *Procureur de la République*, [1976] ECR 1921.

external powers depends on their actual exercise; until they are exercised, the Member States' competence continues, subject to their basic Treaty obligations under (for example) Articles 5 and 7 EEC.[13]

As the intergovernmental nature of the CFSP indicates, this aspect of the Union comprises an aggregation or pooling of existing Member State powers. The theory of exclusivity would therefore imply that development in the external powers of the European Community would result in a transfer of competence not only from the Member States individually but also from the CFSP pillar to the Community pillar of the Union.[14] However legally correct this theoretical position may be, it is unlikely to be reflected in practice, given the pragmatic approach taken by the the Community to the question of Member State participation in its current external relations policy.

Although the theory of exclusivity has been maintained fairly consistently in respect of the common commercial policy (with corresponding arguments about the exact scope of the commercial policy), in practice the Commission, as mouthpiece for the voice of the Community, often struggles rather obviously to maintain coherence in the face of very vocal Member States attempting to protect their own interests.[15]

In other areas the Community institutions (in practice, the Commission) have been prepared to accept continued Member State participation in agreements themselves, through the mixed agreement procedure, even where it is strictly not necessary legally. The agreement establishing the European Economic Area, for example, is to be concluded as a mixed agreement by the Member States individually as well as by the Community,[16] as a result of its significance in the development of the Community's wider European policy. This tendency to combine Member State and Community involvement in external action is likely to increase as a result of the development of a CFSP based on "concerted and convergent action"[17] by the Member States alongside the current tendency of the Community to introduce a political dimension into wide-ranging association agreements.[18]

Although the Union has as one of its objectives the assertion of its identity on the international scene (Art B TEU), and the Presidency is to represent the Union in matters coming within the CFSP, no express Treaty-making powers are given to the Union. Treaties, therefore, need to be concluded either by the

---

[13] See Cases 3,4 & 6/76, *Officier van Justitie* v *Kramer* [1976] ECR 1279.

[14] The possibility of transfers of competence from one pillar to another is expressly envisaged in the context of justice and home affairs: see Art K.9 TEU which provides for the possible future application of Art 100c EEC to areas referred to in Art K.1 TEU.

[15] As, for example, the French Government's defence of the interests of French farmers in the context of the EC's GATT negotiating position.

[16] As an Association Agreement based on Art 238 EEC.

[17] Art J.2(1) TEU.

[18] For example the Association Agreements negotiated with Hungary, Poland and the Czech and Slovak Republics, which include provision for political dialogue. The Commission has said that in formulating the Community's policy towards central and eastern Europe it is moving towards the creation of a "European Political area" (see its June 1992 paper on "The Challenge of Enlargement", Bull EC Supp 3/92); this policy of strengthening political dialogue alongside trading links and commercial co-operation has now been endorsed by the Member States in the conclusions of the Copenhagen summit of June 1993.

Member States themselves, or by the European Community (where matters within EC competence are affected) or both, under the mixed agreement procedure.

We thus have yet one more example of the way in which the European Union Treaty will foster the already apparent move away from the placing of Community and Member State competence in separate and exclusive compartments and towards varieties of shared competence under the general rubric of subsidiarity.

Scope of the Common Foreign and Security Policy

The CFSP is a successor to, and builds on the experience of, European Political Co-operation (EPC), established during the 1970's and formalised in Title III of the Single European Act (SEA) of 1986.[19] There is thus a precedent for the co-existence of intergovernmental and European Community action. There are nevertheless some significant differences between EPC and the CFSP,[20] and from the point of view of the issue of respective competences the most important are the increased level of obligation imposed on the Member States in the implementation of the CFSP and the increased involvement of the institutions, in particular the Council of Ministers, in the formulation of policy. Whereas, for example, the SEA only requires the Member States to "*endeavour* to formulate and implement a European foreign policy",[21] under the European Union Treaty the "Union and its Member States *shall* define and implement a common foreign and security policy".[22] The SEA envisages, as does the TEU, the formation of common positions, but whereas the SEA states that these are to "constitute a point of reference for the policies" of the Member States,[23] the CFSP requires that Member States "shall ensure that their national policies conform to the common position".[24]

Second, EPC was not intended to lead to autonomous action; action was to be carried out by the Member States individually (though acting "as a cohesive force"[25]) or via decisions of the Council of Ministers acting as an institution of the European Communities where, for example, economic sanctions affecting trading relations were employed.[26] The CFSP envisages not just the definition of common positions to which national policies must conform, but also the adoption of joint action by the Council of Ministers.[27] Where a decision on joint

---

[19] Arts 2, 3(2) and Title III of the Single European Act are repealed by Art P.2 TEU.

[20] See Eaton, *supra*, n 6 at 215.

[21] Art 30(1) SEA (author's italics).

[22] Art J.1(1) TEU (author's italics).

[23] Art 30 (2)(c) SEA.

[24] Art J.2(2) TEU.

[25] Art 30(2)(d) SEA.

[26] For example, the sanctions imposed against Iraq on 4 August 1990, two days after the invasion of Kuwait (OJ 1990, L213).

[27] Art J.3(1) TEU. Although joint action will generally be decided upon unanimously, the possibility of qualified majority decision-making exists: Art J.3(2) and Art J.8(2) TEU.

action has been taken Member States are expressly committed to supporting it and the possibility of acting unilaterally is highly circumscribed. The form joint action may take is (unsurprisingly) not specified, but the Council is given the necessary decision-making powers "on the basis of general guidelines adopted by the European Council" in order to ensure "the unity, consistency and effectiveness of action by the Union".[28]

Where joint action impinges on the EC's powers, the Council may need to take decisions based both on the TEU and on the EC Treaty. This raises a further issue.

Alongside the procedural evolution, that may be seen within the CFSP, from co-operation between Member States, through the defining of common positions to the adoption of joint action by the Council of Ministers, an evolution in substantive competence may also be observed. The common security policy is intended to lead to the framing of a common defence policy, and this in turn to lead (possibly) to a common defence.[29] Action in respect of issues with defence implications is to be taken through the Western European Union (WEU)[30] rather than by the Council of Ministers under the joint action procedure; the intergovernmental nature of the action is thus stressed. It is not hard to envisage a situation where action is being taken either simultaneously or in quick succession by the Council of Ministers under both its CFSP powers of joint action and its EC powers, and by the WEU implementing the common defence policy of the Union. Although the respective areas of competence may remain theoretically distinct, in practice implications arise for the autonomy of the Communty's external policy, particularly in the commercial sphere.

One instance of this is provided by one of the examples of so-called "variable geometry" resulting from the Maastricht negotiations and the Edinburgh 1992 Summit: the Danish opt-out from the common defence policy. Imagine a scenario where, as part of a policy of common defence (with which Denmark was not associated) the Council of Ministers agreed (by qualified majority under Art 228a EEC[31]) on the use of economic sanctions. Presumably Denmark would be obliged to accept these sanctions as part of its EC obligations, in spite of not having been involved in the initial decision to take such a measure. The Commercial Policy of the Twelve is thus directly and substantively affected by decisions taken by Eleven in a different forum and under different procedural rules.

---

[28] Art J.8(2) TEU.
[29] Art J.4(1) TEU.
[30] All Member States except Denmark, Greece and Ireland are members of the WEU. See Declaration 30 attached to the TEU on the relatons between the WEU, the Union and the Atlantic Alliance.
[31] Art 228a EC (added by the TEU) provides: "Where it is provided, in a common position or in a joint action adopted according to the provisions of the Treaty on the Union relating to the common foreign and security policy, for an action by the Community to interrupt or to reduce, in part or completely, economic relations with one or more third countries, the Council shall take the necessary urgent measures. The Council shall act by a qualified majority on a proposal from the Commission." Art 73g(1) (also added by the TEU) envisages the possibility of this action encompassing restrictions on capital movements and payments with respect to third countries.

Relationship between the CFSP and European Community powers

As we have seen, the EEC has external competence over the whole range of activity covered by the EEC Treaties themselves, including not only commercial relations, but also for example action on the environment. Many matters traditionally within the "foreign policy" of a state – and particularly those with economic implications – are therefore within the Community's powers, although the term "foreign policy" has never been used in this context. As the Union seeks to develop the political and security aspects of its foreign policy, it will find that its policies and action will frequently have a Community dimension. This is particularly true where the Union seeks to apply pressure on third countries and use its economic weight to achieve political ends. Within the EPC it was not unusual for a political decision to be taken within the framework of political co-operation which was then implemented in the form of economic sanctions by the Council of Ministers.[32] This process has been formalised by a new Article 228a, added to the EEC Treaty by the TEU.[33]

On the one hand, the Union will still need to rely on Community-based powers to support its policy. On the other hand, the Commercial Policy of the Community – and within its exclusive competence – will find itself affected by political decisions taken within the CFSP pillar of the Union. In both cases the decision will be taken by the Council of Ministers, but this conceals rather than resolves the problem: the effect on the institutional balance in decision-making both within the Council itself and between the Council and the other institutions, in particular the European Parliament and the Court of Justice. These points will be considered further below.

The foreign policy of the Union, formulated within the CFSP, may also need to be given effect through the political dimension to external Community agreements. This political dimension does not just include provision for political dialogue but also the establishment of political criteria attached to economic concessions. States seeking increased access to the Community market, and economic aid and co-operation are increasingly meeting an insistence on the inclusion of firm commitments on human rights, multi-party democracy, and minority rights.[34] Again the economic strength of the Community is being used to further political objectives of the Union. As we have seen, the Union does not possess its own treaty-making powers, so the Member States will not be replaced by the Union, and such agreements with third countries will still need to be mixed.

The political dimension to the Community's external relations will also be affected by the co-operation envisaged within the Union in the field of Justice and Home Affairs, for example over immigration policy.[35] It is not difficult to

---

[32] Action in relation to Iraq has already been mentioned: see *supra*, n 26; such action has also been used, for example, in relation to Argentina at the time of the Falklands war, and currently against Serbia.

[33] See *supra*, n 31.

[34] See, for example, the agreements with the Baltic states and with Romania and Bulgaria.

[35] Art K.1 TEU.

see how the Council of Ministers may wish to use the common policy on vis-as[36] as an element in its relations with third states, whether within the context of the Community (an association agreement for example) or within the CFSP itself.

The pattern which is emerging is in some ways a reflection of the relationship within the Communty's commercial policy between participation in international fora (Art 116) and negotiation and conclusion of agreements (Arts 113 and 114). In Opinion 1/78 *(re the Natural Rubber Agreement)*[37] an agreement had been negotiated within UNCTAD (the United Nations Conference on Trade and Development). The Council of Ministers argued that the appropriate procedure was that provided for in Article 116, that is, "common action" by the Member States themselves within such international organizations "of an economic character". This common action should extend, the Council argued, to the conclusion of the agreement itself by the Member States, rather than direct Community involvement in the negotiation (by the Commission) and conclusion (by the Council). The Court ruled that although Article 116 provided a general framework for the Member States, it did not derogate from the external competence of the Community itself. Therefore, whenever discussions within an organization reached the point of an agreement being envisaged, the procedures of Article 113 and 114 should come into play and the Community institutions should be fully involved; the Council could not restrict itself to acting purely as the co-ordinator of the Member States' individual views.

Article 116 is repealed by the TEU, and the necessary co-ordination provided for in the Union Treaty itself. Article J.2(3) requires the Member States to co-ordinate their action in international organizations and at international conferences and to uphold the common positions in such fora, even in cases where not all Member States take part. Two limitations found in Article 116 are removed, reflecting the new provision's presence in the Union Treaty rather than the EEC Treaty: the co-ordination is to take place in all international organizations, not just those of an economic character; and the co-ordination is not limited to "matters of particular interest to the common market". In addition, the Presidency is to express the position of the Union in such organizations and conferences (Arts J.5(2)) and Member States who do not participate are to be kept informed by those who do; express mention is made of the United Nations Security Council (Art J.5(4)).

The logic of the position of the Court in Opinion 1/78 would suggest that wherever either co-operation within Article J.2 or joint action within Article J.3 leads to the possibility of concluding an international agreement falling within the competence of the Community, action should proceed under the relevant provisions of the EEC Treaty (now Art 228) rather than under these CFSP provisions. Any agreement wholly or partly outside Community competence would have to be concluded by the Member States or under the mixed

---

[36] Art 100c EEC, as amended by TEU. Note that other aspects of justice and home affairs may be added to this article, under para 6 and Art K.9 TEU.

[37] See *supra*, n 10.

procedure. The new procedures and the development of the CFSP should not however, if Article M is to believed,[38] derogate from the Community's existing treaty-making powers. It will not therefore be possible for the CFSP to operate in isolation from the Community's external policy or remain unaffected by developments in the scope of that policy. We can now turn to look at some of the institutional aspects of this relationship.

Institutional implications

It is tempting to regard the common foreign and security policy as an over-arching Union policy, within which the Community's own external powers, such as its common commercial policy, operate as a *lex specialis*. However, the different legal and policy contexts and in particular the different institutional powers preclude this solution. The Community's commercial policy for example has its own imperatives, based *inter alia* on its GATT obligations and internal market priorities. It appears from Articles A and B TEU that the European Community and its policies should work alongside the CFSP within the Union and its "single institutional framework".

Does the single institutional framework have any real existence outside the rhetoric of the Union Treaty? The reality appears to be that the Community institutions (or some of them) are being asked to operate under a different set of rules. This difference is not of the same nature as the differences that exist within the EEC Treaty itself (for example between Art 113 and Art 235, or between Art 100a and Art 130s). It is postulated upon a premise as to the nature of the CFSP as primarily concerned with co-ordinating the actions of the Member States themselves, through formulating common positions and joint action, and subject to political control rather than the legal control of the Court of Justice. The CFSP is clearly envisaged by the Member States as operating outside the "new legal order" of Community law, whether or not the term "intergovernmental" is used. When one considers the importance attached by the Court to the existence of this new legal order in formulating the characteristics of the law made by the Community institutions and the respective responsibilities of the Member States and institutions, it becomes clear that the difference is not purely technical or theoretical. What, then, are the substantive differences in the law-making functions of the institutions under the two pillars?

First, the Commission possesses a right of initiative within the European Community, together with the role of negotiator in respect of international agreements. Within the CFSP (as with the EPC), the Commission is merely to be "fully associated" with the work carried out.[39] It is the European Council which has the initiating, policy-forming role.[40]

Secondly, the European Parliament has the right to be consulted "on the

---

[38] See *supra*, n 6.
[39] Art J.9 TEU.
[40] Art J.8 TEU.

main aspects and the basic choices of the common foreign and security policy", and to be kept informed.[41] A similar general right to be consulted also exists in respect of the EC's external powers, with two exceptions. On the one hand there is no such right in relation to the common commercial policy (that is, based on Art 113 EEC, but including economic sanctions under Art 228a). On the other hand, certain (increasingly used) types of external agreement require the assent of the Parliament, including association agreements and others establishing an institutional framework for co-operation.[42] For the Parliament, therefore, the question will be whether it can carry forward its strengthened position into the CFSP or whether, without the protection of the Court of Justice, its political role will be sidelined by the political decision-making within the Council of Ministers.

Thirdly, there are differences in the voting rules for the Council of Ministers. In the context of the CFSP the general rule is for substantive decisions to be taken unanimously. It is possible for decisions on joint action to be taken on a qualified majority basis, but only after a unanimous decision to that effect.[43] Within the Community, decisions concluding agreements with third states are generally subject to qualified majority voting (the exceptions are association agreements based on Art 238 EEC and those which cover a field for which unanimity is required for the adoption of internal rules, such as taxation). Other commercial policy acts, such as alterations of the common customs tariff, the imposition of quotas and anti-dumping duties, and economic sanctions under Article 228a, are all taken by qualified majority vote. In general, therefore, joint action will require unanimity unless economic measures are envisaged, in which case the Council will need to act by qualified majority under the EC Treaty. Underlying these voting rules is a tension between the Council of Ministers as a Community institution and as a Council of representatives of the Member States,[44] a tension which has been responsible for many of the inter-institutional disputes within the Community and which is likely to be increased by the functions given to the Council within the CFSP.

Fourthly, and most important, the Court of Justice has no jurisdiction over the CFSP, including action taken by the Council of Ministers, unless this translates itself into Community action. Although there is an argument, outlined above, that the Court of Justice has jurisdiction to determine the borderline between the CFSP and Community action, as part of its general "constitutional" jurisdiction over the scope of the Community's powers, it is not easy to see how that jurisdiction can be exercised in cases where the Council claims to be acting under the CFSP. Not only will the scope of the CFSP itself be subject

[41] Art J.7 TEU.

[42] Art 228(3)EEC, as amended by TEU. The Parliament's influence in the external context is growing: witness its refusal to assent to the association agreement with the Czech and Slovak Federation in 1992 on the ground that the constitutional position was unclear following the decision to split the Federation into separate states. It was, also, the Parliament that insisted on the Commission referring the revised draft agreement on the European Economic Area to the Court of Justice for a second time under Art 228, so that the Court might examine several important changes to the agreement.

[43] Art J.8(2) and J.3(2) TEU. Issues having defence implications are not in any case subject to this procedure: Art J.4(3) TEU.

[44] Art 2 of the Merger Treaty 1965.

to political rather than judicial control, which is what the Member States clearly desired, but its relationship with the Community's policies will also in practice be determined by the Council itself rather than the Court. Recent battles over questions of legal base have led some commentators to doubt whether the Court has at its disposal the necessary means for developing as an effective constitutional court.[45] This position is unlikely to improve if unchallengeable decisions as to competence are taken by the political institutions without any guarantee of consistency or conformity with prior caselaw.

Recently the Court of Justice had the opportunity to consider the question of the autonomy of European Community law, in its first Opinion on the draft European Economic Area (EEA) agreement.[46] The Community had insisted on the preservation of the autonomy of the EEC decision-making process as one of the fundamental principles underlying the negotiations leading to the agreement,[47] and this led to a restrictive view being taken of the involvement of the EFTA states in formal decision-making within, in particular, the Council of Ministers. Any possibility of giving the Council of Ministers a wider role as legislator for the whole EEA (with corresponding wider membership) was rejected. The negotiators originally took a different view of the Court of Justice, and attempted to create an EEA court containing members of the European Court of Justice as well as members from the EFTA states. However, the Court of Justice ruled that "the autonomy of the Community legal order" would be threatened were such a joint court to be given jurisdiction over questions relating both to the respective competences of the Community and the Member States, and to the interpretation of provisions which are identically-worded to provisions of existing Community law.[48]

It is envisaged that the membership of the Union and European Community should be identical (it will not be possible to become a member of the Community without joining the Union as a whole). Nevertheless, in the relationship between the CFSP pillar and the European Community there is (as with the EEA) an attempt to create two separate decision-making processes which are intended to work together consistently while respecting and maintaining the *acquis communautaire*.[49] The European Court has pointed out the dangers of granting institutions which are outside the Community legal process – such as, here, the European Council and the Council of Ministers acting within the CFSP – powers which will have an impact on the Community legal order. The possibility of opt-outs from parts of Union policy (such as defence) underlines the problem. The more general point is that Community policy is developed as

---

[45] See, for example, Weatherill, "Regulating the internal market: result orientation in the House of Lords", (1992) 17 EL Rev, 299 at 313–314.

[46] Opinion 1/91 (*re the draft treaty on a European Economic Area*) [1992] 1 CMLR 245. For an earlier example see Opinion 1/76 (*re draft agreement establishing a European laying-up fund for inland waterway vessels*) [1977] ECR 741.

[47] This was one of the so-called "Interlaken principles" set out by Commissioner de Clerque in 1987; the other principles were that the development of relations with the EFTA states should not hold back the process of European integration (in particular the internal market programme), and that any agreement should respect the need to balance benefits and obligations within a new relationship.

[48] Opinion 1/91 at paras 32–46.

[49] See Art C TEU.

a result of a complex interaction between the competing priorities of the Commission, the Council and the Parliament, under the control of the Court which is concerned to ensure respect for the fundamental principles of Community law as well as the balance between the institutions. Decision-making within the CFSP will have a different dynamic as well as being subject to different procedures. It is doubtful whether it is sufficient merely to charge the Council and Commission with responsibility for ensuring consistency for the Union's "external activities as a whole in the context of its external relations, security, economic and development policies"[50] without providing an appropriate legal framework for the solution of inevitable conflicts.

The autonomy of the Community institutions was fiercely defended in the EEA negotiations. The importance of preserving, and indeed building upon, the *acquis communautaire* is recognised not only in the statements of political intent in the Union Treaty, but also in a practical way in the EEA negotiations, and in those with the Central and Eastern European states. Third countries wishing close associative relationships with the Community are increasingly required to align their internal laws to the Community model. The central, almost front-line position which is thus given to the Community's legal order in the context of "widening" points towards the need for legal solutions to a crucial question in the context of "deepening" integration: the determination of the interrelationship between the new pillars of the Union and Community institutions and their respective competences.

Article B TEU suggests that a starting point in the search for a legal solution may well be the principle of subsidiarity, which has developed as a response to questions of shared competence. It provides that the objectives of the Union shall be achieved "while respecting the principle of subsidiarity as defined in Article 3b of the Treaty establishing the European Community". That this is only a starting point, and not a complete solution is illustrated by the unanswered questions still clustered around that concept, including the question of whether it is even a principle subject to *legal* analysis and definition.[51] It would nevertheless be a positive step if the principle of effectiveness (a central element of subsidiarity) were to form the basis for deciding questions of competence rather than (as perhaps seems more likely) pragmatic and *ad hoc* voting decisions within the Council of Ministers.

MARISE CREMONA

---

[50] *Ibid.*

[51] See Toth, "A legal analysis of subsidiarity" in this volume 37.

Part 8

Justice and Home Affairs

Chapter 17

Expanding External and Shrinking Internal Borders: Europe's Defence Mechanisms in the Areas of Free Movement, Immigration and Asylum

What are we waiting for, assembled in the marketplace?
The barbarians are due here today . . .
Night has fallen and the barbarians have not arrived
And some of our people just in from the border say
There are no barbarians any longer.
Now what will become of us without barbarians?
Cavafy, "Waiting for the barbarians"[1]

Institutional arrangements

In the three-ring circus of the European Union as established by the Maastricht Treaty on 7 February 1992, the provisions on co-operation in the fields of Justice and Home Affairs belong to the third ring. Title VI of the Treaty on European Union – embracing Articles K-K.9 – deals with forms of co-operation among the Member States in a number of areas, inside the Union, but outside the European Community. This implies that the framework for co-operation is primarily intergovernmental and that the involvement of Community institutions is marginal or less pronounced. Article K.1 lists a number of areas which are to be regarded as "matters of common interest" to the Member States in their efforts to achieve the objectives of the Union. The central, though not exclusive, objective to be kept in mind in Title VI is the free movement of persons, one of the fundamental freedoms of the Community, as mentioned in Articles 3 (under c) and 7.A (originally, since the SEA, Art 8 A). The following nine items are mentioned:

(1) Asylum policy;
(2) Rules governing the crossing by persons of the external borders of the Member States and the exercise of controls thereon;
(3) Immigration policy and policy regarding nationals of third countries:

---

[1] With thanks to Doris Edel, *Identiteit en Integratie; Ierland en Europa in de vroege middeleeuwen*, Utrecht, inaugural address, 18 February 1993.

(a) conditions of entry and movement by nationals of third countries on the territory of Member States;

(b) conditions of residence by nationals of third countries on the territory of Member States, including family reunion and access to employment;

(c) combatting unauthorised immigration, residence and work by nationals of third countries on the territory of the Member States;

(4) Combating drug addiction in so far as this is not covered by (7) to (9);

(5) Combating fraud on an international scale insofar as this is not covered by (7) to (9);

(6) Judicial co-operation in civil matters;

(7) Judicial co-operation in criminal matters;

(8) Customs co-operation; and

(9) Police co-operation for the purposes of preventing and combating terrorism, unlawful drug trafficking and other serious forms of international crime, including if necessary certain aspects of customs co-operation, in connection with the organization of a Union-wide system for exchanging information within a European Police Office (Europol).

We will focus our attention on the first three topics as those are concerned with asylum and immigration, including policy regarding nationals of third countries. In this short contribution it is not possible to deal with topics such as police co-operation,[2] the avalanche of non-Community frameworks for dealing with migration and asylum, the developments of a common visa policy; the position of third country nationals under association agreements and the like, *etc*. This should not be taken to imply that these other topics are not important, or that there is nothing to report on their progressive implementation. Thus, a judicial co-operation working group on civil matters is considering a number of subjects, including the extension of the Conventions of 19 June 1980 on the law applicable to contractual obligations (the Rome Convention) to the Member States of the European Free Trade Area; establishing an EC common position in respect of negotiations within the framework of the Hague Conference on Private International Law on new conventions; considering extension of the Brussels Convention 1968 to matters of personal status and family law; and other topics.[3] These working groups have, up until now, been operating under the auspices of European Political Co-operation, although this has been conceived of as a forum for co-operation in the sphere of foreign policy. Article 30 (10) of the SEA provides for the establishment of working groups, of which the one on civil matters may be mentioned here, as well as the one on criminal law

---

[2] See the excellent contribution by den Boer, "Immigration, Internal Security and Policing in Europe", in the Working Paper Series *A System of European Police Co-operation after 1992*, University of Edinburgh and "Europe and the Art of International Police Co-operation: Free Fall or Measured Scenario?" in this volume, 279. See also: Mols (ed.), *Dissonanten bij het akkoord van Schengen* (1990); Fijnaut, Stuyck, Wytinck (eds), *Schengen:Proeftuin voor de Europese Gemeenschap?* Politiestudies 7 (1992).

[3] See Memorandum from the UK for the European Committee on Legal Co-operation (CDCJ) of the Council of Europe, 13 October 1992, CDCJ (92) 40 restricted. There is of course the problem of demarcations with *e.g.* the work of The Hague Conference for PIL, of which the existing conventions should be ratified first by all Member States. See on the topic Duintjer Tebbens, "De Haagse Conferentie, de Europese Gemeenschap en de subsidiariteit" (1993), *Nederlands Juristenblad* 669–672, d'Oliveira, '100 jaar Haagse Conferenties – van de onderkant bekeken" (1993), *Nederlands Juristenblad* 657–658.

and drugs. Although these working groups are formally answerable to the European Political Committee, they seem to enjoy a considerable autonomy in practice. The Union Treaty makes the working groups responsible to the Council (of ministers of Justice and the Interior).

This brings me to the procedural aspects of the co-operaiton in the fields of Justice and Home Affairs in Title VI in the areas of asylum and immigration. Although other institutions of the EC are, in various degrees, involved in the work under Title VI, it is first and foremost the Council where the decision-making process culminates. It is the Council which may adopt, according to Article K.3, such acrobatic stances as "joint positions", "joint action" (without prejudice to the principle of subsidiarity); it may furthermore "draw up conventions which it shall recommend to the Member States for adoption in accordance with their respective constitutional requirements."[4] The initiative for these measures in the area of asylum and migration[5] lies with either any Member State or with the Commision. Whether this will mean in practice that the Member States will stay passive in expectation of proposals by the Commission – that is how Professor Taschner assesses the situation on the basis of his long experience with the Commission[6] – remains to be seen. I have some reasons for doubt. In the first place, the institutional framework of Title VI mandates in Article K 4 the setting up of a Co-ordinating Committee consisting of senior officials of the Member States, which will not only co-ordinate activities of the Council, but shall also contribute to the preparation of the Council's discussions in the areas referred to in Article K and in Article 100c of the Treaty, *i.e.* the *visa policy*. Although, according to the courteous wording of Article K.4(2), the "Commission shall be fully associated with the work in the areas referred to" in Title VI, the real impetus and initiative seem to come largely from the Co-ordinating Committee. It should be borne in mind that the European Council at Rhodes (2–3 December 1988) instituted a Group of Co-ordinators with tasks which are very similar to those laid down in Article K.4.[7] Thus the Union Treaty provides for a formal, legal foundation for this Group of Co-ordinators which has already been operational for some years, a not uncommon phenomenon in the EC as elsewhere. Indeed, the Union Treaty has been described as a victory of the Member States over the Commission in the areas of immigration, asylum and nationals of third countries.[8]

One of the fora which this group co-ordinates is that of the *ad hoc* immigration working group, which has been set up by decision of the London summit of the Trevi group Ministers back in October 1986. This *ad hoc* immigration working group operates by and large in areas as defined in Article K.1, and is divided in

---

[4] Taschner, 'Asyl- und Einwanderungsrecht aus europäischer Perspektive", in Hailbronner (ed), *Asyl- und Auswanderungsrecht im europäischen Vergleich*, Bd 1, Schriftreihe der europäischen Rechtsakademie Trier, (1992) 113–119 at 117, characterises this provision as "eine ungeschickte, wohl mit heisser Nadel genähte Vorschrift".

[5] For the topics mentioned in Art K.1 under 7 to 9, the initiative of the Commission is excluded.

[6] *Supra* n 4 at 117.

[7] See Towle, *The Development of a policy on asylum for the European Community; in the context of the completion of the internal market* (Florence, EUI 1993) 185 *et seq.*

[8] Fernhout, "De Verenigde Staten van Europa zijn begonnen, maar voor wie?", inaugural address, Nijmegen (1992) at 13.

263

several subgroups, such as the one on Asylum. The Maastricht Union Treaty reinforces the existing intergovernmental co-operation and broadens its tasks somewhat.[9] In this intergovernmental framework with its high frequency meetings machinery, it becomes less probable that the Twelve will allow the Commission to play an important role.

The role attributed to the European Parliament is even more dwindling. It will regularly be informed by what is called "the Presidency" of discussion in the areas covered by Title VI and be consulted on principal aspects of activities in these areas. The views of the European Parliament will duly be taken into consideration, says Article K.6, and it furthermore condescendingly grants the Parliament the right to ask questions of the Council and even to make recommendations to it. The restricted roles of Commission and Parliament mirror the fact that we are in the third ring of intergovernmental co-operation with just a few Community flags waving more or less symbolically. Thus the conventions to be drawn up by the Council "may stipulate that the Court of Justice shall have jurisdiction to interpret their provisions" (Art K.3(2); the administrative expenditure entailed for the European institutions by the provisions of Title VI are to be charged to the Community budget, and the operational expenditure may likewise be charged to the budget of the Communities (Art K.8(2). Thus a lot of "mays" connect the intergovernmental co-operation in the fields of justice and home affairs with the Community legal order, first and foremost the famous *corridor*[10] of Article K.9, leading from the third ring to the first. This provision opens the possibility for the Council to decide unanimously, on the initiative of the Commission or a Member State,[11] to apply Article 100c of the Treaty to action in areas referred to in the catalogue of Article K.1(1) to (6). Article 100c, inserted by the Maastricht Treaty in Title V of the EC Treaty, empowers the Council to determine the third countries whose nationals must be in possession of a *visa* when crossing the external borders of the Member States. Here, in the first ring, the Commission exercises its right of exclusive initiative, though on occasion prompted by a Member State (Art 100C (4)), and the European Parliament shall be consulted before the Council takes a decision, for which unanimity is required. As from 1 January 1996, however, a qualified majority for the decisions concerning visas will suffice.

In turn, paragraphs (6) and (7) of Article 100c refer to Title VI of the Union Treaty and to the Schengen and Dublin Conventions and the like.

Article K.9 – the bridge – allows the Council to communitarise one or more of the topics listed in Article K.1 under (1) to (6) and then to shift them from intergovernmental co-operation on matters of common interest to the Community framework. This shift may eventually entail decision-making in Council by qualified majority. But this shift cannot take place before the Member States have ratified this extension of Community competences, which means involvement of all national Parliaments, the celebration of referendums, *etc*. One

---

[9] *Cf* Widgren, "The need to improve co-ordination of European asylum and migration policies", in Hailbronner (ed), *op cit*, n 4 at 101.

[10] La passerelle, das Brückchen, *etc*.

[11] Commission and Member States have changed places compared to Art K.3 (2).

organizational arrangement of Title VI has already found its way into the Community framework: the Co-ordinating Committee set up by Article K.4 will contribute, according to Article 100d, to the preparation of Council proceedings in the area of visa policy.

The Declaration by the Maastricht Conference on asylum, annexed to the Union Treaty, directs the Council to consider, *by the end of 1993*, the possibility of expanding Community competence to asylum policies. It mentions a "report" on the basis of which this consideration will take place, without it being clear, however, who will draw up this report: the Commission, the Co-ordinating Committee, the Presidency? Even if it is assumed that the Union Treaty will have entered into force in the course of 1993 – one would rather forecast the weather than the outcome of the decision-making process in the United Kingdom and Denmark – it is doubtful whether the Council will take a positive view on insertion of elements of Title VI into the Community legal order. My prediction is that the Member States will not easily give up their manifest resistance against communitarization of their migration and asylum policies, their border control mechanisms, work immigration policies etc, and will be satisfied for the time being with existing forms of collaboration in intergovernmental settings.[12]

Developments concerning crossing of borders, immigration and asylum

Although a tendency has existed for a long time to consider migration and asylum as two totally different topics, it becomes more and more clear that they converge and to a certain extent overlap, both in terms of the persons involved and in the concepts as used and constantly revised. The attempts at distinguishing sharply between "genuine" asylum-seekers and "economic" refugees, between political refugees and others, must be taken for what they are: not exercises in ontology, but methods to sell restrictive measures, and to seal off the external borders of the EC territories.[13]

Personally, I am reminded of the Swiss border police instructions – some 50 years ago – which were only changed a week after D-day, at the end of World War II, on 12 July 1944, and which read: *"Flüchtlinge nur aus Rassegründen sind keine politische Flüchtlinge"* (refugees for reasons of race only are not political refugees).[14] From that date on the police instructions changed, and foreigners "who for political *or other reasons* really ran the risk of life and had no other country to turn to than Switzerland", would be accepted for entry. Thus, half a year later, a group of some 1,500 Jewish refugees were released from concentration camps and allowed to enter Switzerland, after long and difficult

---

[12] *Cf* Drüke, "Asylum Policies in the European Community without internal borders". *CCME Briefing Paper* (No 9 October 1992), 23.

[13] *Cf* d'Oliveira, "European Community refugee policy", (1991) *Migrantenrecht*, 67–82.

[14] *Cf* Hässler, *Das Boot is voll. Die Schweiz und die Flüchtlinge 1933–1945* (1989), 290.

negotiations between the Swiss and the German Nazi government and in exchange for money and trucks to maintain the latter's war efforts. In this way my grandmother survived her internment in the concentration camp of Theresienstadt, and found herself interned in a Swiss camp.

It is not at all ludicrous to suppose that in 50 years time the restrictive definitions of "genuine" refugees in our days may arouse the same kind of indignation as we experience at the Swiss exclusion of Jews, gypsies and others from the definition of political refugees. The Swiss, by the way, were not the only country with restrictive definitions during World War II, or shortly after.[15]

It is evident in the second place that the distinction between political and economic refugees does not hold water. Thus, Professor Nascimbene remarks in a recent paper concerning the Albanian refugees in Italy:

"The obligation to leave one's country can therefore take on different aspects of a political nature, which are often difficult to distinguish from economic motives, as in the case of socialist regimes, where the economy is a direct emanation of the political system."[16]

The same goes for capitalist regimes. The number of refugees taken up by Western European countries who were fleeing from socialist countries during the cold war, suggests that in that period a high percentage were considered to be political refugees although many had only, or primarily, economic motives, and had less to fear than, say, Tamils in the past decades.[17] In other words: there are strong political motives or reasons in defining refugees as genuine political or criminal economic asylum seekers. The depravity of the Communist regimes was measured by the huge number of genuine refugees they created. The more the better!

The growing number of asylum-seekers, in the last ten years, is not only caused by well-known factors, such as globalization of mobility, increased specific information concerning conditions in various potential host countries, the ongoing and new instabilities in many regions of the world, including Europe, after the falling apart of the totalitarian socialist world, but also by the lack of an immigration policy in Western Europe. If the only official gate giving access to fortress Europe is called asylum, many are tempted to try to pass as asylum-seekers. In this sense the growing numbers of asylum-seekers are in part an *artefact* resulting from the lack of migration law in the broad sense of the EC Member States. All migration towards the EC is funnelled through the asylum tube, if not through the tourist pipe.

It is well known that the Member States have always stood firm on the principle that migration was a topic falling outside Community competence. The two Declarations connected to the SEA bear witness of this standpoint.[18] Nevertheless

---

[15] *Cf* on the precarious positions of foreign Jewish persons in and after World War II *e.g.* in Belgium: Caestecker, *Vluchtelingenbeleid in de na-oorlogse periode* (1992) 63.

[16] Nascimbene, "The Albanians in Italy: the right of asylum under attack?" (1991) *International Journal of Refugee Law*, 714–720 at 716.

[17] The criminal way in which Tamil asylum seekers were treated in Denmark led to the resignation and impeachment of ministers. MNS March 1993, 12.

[18] General Declaration on the Arts 12–19 of the Single European Act and the Policital Declaration by the Governments of the Member States concerning the freedom of movement of persons.

the topic of crossing borders by non-Member State nationals is interfaced with that of the achievement of the internal market, defined as an area without internal frontiers in which the freedom of movement of persons is ensured. The controversy on the meaning of the word "persons" in Article 8.A and in Article 3 of the Treaty, which isolates the United Kingdom from the other Member States, is still blocking any Community-wide solution, although, as Richard Plender remarked "the draftsmen of the EEC Treaty intended to establish a common policy for workers in the Community, irrespective of their nationality".[19] This historical interpretation has given way to a teleological one which restricts the freedom of movement to workers and other persons who can claim in addition the nationality of one of the Member States.

There is one category of non-nationals of Member States which derives freedom of movement from EC legislation: the groups of family members as defined in several Directives.[20] The large groups of non-Member State nationals, however, who have established themselves in the territories of the Member States as workers or as a result of family reunification or formation have systematically been excluded from the Community framework. Although they form part and parcel of the population of the countries of the EC, many have been born there, received their education in these countries etc, their position is grossly neglected both by the EC and in intergovernmental co-operation. Professor Groenendijk rightly remarks that there is "more attention for exclusion of new immigrants than for the position of settled immigrants".[21]

There is one important factor which necessitates dealing with these non-nationals of Member States: *the completion of the internal market.* If the EC is seriously considering the abolition of internal borders, then it is difficult to conceive of systems of systematic internal border checks which allow nationals of Member States to pass blindly and which would still include controls of third country nationals. This may be one of the reasons why the "firm political will", expressed in a Declaration concerning Article 8.A of the Treaty, annexed to the SEA, to take the necessary decisions to bring about the internal market before 1 February 1993 has proven to be just not good enough. The phrase with which this Declaration continued, *viz* that the deadline of 31 December 1992 did not create any legal consequences, showed already the afterthoughts accompanying this firm stand.

The Commission takes the position that a declaration cannot change the binding force of a Treaty provision, and has considered taking measures against countries which have not implemented Article 8.A by 1 January 1993, or interpret the provision in such a way as to exclude third country nationals from the

---

[19] Plender, "Competence, European law and nationals of non-Member States", (1990) ICLQ, 559–610.
[20] See van Nuffel, "L'Europe des citoyens: vers un droit de séjour généralisé", (1992) *Revue de Marché Commun*, 89 *et seq.*
[21] Groenendijk, "Europese migratiepolitiek na Maastricht: uitbreiding en beperking van vrijheden", (1991) *Migrantenrecht* 76–86 at 78.

freedom of movement within the internal market.[22] This will presumably take the form of placing a complaint at the Court of Justice against states that refuse to accept the consequences of Article 8.A of the SEA.[23] Dr Bangemann's successor, the new European Commissioner for the Internal Market, Mr V d'Archirafi, took a more cautious stand in a meeting of European Parliament's Committee on Civil Liberties and Internal Affairs. This was not appreciated and led to a Resolution by the Parliament inviting the Commission to take action against Member States failing to fulfill their obligations under Articles 8a, 100 and 235 of the Treaty. In case the Commission and Council come up with answers falling short of the demands of Parliament, "it will not hesitate to use all the measures at its disposal, and in particular its right under Article 175 of the EEC Treaty to obtain that the obligations clearly deriving from Article 8A are fully complied with and applied without delay".[24] Thus the new cautiousness of the Commission is met with a collision course by the Parliament, which may lead eventually to a decision of the Court of Justice.

Part of the problem of established immigrants is being solved by increasing opportunities of acquiring the nationality of the Member States, and thus by becoming citizens of the Union. In several countries the opposition against naturalization of ethnic minorities is diminishing, as is the resistance against plural nationality.[25] This changing attitude has led to the signing of a Protocol to the Strasbourg 1963 Convention on reduction of cases of plural nationality, and the abolition of provisions in the national legislation of several Member States, which prohibited voluntary acquisition of a nationality without shedding the original one. Italy and the Netherlands are examples of this evolution. Resident third country nationals thus become, in growing numbers, nationals of Member States as well, and enjoy the rights and entitlements which this status entails. The recent *Micheletti* case[26] illustrates this phenomenon, although the Member State nationality was acquired there by birth. There are even non-nationals of Member States, enjoying freedom of movement, who can be detected only with difficulty, as they have been given documents in which it is stated that they are nationals of a Member State. This is the case with the Moluccans, a group of

---

[22] The Commission Communication of 6 May 1992 (Bull EC 5–1992) "sets out the Commission's interpretation of Article 8a of the Treaty, which requires the Community to adopt measures with the aim of progressively establishing the internal market – defined as "an area without internal frontiers in which the free movement of goods, persons, services and capital is ensured in accordance with the provisions of this Treaty" – over a period expiring on 31 December 1992. The Council, Parliament and the Member States are urged to ensure that all appropriate measures are adopted by the deadlines set. The Commission takes the view that Article 8a imposes on the Community and on the Member States an obligation in terms of results which can be met only if all controls at internal frontiers (covering individuals, goods, services and capital) are abolished on 31 December 1992 and which leaves no margin for discretion. It points out that, while the abolition of internal border controls does not deprive Member States of their power to act on their territory and up to the frontier of that territory, the crossing of a border may no longer give rise to controls; any action taken must form part of monitoring arrangements covering the whole of the territory in question".
[23] *Agence Europe*, 2 January 1992.
[24] MNS March 1993. See for the latest developments, MNS May 1993.
[25] See d'Oliveira (ed), *Plural nationality, changing attitudes* (forthcoming).
[26] ECJ 7 July 1992, Case C-369/90 *Micheletti* v *Delegacion del Gobierno en Cantabria*, not yet reported; (1993) 30 CML Rev 623–638, with my casenote.

about 40,000 persons, allowed to settle in the Netherlands by court order after the independence of the Indonesian Republic, as they were denied their independent Moluccan islands republic and had collaborated too much with the Dutch colonial powers to stay safely in Indonesia. They possess Indonesian or Dutch nationality, and some of them are stateless. On the basis of a law passed in 1976, the non-Dutch segment of this group got the status of being treated as Dutch for most purposes (franchise and military service excepted) and this implied that they could avail themselves of Dutch aliens passports. As there were problems with this travel document, the government decided resolutely to grant them Dutch passports in which it was indicated that their nationality was Dutch, although as a matter of fact they could be Indonesian or stateless. A white lie, which the authorities of the other EC Member States have to accept, given the Directives and caselaw on the subject, and which oblige Member States to take the valid travel documents of Moluccans at face value.

Similar remarks can be made concerning other groups of non-nationals of Member States who acquire in one way or other the nationality of a Member State: I refer to the 18 million nationals of the former GDR and the so-called *Aussiedler*, who, according to Article 116 of the German Basic Law are to be considered Germans. The accession of the five East-German *Länder* through the unification of Germany has caused little or no public or political concern, although their impact on the economic recession of the EC is enormous. These new EC Member State nationals outnumber by far the groups of asylum seekers in the EC. Their political characterization as Member State nationals has suppressed the most arguable view that they are asylum seekers or even economic migrants *sur place*.

Most developments concerning what is sometimes called "extracommunitarians" (a term with extraterrestrial and basically racist overtones) have taken place outside the framework of the EC, although linked with it through the connection with the freedom of movement. Schengen and Dublin are the keywords.

Schengen and Dublin

The Schengen Convention on the gradual abolition of checks at the common borders of France, the Federal Republic, Belgium, the Netherlands and Luxembourg of 14 June 1985 was the surprising outcome of what can be described as a "symbolic French German move" to relax the checks at the common French-German border.[27] It had little to do with the completion of the internal market, although it was not alien to the topic of the freedom of movement. It certainly represents a fair example of Europe at two speeds.

This is not the place to spell out the details of the Schengen Convention 1985 or the Schengen Implementing Convention of 19 June 1990 and its 142 Articles, its Final Act with six Declarations, a Protocol, a Common Declaration, *etc.*[28] I will

---

[27] Schutte, "Schengen: its meaning for the free movement of persons in Europe" (1991) 28 CML Rev 549–570.
[28] See for the impact of Schengen on the freedom of movement generally, O'Keeffe, "The Schengen Convention: a suitable model for European integration?" (1991) 11 YEL (11); (1992) 185–219, who considers, with others, that many of these provisions are seriously flawed.

deal here only with some selected topics. The Dublin Conventions are the result of a series of negotiations in an intergovernmental framework with a view to the creation of an internal market as defined in Article 8a which was introduced by the SEA 1986. On the basis of the Palma Document two instruments have been prepared, one on determining the state responsible for examining applications for asylum lodged in one of the Member States of the EC, concluded on 15 June 1990, and a draft convention on checks at the external borders, which has up till now not reached a final stage primarily due to the fact that some countries found a skeleton in their common cupboard, dating from the year 1713 (Treaty of Utrecht).

Djabal al Tarik (Tarik's Hill), nowadays commonly known as Gibraltar, captured in 1704 by an Anglo-Dutch fleet has ever since been a bone of contention between Spain and the United Kingdom. The conflict now takes the form of differing views on the interpretation of Article 8a of the Treaty. Is the narrow border between the rock and Spain an internal or an external border? At the Meeting of Ministers with responsibility for immigration on 30 November and 1 December 1992 in London, "deep regret" has been expressed that no solution had yet been found, and the Ministers "urged the parties concerned to redouble their efforts under the Danish presidency".[29] Talks about this "colony" resumed in early March 1993 between Spain and the United Kingdom, which eventually and temporarily may lead to some form of dual sovereignty over Gibraltar.[30]

Spain is firm in its position that, according to the Treaty of Utrecht, 1713, should the United Kingdom renounce its sovereignty over Gibraltar, this could only be transferred to Spain; the UK proposal to draw up a Magna Carta or Constitution of Gibraltar was certainly a windfall for the local movement for independence. All has become quiet on the Gibraltar front[31] since; it will take quite some time before parties will leave their entrenched positions, and this implies that the Schengen Implementing Convention will in all probability arrive first in this tortoises' race towards entry into force.

The Member States seem physically to panic at the sight of abolition of internal borders. This is the only explanation for the definitions given in the instruments of Schengen and Dublin for what are to be considered as internal and external borders: the internal borders are shrinking whereas the external borders have grown out of proportion. The internal market is established by defining internal borders away: nearly all air and seaports are called external and even the Channel Tunnel between England and France is considered "external"! The United Kingdom seems to forget its continental (pre)history, when the rivers Thames and Humber were tributaries of the river Rhine, but it is certainly not the only country to inflate its external borders.[32]

In the area of travel by non Member State nationals to and through the

---

[29] Draft Conclusions V.

[30] Gibraltar itself has the ambition to become an autonomous Member of the EC, a prospect as abhorrent to Mr Solana (Spain's foreign minister) as it is to Mr Hurd (*The Independent*, 1 March 1993); *De Volkskrant* 1 March 1993.

[31] *Agence Europe*, 3 March 1993, 5.

[32] See *e.g.* Art 4(4) of the Schengen Supplementary Agreement.

territories of Member States, the Schengen Implementing Agreement seems nearest to entering into force. Although the Ministers concerned originally had in mind the creation of a common territory between the contracting parties by the end of 1990, even today the Agreement is still dormant. This despite the fact that *e.g.* Article 4 mentions "that *as from 1993* passengers on flights from third States who board internal flights wil first be subject, upon arrival to . . . checks in the airport of arrival of their external flight". The deadline has now been extended to 30 June 1993.[33] The five founding members to the Schengen Treaties have been joined by several other Member States: Italy, Spain, Portugal and Greece. The original Schengen countries have to ratify each of these accessions. For various reasons the United Kingdom, Ireland and Denmark have preferred to stay out of this incremental association, which at least avoids this instrument's Gibraltarian petrification.

It is extremely doubtful whether the newest deadline will be met. Although the approval procedure of the Supplementary Convention has been completed in Spain, France, Belgium, Luxembourg, Portugal and the Netherlands,[34] other parties are lagging behind, especially Germany, which wants to revise the constitutional provision on asylum first. A new deadline is whispered about: 1 September 1993. We will wait and see. The present writer, for one, would be astonished if the entry into force were to happen at all in 1993. According to its Article 139, the Supplementary Convention will enter into force between one and two months after deposit of the final instruments of ratification by the five original parties, by which date the provisions concerning the setting up, activities and jurisdiction of the Executive Committee shall apply;"The other provisions shall apply as from the first day of the third month following the entry into force of this Convention" (Art 139 (2)).

In Portugal President Soares has postponed his approval of the Bill on ratification of the Schengen Convention, presumably in connection with the new Aliens Act which has met with criticism from Brazil.[35] Schengen entails changes in the existing regime for Brazilian (and Portuguese) nationals as laid down in several bilateral agreements which allow each others" citizens to take up residence, exempt from visa requirements etc.[36]

Although Dublin has run on to the rock of Gibraltar and Schengen has met with delays, still progress is being made in harmonization of immigration and visa policies, be it in sometimes informal ways.

The nine Schengen Member States have invited the states involved in the enlargement negotiations – Austria, Finland and Sweden – to join them in their interpretation of Article 8a SEA as setting the objective of the elimination of controls on persons at the Community's internal frontiers. They have

---

[33] MNS February 1993.

[34] The Dutch Senate approved the endorsement-bill on 23 Februray 1993 and accepted the accession of Italy on the same date. *Stb.* 1993, Nos. 138, 139, 140.

[35] MNS February 1993, 4. See also *Le Monde*, 18 February 1993.

[36] *Cf* the Treaty on Friendship and Consultation between Portugal and Brazil, 16 November 1953, the Convention of Brasilia on the Equality of Rights and Duties between Portuguese and Brazilians, September 1971, and an Exchange of Notes from 1960 exempting Brazilians from visa requirements provided they were arriving in Portugal for business, transit or tourism, and would not stay for a period exceeding six months.

271

furthermore invited them to adhere to the Schengen Agreement and Convention in due time,[37] and to conduct negotiations to this effect in parallel with the negotiations with the EC. Switzerland, although more aloof concerning the European Economic Area, has shown interest in the Bangemann-wave.[38]

Visa policy

As long as Maastricht has not entered into force, which, as we have seen, has communitarised in Article 100c the visa policy of the Member States, any co-operation among the EC Member States is necessarily intergovernmental. Under the Schengen Implementing Agreement, Chapter 3 of Title II deals with a common policy concerning short stay visa (Art 9 (6)), whereas visa for periods longer than three months remain in the hands of each contracting state; the implication for the other parties being only to allow transit (with some exceptions) to travel towards the issuing country. Under Article 100c of the Union Treaty a more general visa policy could be adopted, which may even transform itself gradually into a genuine migration policy.

As long as the Schengen Implementing Agreement has not yet entered into force, the forms of co-operation are rather undefined but definite. The Schengen Ministers have decided in their meeting in Madrid in mid-December 1992 to develop:

– basic criteria for inclusion of third countries in a common list of countries from which persons would need a visa;
– a uniform visa label, non-counterfeitable, for three-month visas;
– and to start drawing up a provisional list of some 120 countries and their various positions as to visas, which would be harmonised as much as possible with the existing list of the Benelux countries.

At present three lists already exist:

(1) a list of countries which require a visa;
(2) a list of visa-exempted countries; and
(3) a list of countries on which a common decision has not yet been made.

It is to be noted that the list of visa-countries has been greatly expanded under the influence of France. Although in various Schengen countries this list is considered to be confidential or secret, it has been made public in an annex to a report by the Dutch Government to the second chamber of Parliament.[39]

Asylum

As for paracommunitarian activities concerning asylum, we dispose of two more or less identical instruments: the Chapter on asylum in the Schengen Supplementary Convention, and the Dublin Convention determining the state

---

[37] *Europe*, 4 February 1993.
[38] *Europe*, 29 January 1993.
[39] See INS January 1993. Recently Belgium has requested the other Benelux and Schengen countries not to provide President Mobutu of Zaire and his family with a visa. See *De Volkskrant*, 25 February 1993. The fate of this request is unknown to me.

responsible for examining applications for asylum lodged in one of the Member States of the European Community, 15 June 1990. This last Convention has been ratified by five Member States: Denmark, Greece, Ireland, the United Kingdom, and, recently, Italy.[40] It is still in need of seven more ratifications before it can enter into force.

Both Schengen and Dublin offer a procedure for deciding which state shall have to process asylum applications lodged in one of the Member States. It does not attempt to harmonise substantive rules concerning asylum as is explicit in Article 3 (3) which states that the "application shall be examined by that state in accordance with its national laws and its international obligations".[41]

The stated motives for the asylum Conventions are the reduction of "orbiting" of asylum seekers, and to reinforce the legal position of asylum seekers by guaranteeing that their applications will be examined by one of the Member States. This so-called "improvement" is bought by the asylum seekers with heavy setbacks. The most important one is the reduction of multiple asylum requests. It is extremely doubtful whether this reduction is in conformity with the Geneva Convention. The Dutch Council of State addressed this issue and considered that each state party to the Geneva Convention has an individual responsibility to comply with the Convention and is not allowed to delegate this responsibility to some other States.

This problem becomes moot only after substantive harmonization of rules concerning asylum in the Member States *to the Geneva Convention*.[42] Is speaking with one voice by 12 Member States acting in good faith towards the other parties to the Geneva Convention whose burden will be increased in this way? This problem will become even weightier if parallel conventions with countries surrounding the EC are concluded.[43] And what about the compatibility of this system of exclusion of what is called asylum-shopping with Conclusion No 12 (XXIX) of the Executive Committee of the UNHCR which reads:

"The Executive Committee ... further recognizes that a decision by a Contracting State not to recognize refugee status does not preclude another Contracting State from examining a new request for refugee status made by the person concerned".[44]

Although these Conclusions are not binding on the contracting states, it is beyond doubt that the Executive Committee starts from the assumption that each state has an *individual* responsibility to deal with asylum requests. The Schengen and Dublin instruments, however, put into place a system in which the (negative) decision by one country on a request for asylum will be recognised in all other contracting states. This recognition implies: (a) that new

---

[40] MNS, February 1993, 6. See for Italy, Law 523 of 23 December 1992.
[41] *Cf* Schengen Art 32: "in accordance with its national laws". See also Art 28 in which "obligations under the Geneva Convention of 18 July 1981" are reaffirmed.
[42] See Herwig Verschueren, "Het vrije verkeer van personen in de Schengen Verdragen", in Fijnaut, Stuyck, Wytinck (eds), *Schengen: Proeftuin voor de Europese Gemeenschap?* (1992) 13–54 at 47; D'Oliveira, "European Community Refugee Policy", (1991) *Migrantenrecht*, 67–82.
[43] See *infra*, 275.
[44] *Cf* Jaeger, "Asiel en de Verdragen van Schengen", *Delikt en Delinkwent* (1991), 762–768.

applications in other contracting states will not be considered, and (b) that these countries will co-operate in expelling the applicants to third countries. Thus the contracting states act as if they were only one state.

There are furthermore, defects in both instruments in their relationships with other conventions, especially those concerning human rights and fundamental freedoms. In several places mention is made of the Geneva Convention and Protocols,[45] but reference to the European Convention on Human Rights and Fundamental Freedoms (1951) *e.g.* is blatantly absent. Article 3 of this Convention is one of prime importance to asylum seekers as it prohibits their refoulement. Article 6 concerning access to justice and its underlying principles of procedural justice has its importance as well. Reference to the Rome Convention has, however, been made in one of the recommendations of the Immigration Ministers in their meeting of 30 November – 1 December 1992, *viz* the recommendation on expulsion practices.

Then there is Article 3 of the Geneva Convention stating that "the Contracting States shall apply the provisions of this Convention to refugees without discrimination as to race, religion or country of origin." Is the definition of "alien" for the purposes of the Dublin Convention in its Article 1 compatible with this non-discrimination clause? "Alien" is defined as "any person other than a national of a Member State". A similar definition is to be found in the Schengen Convention, Article 1. This definition excludes asylum seekers from the other Community Member States from the regime of the Dublin Convention. If this regime is indeed what it professes to be, an improvement of the status of asylum seekers by guaranteeing them that at least one state will deal with their request, then it boils down to (reverse) discrimination to exclude nationals of Member States.[46] In all probability the Conventions do not primarily aim at improving the situation of asylum seekers, but at building a fortress Europe by a common effort. In my opinion, the Conventions are either containing new guarantees for asylum seekers, and in that case the definition of "aliens", excluding Member State nationals, is discriminatory contrary to *e.g.* Article 3 of the Geneva Convention, or indeed its hidden aim is a *deterioration* of their status and in that case preferential treatment of nationals of other Member States may be allowed under international law. One may ask whether the Member States are of the opinion that asylum seekers who originate from or are nationals of Member States do not exist; that Member States are safe countries; that the freedom of movement will take care of the problem of Member State nationals seeking access as asylum seekers in other Member States. All these assumptions are highly doubtful. Clear, however, is the origin and thrust of these conventions as flanking measures to the introduction of the internal market.

---

[45] Dublin, Preamble, Art 2; Schengen Art 28, Art 135.

[46] See d'Oliveira, "De EG discrimineert zijn eigen asielzoekers", (1991) *Nederlands Juristenblad*, 442, also *ibid*, "Fortress Europe and (extra-communitarian) Refugees: co-operation in sealing off the external borders, in Schermers *et al* (eds), *Free Movement of Persons in Europe: Legal Problems and Experiences*, Asser Institute Colloquium on European Law, Session XXI (1993) 166–182.

Recent developments

That the primary objective in the field of asylum is reducing the flow of asylum seekers can be shown by two developments.

In the first place we witness the conclusion of agreements – bilaterally or multilaterally – with third countries concerning readmission of "irregular migrants" and other matters

Thus, a readmission Agreement has been concluded between the Schengen countries and Poland, 29 March 1991.[47] This obliges the countries involved (read: Poland) to readmit persons found in the Schengen area who entered through the Schengen-Polish border in an irregular way, overstayed, *etc*. This not only concerns Polish nationals, but also other persons crossing the Polish border without adequate documents. According to its Article 6, the agreement is already provisionally applicable and will come into force after ratification by two states.[48] These agreements have the effect of establishing reinforced border controls in the third countries, not only at the frontier with Schengen countries, but also elsewhere, at the "far end", in order to prevent irregular entries into the Schengen area, and to prevent the third countries to incur costs of readmission.[49]

Similar arrangements are being concluded with Hungary and former Czechoslovakia, while at the southern flank negotiations have started between Morocco and Spain, and France is urging for a multilateral readmission agreement to be concluded with the Maghreb countries. Thus a *cordon sanitaire* is formed around the Schengen countries at the expense of the developing countries adjacent to the EC in order to prevent and counter irregular migration: a new iron curtain.[50] In return continued development aid or its defrosting is offered, or the withdrawal of visa requirements for the nationals of the states involved, contribution to the costs of readmission, lifting of trade barriers *etc*. In this way Hungary has refused, in the first half of 1992, some 500,000 persons at the Rumanian border. Morocco has become reluctant in issuing passports to its nationals, and is now willing to readmit undocumented Moroccans when expelled from Member States such as the Netherlands, as it is aided in return by the EC institutions in its territorial claims on the Western Sahara.[51]

One of the Principles accepted after the European Council in December 1992 states:

---

[47] Trb 1991, No 65.

[48] Ratifications have been obtained in France, Germany, Italy, Luxembourg and Poland.

[49] *Cf De Volkskrant*, 18 February 1993; *Financial Times*, 10 February 1993, on Poland; *De Volkskrant*, 22 December 1992, on the Tchech Republic and Hungary.

[50] *Cf* Kay Hailbronner, "Perspektiven einer Europäischen Asylrechtsharmonisierung nach der Maastrichter Gipfelkonferenz", in: *ibid, Asyl- und Einwanderungsrecht in Europäischen Vergleich* (1992) 146: "das Abkommen mit Polen (ist) als Beginn eines 'cordon sanitaire' kritisiert worden, mit dem sich die E.G. Staaten künftig von Asylbewerbern aus Ost-Europa abschotten wollten. Diese Bedenken sind nicht ganz von der Hand zu weisen wenn – wie beabsichtigt – vergleichbare Abkommen mit anderen osteuropäischen Staaten geschlossen werden sollten."

[51] MNS January 1993, 3. *Cf* Principle 7, Conclusions of the Presidency, Edinburgh, 12 December 1992: "In their relations with third countries, they will take into account those countries" practices in readmitting their own nationals when expelled from the territories of the Member States." In other words: no readmittance, no favours.

"Where appropriate, they will work for bilateral or multilateral agreements with countries of origin or transit to ensure that illegal immigrants can be returned to their home countries, thus extending co-operation in this field to other States on the basis of good neighbourly relations."[52]

This boils down to exporting the EC problems with refugees and other undesirables to countries which lack the infrastructure to cope with it.[53] These "good neighbourly relations" lead regularly to events, reported in the newspapers, whereby hundreds of migrants and asylum seekers drown in *e.g.* the Gibraltar Straits or in the Greek waters.[54] It is, as the German writer, Magnus Enzensberger remarks, ironic and perverse that the threat of immigration in Europe is using the metaphor of the full boat, where, as a matter of fact, boats full of asylum seekers are sunk before arriving in Europe.[55]

In the second place the work that is being carried out towards harmonization of elements of substantive asylum law shows the tendency to be as restrictive and deterrent as possible. At the meeting of the Migration Council in London in early December 1992, several decisions have been taken, in the form of resolutions or otherwise, concerning topics such as "manifestly unfounded applications for asylum", on "countries in which there is generally no serious risk of persecution" (persons coming from these countries having the burden of proof that their applications are not manifestly unfounded) or the use of the novel concept of "host third countries" to reduce even more the granting of asylum in EC countries,[56] the establishment of a clearing house, *i.e.* a centre for information, discussion and exchange on asylum, which is already operational, etc. The Ministers involved expressed the wish that all these harmonising, read "restrictive", elements should be laid down in a binding convention.[57] New obligations are furthermore imposed on carriers: I mention the duty to *copy* documents offered by passengers at boarding stations, which will increase the chance again that asylum seekers may be stuck in the country from which they seek refuge.

The progress in harmonization of measures to restrict the influx of asylum seekers is more a cause for concern, as the development of an immigration policy for third country nationals seeking work in the Community Member States is barely advancing. The conclusion of the meeting of immigration ministers, London, 30 November – 1 December 1992, mentions the efforts of

---

[52] See also Part IV of the Recommendation on expulsion by the Immigration Ministers of 30 November – 1 December 1992 on readmission agreements.

[53] See *Financial Times*, 10 February 1993; *De Volkskrant*, 18 February 1993.

[54] See *e.g. De Volkskrant* 15 September 1992, which mentions five Moroccans drowning off the Spanish coast; since Spain instituted visas for Moroccans, Tunisians and Algerians, in May 1991, hundreds of Maghreb boat people have drowned according to the "Guardia Civil"; Christian Iraqi asylum seekers, transported by Turkish fishing boats, drown regularly and are kept off by the Greek coast guard near the Turkish coast. Yugoslav refugees have been shot at the Italo-Jugoslavian border; Albanians suffocate in containers (see *La Repubblica*, 31 January 1992) etc.

[55] Enzensberger, *Die Große Wanderung* (1992).

[56] The idea is to first look for a *non* EC country where the applicant had already been granted protection or had an opportunity to make contact with the authorities to seek protection, or where there is clear evidence of admissibility to the country. This new subterfuge will of course lead to orbiting and to social dumping.

[57] See Letter of the Dutch Minister of Justice, 15 December 1992 with annexes (21.503–23.407).

the *ad hoc* Group on immigration and invited this group to round off their discussions before the ministers' meeting in June 1993.[58]

The secrecy and isolation with which the negotiations in the fora concerned with Schengen, Dublin, the EC and other bodies is surrounded is notorious, as is the lack of parliamentary and judicial control. The isolation in which the many civil servants – this new class of nomads travelling frantically from seaside resort to arcadic mountain village – are operating has spoiled the broth. It is very difficult to mend political and technical mistakes once they have been agreed upon by the Eurocrats and national administrations. The procedural *vitium originis* shows in the substantive results. These have been called, rightly so, "an insult to democracy".[59] That is why, as an afterthought, several countries are now urging for improved forms of parliamentary and judicial control. Under pressure of the Dutch parliament the Dutch minister involved has introduced some draft protocols to the Schengen partners: *one* to define specific competences of the European Court of Justice under the Schengen Implementing Convention; and *one* to all Member States of the EC concerning the Dublin Conventions and other paracommunitarian instruments implementing the freedom of movement of persons.[60]

A common position on these reinforcements of the situation of those subjected to the provisions of these treaties has not yet been reached; Belgium is in favour, France is against judicial control and harmonization.

The UNHCR has proposed to put into place an independent committee which would have the task of answering preliminary questions concerning the interpretation of the various European instruments concerning asylum which would arise pending (administrative) proceedings in the countries of the contracting parties. This would split up the machinery of application of the Schengen Implementing Agreement in a part concerning asylum, and all other matters; it is not clear whether this Committee would give binding interpretations: in this respect the Dutch proposal is an improvement. The Executive Committee under this Agreement cannot be considered as exercising judicial control on the decisions of the contracting parties.

As for strengthening parliamentary controls the Dutch Minister of Justice promised the Second Chamber (21 October 1992) to inform Parliament in time before the November/December 1992 meeting of the Immigration Ministers about the agenda, the intended Dutch position and the draft conclusions. He furthermore promised not to take a definite position on resolutions which had not been presented before to Parliament for discussion. The Dutch situation is now aligned to the Danish one: in the conclusions of the December meeting more or less identical reservations by the two ministers are minuted. Further-

---

[58] The Draft Resolution on Harmonization of National Policies on Admission for Employment, prepared by the *Ad Hoc* Group on Immigration, has, in other words, not met with approval from the Ministers. Neither did it succeed in receiving applause from the Standing Committee of Experts on International Immigration in an early Comment of 22 October 1992. Not that approval by this excellent committee was to be expected.

[59] Standing Committee of Experts on International Immigration Refugee and Criminal Law in its comment on results of the December 1992 meeting.

[60] See (1993) *Nederlands Juristenblad*, 207.

more, it has been agreed that future decisions of the Schengen Executive Committee (Arts 131–133, Title VII) do not become final unless explicitly or
implicitly approved of by the Dutch Parliament (see Art 132 (3)). In this way in
the Netherlands and elsewhere political influence, scrutiny and control may be
injected in a system which is badly in need of democratic legitimation. National
parliaments are being given the opportunity to step in where Community institutions are helpless in their democratic deficit;[61] it is to be hoped that they will
avail themselves of this opportunity to scrutinise proactively the developments
in the various arenas concerned with migration and asylum.

Postscript (1 May 1993)

My scepticism concerning an entry into force of the Schengen Implementing
Agreement has been reinforced and corroborated greatly by the announcement
by the French Government that it has no intention of depositing its act of
ratification in 1993. The French Deputy Minister for European Affairs, Mr
Lamassure, has declared that the preconditions for the putting into effect of the
freedom of movement of persons under the Schengen Agreement "ne seront
réunies ni d'ici la fin de l'année 1993, ni même sans doute avant une période
assez longue."[62] It is ironic that the new French Government with Mr Pasqua
responsible as Minister for Internal Affairs is not at all inclined to stick to an
agreement which at the time of ratification – 4 June 1991, during the first
cohabitation, had been staunchly defended by Mr Pasqua acting in the same
capacity. France has struck a blow in this way against the establishment of the
internal market and its abolition of internal borders. France does not trust its
internal border with Italy and is afraid of the influx through this area of North
African irregular migration. It furthermore disagrees fundamentally with the
Dutch approach to the use of soft drugs, which is followed in Spain and, by the
abrogative referendum, in Italy which obliges the (which?) Italian Government
to decriminalise the use of soft drugs, a measure which was introduced on the
initiative of the criminal Secretary-General of the PSI, Bettino Craxi, only a few
years ago. This French position makes a decision by the European Court of
Justice only more urgent.

One cannot but think that the difficulties which the Schengen and Dublin
instruments have so far encountered, and which are largely based on mistrust in
the capacity of some contracting parties in putting their provisions into effective
operation, show unambiguously that of the four fundamental freedoms the
freedom of movement of persons is the lesser one in an organisation which does
not stop telling us that this is citizens' Europe. The European Community seems
to fear its citizens as much as it fears uncontrolled migration, and makes clear
again that, whatever the name, it is still an overwhelmingly economic enterprise.

HANS ULRICH JESSURUN D'OLIVEIRA

---

[61] See Groenendijk, Three questions about free movement of persons and democracy in Europe, *op cit*, n
46, 391–402.
[62] *Le Monde*, 3 May 1993.

Chapter 18

Europe and the Art of International Police Co-operation: Free Fall or Measured Scenario?[1]

The inclusion of European police co-operation in the third pillar of the Maastricht Treaty entails both a continuation of as well as a rupture with the past. On the one hand, EC Member States have reinforced a number of matters by means of Article K.1 which have been subject of common interest for several years (in particular immigration policy, the combating of drug addiction and international fraud, and customs co-operation); on the other hand, the signatories have taken on new challenges (in particular asylum policy, judicial co-operation in civil and criminal matters, and police co-operation) which imply a widening of the legal-functional scope of the European Community. Yet, as d'Oliveira notes in his contribution to this volume,[2] the matters have been concluded on an entirely intergovernmental basis, which encourages speculation about the "boundaries" of the European Community. One of the problems this chapter seeks to deal with is the possibility of expanding EC competences into the field of police and judicial co-operation, and of absorbing intergovernmental instruments and structures into the wider EC institutional framework. It addresses these questions by regarding the field of police co-operation as a policy-making process which interacts directly with the wider context of European integration, that is, first, political and legal concepts of federalism and the potential "transfer of sovereignty" to supranational bodies, and second, the concept of Europe's internal security.

Context, history and background

The completion of the internal market and the realization of a "People's Europe" has entailed the abolition of border controls on people at all internal borders of the European Community; nine of the 12 Member States, who together have

---

[1] This chapter has been written on the basis of research conducted within a project on 'A System of European Police Co-operation after 1992', which is funded by the Economic and Social Research Council.

[2] 'Expanding external and shrinking internal borders: Europe's defence mechanisms in the areas of free movement, immigration and asylum' in this volume, 261.

signed the Schengen Agreement, have agreed to abolish these controls by 1 December 1993.[3] As border controls have traditionally been relied on as a means to protect internal security,[4] their abolition has certain repercussions for policing. First, the abolition may encourage the real and potential growth of transnational crime, which is assisted by increased mobility and by the exploitation of lacunae in national and European legislation. Only through co-operation will it be possible to monitor the movements of internationally active criminals. Secondly, it may involve a qualitative change in the policing-task, as there will be a shift from systematic to selective border controls, associated with the increased use of (international) intelligence.[5] There will also be a shift from external to internal controls, which will require the police to be more selective; however, the targeting of suspect citizens may lead to charges of discriminatory conduct, and as police organizations are well aware of the importance of public confidence and support, they will be wary of making these internal controls too obvious. The realization that this new set of circumstances will equally affect the police organizations in all EC Member State, has inspired police forces to act jointly to amplify these mutual professional concerns.

These factors, in combination with the reinforcement of co-operative efforts as laid down in the Maastricht Treaty, have caused a *momentum* in what has been a long-term policy-making process. In the last two decades, Europe has witnessed the creation of a large number of co-operative structures, of which Trevi, Schengen and Europol have been the highlights.[6] The practical momentum of European police co-operation has been accompanied by a number of positive and negative factors. The positive factors include the drive for European integration, the infrastructural facilitation, and the mutual trust and co-operation which has gradually been shaped between the EC Member States.[7] The largest negative factor has been the concern about the "loss" of *national sovereignty*. Schutte[8] formulates the issue as follows:

"It seems, ... that the member states continue to resist the transfer to a supranational, communitarian authority of control over the issues outlined above on the ground that they are very closely bound up with questions of law enforcement. Thus, we see hardly any new powers conferred on Community institutions."

The Member States are not ready to consider the European Political Union as a "regional model for the development of supranational criminal justice".[9] The fear of having to compromise national sovereignty is responsible for the divergent interpretations of Article 8A of the Single European Act, for the conflicting views about national policies *vis-à-vis* drugs and terrorism, for the

---

[3] *Financial Times*, 1 July 1993.

[4] Den Boer, 'The quest for European policing: rhetoric and justification in a disorderly debate', forthcoming in Anderson and den Boer (eds) *Policing across National Boundaries* (Pinter, London, 1994).

[5] *Cf* Stüer, *Personenkontrollen an den Europäischen Binnengrenzen und ihr Abbau* (1990) 213.

[6] For more detail about these, see den Boer and Walker, 'European policing after 1992', (1993) 31 JCMS, 3–28.

[7] See *supra*, n 6, at 10 *et seq.*

[8] Schutte, 'The European market of 1993: test for a regional model of supranational criminal justice or of interregional co-operation in criminal law', (1991) 3 *Criminal Law Forum* 1, 55–83 at 83.

[9] *Ibid.*

painfully slow process of harmonization between criminal justice systems, for the competition between Member States about the location of major international policing institutions (such as Europol), and for the lack of clarity about Community powers with respect to the immigration of non-EC citizens. It is therefore accurate to describe the policy-making process on European police co-operation as a series of political boosts succeeded and often hampered by political, legal and technical realism. In particular the policy-making process surrounding the Schengen Agreement and Europol have made it abundantly clear that a great deal of political and legal problems have to be solved both *in retrospect* and *in anticipation*, thereby severely delaying the implementation of decisions.

One could argue that as a number of issues in the third pillar were already a matter of common concern before the Treaty was drafted, most of it would go ahead even if the Treaty were not ratified. As far as Denmark was concerned, the outcome of its referendum would *not* negatively affect its participation in the co-operation on Justice and Home Affairs.[10] On the other hand, however, the need for unanimity in the Council on justice and home affairs issues was emphasized in an accompanying unilateral Declaration by Denmark, by means of which special voting majorities are required to ratify developments in this field.[11] This does not discredit the argument that the very intergovernmental character of the third pillar paralyses the obstacles thrown up by political disagreement.

The third pillar of the Maastricht Treaty *consolidates* and *formalises*[12] initiatives which have already been undertaken in the realm of law enforcement. An important side-effect of this is that it will create some order in the chaos[13] which was brought about by the previous establishment of several intergovernmental structures which engaged in problems related to international crime or international law enforcement.[14] The new Co-ordinating Committee (Art K.4) will bring into effect a more structured (channelled) communication between the responsible ministries and law enforcement agencies, and will streamline the link between policy-making and financial resources. Its accountability will, however, not necessarily be increased, given the fact that it will retain an intergovernmental character. The problems of legal and democratic control will be discussed later in this chapter.

The third pillar leaves a number of issues unresolved, which are in part legal, in part technical. One of the first and foremost unresolved issues is that of the *extent* of international police co-operation, both in terms of *remit* and in terms of *functional intensity*. As we have seen in the recent past with Trevi and as we will

---

[10] See Conclusions of the Presidency, Edinburgh, 12 December 1992, Part B – Denmark and the Treaty on European Union.

[11] Walker, 'The International Dimension', in Reiner and Spencer (eds) *Accountable Policing: Effectiveness, Empowerment and Equity* (London, IPPR, 113–171; Annex 3.

[12] Fernhout, 'The United States of Europe have commenced. But for whom?', (1993) *Netherlands Quarterly of Human Rights* 3, 249–265.

[13] *Cf* van Outrive, *Second Report of the Committee on Civil Liberties and Internal Affairs on the entry into force of the Schengen Agreements*, 1992, European Parliament Session Documents, A3–0336/92, 17.

[14] Winter, 'Institutionelle Strukturen der Europäischen Union', (1993) 46 *Die Öffentliche Verwaltung* 173–184 at 180.

see in the future with Europol, the remit of these organizations is incremental in the sense that more tasks are being brought under the umbrella of these institutions.[15] Trevi expanded its remit from terrorism to police training, the internal market and even immigration. Europol, which is initially set up as a European Drugs Unit, is likely to expand its remit to include organised crime and fraud in the first round. The limits of, and opportunities for, future expansion of Europol will however be anchored in the Europol Convention, which is currently being drafted.

Relation between competence, sovereignty and harmonization

The move towards integrating the field of International Co-operation in Justice and Home Affairs into the institutional clockwork of the EC may be read as a political manifestation of the growing willingness to link crime and criminal justice issues with other issues on the European agenda, such as health, education, employment and migration. It is along this line of interpretation that the intergovernmental character of the chapter on Justice and Home Affairs can be characterised as (potentially) *transitional*, in the sense that these issues could in the future be made into an integral part of the European Union. Schutte,[16] who is sombre about this latter possibility, believes that "gradual integration may ultimately create the necessary substantive and institutional preconditions for the emergence of a genuine European model of interregional co-operation in criminal justice". In a similar vein, O'Keeffe[17] argues that:

"(O)ne conclusion to be drawn from the Union Treaty provisions and from the work programmes on immigration and asylum is that one may be assisting at the start of a very slow evolutionary process, whereby there may be a very gradual transfer of competence to Community institutions."

Fernhout[18] notes that in the Maastricht Treaty:

"the route towards Community powers in this area is deliberately left open and indeed, the first step in that direction has been taken. A new section 100c of the EC Treaty brings visa policy under Community authority. Section K9 of the Union Treaty grants the Council the opportunity, by means of a unanimous decision, to declare certain matters, which are currently dealt with through co-operation in the field of justice, as coming under the authority of the Community in future."

---

[15] Bigo, 'The European internal security field: stakes and rivalries in a newly developing area of police intervention'; den Boer, 'The Quest for European Policing: rhetoric and justification in a disorderly debate', in Anderson and den Boer (eds), *supra*, n 4.
[16] Schutte, *supra*, n 9 at 83.
[17] O'Keeffe, 'The Schengen Convention: a suitable model for European integration?', (1991) 11 YEL, 185–219 at 216.
[18] Fernhout, *supra*, n 12.

It is in this light perhaps interesting to consider the future development of the Schengen (Implementation) Convention. Apart from the fact that its provisions are merely applicable if compatible with Community law (Art 134), and the fact that it excludes non-EC Member States from becoming parties to the Convention (Art 140), the Schengen Agreement may be uplifted and integrated in the European Community legal framework. The European Parliament Committee on Civil Liberties and Public Affairs, which has monitored the Schengen developments, sounds cautious about this prospect, however, as "there is a danger that a body of law will develop over which neither the Commission nor Parliament has any influence".[19] O'Keeffe[20] clarifies this by noting that police co-operation within the European Community would have a basis both in Schengen as well as in the Maastricht Treaty. He says that it is likely that both will be very similar, "with the Schengen rules being used as a precedent".[21] More boldly, some predict that in due course the Schengen Agreement will be replaced by "the wider Europol initiative".[22] The latter would indicate a move from the current two-tiered system of European integration to a one-tiered system which would include all EC Member States, and (if the reading about the hybrid character of the current intergovernmental arrangements is correct) it would indicate a move toward future inclusion into the legal and political framework of the European Community: intergovernmental initiatives such as Schengen are gradually superseded by Community instruments.[23]

The potential for institutional integration is still obscure however. First, a clear direction is lacking in the determination of policies that focus on international crime and cross-border policing. A major source of indecision about crime "fighting" in Europe is whether it should be *preventive* or *repressive*.[24] In the case of a preventive policy, the associative links between crime and social-economic situations (social deprivation) would have to be looked into; between crime and health concerns (for example the link between drug addiction and disease); between crime and legal loopholes (for example the exploitation of legal gaps by organised crime); between crime and political anomaly (opportunities for corruption); and between crime and policy vacuums (criminal exploitation of unavailability of legal options for environmental dumping for instance). A "European Crime Prevention Programme" would have to be linked up with on the one hand a "Social Programme for Europe", and with on the other hand a "European Crime Control Programme". If, however, a repressive policy were to be adopted, not the causes and intentions behind criminal activities, but the methods and techniques of crime-fighting would become the principal object of concern. In this line of thought, organised crime, fraud, terrorism, drug-trafficking and the trade in women would be regarded as

---

[19] Van Outrive, *supra*, n 13 at 20.

[20] O'Keeffe, *supra*, n 17 at 204 and 216.

[21] The Italian Minister of Schengen Affairs, Sr Giuseppe Lo Iacono, suggested that Schengen is a good laboratory for free movement throughout the whole EC, and argued in favour of a pragmatic 'trial and error' approach (personal interview, Rome, 15 June 1993).

[22] Van Outrive, *supra*, n 13 at 25.

[23] *Ibid* at 28.

[24] *Cf* Walker, *op cit*, n 11.

a series of phenomena that should be suppressed with the increased use of intelligence, internal controls, and operational powers. A "European Crime Control Programme" should be properly balanced by a "European Crime Prevention Programme", but the question of policy-linking and institutional integration comes down to which discursive domain the European politicians would like matters to belong: the socio-economic or the legal domain.[25]

Furthermore, the institutional relationship between some intergovernmental institutions and EC institutions is unclear[26] or unsatisfactory. Although Article K.4 of the third pillar makes some firm statements about the type of relation between the members of the Co-ordinating Committee and the European Parliament and the European Council respectively, these statements do not express a firm commitment to institutional integration and accountability. As with regard to other intergovernmental structures, which do not cover the whole EC, but large parts of it, such as Schengen, it is unclear to whom the Schengen groups are accountable and how in the future they could be integrated in a wider organizational framework (see above); the European Commission attends meetings, of the Schengen central negotiating group and the Council of Ministers, as an observer.[27] But there is also uncertainty concerning the mutual integration of European Community law enforcement initiatives – for instance the European Community's own anti-fraud unit (UCLAF), which has administrative powers to investigate fraud[28] – and intergovernmental initiatives.[29] Finally, there is little explanation in the third pillar about how European Community legislation in the area of law enforcement ties in with intergovernmental agreements and conventions,[30] in particular instruments regarding *insider trading*,[31] *illegal substances*,[32] *money laundering*,[33] and *firearms and ammunition*.[34]

The vagueness about institutional integration also leaves the fate of legal control and accountability undecided. The role of the European Court of Justice and the European Court of Human Rights is rather vague, although according

---

[25] *Cf* Winter, *op cit*, n 14.

[26] *Cf* Walker, *op cit*, n 11.

[27] Van Outrive, *supra*, n 13, at 14.

[28] "Such powers include obtaining information from the member states, participating in investigations by member states of irregularities, initiating controls to be exercised in conjunction with officials of member states, requiring member states to establish inspection offices especially for this purpose, obtaining copies of information exchanged between the administrative services of member states, and receiving reports on the results of investigations undertaken and proceedings brought." ... "Moreover, Commission officials are being vested with greater operational powers, even though these may be exercised as yet only jointly with national authorities." These powers include the right to enter premises, to inspect administrative records, to take samples and conduct interviews and to gather evidence otherwise. Schutte wonders if this information would be admissible as evidence in the national courts. Schutte, *supra*, n 16 at 67–68.

[29] *Ibid*; Reinke, 'The EC Commission's anti-fraud activity', in Anderson and den Boer (eds), *European Police Co-operation*, Proceedings of a Seminar, University of Edinburgh, Department of Politics (1992) 13–30.

[30] *Cf* Schutte, *supra*, n 8, at 66.

[31] Council Dir 89/592 co-ordinating regulations on insider trading.

[32] Council Reg 3677/90 laying down measures to discourage the diversion of certain substances.

[33] Council Dir 91/308/EEC on prevention of the use of the financial system for the purpose of money laundering.

[34] Council Dir 91/477/EEC, which has made the acquisition and possession of weapons subject to common rules based on a Community list of authorised weapons.

to Article K.3 of the third pillar, international conventions drawn up in the field of justice and home affairs may stipulate that the Court of Justice "shall have jurisdiction to interpret their provisions and to rule on any disputes regarding their application, in accordance with such arrangements as they may lay down". Jurisdictional questions about hypothetical situations in which European citizens become subject of (illegitimate) international law enforcement action remain, however. From the jurisprudence of the European Court of Justice it has become evident that it was the "intention of the drafters of the Community treaties that European Community law is a community of law without a criminal law",[35] and that the "enforcement of law through the criminal law, including the enforcement of Community law through the criminal law, has been left exclusively to the member states".[36] The resistance against the creation of a European criminal justice system is immediately related to concerns about "the transfer of sovereignty" to a supranational body.

This concept of "transfer" itself is controversial however. According to Hay,[37] it is the question whether, the exercise of sovereignty by supranational organizations, such as the European Community, actually represent a lessening of state sovereignty. Apart from characterising the link between the "transfer of sovereignty" and "federalism" (so often made by politicians) as "wholly conceptualistic", Hay admits that supranational organizations undoubtedly show "analogies to federal entities in their supranational concentration of functions and powers and in their indirect jurisdiction over persons living in the member states."[38] The other, more profound, complication with the concept of "transfer of sovereignty" is that the supreme authority of the state and the primacy of national law over international law can only be considered as *juristic hypotheses*,[39] or even "fiction, when measured by the degree of actual interstate co-operation, factual interdependence, and reciprocal commitment".[40] It is argued by Kelsen[41] that as no strict division is possible between national and international law, the latter is considered part of the first; stronger even, international law can only be valid for a state if its legal order "contains a norm stipulating that the relations of this state to other states are subject to international law." In this interpretation, it depends on the normative authorization, given by the nation state to the supranational entity, whether or not the latter can legitimately exercise legal competence.[42] Hence, the core of the problem must lie in the divergent interpretations about the extent to which this authorization should reach, and the extent to which competences or new powers (not sovereignty) should be transferred or given to the Community.[43] As this interpretation is a

---

[35] Schutte, *supra*, n 8.
[36] Schutte, *supra*, n 8 at 55.
[37] Hay, *Federalism and Supranational Organizations: Patterns for New Legal Structures* (1966) 32.
[38] *Ibid*.
[39] Kelsen, *General Theory of Law and State* (1946) 383 *et seq*.
[40] Hay, *op cit*, n 37 at 67. This is a paraphrase of the views of Loewenstein.
[41] *Supra*, n 39 at 382.
[42] See also MacCormick, 'Beyond the Sovereign State' (1993) 56 MLR, 1–18 at 3.
[43] *Cf* Hay, *op cit*, n 37 at 65.

variable of the political consensus that can be achieved between the parties, the concept of sovereignty can be considered as dynamic.[44]

The battle about national sovereignty will be fought especially in relation to the harmonization of criminal laws and the "transfer" of criminal justice powers to the European Commission and the European Court of Justice. More than anyone else, the law enforcement professionals throughout Europe would like to see more harmonization between laws, to remove the legal-technical obstacles which they encounter in international criminal investigations.

Lack of legal harmonization

The difference between criminal laws and laws on criminal procedure confronts law enforcement officials, first of all with problems of *legal semantics*, in the practice of cross-border policing. A good example of discrepant legal definitions is the concept of *ordre public*, which may in the future become subject of a communitarian focus as phenomena such as football hooliganism and racist demonstrations have begun to take on an international dimension; furthermore, "legislative and social policy profile of the EC increases the likelihood of public order protests ... against European institutions and policies".[45] Within the EC Treaty, the concepts of *ordre public* and "internal security" are not concretised in Article 48 paragraph 3 and Article 56 paragraph 1.[46] The process of finding a common definition for these concepts[47] will primarily depend on the role assigned to the European Court of Justice in these matters.[48] Secondly, they have to cope with *operational differences* in the practice of cross-border police co-operation, which is related to the differences between national criminal procedures. In particular, rules on how to obtain criminal information and/or intelligence, arrest, hot pursuit, questioning, and pre-trial investigation differ quite substantially. Thirdly and finally, there are considerable differences in the *conduct of criminal trials* in the EC Member States. Rules on witnesses, evidence, pleadings and interrogation diverge, which affects the role of the police (as reporter of evidence or as witness) considerably. For example, rules of how to conduct "fair trial" vary widely throughout the Community,[49] which hampers law enforcement co-operation. It should be noted that the Council of Europe has done most of the pioneering work in the area of judicial co-operation in criminal matters; the legal arrangements which have been elaborated in its framework are now

---

[44] *Ibid* at 68.

[45] Walker, 'European integration and European policing: a complex relationship', in Anderson and den Boer, *op cit*, n 4.

[46] For a more elaborate interpretation of these clauses in relation to Article 8A of the EEC Treaty, see Timmermans, 'Free movement of persons and the division of powers between the Community and its Member States', in Schermers, *et al* (eds) *Free Movement of Persons in Europe* (1993) 358 *et seq.*

[47] Stüer, *op cit*, n 5, 202.

[48] Bongen, *Schranken der Freizügigkeit aus Grunden der Offentlichen Ordnung und Sicherheit im Recht der Europäischen Wirtschaftsgemeinschaft,* (1975).

[49] Gomieu, 'The future of fair trial in Europe: the contribution of international human rights legal and political instruments', (1991) 9 *Netherlands Quarterly of Human Rights*, 263–290.

generally regarded as the "body of law governing co-operation in criminal matters among the European Community Member States".[50]

Also the lack of harmonization of rules on *mutual judicial assistance and legal aid* is a problem.[51] There was considerable disquiet for example in Britain about the lack of a sound extradition arrangement with the Republic of Ireland, although recent Irish moves have been much appreciated by the British Government.[52] Finally, the harmonization of national criminal justice *policies* is a rather substantial problem. Disagreement and controversy for example exist with regard to the lenient Dutch drugs policy, and the criticism it receives from France and Germany for "exporting" its problems.[53]

The legal deficit

The absence of a clear legal direction in the development of European crime control is coupled with the lack of information about citizens' rights and duties.[54] The variation in criminal procedures, which we mentioned above, will be to the detriment of the citizen, if and when law enforcement co-operation will be intensified.[55] Furthermore, the intensification of mutual assistance in criminal matters within the framework of Schengen has not been complemented by an increase in mutual legal aid for suspects.[56] O'Keeffe[57] notes that the Schengen Convention strengthens the position of the prosecution, without mentioning the rights of the defence: "The balance between the parties in the case is altered. The defence does not have independent access to the foreign networks available to the police, even though it may have legitimate need thereof". A pressing question which ought to be raised is whether this imbalance in the Schengen Agreement is prophetic for police and judicial co-operation which has been arranged under the auspices of Title III of the Maastricht Treaty.

Moreover, there may be a particular problem concerning citizens who live in the European Community but who are not included in EC citizenship.[58] Members of *ethnic minority groups* are vulnerable to the abuse of human rights in Europe, especially more so in the light of the increased reliance on internal

---

[50] *Schutte, supra*, n 8 at 77.

[51] *Cf* Wöretshofer, 'Het Schengen-akkoord, dwangmiddelen en rechtsbescherming', in Mols (ed) *Dissonanten bij het akkoord van Schengen*, (1990) 110–118.

[52] *E.g. Irish Times*, 12 April 1990, 'Legislation urged to close 'loopholes' in extradition cases'; *Financial Times*, 21 November 1991, 'Brooke satisfied over extradition'.

[53] See *e.g. Le Figaro*, 4 December 1992, 'Drogue: le mauvais example d'Amsterdam'; *NRC Weekeditie*, 9 March 1993, 'De Franse angst voor nederwiet'; *NRC Weekeditie* 20 April 1993, 'Franse minister bestrijdt Nederlands drugsbeleid'; *Independent*, 6 May 93, 'Drug-tourism is side-effect of Maastricht'.

[54] Van Outrive, *supra*, n 13 at 6.

[55] *Ibid* at 8 and 21.

[56] *Ibid* at 20.

[57] O'Keeffe, *op cit*, n 17 at 203.

[58] See *e.g. Annual Report* of the Committee on Civil Liberties and Internal Affairs on respect for human rights in the European Community, Karel de Gucht (Rapporteur), European Parliament Session Documents, 27 January 1993, A3–0025/93 at 43.

controls which involve identity checks, and checks of hotel and employment registers.[59] If they fall victim to misuse of (international) police data they may face difficulty in appealing to the European Court of Human Rights, even though police and judicial co-operation conducted under Title III will be "in compliance with the European Convention of Human Rights" (Art K.2). On a more positive note, Fernhout[60] argues that the "Court of Justice has to an increasing extent included immigrants in Community law". However, given the institutional heterogeneity of the Community, it is the question whether the Court would also take up matters which normally fall under the auspices of intergovernmental agreements on police co-operation.

Moreover, there is the problem of *data protection*. The problem at the moment is that there are no general communitarian provisions for the various means of exchanging police data between the EC Member States. Each agreement has its own provisions: the Schengen Implementation Convention includes rules on how to protect data exchanged in the context of the Schengen Information System, mainly with reference to national data protection laws (between which there are considerable variations[61]) and the Council of Europe Convention on data protection;[62] Europol will also have its own data protection provisions, which will be laid down in its Convention which is currently being drafted. The Ministerial Agreement[63] concluded in Copenhagen on June 1993 reveals, however, that personal information will be communicated between liaison officers, who act in accordance with the provisions of national laws, and on the basis of bilateral agreements; the transmission of personal information to non-Member States or to international organizations will not take place. It should be noted that concerning Europol, there are already political noises about the stringency of, in particular the German and Dutch data protection laws, hindering the exchange of police data. The only solution for communitarian data protection provisions on the use of police data could have been offered by the (draft) EC Data Protection Directive. However, its remit is restricted, in that it primarily covers the private sector; in cases where it concerns the public sector police data is generally excluded.[64]

Finally, there is the problem of how to organise *international judicial monitoring* of cross-border policing. The Committee on Civil Liberties and Public Affairs calls for the monitoring of the Convention implementing the Schengen Agreement, and "considers the Court of Justice in Luxembourg to be the appropriate body for this purpose".[65] The Schengen Secretariat is currently studying possible jurisdiction by the Court of Justice in Luxembourg.[66] The

---

[59] Den Boer, *Immigration, Internal Security and Policing in Europe*, (1993), Working Paper VIII, A System of European Police Co-operation after 1992, Department of Politics, University of Edinburgh.
[60] Fernhout, *supra*, n 12.
[61] See Raab, 'Police co-operation: the prospects for privacy', in Anderson and den Boer (eds) *op cit*, n 4.
[62] Baldwin-Edwards, and Hebenton, 'Will SIS be Europe's 'Big Brother'?', in Anderson and den Boer (eds) *op cit*, n 4.
[63] *Ministerial Agreement on the Establishment of the Europol Drugs Unit*, Copenhagen, 2 June 1993, at 4.
[64] Raab, *op cit*, n 61.
[65] Van Outrive, *supra*, n 13 at 8.
[66] *Ibid*, 14.

Ministerial Agreement on Europol does not contain legal provisions on its legal accountability, but the expectation is that this will be arranged in the Europol Convention.

The democratic deficit[67]

The intergovernmental structure of European police co-operation implies a lack of formal democratic powers by the national parliaments and the European Parliament to exercise direct control over European policing bodies.[68] Even although the K4-Committee will have structured and institutionalised links with the European Parliament (see Art K.6, where it says that the Presidency shall regularly inform and consult the European Parliament and that the Parliament may ask questions of the Council or make recommendations to it), there will be other "floating" intergovernmental structures with an impact on international police co-operation which will not be subject to the arrangements made in Title III. A striking example is the Schengen central negotiating group, which consists of senior officials of the Schengen Member States, and is sub-divided into a number of working parties, such as ORSIS ("Orientation", Schengen Information System), Schengen I (Police and Security) and Schengen II (Movement of Persons[69]). Meanwhile, Europol's democratic accountability is at the moment unclear, although the Ministerial Agreement (1993) provides in the submission of a six-monthly written report by the co-ordinator about management and activities.

Furthermore, in the future there may be a lack of "bottom-up" subsidiarity,[70] which could be seen as a form of social legitimacy[71] and active citizen's control from below over policing activities. As policing accountability is displaced from the local/regional level to the international level, anonymity and distance between citizens and police will be reinforced. Moreover, as national governments introduce intergovernmental measures, consequential upon the consolidation of Europe's internal security apparatus, these cannot be disputed at any suitable international forum. Walker[72] notes, in this context, that the "vital nexus between effectiveness, active consent and public answerability is much less well established" in the international system.

---

[67] Bogdanor and Woodcock, 'The European Community and Sovereignty', (1991) 44 *Parliamentary Affairs* 481–492 at 482, define the democratic deficit as 'the lack of accountability of the Council of Ministers due to the insufficient powers of the European Parliament'.

[68] Van Outrive, *supra*, n 13 at 6, 8 and 14.

[69] *Ibid* at 14 and 16.

[70] 'Subsidiarity' is here defined wider than in the Conclusions of the European Council in Edinburgh (December 1992), which sees it as analogous with transparency and openness in the decision-making process of the Community.

[71] Weiler, 'The Transformation of Europe', (1991) 100 Yale LJ, 2403–2483 at 2469.

[72] Walker, *op cit*, n 11 at 38.

Future of Europe's internal security

As the geographical and the political shape of Europe is in a state of flux,[73] fragmentation, enlargement and integration have their effects on the re-conceptualization of a new European internal security. On the one hand there are signs of increasing regionalization and fragmentation, in Western as well as in Eastern Europe. As far as the regions in the European Community are concerned, there are numerous hot-spots where there is political pressure for more regional autonomy (Catalunya, Flanders and Wallonia, the German *Länder*, Scotland, etc). At the same time the enlargement of the European Community is on the agenda,[74] with a possible future inclusion of the EFTA states and some Eastern European states.[75] Enlargement negotiations have started with Austria, Sweden and Finland at the beginning of 1993. As these pressures and developments will profoundly affect the political map of Europe, they will also have an impact on considerations about Europe's internal security. Whereas increased regionalization will have consequences for the organizational and operational aspects of law enforcement, and indirectly also for opportunities for interregional police co-operation, the anticipation to enlargement begs the question whether EFTA states and Eastern European states should not already be involved in negotiations about the future of pan-European police co-operation.[76]

At the same time, national party politics are an important determinant of the issues which appear on Europe's internal security agenda.[77] It is significant that the push for the introduction of restrictive compensatory measures has been strongly supported by the ruling parties and governments in the EC Member States, whether they stand on the right, left or centre. This support has either been the product of a prevailing conservative ideology, such as in the United Kingdom and recently also in France, where exclusionary and restrictionist measures have been promoted to prevent even greater competition for employment, to avoid having to compromise internal security, and to avoid extremist reactions, or it has been the product of concessions to an essentially right-wing electorate (the Netherlands). The concluded agreements (Dublin, Schengen etc) and the planned establishment of new control measures (Europol, European Information System) are the manifestation of a European internal security ideology which predominantly aims at exclusion and control. It is very much the question whether future changes in the arena of national party politics will turn the tide of Europe's internal security apparatus, and whether there will be more consideration of legal and democratic control, and of human rights, international legal aid and data protection.

As international law enforcement bodies are increasingly expanding their

---

[73] *Cf* Pastore, *'Boundary' conflicts around and inside the European Community*, Paper presented to the 20th Annual Conference of the European Group for the Study of Deviance and Social Control (Padova, 4–6 September 1992), *mimeo*.

[74] See for example Conclusions of the Presidency, Edinburgh, 12 December 1992.

[75] Federal Trust for Education and Research, *Europe's Future: Four Scenarios*, (1991).

[76] Den Boer, *Police Co-operation after Maastricht*, (Research Paper No 2/92, University of Hull, ECRU).

[77] See *e.g.* 'Extreme Right in Europe', 45 *Parliamentary Affairs* (1992 special issue).

remit, concerns about phenomena which could jeopardise the internal security are frequently concatenated (a process whereby international crime is placed on the same continuum as illegal immigration) and together constitute an "internal security continuum".[78] This prevailing semantic interconnection also has repercussions for the linkage between these issues in the actual development of an "supranational security apparatus".[79] International crime and illegal immigration are increasingly often mentioned in combination with one another. Subtle, but indicative of this ideological interconnection is a phrase used by the European Council, when it talked about the work necessary to achieve free movement of people, "without creating dangers for public security and compromising the fight against illegal immigration".[80]

But even though internal security considerations of European governments are uniform in their desire to exclude and control, one may wonder whether the current multi-speed process of European integration will have an impact on the interpretation and application of internal security measures. It suffices to refer to the controversy between the United Kingdom and the European Commission, and her European counterparts, which has been caused by the divergent interpretation of Article 8A. Future controversies may include the qualitative enforcement of internal controls and the intra-European checks on EC citizens. Van Outrive[81] points out that the Schengen parties have not yet tackled the interpretation of the terminology used in Articles 95–100 of the Convention Implementing the Schengen Agreement, such as "danger to internal security", "public policy", and "serious criminal offence". It is therefore not necessarily the case that fewer partners reach an easier consensus about the interpretation of internal security concepts.

MONICA DEN BOER

[78] Bigo, 'The European internal security field: stakes and rivalries in a newly developing area of police intervention', in Anderson and den Boer (eds) *op cit*, n 4.

[79] Pastore, *supra*, n 73, at 10.

[80] Conclusions of the Presidency, Edinburgh, 12 December 1992, 17.

[81] Van Outrive, *supra*, n 13 at 17.

Part 9

Social Policy

Chapter 19
Twin-track Social Europe – the Inside Track

Introduction

The purpose of this article is to assess the changes introduced by the Treaty of Maastricht into the social policy provisions contained in the main body of what is now the EC Treaty.[1] Thus, if the deliberations of the Heads of State and Government at Maastricht in December 1991 and the formalization of those deliberations into Treaty form can be said to have created a twin-track Social Europe comprising, on the one hand, the main body of the Treaty and, on the other hand, the Social Policy Protocol (SPP) and Social Policy Agreement (SPA), this article follows the inside track, looking at social policy developments from the perspective of the core elements of the Treaty to which all Member States have assented.

The reasons for this focus are two-fold. First, the novel legal arrangements dreamed up by the policy-makers in Maastricht are the central concern of a related paper by Erika Szyszczak in this book, and they have, moreover, already been discussed in detail elsewhere.[2] Secondly, from diverse parts of the new EC Treaty it is possible to gather together a range of changes in terms of statements of principle, substantive content and general emphasis which, although disappointing in as much as the expectations for change in the social policy provisions before the Maastricht meeting had been high, are nonetheless worthy of comment in their own right.[3]

It is vital, in the welter of discussion about the SPP and the SPA, not to lose sight of the continuing role of the Treaty itself at the core of both existing and future EC social policy developments. The key phrase is that contained in the SPP: "this Protocol and [the SPA] are without prejudice to the provisions of this Treaty, particularly those which relate to social policy which constitute an integral part of the *acquis communautaire*". The Treaty itself, with the well-established law-making powers to be found in provisions such as Articles 100, 118A and

---

[1] This article adopts throughout the terminology of the Treaty of Maastricht, which renames the EEC Treaty as the 'EC Treaty'.

[2] See Szyszczak, 'Social Policy: a happy ending or a reworking of the fairy tale' in this volume, 313, also Whiteford, 'Social Policy after Maastricht', (1993) 18 ELRev 202; Weiss, 'The Significance of Maastricht for European Community Social Policy', (1992) 8 IJCLLIR 3; Barnard, 'A Social Policy for Europe: Politicians 1:0 Lawyers', (1992) 8 IJCLLIR 15; Blanpain, *Labour Law and Industrial Relations of the European Union. Maastricht and beyond: from a Community to a Union* (1992); Fitzpatrick, 'Community Social Law after Maastricht', (1992) 21 ILJ 199; Shaw, 'Social Policy after the Treaty of Maastricht: a brief comment' [1992] JSWFL 255. For further details on the specific problem of sex equality see Lanquetin & Masse-Dessen, 'Maastricht: consolidation ou remise en cause des principes en matière d'égalité professionnelle',(1992) *Droit Social* 386.

[3] See also Lanquetin & Masse-Dessen, 'Maastricht: consolidation ou remise en cause des principes en matière professionnelle',(1992) *Droit Social* 386.

235, coupled with the statements of principle on Social Policy to be found in the preamble to the Treaty and Articles 2, 3 and 117, offers the framework within which a more proactive social policy could have developed and could still be developed, given the necessary political will. The SPA sets out a parallel set of provisions covering largely the same substantive ground, but with a different institutional basis within which the role of qualified majority voting in the Council of Ministers is substantially increased. The reference to the *acquis communautaire* must be intended to ensure that the SPA will not entirely supplant the existing Treaty, and that recourse will only be had to the Agreement where the alternative would be the adoption of no policy measure at all, due to the blocking vote of the United Kingdom in the Council of Ministers.[3a] The purpose of the SPA was not to allow the United Kingdom to escape all responsibility in relation to Social Policy under the Treaty; it must surely be implicit in the UK's Community obligations that it should continue to support the development of existing policies and actions under the EC Treaty, as amended. However, the weakness of this argument lies in the absence of "a duty to legislate" on the part of the Council of Ministers which cannot be forced to accept specific proposals put forward by the Commission, even where the Parliament is in favour.[4] Certainly, the Council cannot normally be obliged to develop new policy competences, although the new view of the mutuality of the obligations of the Member States and the Community institutions under Article 5 EC which is being propounded by the Court of Justice[5] could be used to support an argument that the Council is obliged to act in order to implement the Community's recognised objectives.

Consequently, one of the key questions for the future within EC social policy will be the precise relationship between the Treaty and the SPA – the two tracks – and, to answer that question, we need a full assessment of the current state of play under the Treaty.

A note on style

The provisions on Social Policy within the EC Treaty have always displayed a number of distinctive characteristics:

– the provisions themselves are physically scattered and diffuse, and are not located in a single chapter or title;
– nor are they organised conceptually around a single statement of "what is Community social policy", along the lines of the definition of an internal market contained in Article 7A;[6]
– in that context, there has always been an unresolved tension between economic and social motives within Community social policy – between

---

[3a] On 12 October 1993, the day when the German Constitutional Court unblocked the coming into force of the TEU, the UK blocked the passage into law of the draft Works Council Directive, thereby triggering what is expected to be the first usage of the SPA.

[4] *Cf* the use of Art 175 EEC by the Parliament in Case 13/83 *Parliament* v *Council* [1985] ECR 1513.

[5] Case C-2/88 Imm *Zwartveld* [1990] ECR I-3365.

[6] Previously Art 8A EEC.

facilitating the completion of the internal market and pursuing agreed policy goals which are focussed on ensuring an increased level of social justice;
- the provisions lack "identity"; unlike the Treaty provisions on which the internal market has been constructed, the Social Policy provisions cannot lay claim to an obvious constituency, not least because there is still not in any true sense either a European labour market or a European trades union movement;
- finally, the provisions of the Community treaties have always been weak in terms of normative content. With the exception of Article 5 (right to non-discrimination on grounds of nationality), Articles 48, 52 and 59 (rights to free movement of persons) and Article 119 (right to equal pay for men and women), no enforceable social rights which individuals could rely upon have been granted by the EEC Treaty. Where the objective of the legislation is not concerned with matters of health and safety (Art 118A), there is little alternative to adopting harmonization legislation on provisions requiring a unanimous vote in the Council of Ministers. Article 118 offers a power under which the Commission can organise consultation exercises involving the Member States, but it cannot require changes in policy at national level or institute policies at the Community level.[7]

The Treaty on European Union (TEU) or Treaty of Maastricht does not significantly alter the position described above; indeed, if anything, it reinforces the poverty of the available provisions in the sense that there is a marked lack of progress towards a comprehensive and coherent body of Social Policy within the framework of the body of the Treaty itself. The creation of the dual arrangement involving the Treaty and the SPA and SPP creates a real danger of the destruction of any cohesiveness which might exist in the Social Policy field. The failures in the context of Social Policy stand in contrast to the progress made towards Economic and Monetary Union, the extension of the powers of the Parliament and the creation of the three pillar structure of European Union, to name but three of the successes of the Treaty of Maastricht. This failure must be seen in context, since Social Policy was one of the areas in which the European Council did ask the Intergovernmental Conference on Political Union to consider whether the extension of policy competence was appropriate.[8]

Policy incoherence and deconcentration of the relevant Treaty provisions remain a problem. For example, the provisions of citizenship and immigration – issues closely linked to the free movement of persons and consequently to Social Policy – are to be found in a number of disparate locations within the Treaty, including Part Two of the EC Treaty ("Citizenship of the Union"), Article 100C EC (visas) and Title VI of the TEU (Justice and Home Affairs). There is, moreover, no attempt in the Treaty to link the Community's labour market policies – of which immigration policy is one aspect, in so far as it is concerned with controlling the access of third country nationals to the legitimate labour market – either to its still nascent social law harmoniz-

---

[7] See on the interpretation of Art 118: Case 281/85. *Germany et al* v *Commission* [1987] ECR 3205.
[8] Laursen, Vanhoonacker & Wester, 'Overview of the negotiations', in Laursen & Vanhoonacker (eds), *The Intergovernmental Conference on Political Union*, Maastricht, EIPA (1992) at 11.

ation programme or to its redistributive structural policies such as regional policy. It is exceedingly difficult, therefore, for the outsider to point to common themes in Community Social Policy.[9] What is undoubtedly true is that while the European Community has made some significant incursions into the social policy field – notably through its regulatory framework guaranteeing the social security of migrant workers, its protection of equal pay for equal work for men and women and more recently its developing body of harmonization legislation in the field of health and safety at work – it has not developed a Social Policy in the style of a national policy, based around an organising principle of social justice or a set of welfare institutions which, if necessary, carry the individual from cradle to grave.

Amendments to the framework and substance of EC social policy contained in the Treaty of Maastricht

The general framework

"Mission statements"

In the Preamble to the TEU the High Contracting Parties indicate their determination:

"to promote economic and social progress for their peoples, within the context of the accomplishment of the internal market and of reinforced cohesion and environmental protection, and to implement policies ensuring that advances in economic integration are accompanied by parallel progress in other fields."

Article B TEU states that one of the objectives of the Union is:

"to promote economic and social progress which is balanced and sustainable, in particular through the creation of an area without internal frontiers, through the strengthening of economic and social cohesion and through the establishment of economic and monetary union . . . ."

Since the Paris Summit in 1972, the Member States have been concerned to promote a public rhetoric in which social affairs are accorded equal status with "pure" economic integration. The rhetoric of the Preamble and of the general principles contained in the TEU and the amended EC Treaty indicates that it is "neo-liberal business as usual", with these provisions apeing those which have long stood largely unheeded in the Treaty of Rome. Progress in the social sphere continues to be expressly linked to overall growth objectives. Moreover, any beefing up of the mission statements which underlie social policy is inevitably purely symbolic; policy progress in the European Community hinges

---

[9] Teague & Grahl, 'European Community Labour Market Policy', (1989) 13 *Journal of European Integration* 167; Majone, 'The European Community between Social Policy and Social Regulation', (1993) 31 JCMS 153.

on a coincidence of political will and normative competence, both of which are relatively weak in the Social Policy field.

The subsidiarity doctrine

Details of this doctrine can be found elsewhere in this book.[10] My comments here are limited to addressing how the application of the principle of subsidiarity might exert a practical influence upon the evolution of Social Policy. Some evidence can be gleaned from the reformulation of Article 3 EC to incorporate references to new policy fields. Article 3 is largely unamended in the social sphere, although Article 3j now commits the Community to a "strengthening of economic and social cohesion"; health protection, education and training, cultural policy and consumer protection are also now formally included in the "activities" of the Community (Art 3o, p and s). The references to health protection, education and culture are phrased in terms of the Community making a "contribution", in this case in areas where it is acknowledged that primary policy competence continues to lie with the Member States. This is one of a number of examples of how subsidiarity is given a legal significance through new or redrafted provisions of the Treaty. In this case, a new form of policy division between the Community and the Member States is contemplated – "the Community contribution" – which can be treated as an example of co-existing competence with the Member States taking the lead.

Whatever the wishes of the UK Government, subsidiarity cannot be used as a justification for challenging the very notion of a Community Social Policy. This was made clear in the Edinburgh Communiqué:[11]

"The principle of subsidiarity does not relate to and cannot call into question the powers conferred on the European Community by the Treaty as interpreted by the Court. ... The application of the principle shall respect the general provisions of the Maastricht Treaty, including the 'maintaining in full of the *acquis communautaire*' ... nor shall it call into question the principle set out in Article F.3 of the Treaty on European Union, according to which the Union shall provide itself with the means necessary to attain its objectives and carry through its policies."

In terms of the implementation of social policy, however, the Communique' carries a sting in the tail. In the detailed comments upon the third paragraph of Article 3b (nature and extent of Community action), it is noted that:

"The form of action should be as simple as possible, consistent with satisfactory achievement of the measure and the need for effective enforcement. The Community should legislate only to the extent necessary. Other things being equal, directives should be preferred to regulations and framework directives to detailed measures. *Non-binding measures such as recommendations should be preferred where appropriate. Consideration should also be given where appropriate to the use of voluntary codes of conduct.*"[12]

---

[10] See Toth, 'A legal analysis of subsidiarity', Steiner, 'Subsidiarity under the Maastricht Treaty' and Emiliou, 'Subsidiarity: panacea or fig leaf?', in this volume at 37, 49 and 65 respectively.

[11] Presidency Conclusions, Edinburgh European Council, 11–12 December 1992, Part A, Annex 1, Basic Principles (Agency Europe 13–14 December 1992).

[12] Author's italics.

It is a well known facet of Community Social Policy, that measures originally intended by the Commission to take legally binding form are sometimes adopted in the end merely as persuasive recommendations or resolutions. The use of such soft law forms is well-established in current Social Policy practice.[13] The difficulty with these measures is, of course, that of securing compliance in the absence of legal obligation, and it is questionable whether they satisfy the requirement of "effective enforcement" referred to above. Furthermore, even where binding measures are adopted, difficulties in achieving the requisite agreement amongst the Member States frequently leaves Social Policy harmonization measures as offering very much a minimum of provision. The recently adopted Pregnancy Directive is an example of the minimal impact of Community law.[14]

The Commission has conceded in the subsidiarity debate that it might need to reconsider some of the proposals which it has placed on the table before the Council of Ministers, and also to facilitate the reconsideration by the Council itself of measures which have already been adopted and which might no longer seem appropriate in the light of the introduction of the subsidiarity principle. The legitimacy of the latter course of action seems questionable in so far as the Community project must be seen as a process in which the Member States gradually transfer competence to the Community within a supranational framework[15] such that reconsideration of earlier measures would appear to be a threat to the *acquis communautaire*. However, it should be noted that the majority of the recent social law Directives do not appear to be under threat. The Commission has commented that:

"the group of directives based on Article 118A of the Treaty is too recent to warrant re-examination. Instead its priority will be to supplement them by implementing all the provisions of the Charter of the Fundamental Social Rights of Workers."[16]

While welcome from the perspective of the maintenance of the body of Community social law, these comments seem somewhat illogical. Being of recent vintage does not render Community legislative measures immune from the "threat" of subsidiarity, if that is how it is to be construed and applied. Indeed, on a "last-in/first-out" approach to the gradual accretion of competence by the Community, surely they would seem the most vulnerable to reconsideration, if they were in fact measures in which the Community had overstepped its role in the health and safety field.

I shall return to the practical application of the subsidiarity principle in the newly amended social policy provisions of the EC Treaty below.[17]

---

[13] *E.g.* Council Rec 92/241 on child care and family responsibilities (OJ 1992 L123/16); Commission Rec 92/131 on dignity at work (OJ 1992 L92/131) and Council Declaration of 19 December 1991 on the implementation of this Recommendation (OJ 1992 L27). The Commission has issued a Code of Practice on measures to be introduced by the Member States to combat sexual harassment.

[14] Council Dir 92/85/EEC (OJ 1992 L348/1).

[15] Case 6/64 *Costa* v *ENEL* [1964] ECR 585.

[16] Annex 2 to Part A of the Presidency Conclusions, Edinburgh European Council; Agence Europe 13–14 December 1992.

[17] *Infra* at 307.

Fundamental rights

According to Article F.2 TEU:

"The Union shall respect fundamental rights, as guaranteed by the European Convention for the protection of Human Rights and Fundamental Freedoms signed in Rome on 4 November 1950 and as they result from the constitutional traditions common to the Member States, as general principles of Community Law".

This follows verbatim the formula long adopted by the Court of Justice in its caselaw on fundamental rights.[18] A number of comments on this provision can be made. First, it is the location of Article F.2 which is the key to its interpretation: the drafters of the Treaty chose to place the Union's commitment to fundamental rights within Title I TEU, outside the jurisdiction of the European Court of Justice. Furthermore, the provision appears to be limited to the Union, and does not extend to the Member States, although the latter have in recent years been held by the Court of Justice to be subject to Community fundamental rights where they act within the scope of Community competence. Finally, the provision is phrased in terms of "respect" for fundamental rights, not in terms of offering rights guarantees to individuals.

The exclusion of Article F.2 TEU from the scope of the jurisdiction of the European Court and the drafting of the provision will have disappointed those, including the Commission and the European Parliament, who have long urged a firmer commitment on the part of the European Community to fundamental rights and who must have hoped for both a catalogue of rights and a legally binding guarantee of individual rights to be included in the Treaty of Maastricht. The link between constitutional maturity and stability and respect for fundamental rights is a cornerstone of liberal democracy. The elaboration of a catalogue of fundamental rights for the European Community and now for the European Union is an endeavour which is fraught with the most acute difficulties in both theory and practice. There are two principal points of contention which continue to bedevil both the judicial protection of fundamental rights as general principles of laws as currently practised in the European Community on the basis of the case law of the Court, and, consequently, the prospects for the elaboration of a Community code or catalogue of fundamental rights.[19] These concern the range of activities subject to Community fundamental rights and the content of the rights to be protected. Both of these issues were touched upon, but ultimately dodged, by the Court in *SPUC* v *Grogan*.[20] This case leaves uncertain the extent to which a Member State may fall foul of the Community's basic economic principles such as freedom of movement for services and persons (which themselves have the status of fundamental rights), where the Member State in question is simply pursuing a specific national constitutional goal based on deeply entrenched domestic cultural commitments – in that case,

---

[18] See for a practical example of the caselaw of the Court: Case 46/87 *Hoechst* v *Commission* [1989] ECR 2859.

[19] See generally on this Lenaerts, 'Fundamental rights to be included in a Community catalogue', (1991) 16 EL Rev 367.

[20] Case C-159/90 [1991] 3 CMLR 689.

the Irish constitutional ban on abortion.[21] The case also leaves unresolved the question of how a conflict between different fundamental rights (here freedom of information and freedom to travel *vs* the right to life of the foetus) should be dealt with where one Member State stands out of line with the others.[22]

If agreement cannot be reached on providing the Community with a catalogue of basic civic and political rights, it cannot be regarded as surprising that the Community is no nearer adopting a "rights-based" approach to Social Policy than it was in December 1989 when the Community Charter of Fundamental Social Rights of Workers was adopted in a declaratory form in Strasbourg by 11 out of the 12 Member States. Rights in the European Community will continue in large measure to play the same role as hitherto, at least as regards the status of individuals. Social rights, including those elaborated in the European Social Charter – the Council of Europe document – as well as the European Human Rights Convention and the Community's own internal documents such as the Social Charter, could potentially be used as the basis for challenges to acts of the Community where these impinge upon individual rights. However, the judicial scrutiny will have to be based on the existing judicial approach rather than on Article F.2 TEU which is likely to be viewed as no more than an aid to interpretation for the Court of Justice. Moreover, it is a moot point whether the Court of Justice would ever be willing to extend its fundamental rights caselaw by reference to open-ended aspirational social rights such as those included in either the Community or the Eurpean Social Charter. The content of such rights is insufficiently certain to permit of judicial enforcement by the Court of Justice.

A further damaging consequence of the failure to include the fundamental rights provision within the EC Treaty and to subject it formally to the jurisdiction of the Court of Justice is that fundamental rights will continue to retain the rather anomalous position of general principles of law. In principle these are superior sources of law, binding both the Community and the Member States where they act within the scope of Community competence. However, general principles of law, even where these take the form of fundamental rights such as the right to sex equality recognised in *Defrenne* v *SABENA (III)*,[23] are not directly effective and capable of giving rise to individual rights which national courts must protect, unlike some of the Treaty provisions from which they stem (*e.g.* Art 119 EC – equal pay for men and women). Had the provisions of Article F.2 TEU been brought within the scope of the jurisdiction of the Court of Justice, it might have been possible for Community fundamental rights to evolve in the hands of the judiciary to acquire the same status in the *national* legal order as other Treaty provisions which are directly effective, thus in part supplanting the role of the Member States in agreeing upon a binding Community fundamental rights code. It is interesting to speculate whether it was the prospect of such a judicial development which persuaded the drafters of the Treaty that it would

---

[21] See also Case C-260/89 *Elliniki Radiophonia Tileorasi (ERT)* v *Dimotiki Etairia Pliroforissis* [1991] ECR 2925; Case 5/88 *Wachauf* v *Federal Republic of Germany* [1989] ECR 2609.

[22] See Phelan, 'Right to life of the unborn v promotion of trade in services: the European Court of Justice and the normative shaping of the European Union', (1992) 55 MLR 670.

[23] Case 149/77 [1978] ECR 1365.

be wisest to locate the commitment to fundamental rights outside the EC Treaty.

Notwithstanding these comments, the formal reference to the fundamental rights which bind the Union, and the implicit invocation of the caselaw of the Court Justice in the text of the article, lends weight to the argument that Community fundamental rights could play a vital role in litigation strategies in which challenges are mounted against the extent to which Member States fail to heed basic rights such as race equality when acting within the scope of Community competence. A good example would be that certain Member States do not effectively prohibit race discrimination in the employment sphere. Thus, discrimination could go unremedied where it affects migrant workers from the ethnic minorities who are benefitting from the freedom of movement granted by Article 48 EC and the relevant secondary legislation and who therefore fall within the scope of Community competence and under the protection of Community law. Although it is difficult to characterise an omission as a violation of human rights, it is nonetheless possible to argue that the Member State in question would be infringing the Treaty by failing to provide effective remedies against discrimination on grounds of colour or ethnic origin. Against this argument it would be ineffective for the Member State to invoke the doctrine of subsidiarity to argue that the observance of rights guarantees in relation to all national legislation is a matter for Member States, even where the issue in question falls within Community competence.

The inclusion of fundamental rights protection amongst the framework provisions of the European Union could also assist attempts to argue that the provisions of the EC Treaty (such as Art 235) could be used to enact protective legislation within particular areas where fundamental rights are exceptionally vulnerable to infringement. Again race discrimination provides a good example.[24] As with any factor which distorts the level competitive playing field within the labour market, it is possible to argue that the disparities between the race discrimination laws of the Member States[25] should be made the subject of harmonization measures in the interests of the single market, at least in as much as they affect employment issues.[26] More convincing a justification for Community action – but one which is even less likely to attract the support of the Member States in the Council of Ministers than the distortion of competition argument – is that in the move towards a new stage of European integration involving the creation of a European Union, the Community should be concerning itself with ensuring the practical enforcement of the basic standards of human decency to which the Union is so piously dedicated. The presence of Article F.2 TEU lends a new dimension to the arguments for the phrase "objectives of the

[24] See generally Szyzsczak, 'The limits of market equality?' in Hepple and Szyszczak (eds), *Discrimination: the Limits of Law* (1992).

[25] Forbes and Mead, 'Measure for measure. A comparative analysis of measures to combat racial discrimination in the Member Countries of the European Community' (Employment Department Research Series, No 1, 1992).

[26] Art 100 EC would be the appropriate legal basis for such measures, since measures concerning the rights and interests of employed persons are excluded from the qualified majority voting provisions of Art 100A.

Community" in Article 235 to be given a broader and more proactive interpretation in the light of the Community's evolving role in western Europe.

Democracy, accountability and legitimacy

These are not issues which strictly pertain to social policy *per se*. It would, however, be useful to comment upon these types of institutional developments from the Social Policy angle, in particular since the link has been made since the 1973 Social Action Programme between participative democracy and the evolution of Community Social Policy. The major institutional innovation of the Treaty of Maastricht which impinges directly upon the Social Policy legislative programme is the establishment of the Committee of the Regions. This Committee of representatives of regional and local bodies established by Article 198a EC matches the ECOSOC in size and composition[27] as well as basic role within the structure of interest representation in the Community. The members of the Committee, whose principal role is to deliver opinions on legislation when consulted by the Council of Ministers and to issue own-initiative opinions in appropriate cases (Art 198c EC), are completely independent in the performance of their duties in the general interest of the Community.

Certain cases of compulsory consultation of the Committee on proposed legislation are prescribed in the Treaty, and these include Article 128 EC (culture), Article 129 (public health) and the revised provisions on Economic and Social Cohesion (Arts 130a-e EC). Consultation of the Committee is not envisaged for measures adopted under Article 118a EC – the central Social Policy law-making power regarding health and safety. Somewhat anomalously, provision is not made for the consultation of the Committee in the context of the implementation of the Community's environmental policy (Arts 130r-t EC), although this is a case where Article 198c(2) might come into play. This provides that the Committee should be informed where the ECOSOC is consulted on a proposal but it is not, allowing the Committee to issue an opinion if it "considers that specific regional interests are involved." By strengthening the input of the "regional perspective" into the Community's legislative process, the Member States are – at least in theory – attempting in a small way to bring the European Community and the European Union closer to the peoples of Europe, as mandated by Article A.2 TEU. The true impact of this institutional innovation, and its ability to underpin the Community's emergent regionalism, remains as yet unproven.[28]

It is also unlikely that the measures introduced by the Treaty of Maastricht to alleviate the democratic deficit in respect of Parliamentary participation will bring about any significant change in the existing balance of power within the legislative process in the social policy field. The key provisions such as Articles 118a and 6 EC[29] have not been altered to introduce co-decision on the part of the Parliament (Art 189b EC) but are still based on the co-operation procedure (Art 189c EC). Articles 100 and 235 retain the "old style" legislative procedure

---

[27] 189 members shared between the Member States according to size and population.

[28] See further on this Häberle, 'Der Regionalismus als werdendes Strukturprinzip des Verfassungstaates und als europarechtspolitische Maxime', (1993) *Archiv des öffentlichen Rechts*, 1.

[29] Formerly Art 7 EEC.

involving consultation of the Parliament and a unanimous vote in the Council. The scope of Article 100a remains unaltered and has not been widened to include social policy harmonization measures. The only exceptions to this continuing policy of limiting the input of the Parliament into social policy are the use of the co-decision procedure for the adoption of the measures implementing the Community's "contribution" in the flanking policy areas of education, culture and public health,[30] the use of the co-decision procedure for the adoption of guidelines on the Trans-European Networks to be funded by the new Cohesion Fund[31] and the requirement of the *assent* of the Parliament for the creation of that fund and for the reorganization of the existing structural funds.[32]

Criticism can therefore be levelled at the failure of the Member States to develop the existing Social Policy competences and law-making powers in the same way that those directly pertaining to the (economic) internal market have been developed. However, it should also be recalled that the provisions of the SPA do not provide for co-decision in respect of Social Policy measures. The institutional innovations of those provisions are limited to extending qualified majority voting and the use of the co-operation procedure. It is hard to see why the Member States should refuse to trust the Parliament with enhanced participation powers in the context of Social Policy, in particular since there is no evidence to suggest, in the areas where its powers have seen a gradual accretion, that it has used these powers other than in the general interest of the Community.

Substantive areas

Citizenship, immigration and the free movement of persons

This important field of Community social policy is amply dealt with elsewhere in this book;[33] consequently the changes brought about by the Treaty of Maastricht are not considered here.

Economic and social cohesion

The Community's principal redistributive policies hide modestly behind a piece of "Euro-jargon" – *economic and social cohesion*. This is the forgotten face of Community Social Policy, where the Member States have found it easier to reach a consensus than in respect of the harmonization programme which involves a more obvious invasion of national interests and national sovereignty and often requires the import of "foreign" provisions into the domestic legal system. Social policy of this nature is also intended to be enabling and facilitative *vis-à-vis* its beneficiaries, rather than restrictive and regulatory, as social policy harmonization measures can sometimes be characterised. Thus although these policies do involve governmental intervention in the market place in order to mitigate some of the harsher effects of the free market, they are not treated with the same suspicion as policies based on harmonization by many of the Member

---

[30] Arts 127–19a EC.
[31] Art 129d EC.
[32] Art 130d; see below.
[33] See d'Oliveira, 'Expanding and shrinking internal borders' in this volume, 261.

States.[34] It is conventional wisdom that some of the Member States who were sceptical of the ability of pure market-led growth alone to regenerate the fortunes of the Western European economy were signed up to support the internal market project on the promise of a reorientation of the Community's financial commitments in favour of the structural policies.[35] This was achieved in 1988. The same comment holds true of the step forward towards Economic and Monetary Union taken in the Treaty of Maastricht; this was sold to the Member States, in part, using the innovation of a new Cohesion Fund, which facilitates the channelling of assistance from the richer Member States towards those with Gross National Products well below the Community average, through support for projects in the fields of the environment and trans-European infrastructure and transport networks (Art 130d EC). The same provision envisaged a reorganization of the existing structural funds[36] as regards their tasks, primary objectives and functioning in order to increase their effectiveness. The legislative procedure for both parts of Article 130d involves a Commission proposal, Council unanimity, European Parliament *assent*[37] and consultation of the ECOSOC and the Committee of the Regions.

Evidence of a high level of commitment amongst the Member States to the structural policies comes not only from the 1988 reforms and the subsequent policy direction of Community regional policy, but also from the fact that alone among the policy developments envisaged by the Treaty of Maastricht, those concerned with the structural funds and the Cohesion Fund have suffered relatively little as a consequence of the delays in ratifying the Treaty. Even if Community regional policy development has less to do with an emerging concept of a "Europe of the Regions" as a basis for Community federalism or with an application of subsidiarity doctrine which effectively empowers the regions in preference to the nation states, and more to do with a trade-off between Member States which have differing stakes in the progress of the integration project, the success is significant and worthy of comment.

A detailed agreement on the content of the Cohesion Fund Regulation was reached at the Edinburgh Summit[38] and detailed financial perspectives based on the "Delors II" plan for the future financing of the Community[39] were agreed which will see a further narrowing of the gap between Community spending on agriculture and on structural actions by 1999.[40] The four countries initially to benefit from the Cohesion Fund – those with GNPs per capita at 90% or less of the Community average – are Spain, Portugal, Greece and Ireland. However,

---

[34] See however the caution of Hochbaum, 'Kohäsion und Subsidiarität – Maastricht und die Länderkulturhoheit', *Die öffentliche Verwaltung* (1992) 285.

[35] See generally Scott and Mansell, 'European Regional Development Policy: confusing quantity with quality' (1993) 18 EL Rev 87.

[36] The most important sources of funding are the European Social Fund, the European Regional Development Fund and the Guidance section of the European Agricultural Guidance and Guarantee Fund.

[37] This is an example of the extension of this requirement for legislative action, originally included in the Single European Act for the accession of new Member States (Art 237 EEC) into the internal policy field.

[38] See Part C, Annex 3 to the Presidency Conclusions, *Agence Europe*, 13 December 1992.

[39] 'From the Single Act to Maastricht and beyond: the means to match our ambitions', COM (92) 2000.

[40] From 35,230 million ECU on agriculture and 21,885 million ECU on structural actions in 1993 to 38,389 million ECU on agriculture and 30,000 million ECU on structural actions in 1999.

for these countries, continued Community participation in infrastructure and environmental projects supported by the new fund may be restricted once two years after the entry into force of the Treaty of Maastricht has elapsed if they fail to obseve the macro-economic conditions on budget deficits laid down in Article 104c(6) with a view to keeping overspending and undisciplined countries firmly on the path towards EMU. In that way, the redistributive allocations made by the Community are explicitly tied to the pursuit by the beneficiaries of certain types of approved macro-economic policies.

The European Council in Edinburgh invited the Commission to set the ball rolling towards the adoption of an interim instrument establishing the Cohesion Fund, based on Article 235, even in advance of the successful completion of the ratification process. Where that approach leaves the assent of the Parliament provided for in the Treaty of Maastricht is not made clear in the Presidency Conclusions.

Education and vocational training

Article 128 EEC was one of the provisions of the original Treaty of Rome which was ripe for reformulation by the Member States. It displayed two serious inadequacies: first, as regards content, speaking merely of "general principles" contributing to "the harmonious development both of the national economies and of the common market", it failed to give sufficient guidance to the Community institutions as to the scope and direction of Community vocational training policy; secondly, as regards procedures, it contained a rather anomalous law-making power under which the Council of Ministers could act by a simple majority and without consulting the European Parliament. The Court of Justice played a decisive part in shaping the precise role of Article 128 EEC as the cornerstone of a suprisingly extensive Community vocational training policy.[41] Through its decision in *Gravier* v *City of Liège*,[42] the Court of Justice pushed the Council into adopting the ERASMUS programme co-ordinating the movement of students in Higher Education within the European Community; the alternative to such planned movements would be unco-ordinated movements with students taking advantage of the rights they derived under the Treaty to freedom of movement, rights of residence and equality of access to educational facilities using Articles 7 and 128 EEC read together. The Court also enhanced the role of Article 128 EEC as a legal basis for Community action, refusing to accept arguments that the rather anomalous form taken by Article 128 precluded its use as a legal basis for the Council Decisions underpinning the Community's vocational training support programmes.[43]

Now the need for such artificiality has gone. Under Article 127 EC as redrafted, the guidelines on policy content are clearer and more extensive, and the anomaly of the legislative power is replaced with the familiar pattern of the co-operation procedure under Article 189c EC. The Community is now

---

[41] See generally Shaw, 'Education and the law in the European Community' (1992) 21 *Journal of Law and Education* 415; Flynn, 'Vocational training in Community law and practice' (1988) 8 YEL 59.
[42] Case 293/83 [1985] ECR 593.
[43] Case 242/87 *Commission* v *Council (ERASMUS)* [1989] ECR 1425; Case 56/88 *United Kingdom* v *Council (PETRA)* [1989] ECR 1615.

responsible for implementing a vocational training policy "which shall support and supplement the action of the Member States, while fully respecting the responsibility of the Member States for the content and organization of vocational training". This clearly shows that the Community holds a competence which is restricted in its purpose and scope, a point elaborated in paragraph 4 of the article where measures harmonising the laws and regulations of the Member States are specifically excluded from those which can be adopted under that law-making power. This would appear to be a specific example of the subsidiarity principle in its narrow legal sense – that of policing the borderline between the respective roles of the Member States and the Community in areas of shared competence.

The measures to be adopted under Article 127(4) should serve the achievement of the objectives laid down in Article 127(2), including the facilitation of industrial change through training and retraining, the improvement of initial and continuing vocational training in order to facilitate vocational integration and re-integration into the labour market, the facilitation of access to vocational training, the stimulation of co-operation between business and educational establishments, and the development of exchanges of information on vocational training issues between the Member States.

Perhaps somewhat surprisingly, the Treaty does not define either vocational training or education. Neither has the Court of Justice offered a positive definition of vocational training, although it is clear from its caselaw since *Gravier*[44] that almost all post-secondary education will be included in the concept of vocational training with the exception of:

"certain special courses of study which, because of their particular nature, are intended for persons wishing to improve their general knowledge rather than prepare themselves for an occupation."[45]

By the same token, general school education cannot normally be considered as vocational training[46] which would appear to be limited by reference to a vocational and consequently economic end. However, the Court has held that Community vocational training measures such as the ERASMUS programme did not fall outside the scope of Article 128 EEC, simply because there is a chance that some students would take advantage of the programme in order to study non-vocational subjects in other Member States.

This distinction remains important in the context of the Treaty of Maastricht, as education is accorded a different status as a Community policy under Article 126 EC. Education is treated, like culture and public health, as a "flanking policy". That is, the Community policy makes a "contribution" to the policies of the Member States – a state of affairs which is not many steps removed from the intergovernmental structures which have previously been used in these policy areas. The key difference is that under Article 126 EC, educational incentive measures are to be adopted by the Council using the co-decision

---

[44] *e.g.* Case 24/86 *Blaizot* v *University of Liège* [1988] ECR 379; Case 197/86 *Brown* v *Secretary of State for Scotland* [1988] ECR 3205.
[45] Case 24/86 *Blaizot* v *University of Liège* [1988] ECR 379 at 404.
[46] Case 263/86 *Humbel* v *State of Belgium* [1988] ECR 5365.

procedure, and recommendations on educational issues are to be adopted by a qualified majority. This is quite different from the consensus-based approach of intergovernmentalism, although it is perhaps still unfortunate that in the case of recommendations no input from the Parliament is foreseen. It can now be anticipated that many of the measures previously adopted by the Council of Ministers on the mixed basis of "Decisions of the Representatives of the Member States, meeting in Council" can now be adopted in the form of Council Recommendations. Funding programmes in the broader educational sphere will also be capable of receiving support out of the Community's own financial appropriations. This gives the Community an increased role through the "carrot and stick" approach of selective funding to encourage the development of educational initiatives which foster the spirit and practice of European integration, including in particular language training, mobility of students and teachers and enhanced mutual recognition, all topics cited expressly in Article 126.

It appears acceptable that the role and nature of Community action should be strictly circumscribed in respect of educational policy to exclude harmonization measures (as it is also with culture and public health), since these are policy areas which are more tangential to the specifically economic objectives of the Community *per se* and more directly related to the wider political objectives of the European Union. They are areas merely emerging gradually into the supranational sphere out of the sphere of intergovernmentalism. It seems less legitimate for the Member States to impose a strict limitation upon the type of measures which the Community can adopt in the field of vocational training – a well-established area of Community competence with strong roots in the Treaty, in secondary implementing measures, in institutional structures such as CEDEFOP and in the caselaw of the Court of Justice. It remains a moot point, it is submitted, whether other provisions of the Treaty such as Articles 100, 100a and 235 could be used as a legal basis for harmonization measures should this prove necessary in the future either to facilitate the completion of the internal market or to attain one of the Community's objectives.

Articles 126(3) and 127(3) EC mandate the Community and the Member States to foster co-operation with third countries in the matter of education and vocational training. The parallelism of the Community's internal and external competences requires no specific Treaty provisions but is recognised by the case law of the Court of Justice on implied powers.[47] This point is further evidenced in practice by the adoption under Article 235 EEC of Council Regulation 1360/90 establishing the European Training Foundation.[48] The aims of the Foundation are to act as a vehicle for the delivery of aid in the form of assistance for vocational training from the Member States of the Euorpean Community (and certain other third countries) to the new democracies of Central and Eastern Europe. The political justification for the Member States acting together in this way, rather than separately, is that it enhances the effectiveness of the aid. The legal justification is that the Community has

---

[47] Case 22/70 *Commission* v *Council (ERTA)* [1971] ECR 263.
[48] OJ 1990 L131/1.

an external competence in relation to vocational training which matches its internal competence.

Despite the increased detail in the redrafted Treaty, there seems little reason to suppose that Community policy in relation to vocational training will change greatly in the light of the new Treaty; in relation to general education it can be expected that most changes which do take place will amount simply to a general intensification of existing co-operative activities.

Culture, public health and consumer protection

In each of these policy areas, the Treaty speaks of the Community making a "contribution". However, whereas culture and public health can be paired with education policy as newly emerging policy areas where Community action is essentially subsidiary to the role of the Member States, the position of consumer protection (Art 129a EC) is rather different as it is a policy area which inevitably impinges upon almost all of the regulatory activities of the Community which focus upon the completion of the single market. Consequently, read in conjunction with Article 100a, as well as the general framework principles of Community law such as Articles 3 and 3b, it would appear that Article 129a generates a duty on the part of the Community to develop consumer protection regulation which is appropriate to resolving the continuing conflict of interests between the "vulnerable" consumer and the free market actor benefitting from the opportunities of the single market.

In the fields of culture and public health, Community measures are in general to be aimed at encouraging co-operation and supplementing Member State policies. The co-decision procedure is to be used for the adoption of incentive measures. Incentive measures allow the Community to target resources and to persuade national policy-makers to shift the domestic agenda in order to attract Community funds which are available. However, one institutional peculiarity of the Treaty of Maastricht is that under Article 128(5) EC, Article 189b is to be used in combination with unanimity in the Council of Ministers for incentive measures in the field of culture. It is unclear how the rigidities in the decision-making process engendered by the requirement of unanimity can be successfully combined with the degree of Parliamentary participation required by co-decision. If the Conciliation Committee is convened, will an agreement in the Committee require unanimity amongst the Council members of that body, a requirement which would run directly counter to the very spirit of conciliation? Nor is it clear why the Member States felt the need to reserve culture as a field for unanimous action, in particular since Article 128(1) EC contains the *caveat* that Community action must respect the "national and regional diversity" of the Member States, while "at the same time bringing the common cultural heritage to the fore". Surely in the light of this explicit reservation, any measures which overstepped the mark by imposing a "Euro-cultural paradigm" would be vulnerable to challenge for violation of the subsidiarity principle. Consequently, there appears little need for a unanimous vote to preserve the rights of dissenting Member States. This must be regarded as an example of excessive sensitivity to the demands of national sovereignty in the Maastricht negotiating process.

Reflections on Social Policy after Maastricht

The point was made earlier in this article that we are following here the inside track of Community Social Policy. This may be a track which is relatively smooth, not pitted with the ruts and bumps which accompany the legal status of the SPP and the SPA, but it is one which appears, regretfully, to be leading nowhere. It is possible that changes in the effectiveness of Community Social Policy will come about through the gradual accretion of competence as discussed in this article. Indeed, Weatherill has remarked optimistically in relation to the new policies added to the Treaty of Rome by the Single European Act and the Treaty of Maastricht that:

"however anodyne the detailed provisions of such new Titles may appear, their real importance lies in the fact of their existence, which generates obligations to pursue the policy sketched by the Treaty."[49]

It is possible that the Court of Justice will spring a surprise by identifying a distinct and enforceable duty on the institutions in its interpretation of the nature of these Community "contributions". It is also possible that the Court of Justice could make some progress towards a rights based Social Policy if it is prepared to make an imaginative use of Article F.2 TEU regarding fundamental rights. It is, however, remarkable that in the age of the Social Charter, the social dimension of the internal market and the Social Policy Agreement between the Eleven that we continue to talk in terms of serious policy initiatives in relation to social affairs emerging from the Court of Justice, in the same way that they emerged out of the Court's caselaw on sex equality and vocational training. It is not only remarkable, but also a source of regret in a Community in which the legislative side of supranationalism is supposed to have been significantly strengthened. It is a comment which continues to reflect a minimalist attitude amongst some Member States to social policy when they are drafting and concluding the founding Treaties of European Union.

JO SHAW

---

[49] Weatherill, 'Subsidiarity and responsibility' (University of Nottingham, Research Papers in Law, No 6, 1993, 5).

Chapter 20

Social Policy: a Happy Ending or a Reworking of the Fairy Tale?

Social Policy, so long the Cinderella of the common market, has been trans-
formed, not into a fairy princess, but into an ugly sister of the internal market. At
the eleventh hour of the Maastricht Summit 1991, when it was clear that no
further compromises could be made to the United Kingdom, the chapter on
Social Policy was removed from the main body of the Treaty on European Union
(TEU) and signed as a Protocol and Agreement fragmenting even further the
potential social dimension of the internal market. This shattering of the legal base
for future Social Policy measures has thrown up in its wake a number of incon-
sistencies and uncertainties as to the legality and scope of Social Policy law and
called into question the future of the European integration process.

At the political level the Maastricht Summit 1991 left unresolved the issue of
whether an integrated social dimension is necessary for the functioning of the
internal market. The United Kingdom Government's argument against Community competence in this area is firmly located within a philosophy of
deregulation. This is seen in the Government's voluntary response to the EC
Commission's monitoring of the implementation of the Social Charter 1989
report:

"In the UK Government's view labour markets work most efficiently with the minimum
of Government intervention. Policies have been directed at removing hindrances to the
free operation of markets and to balancing the needs of employer and employee. Unnecessary regulations have been removed, thereby lessening the burden of Government on
business ..."[1]

The argument is put forward that too rigid a social dimension to the internal
market will reinforce "Eurosclerosis" (a disease caught by too close a liaison with
Brussels) the symptoms being inflexibility, loss of competitiveness and unemployment. The UK Government argues that it is not opposed in principle to all
regulation of the labour market:

"... legislation is sometimes necessary to ensure effective operation of the market, to
protect particularly vulnerable groups or to achieve a fundamental principle of public
policy, for example to combat discrimination ... However, legislation should be confined

---

[1] Second Report From the Commission to the Council, the European Parliament and the Economic and
Social Committee on the application of the Community charter of the fundamental social rights of
workers COM(92) 562 final, 271.

to the minimum necessary consistent with establishing a balance between the needs of employers and employees."[2]

But intervention in areas such as the content of the employment relationship and collective bargaining will impede decision-making at the level of the firm and in the wider context will make European firms uncompetitive with American and Japanese rivals:

"The UK believes that terms and conditions of employment are best determined by employers and employees: they are in the best position to judge what is appropriate, taking account of the circumstances of their particular firm in the labour market."[3]

In contrast, supporters of a social dimension to the internal market argue that its value has an economic as well as a social/human rights dimension. The lack of integration and co-ordination of the Community labour markets has created a social deficit leading to economic imbalances which in turn may lead to chaotic and inflationary wage-setting. Thus the social dimension is necessary for the realization of the economic benefits of the internal market.[4]

The Social Charter 1989 was a symbolic breakthrough in providing an agenda for a limited social dimension to the internal market. But progress has been slow, with many of the Commission's proposals being watered down, particularly by the United Kingdom in the Council of Ministers.[5] Even this limited framework has received criticism. Two examples give a flavour of the views held. Health and safety measures are considered too costly for the poorer Community states:

"... poorer countries just like poorer people can less afford to be "choosey". Low wage countries and small firms will be disadvantaged by ambitious legislation of this type."[6]

The proposals relating to "atypical" work are attacked in that they neglect the role of choice. Part-timers for example, may want jobs with less training which offer higher starting salaries. It is argued that the Commission has failed to offer a diagnosis of the growth of atypical work – the market's way of escaping onerous restrictions. The Social Charter 1989 is criticised in that it seeks to impose uniformity on Member States which have very different systems of labour regulation. Thus, a basic question arises as to whether the Community should remove areas of competition. Addison and Siebert think not:

"... the Commission's quest for harmonization, and its selection of "models" in this regard, is inappropriate. Systems of regulation and industrial relations evolve. Their survival is an indicator of their internal appropriateness, *not* of their generalisability."[7]

---

[2] *Ibid.*

[3] *Ibid.*

[4] See, for example, Grahl and Teague, 'Integration theory and European labour markets', (1992) 30 *British Journal of Industrial Relations* 515–527.

[5] *Supra*, n 1.

[6] Addison and Siebert, 'The EC Social Charter: the nature of the beast', (1993) *National Westminister Bank Quarterly Review* 13–28 at 14.

[7] *Ibid* at 18.

The Social Policy Protocol and Agreement were intended as a way out of this political, economic and legal stalemate. The legal framework in which this escape is attempted is structurally so unsound that it has left many issues unresolved. Some of the most problematic areas will now be discussed.

The Social Policy Protocol and Agreement

The Social Policy Protocol authorises the 11 Member States to have recourse to the "institutions, procedures and mechanisms of the Treaty for the purposes of making and applying amongst themselves acts and decisions required to give effect to the Agreement annexed to the Protocol". By way of derogation from Article 148(2) EEC a new form of qualified majority voting is introduced. The Agreement on Social Policy is annexed to the Social Policy Protocol. Article 1 states:

"The Community and the Member States shall have as their objectives the promotion of employment, improved living and working conditions, proper social protection, dialogue between management and labour, the development of human resources with a view to lasting high employment and the combatting of exclusion. To this end the Community and the Member States shall implement measures which take account of the diverse forms of national practices, in particular in the field of contractual relations, and the need to maintain the competitiveness of the Community economy."

Article 1 is a departure from Article 117 EEC. The Member States are no longer obliged to promote improved working conditions to "make possible their harmonization while improvement is being maintained". The new provision only obliges the Member States to promote employment and to improve living and working conditions. The inclusion of the words "the Community" raises the question as to whether competence in this area has been transferred to the Community. The inclusion of the words "the Community" would seem to indicate this is so[8] and yet as we shall discover later it is not entirely clear whether measures taken under the Agreeement are to be regarded as *Community* legal measures or whether they operate outside the Community legal order at the level of intergovernmental agreements.

The precise legal scope of Article 117 EEC is still being clarified. Thus, the relationship between Article 1 of the Agreement and Article 117 EEC may prove problematic. Nielsen and Szyszczak,[9] for example, argue that Article 117 EEC is circumscribed by Article 118 EEC. The Court of Justice has held that Article 117 EEC is only programmatic, but this does not mean that it is devoid of legal effect:

---

[8] See the statement by Mr Eric Forth MP, the then Parliamentary Under-Secretary of State, Department of Employment: the Agreement 'sought to shift the balance of policy from the Member States to the Community', in House of Lords Select Committee on the European Communities *7th Report*, Session 1991–92 *Social Policy After Maastricht*, HL Paper 42, HMSO (1992) 18.

[9] *The Social Dimension of the European Community* 2nd ed. (1993) ch 1.

"The fact that the objectives of Social Policy laid down in Article 117 are in the nature of a programme does not mean that they are deprived of legal effect. They constitute an important aid, in particular for the interpretation of other provisions of the Treaty and of secondary legislation in the social field."[10]

This is an important point. Since Social Policy measures are often enacted in the form of *soft law*, Article 117 EEC provides a Treaty base for the interpretation of such measures. More recently the Court has ruled that Article 117 EEC does not give rise to direct effects for individuals before national courts and it cannot be used to review the compatibility of measures taken by the Member States with Community law.[11]

Article 2 of the Agreement performs a function similar to Article 118 EEC, in that it would seek to circumscribe Article 1 of the Agreement:

"With a view to achieving the objectives of Article 1, the Community shall support and complement the activities of the Member States in the following fields:
– improvement in particular of the working environment to protect workers' health and safety;
– working conditions;
– the information and consultation of workers;
– equality between men and women with regard to the labour market opportunities and treatment at work;
– the integration of persons excluded from the labour market, without prejudice to Article 127 [EEC] ...".

This article is again a departure from the existing Treaty provisions contained in Articles 118 and Article 118a EEC. In particular, the range of areas covered is wider, providing a legal basis for provisions relating to working conditions. Legal uncertainty arises in connection with the fact that the legal parameters of the original Article 118 and 118a EEC are still relatively unexplored,[12] thus questions emerge as to the exact scope of the new Article 2 and its relationship with Article 118 and 118a EEC. Of fundamental importance is the issue as to whether these are the only areas where the Community has competence, or merely a statement of priority areas necessary to fulfil the aims of Article 1.

Although not openly articulated, this new provision would seem to override Article 100a(2) EEC which requires unanimity voting in the field of "the rights and interests of workers". In the past the UK Government has argued for an expansive interpretation of this article to embrace all labour law issues not covered by Article 118a EEC, which in turn has been interpreted narrowly by the United Kingdom.[13] In Germany also there have been

---

[10] Case 126/86, *Zaera* v *Insituto Nacional de la Seguridad Social* [1987] ECR 3697, para 14.

[11] Joined Cases C-72/91 and C-73/91 *Firma Sloman Neptun Schiffahrts AG* v *Seebetriebsrat Bodo Ziesemer der Sloman Neptun Schiffahrts AG*, not yet reported.

[12] See Joined Cases 218, 283–85 & 286/85 *Germany and others* v *EC Commission* [1987] ECR 3203; Opinion 2/91 *Re ILO Convention No 170*, not yet reported.

[13] See the discussion of the various interpretations of Art 100a(2) EEC by Bercusson, 'Fundamental social and economic rights in the European Community' in Cassese *et al* (eds) *Human Rights and the European Community: Methods of Protection, Vol II* (1991) and Vogel-Polsky 'What future is there for a social Europe following the Strasbourg Summit?' (1990) *Industrial Law Journal* 65–80.

moves to interpret terms such as "working and economic conditions" narrowly.[14] In the future Article 100A(2) EEC may be narrowed down or may become, like Article 118a EEC, an embattled chess piece in future litigation in the "legal base game".[15]

In the *Titanium Dioxide* case, *Commission* v *Council*,[16] the Court of Justice developed a broad interpretation of Article 100a(1) EEC setting the framework in which to tackle the disputes over the correct legal base for a piece of secondary legislation. The application of this case to Article 118a EEC and other Social Policy measures on the one hand paves the way for a broader role for Article 100a(1) EEC in the sphere of labour market regulation, but on the other hand could reduce the ambit of such measures to economic and competition issues only. It may not be so easy to apply the criteria to the application of Social Policy measures and the outcome may give rise to absurd results. For example, in the Vredling Proposal[17] for a Directive on the information and consultation of workers, the proposals are linked to the existing forms of worker representation. This proposal could be implemented by a qualified majority vote. In contrast, the proposed Directive establishing a European Works Council in Community-wide undertakings and groups of undertakings would require unanimity voting since it envisages new modes of representation.[18] Weiss points out that precisely the same subject matter is being regulated and that this example:

"... reveals sharply a lack of clarity and the absence of conceptual thinking in the drafting of the Protocol."[19]

Rhodes argues that the general provisions concerning the common/internal market must take priority over Article 2 of the Agreement, thus leaving the scope of labour market harmonization unaltered.[20]

Another area where the Agreement might conflict with existing Community law is Article 6(3). This provision purports to allow the Member States to use positive action as a means "to make it easier for women to pursue a vocational activity or to prevent or compensate for disadvantages in their professional careers".[21] Article 119 EEC does not contain such a provision but Article 2(4) of the Equal Treatment Directive[22] allows the Member States to take measures "to promote equal opportunity for men and women, in particular by removing existing inequalities ...". This provision was interpreted restrictively by the

---

[14] See Weiss, 'The significance of Maastricht For European Community Social Policy', (1992) 8 IJCLLIR 3–14.
[15] Wedderburn, *The Social Charter, European Company and Employment Rights. An Outline Agenda* (1990); Barendts, 'The internal market unlimited: some observations on the legal base of Community legislation', (1993) 30 CML Rev 85–109.
[16] Case C-300/89 [1991] ECR I-2867. *Cf* Case C-155/91 *Commission* v *Council* not yet reported. Here the ECJ held there was no justification to utilise Art 100a(1) where the harmonization of the conditions of the market within the Community had only an *ancillary* function in the legal measure to be adopted.
[17] OJ 1983 C217/3.
[18] COM (90) 581 final. See Nielsen and Szyszczak, *op cit*, n 9, Ch 5.
[19] *Supra*, n 14 at 8.
[20] Rhodes, 'The future of the 'social dimension': labour market regulation in post 1992 Europe' (1992) XXX JCMS 24–27.
[21] *Cf* Lanquetin and Masse-Dessen, 'Maastricht: consolidation ou remise en cause des principes en matière d'égalité professionelle', (1992) 4 *Droit Social* 386–390.
[22] Council Dir 76/207/EEC (OJ 1976 L39/40).

Court of Justice in *Commission* v *France*[23] in that any positive action measures must be of a specific rather than a general nature applying to areas where existing inequalities are shown to exist.

Implementation of Social Policy by collective agreements

Bercusson argues that one outcome of the TEU was a quantum leap for collective bargaining.[24] This was achieved in Article 2(4) which states:

"A Member State may entrust management and labour, at their joint request, with the implementation of directives adopted pursuant to paragraphs 2 and 3."

Bercusson, however, is not uncritical of the framework for facilitating collective bargaining, describing it as "bargaining in the shadow of the law".[25]

Article 3 extends the social dialogue first initiated in Article 118b EEC:

"1. The Commission shall have the task of promoting the consultation of management and labour at Community level and shall take any relevant measure to facilitate their dialogue by ensuring balanced support for the parties.
2. To this end, before submitting proposals in the Social Policy field, the Commission shall consult management and labour on the possible direction of Community action.
3. If, after such consultation, the Commission considers Community action advisable, it shall consult management and labour on the content of the envisaged proposal. Management and labour shall forward to the Commission an opinion or, where appropriate, a recommendation.
4. On the occasion of such consultation, management and labour may inform the Commission of their wish to initiate the process provided for in Article 4. The duration of the procedure shall not exceed nine months, unless the management and labour concerned and the Commission decide jointly to extend it."

Article 4 provides the mechanisms whereby:

"1. Should management and labour so desire, the dialogue between them at Community level may lead to contractual relations, including agreements.
2. Agreements concluded at Community level shall be implemented either in accordance with the procedures and practices specific to management and labour and the Member States or, in matters covered by Article 2, at the joint request of the signatory parties, by a Council decision on a proposal from the Commission.
The Council shall act by qualified majority, except where the agreement in question contains one or more provisions relating to one of the areas referred to in Article 2(3), in which case it shall act unanimously."

---

[23] Case 318/86 [1988] ECR 6315. See also Case 111/86 *Delauche* v *Commission* [1987] ECR 5345.
[24] 'Maastricht: a fundamental change in European labour law' (1992) 23 *Industrial Relations Journal* 177–190.
[25] *Ibid* at 185.

First, we must reconcile these provisions with the caselaw of the Court of Justice. The Commission has brought actions under Article 169 EEC against Member States who have relied upon collective agreements in order to implement the earlier Social Policy legislation.[26] In its judgments the Court pointed to the weaknesses of using collective agreements to implement Social Policy obligations *viz:* collective bargaining lacks a normative quality, it does not benefit non-trade union members, it does not apply to organizations outside of the employers' association, it does not exist in all economic or industrial sectors and even where it does exist it may not cover the exact scope of Community obligations. The Court was prepared to hold that a Member State may in the first instance use collective agreements but these must be underpinned by legislation where there was not adequate coverage or the substantive content of the agreements did not coincide with the Directive's obligations.[27] In *Commission* v *French Republic*[28] the Court of Justice held that a Member State must observe Community rules and abide by agreed deadlines when using collective bargaining as a means of implementing Community obligations.

The Social Charter 1989 accepted that Social Policy measures might be implemented by collective bargaining, but the Charter did not facilitate or protect the role of trade unions in carrying out such a task. There are conflicting impressions of the *Val Duchesse* talks conducted under the auspices of Article 118b EEC. Gospel argues:

"Major obstacles stand in the way of developing the so-called social dialogue between European employers and trade unions begun at Val Duchesse in 1985. Not least, these include employer opposition, the weakness of the representative organizations on both sides of industry, and problems of implementing any such agreements."[29]

In contrast the Commission is more positive, stressing the contribution made by the social dialogue to the implementation of the Social Charter 1989 with the adoption of six joint opinions.[30]

There is some ambiguity as to *when* the special procedure in Article 3(4) should be initiated. Should consultation occur before and/or after the Commission produces its envisaged proposal? This seems a crucial point overlooked in the drafting of the article and yet, as Bercusson argues, the timing of the consultation may be relevant to the outcome.[31]

The principle of the autonomy of the social partners may give rise to further litigation at the national level and even before the Commission and Court administering the European Convention of Fundamental Human Rights and Freedoms 1953. The Court of Justice did not address the issue in *Nimz* v *Freie und*

---

[26] See Adinolfi, 'The implementation of Social Policy Directives through collective agreements', (1988) 25 CML Rev 291–316; Lyon-Caen, 'Collective bargaining and Community legal instruments' Paper presented to a Conference on the Legal Formulation and Implementation of the Social Dimension of the Internal Market, Florence, 4–6 December 1989.

[27] Case 143/83 *Commission* v *Denmark* [1985] ECR 427.

[28] Case 312/86 [1989] ECR 6315.

[29] 'The Single European Market and Industrial Relations: an Introduction' (1992) 30 *British Journal of Industrial Relations* 483–494.

[30] *Op cit*, n 1 at 4.

[31] *Ibid* at 185.

Hansestadt Hamburg.[32] Here it was alleged that a provision contained in a German collective agreement was contrary to Community law. In its ruling the Court of Justice stressed the supremacy of Community law and that it was open to the national courts to apply Community law without waiting for the modification of a collective agreement through collective bargaining. Thus, it would seem possible to test the compatibility of Community-based collective agreements with the *acquis communautaire* but a more fundamental issue of whether the autonomy of the social partners is a right protected under Community law is unexplored.

Even so, there may be limitations upon the amount of protection available under the *acquis communautaire* to individuals and the litigation could easily be used by the Member States to limit the application of collective agreements. The *Nimz* ruling underlines the importance of a legislative floor of rights to provide a safety net for workers fully or partially excluded from rights derived from collective agreements and the role of Community law in providing a quasi-constitutional standard by which infringements of human/social rights may be tested.[33] The Court of Justice has interpreted the equality principle and the free movement principle liberally, elevating both areas into the realm of fundamental rights protected by Community law.[34] In other areas relating to employment rights the Court has not been so generous, leaving many crucial definitions to national law.[35]

Obligation to implement collective agreements

A Declaration contained in the final Act states:

"The Conference declares that the first of the arrangements for application of the agreements between management and labour Community-wide referred to in Article 118B(2) will consist in developing by collective bargaining according to the rules of each Member State, the content of the agreements, and that consequently this arrangement implies no obligation on the member states to apply the agreements directly or to work out rules for their transposition, nor any obligation to amend national legislation in force to facilitate their implementation."

Uncertainty arises as to the legal effect of such a Declaration.[36] The Declaration merely instructs the Member States to develop the content of the Community agreements. There is no obligation to apply the agreements directly, or to transpose them or even facilitate their implementation. In many respects, therefore,

---

[32] Case C-184/89 [1991] ECR I-297.

[33] See Docksey, 'The principle of equality between women and men as a fundamental right under Community law' (1991) 20 ILJ 258–280.

[34] See Arnull, *The General Principles of EEC Law and the Individual* (1990); Docksey, *ibid.*

[35] See Szyszczak 'L'Espace Sociale Europeenne: reality dreams or nightmares?' (1990) 33 *German Yearbook of International Law* 284–307.

[36] *Cf* the discussion by Toth, 'The legal status of Declarations Annexed to the Single European Act 1986' (1986) 23 CML Rev 803–812 who argues that the Declarations attached to the Single European Act 1986 have no legal effect.

it would seem that this Declaration has limited legal significance and is not justiciable.

Creation of a variable geometry

Curtin notes that it is a striking feature of the TEU that it is encumbered with a large number of Protocols and Declarations.[37] Unlike the original Treaty of Rome 1957 and the Single European Act 1986 the Protocols to the TEU provide dangerous precedents in that they pander to special pleading on the part of the Member States leading to what Curtin categorises as the "hijacking of the *acquis communautaire*".[38] With the Social Policy Protocol and Agreement a new precedent has been set, allowing the Community institutions to develop and apply rules which have the force of law in 11 out of the 12 Member States.

The concept of a "two-speed" or "twin-track" Community is not new.[39] A number of phrases have emerged to describe the idea: "Europe à géométrie variable", "Europe à la carte", "abgestufte Integration". The idea is traceable back to an address given to the Organisation Française du Mouvement Européen in Paris on 19 November 1974 by the then Chancellor of West Germany, Willy Brandt. The following year a formula for such a strategy was drawn up in the Tindemans Report[40] in the context of economic and monetary policy. Tindemans argued that it must be possible to develop within the Community framework an overall concept of European Union. Those Member States which are able to, have a duty to forge ahead; whereas those States which have reasons for not progressing, which the Council of Ministers on a proposal from the Commission acknowledges as valid, do not do so. But, at the same time it was envisaged that the Member States would receive from other states any aid or assistance that could be given to them to enable them to catch up with the other Member States and they would take part, within the joint institutions, in assessing the results obtained in the field in question.[41] At this juncture it should be noted that the aim is towards uniformity and conformity with Community policies and the regulation of the Member States lagging behind is firmly within the institutional structure of the Community. Thus, this analysis is not applicable to the Social Policy issue under discussion here, since the Protocol and Agreement represent a difference between the United Kingdom and the other Member States over the content of Community policy in this field. While the political debate as to the viability of a "twin-track" Europe continues, the legal debate is even more hazy.

Grabitz and Langeheine argue that a two-speed Europe is compatible with

---

[37] 'The Constitutional structure of the Union: a Europe of bits and pieces' (1993) 30 CML Rev 17–69.

[38] *Ibid* at 44.

[39] See Shaw, 'Twin-track social Europe – the inside track' in this volume, 295.

[40] European Union: Report by Mr Leo Tindemans, Prime Minister of Belgium, to the European Council, (Bull EC Supp 1/76).

[41] *Ibid* at 20–21.

the Treaty provided that it is not used in "core areas" of the common market and external relations and provided that all the Member States agree, that is, it cannot be used in areas governed by majority voting.[42] Ehlermann disagrees with this analysis arguing that under Community law consensus is not a valid argument in favour of legality.[43] The EC Commission has maintained that a "twin-track" Europe would require a Treaty amendment.[44] Article 236 EEC requires an intergovernmental conference and a unanimous vote for a Treaty amendment.[45] Although the Protocol satisfies these criteria the Agreement clearly does not unless one sees the annexation of the Agreement to the Protocol as satisfying the criteria. The dominant view seems to be that by virtue of Article 239 EEC the Protocol and Agreement are an integral part of the EC Treaty. However, in the Final Act the Heads of State or Government sign the TEU and the Protocols as separate documents, providing an alternative legal argument that the Protocol and Agreement are *separate* agreements.

A less pessimistic view would be to categorise the Social Policy Protocol and Agreement as a transitional stage. Weiss, for example, suggests that we could contextualise the Agreement as an attempt to strengthen the Community Charter of Fundamental Social Rights of Workers 1989 (an aim expressly declared in the Preamble to the Protocol) in an attempt to broaden the acceptance of a need to create a social dimension to the internal market. This may in turn lead to a re-drafting of the Treaty in terms amenable to all 12 Member States. Protocols were used in the original Treaty of Rome 1957, but not in the Single European Act 1986, arguably as a form of transitional arrangement in the movement towards full integration. This is not the case with the TEU where the Protocols facilitate derogations from the *acquis communautaire* despite express statements towards preserving it.

Community law ... or not?

The Agreement refers to the Council adopting "Directives" in the areas listed in Article 2(2). Are these "Directives" the same kind of legal acts envisaged in Article 189 EEC – with all the attendant caselaw of the Court of Justice applying as to the legal scope of the measures? At first sight the answer would appear to be in the affirmative. The Agreement refers to the Council adopting such acts, by a qualified majority vote, in accordance with Article 189c EC and the Protocol forms an integral part of the Community legal order. A closer reading of the wording of the Protocol might elicit a negative response. The Protocol refers to the 11 "for the purposes of taking among themselves and applying as far as they are concerned" the necessary acts and decisions to give

---

[42] 'Legal problems related to a proposed 'two-tier system' of integration within the European Community' (1981) 18 CML Rev 33–48.
[43] 'How flexible is Community law? An unusual approach to the concept of 'two speeds" (1984) 82 *Michigan Law Review* 1274–1293.
[44] *Ibid.*
[45] *Ibid.* See also Case 43/75 *Defrenne* v *Sabena* [1976] ECR 455.

effect to the Agreement. This would seem to indicate that the measures taken are not to be considered a part of Community law but are a form of inter-governmental agreement.[46] Such a view is reinforced by the statement in the Protocol that the Protocol and Agreement are without prejudice to the pro-visions of the Treaty which constitute an integral part of the *acquis communautaire*. In the United Kingdom the then Parliamentary Under-Secretary of State, De-partment of Employment, Mr Eric Forth stated that the new agreements ". . . would be a self-styled Directive agreed by the 11 enforceable in the 11 countries but not Community law as such."[47] This argument is put forward by Curtin:

". . . the directives . . . are not synonymous with directives as defined in Article 189 EEC and the drafting sloppiness revealed by the use of the same terminology can only be regretted."[48]

The legal situation is complicated further when we consider the issue of sub-sidiarity contained in Article 3b of the TEU. In areas where the Community does not have exclusive competence it is arguable that the 11 Member States could implement the Agreement at the national level. Difficult questions arise as to enforcement and judicial review by legal persons and the policing of any recalcitrant Member State which fails to implement appropriate measures.

A salient lesson we have learnt from the past experience of Community Social Policy law is that, for its implementation, enforcement and expansion, it is heavily reliant upon individual litigants at the national level and the access to the Court of Justice provided by Article 177 EEC.[49] The effectiveness of the Social Policy Protocol and Agreement is thus called into question if any ensuing commitments undertaken by the Member States are not directly enforceable in the national courts.

Are all the Institutions borrowed?

The Protocol authorises the 11 Member States to "borrow" the "institutions, procedures and mechanisms of the Treaty". This raises the issue of whether it is only the legislative mechanisms which are "borrowed" or also the Court of Justice. If the latter is also "lent" does this include the wide jurisdiction of the Court to hear infringement actions under Article 169 EEC and 170 EEC, judicial review, Article 173 EEC, failure to act, Article 175 EEC and, of course,

---

[46] Vogel-Polsky, *Evaluation of the social provisions of the Treaty on European Union agreed by the European Summit at Maastricht* DOC en/cm/202155 PE 115.405/I.

[47] House of Lords *op cit* at 20. But compare his earlier statement 'The apparent intention of the other Member States is however to regard any such measures as if they had been adopted under the Treaty so they would adopt what they would call 'Directives' and would accept that these imposed upon them the same obligations of implementation and enforcement as do Community measures in their own right.' House of Lords *op cit* at 13.

[48] *Supra* n 37, at 58.

[49] Art 169 EEC has been utilised but it would seem that the Court of Justice would prefer to structure its constitutional role through rulings given under Art 177 EEC. See Mancinini, 'Labour Law and Com-munity Law' (1985) XX *Irish Jurist* 1–16.

the access of national courts via Article 177 EEC? Curtin[50] argues for a wide interpretation of these words. If the Court does have jurisdiction over inter-governmental agreements this would be a departure from current practice in Article 31 of the Single European Act 1986 and the parts of the TEU dealing with intergovernmental activity (Title V and VI) where the Court's jurisdiction is specifically excluded.[51]

The compatibility of the Social Policy Protocol and Agreement with the Treaty of Rome 1957 and the *acquis communautaire* may be tested before the Court of Justice in a number of ways which are not contingent upon the Court being "lent" under the Protocol.[52] One can foresee a wide range of disputes before national courts where the Court may be asked to provide preliminary rulings on the interpretation of measures enacted at the national level under the Social Policy Agreement where the compatibility of the new measures is tested against the *acquis communautaire*. Under Article 177 EEC the Court has jurisdiction to rule on "the interpretation of this Treaty" and "the validity and interpretation of acts of the institutions of the Community." There would be jurisdiction to test the compatibility of the Protocol and Agreement against the original Treaty of Rome 1957 in so far as it may be argued that the Agreement is at variance with the original Treaty. Similarly the acts of the institutions "borrowed" under the Protocol may be subject to review on the grounds of the compatibility of the acts with the *acquis communautaire* of the Treaty of Rome 1957. In the past the Court has utilised Article 5 EEC as a constitutional basis for defining the obligations of the Member States but in *Zwartveld*[53] and *Stergios Delimitas*[54] the Court extended Article 5 EEC to impose an obligation upon the Commission to support the enforcement of Community law at the national level.[55] Thus there would seem to be ample opportunity to create a test case in order to tempt the Court into taking jurisdiction over the issue of the legality of the Protocol and the Agreement.

Equally, we might contemplate challenges under Article 173 EEC concerning the legal base of future measures made under the "old" Treaty provisions and perhaps under the Agreement. Again, will the Court be able to find jurisdiction to review measures taken under the Agreement? Given the Member States willingness to utilise such procedures and also the confidence the European Parliament has gained we can imagine a variety of scenarios for future litigation. Will the United Kingdom or the European Parliament argue that measures taken under the Agreement are *ultra vires* since both actors have been excluded from the conventional treaty forum? At the time of writing the new Minister of State for Employment, Mr Hunt, has threatened the Council and the Com-

---

[50] *Op cit.*
[51] Note, however, the exception in Art L TEU relating to Art K 3(2)(c), third sub para.
[52] For a discussion of how the Social Policy Protocol and Agreement may be binding on the UK see Barnard, 'A Social Policy for Europe: Politicians 1: Lawyers 0' (1992) 8 IJCLLIR 15–31.
[53] Case C-2/88 [1990] ECR I-3365.
[54] Case C-234/89 [1991] ECR I-935.
[55] See Temple Lang, 'Community Constitutional law: Article 5 EEC Treaty' (1990) 27 CML Rev 645.

mission with an action under Article 173 EEC, after the Council agreed to a common position on the working time Directive on the basis of Article 118a EEC at the Labour and Social Affairs Council Meeting on 1 June 1993.[56] Thus, the *possibility* of similar threats of litigation is not to be dismissed. The extent to which legal persons in the form of individual litigants, employers" representatives or trade unions will be able to establish *locus standi* will presumably be limited.[57] Yet, trade unions have an enhanced role under the procedures set out in Articles 3 and 4 of the Agreement and, as outlined above, the procedures themselves lack precision and clarity. Will the Court be able to find a legal interest that has been violated?

The issue of a failure to act brought under Article 175 EEC is unlikely to arise. Arguably a Member State or a trade union or an employers' association may have a legitimate interest in wanting to push the 11 Member States into negotiations under the Agreement. The question arises whether the Council or the Commission have failed to act "in infringement of this Treaty". The issue may arise as to the legality of the Agreement with the Treaty and the conclusion that if the Protocol is not compatible with the Treaty a failure to act under it is not an infringement of Article 175 EEC. Even if the Court of Justice decides otherwise it is most likely that the scope of Agreement is of insufficient substance for the Court to declare that there has been a failure to act. A parallel might be drawn with *European Parliament* v *Council*[58] concerning an allegation that the Council had not conducted a common transport policy. The Court concluded that the Council was obliged to conduct a common transport policy, but the Council was not in infringement of the Treaty of Rome since the Treaty did not clarify what the substance of the common policy was to be.

It remains to be seen how the Court of Justice will react to questions concerning the legality of the Social Policy Protocol and Agreement. From past caselaw[59] one suspects the Court will not take kindly to any undermining of the constitutional base of the Community or the diluting of the homogeneity of the Community legal order, the development of which, the European Court has indicated can only take place within the Community legal order itself.[60] In *SpA International Chemical Corporation*[61] the Court stressed that the uniform application of Community law is imperative and in *Ramael* v *Receveur des Douanes*[62] the Court held that the Member States and the institutions must use their powers with the unity of the market in mind.

---

[56] COM(90) 317 final. See 'Hunt to fight EC Directive', *The Independent*, 1 June 1993.

[57] See Rasmussen, 'Why is Article 173 interpreted against Private plaintiffs?' (1980) 5 ELRev 112–127.

[58] Case 13/83 [1985] ECR 1513.

[59] Case 294/83 *Parti Ecologiste 'Les Verts'* v *European Parliament* [1986] ECR 2041.

[60] Opinion 1/9, *Re The Draft Treaty on a European Economic Area* [1991] ECR I-6079.

[61] Case 68/80 [1981] ECR 1215.

[62] Case 81/77 [1978] ECR 927.

A fairy tale ending?

The apparent haste with which the Heads of State or Government sought to embrace a wider legal basis for Social Policy in the TEU has resulted in ambiguities in the terminology and the legal effect of the Social Policy Protocol and Agreement. The official view is that this was a pragmatic solution to the UK's intransigence with the hope of achieving a fairy tale end to Social Policy's "Cinderella" status. While feminists may baulk at the use of such terminology, it is perhaps appropriate, to describe and locate the TEU within the continuum of the Community's attitude towards Social Policy. An historical analysis of Community Social Policy reveals that the weaknesses and incoherence resulting from political differences combined with a tenuous legal base created a fragmented and piecemeal attitude towards Social Policy. Some progress was made to consolidate the failure of the Single European Act 1986 to put Social Policy squarely within the internal market programme by the acceptance of the Social Charter 1989. While there are criticisms to be made of the approach of the Social Charter it has provided some dynamic to the enactment of Social Policy measures in recent years when compared with the political stalemate of the 1980s.[63] Some optimists argue that maximum advantage may be taken of Article 118a EEC to minimise the resort to the Agreement.[64] In order to avoid the use of the veto under Articles 100, 100a(2) and 235 EEC the Commission has utilised Article 118a EEC. This, in fact, has kept the United Kingdom within the Community fold, but at the cost of weakening some of the Commission's original proposals. One suspects the Commission and the other Member States are beginning to lose patience with the United Kingdom. This is seen in the adoption of a common position on the working time Directive by the 11 Member States with the UK's abstention, despite generous concessions. Pragmatically this may produce results. But, if increasing resort is made to the Agreement, the ensuing measures, when combined with the Social Policy measures envisaged in the main body of the TEU, will result, to borrow Curtin's[65] phraseology, in a Social Policy of "bits and pieces".

The Social Policy Protocol and Agreement have been recommended to us as the way forward, to develop the social dimension to the internal market.[66] A pessimist might argue the route taken is a step backwards. After the acceptance of the need for a social dimension to the internal market the Protocol and Agreement make this issue into a peripheral aspect, lacking the force of binding Community obligations. Whatever one's view, the outcome is unfortunate, both for the political and constitutional coherence of European integration[67] and for

---

[63] See Hepple, 'The crisis in EEC labour law' (1987) 18 ILJ 77–87; Nielsen and Szyszczak, *op cit*, n 9.
[64] See earlier arguments for a broad interpretation of Art 118a in Hepple, *ibid.*
[65] *Supra*, n 37.
[66] Even the fiercest critics of the social dimension express concern over the potential impact of the Protocol and Agreement, see Addison and Siebert, 'The Social Charter: Whatever Next?' (1992) 30 *British Journal of Industrial Relations* 495–513.
[67] *Cf* the idea of European Citizenship discussed in this volume and the European Parliament's draft European Citizen's Statute, European Parliament, Social Affairs, Draft Report on the European labour market after 1992, Part XI: The European Social Model, EP 151. 130/IX of 30 May 1991; Resolution A3-O238/92 of 8 July 1992.

the protection of individual rights in the delicate process of restructuring and adapting to a changing economic climate. Fairy tales have been at the heart of the oral history of Europe's poorest people and have constantly been retold and reworked to accommodate changing situations. The truth is, outside of Disneyland, there are few "fairy tale" endings and this would seem to be the same fate for Social Policy after Maastricht.

ERIKA SZYSZCZAK

Chapter 21
Legal Issues concerning the *Barber* Protocol

Introduction

One of the striking features of the Treaty on European Union (TEU) is the annexation to the Treaty of various Protocols dealing with specific issues.[14] This article discusses some of the legal issues arising from one of the Protocols annexed to the TEU, Protocol No 2 on Article 119, also known as the "*Barber* Protocol".[15]

The Protocol

In tracing the history of the Protocol it may be opportune to begin with Directive 79/7/EEC concerning equal treatment in social security[16] and Directive 86/378/EEC concerning equal treatment in occupational social security schemes.[4] During negotiation of these Directives, the Member States were unable to reach agreement on the equalization of state pensionable ages. As a result, both Directives include a derogation provision on that matter. Accordingly, instead of completing the equal treatment principle in all matters relating to state social security and occupational social security, Article 7 of Directive 79/7 and Article 9 of Directive 86/378 permit Member States to continue to treat women and men differently in the "determination of pensionable age for the purposes of granting old-age or retirement pensions, and the possible implications for other benefits".

When the Court of Justice was called upon to interpret Article 119 in the *Barber* case,[5] in accordance with a long line of established precedent,[6] the Court interpreted Article 119 broadly, holding that benefits paid under a private "contracted-out" occupational pension scheme constituted "pay" and fell within Article 119.[7] However, since, in the light of the aforementioned derogation

---

[1] See Curtin, "The Constitutional structure of the Union: a Europe of bits and pieces" (1993) 30 CML Rev, 17–69.

[2] Henceforth "the Protocol".

[3] OJ 1979 L6/24.

[4] OJ 1986 L225/40.

[5] Case C-262/88 *Barber* v *Guardian Royal Exchange* [1990] ECR 1889.

[6] Case 69/80 *Worringham* v *Lloyds Bank* [1981] ECR 767; Case 23/83 *Liefting* v *Directie van het Academish Ziekenthius* [1984] ECR 3225; Case 192/85 *Newstead* v *Department of Transport* [1987] ECR 4753; Case 170/84, *Bilka-Kaufhaus GmbH* v *Weber von Hartz* [1987] ICR 110; Case 171/89, *Rinner-Kühn* v *FWW Spezial Gebaudereinigung GmbH & Co KG* [1989] ECR 2743.

[7] See Honeyball and Shaw, "Sex, law and the retiring man" (1991) 16 EL Rev. 47–58 at 55.

provisions, it was reasonable to believe that Article 119 did not apply to contracted-out pension schemes, "overriding considerations of legal certainty"[8] required that the Court of Justice limit the effect of its judgment *ratione temporis*. In the now notorious paragraph 45 of its judgment, the Court of Justice held:

"It must therefore be held that the direct effect of Article 119 of the Treaty may not be relied upon in order to claim entitlement to a pension with effect from a date prior to that of this judgment, [*i.e.* 17 May 1990] except in the case of workers or those claiming under them who have before that date initiated legal proceedings or raised an equivalent claim under the applicable national law."

It is unsurprising, given the cost elements involved,[9] that the precise meaning of paragraph 45 has been a matter of fierce debate.[10] Does the judgment mean: (a) that the principle of equal pay applies only to new pension schemes set up after 17 May 1990; or (b) that only workers who become members of and pay contributions to an occupational pension scheme after 17 May 1990 may claim equal pay; or (c) that equality applies only to benefits in respect of employment after that date; or (d) that equality applies to all pensions payable for the first time, or to all pensions payments made, after 17 May 1990?

The Member States sought to clarify the ruling in paragraph 45 of the *Barber* judgment by means of the Protocol. The Member States chose to interpret paragraph 45 so that Article 119 applies only to benefits under occupational social security schemes that are attributable to periods of employment after 17 May 1990. The interpretation chosen by the Member States (and there is no doubt that the powerful pension funds lobby in the UK and the Netherlands played a part in the decision) will mean, in effect, that the principle of equal pay will not be extended to occupational pension schemes in full for another 40 years or so.[11] Thus, the clauses permitting Member States to derogate from the principle of equal treatment by preserving discriminatory state pension ages, and the consequences thereof for other benefits, found in the directives concerned with sex discrimination in social security, are effectively maintained.

In summary, in the *Barber* case, the Court of Justice, in as far as it was competent to do so, attacked the exclusion from the sex discrimination Directives of the politically contentious issue of pensionable ages. The response of the Member States was the agreement found in the Protocol, that occupational pension schemes would be equalised only in respect of periods of employment after the date of the judgment, thus effectively restoring the political compromise found in the provisions of the Directives, but, in view of its inconsistency with the principle of non-discrimination, virtually interpreted away by the Court of Justice.

---

[8] *Barber, supra*, n 5, para 44.

[9] The cost to British industry was estimated at between £5 billion and £40 billion, depending upon the precise interpretation to be adopted. See House of Commons Foreign Affairs Committee, *Europe After Maastricht*, Session 1991–92, 2nd Report, 70, paras 11–14.

[10] See, for example, Fitzpatrick, "Equality in occupational pensions – the new frontiers after *Barber*", (1991) 54 MLR 271–280, at 278; Honeyball and Shaw, *supra*, n 7 at 56; Hudson, "Some reflections on the implications of the *Barber* decision" (1992) 17 EL Rev 163–171 at 167; Shrubsall, "Sex discrimination and pension benefits" (1990) 19 ILJ 244–250 at 248; Watson, "Social Policy after Maastricht" (1993) 30 CML Rev 481–513 at 510 n 59.

[11] That is to say, the working life of the youngest members of pension schemes as at 17 May 1990.

The status of the Protocol

The Protocol affirms the construction of the Court of Justice of the concept of "pay" in the context of Article 119. The provision of the Protocol is not inconsistent with the ruling in *Barber*[12] ; it may even express precisely what the Court of Justice intended.[13] However, inclusion of the Protocol in the TEU does beg the question of its precise status. In particular, is the Protocol an "amendment" of Article 119, an "interpretation" of Article 119, or neither? Opinion is divided on this matter[14] ; moreover, there are difficulties with each conclusion.

If the Protocol *amends* Article 119, in such a way that Article 119 does not apply to benefits under occupational social security schemes attributable to periods of employment before 17 May 1990, then the Protocol takes the form of retroactive legislation. Retroactive legislation is in principle repugnant to the rule of law, and in breach of the general principle of legal certainty according to which the effect of the law in certain circumstances must be reasonably clear and predictable.[15] Therefore, the legal relationships of individuals and the legal consequences of certain acts should not be altered after the fact, but knowable and certain at the relevant time.

Although legal certainty and non-retroactivity are recognised as general principles of European Community law,[16] there have been instances in which the institutions have lawfully enacted retroactive legislation.[17] For example, in the *Roquette*[18] and *Maizena*[19] cases, the Court of Justice was not prepared to annul a Regulation on grounds of retroactivity, where the Regulation was introduced to replace a previously annulled Regulation. In the interests of continuity in legal relations and to maintain the restored certainty of the position, the retroactive legislation was held to be a valid provision of Community law. Given that, in the case of the Protocol, the principal concern was the promotion of legal certainty, it seems that there can in fact be few objections to the Protocol as an amendment to Article 119 on the grounds that it constitutes retroactive legislation.

A more significant objection to the assertion that the status of the Protocol is that of an amendment to Article 119 is that on its face the Protocol suggests no such intention on the part of the Member States. The Protocol reads "for the purposes of Article 119", thereby suggesting that Article 119 itself remains intact, and the Protocol does not amend it, but gives an interpretation of Article 119 in the context of benefits accrued under occupational social security schemes. Had the Member States intended to amend Article 119 the appro-

---

[12] See Hudson, *supra*, n 10.

[13] See the submissions of the Advocate General in joined Cases C-109/91, C-110/91; C-152/91 & C-100/91, *Ten Oever v Stichting Bedrijfspensioenfonds voor het Glazenwassers-en Schoonmaakbedrijf; Moroni v Firma Collo GmbH; Neath v Hugh Steeper Ltd; Coloroll Pension Trustees Ltd v Russell, Mangham and others*, not yet reported; see also the judgment of the Court of 6 October 1993 in *Ten Oever*, not yet reported.

[14] See, for example, Curtin, *supra*, n 1, at 51 ("interprets"); *cf* Hudson, *supra*, n 10, at 163 ("amends").

[15] See Arnull, *The General Principles of EEC Law and the Individual* (1990).

[16] See, for example, Case 63/83 *R v Kirk*, [1984] ECR 2689; Case 80/86 *Officier van Justitie v Kolpinghuis Nijmegen* [1987] ECR 3986.

[17] See Schermers and Waelbrock, *Judicial Protection in the European Communities* (1992), 5th ed 59–63.

[18] Case 138/79 *Roquette Frères v Council* [1980] ECR 3333.

[19] Case 139/79 *Maizena v Council* [1980] ECR 3393.

priate place for such an amendment would have been within the provisions of Article G TEU. That the Member States chose instead to annex a Protocol to the TEU suggests strongly that they had in mind not an amendment to Article 119, but an authoritative interpretation of Article 119.

However, if the status of the Protocol is an authoritative *interpretation* of Article 119, this also poses fundamental difficulties. The Protocol then constitutes no less than a serious threat to the institutional balance of the European Community. The governments of the Member States, in response to a politically difficult judgment from the Court of Justice and under pressure from certain powerful interest groups, have, in adopting the Protocol, carried out the function of giving an authoritative interpretation of a provision of the Treaty of Rome. In doing so, they have usurped the function of the Court of Justice.

In order that the European Community be sustained and advanced by integration through law, it was necessary to provide, in the founding Treaty of Rome, for a Community court with jurisdiction to give binding and authoritative interpretations of measures of Community law. Uniform application of Community law, upon which the European Community legal system is founded, would be jeopardised if bodies other than the Court of Justice were empowered to give authoritative interpretations of Community law. Furthermore, the principle of separation of powers, a fundamental aspect of the rule of law, upon which the Community is founded, would be placed in jeopardy.[20]

If the Protocol interprets Article 119, then, given the Court's interpretative competence in the current *acquis communautaire*, and the assertions in Articles B and C TEU that the *acquis* is to be maintained in full, can it be said that the Court is bound in principle by the interpretation given by the Protocol? Why, as a matter of principle, rather than practice, should the interpretation reached by the heads of state of the Member States be preferred to a conflicting interpretation reached by the Court? By this logic, it seems that there is nothing to prevent the Court from reaching a conclusion on the proper construction of Article 119 EEC, in the light of the *Barber* decision, which differs from that in the Protocol. That the Court is entitled to do so *before* the TEU is ratified and enters into force is relatively non-contentious.[21] What is far more contentious is the question of whether the Court could refuse to apply the interpretation enacted in the Protocol *after* the TEU is ratified. If the Court were to adopt such a position, this could only be by means of a challenge to the Protocol as "unconstitutional".[22]

If the Protocol neither amends nor interprets Article 119, is there any other way in which its status can be characterised? The Protocol is clearly intended to have legal effect, and so cannot be considered to be in the nature of a recommendation of the Member States to the Court. The Protocol does not affect the ruling in the *Barber* case itself. Nor can it be said (at least on its face) to be an interpretation of the ruling in paragraph 45 of the *Barber* case. It seems impossible to make sense of the Protocol unless it has a status akin to legislation, albeit

---

[20] See below.
[21] But see Hudson, *supra*, n 10.
[22] See below.

primary legislation in the Community context. Naturally there is scope for legislative reform of judicial precedent in EC law, as in other legal systems. That said, the objections raised above are not avoided by this observation, and difficulties pertaining to the status of the Protocol remain.

In practice, it seems likely that the Court will demur to the Protocol as a *fait accompli*.[23] Several references from national courts concerning the application of the *Barber* decision are before the Court at present.[24] The opinion of Advocate General van Gerven suggests that the solution favoured by the Member States (expressed in the Protocol) should be followed by the Court in making preliminary rulings in these cases. The existence of the Protocol may contribute to a good faith reliance on that interpretation of Article 119 promulgated by the Protocol, especially where it is borne in mind that the Court has accepted that good faith exists where the Community institutions themselves have helped to create a particular impression of Community law.[25] This principle could be extended from good faith in the acts of the *institutions* of the Community, to good faith in the acts of the *Member States*, acting in a Community context.

The Protocol and the separation of powers

The European Community is a "Community based on the rule of law".[26] The concept of the rule of law comprises several related components: government according to law, equality before the law, *nulla poene sine lege* and the separation of powers. Separation of powers is "an essential structural guarantee of democracy",[27] since it protects individual subjects within a legal system from a concentration of power, in a single arm of government, without "checks and balances". Separation of powers traditionally requires that the three functions of government, legislative, executive and judicial, be exercised by separate organs of the state.[28] In the European Community, exercise of judicial power is the responsibility of the courts of the Member States, the Court of First Instance and the Court of Justice. Article 177 confers upon the Court of Justice jurisdiction to give preliminary rulings on the interpretation of provisions of Community law. In this context, the Court is acting as a "supreme court", by providing binding interpretations of provisions of Community law, thereby protecting the uniform application of Community law in all the Member States.[29]

---

[23] See Curtin, *supra*, n 1, at 51 and Prechal cited therein. The judgment in *Ten Oever, supra*, n 13, bears out this assertion. The Court held that para 45 of *Barber, supra*, n 5, requires equal treatment in occupational pensions "only in relation to benefits payable in respect of periods of employment subsequent to 17 May 1990" (para 17); that is, the Court adopted the interpretation favoured by the Member States in the Protocol.

[24] Joined cases *Ten Oever, Moroni, Neath, Coloroll, supra*, n 13.

[25] For example, by the Commission failing to bring an action under Art 169 to challenge a state of affairs contrary to Community law; see Case 43/75 *Defrenne* v *SABENA* [1976] ECR 455.

[26] Case 294/83 *Parti écologiste "Les Verts"* v *European Parliament* [1986] ECR 1339.

[27] Lenaerts, "Some reflections on the separation of powers in the European Community" (1991) 28 CML Rev 11–35 at 11.

[28] Although Lenaerts, *supra*, n 27 at 13, suggests that a functional rather than an organic division may also be appropriate.

[29] See Lenaerts, *supra*, n 27 at 32.

There are two effects of a judgment of the Court of Justice under the preliminary rulings procedure. The judgment decides the case in question, and, although not in a formal sense, lays down a precedent for future cases. Moreover, as the Court explained in *Denkavit*:

"The interpretation which, in the exercise of the jurisdiction conferred upon it by Article 177, the Court of Justice gives to a rule of Community law clarifies and defines where necessary the meaning and scope of that rule as it must be or ought to have been understood and applied from the time of its coming into force."[30]

The interpretation given by the Court must therefore, as a general rule, be applicable to legal relationships arising before the judgment.

Since the effect of this rule could have devastating effects in certain cases, the Court of Justice has long recognised exceptions to the rule.[31] By considerations of good faith, legal certainty, and even the practical effects of its judgment, the Court of Justice is empowered to determine the temporal effect of its rulings. This power is an essential component of the exercise of its judicial function: in the *Denkavit*[32] case the Court ruled that it is for the Court of Justice alone to decide upon the temporal restrictions to be placed on the interpretation that it lays down.

In enacting the Protocol, a non-judicial organ of government of the European Community, that is, the Member States acting in an intergovernmental conference, (at least according to one view of the status of the Protocol) gave an authoritative interpretation of a provision of Community law. Moreover, the Member States determined the precise temporal effect of the *Barber* ruling. In other words, the Member States usurped the judicial function, which, in accordance with the doctrine of separation of powers, ought properly to be exercised by the judicial organ of the European Community, the Court of Justice.

The Community is a legal entity *sui generis*, not an intergovernmental organization. As Lenaerts points out, (in the context of the Commission's monopoly of legislative initiative), one of the principal functions of the rule of law in general, and the separation of powers in particular, in the context of the European Community, is to protect the Community interest from the influence of intergovernmentalism.[33] Similarly, in the context of the Court's monopoly of interpretative competence, the preservation of separation of powers can effectively protect Community law from intergovernmentalism. The *Barber* Protocol, therefore, is particularly disturbing, since it is evidence of the breakdown of the separation of powers in the European Community, and, by extension, evidence of the mistrust of the Member States of the roles of the Community institutions in a Community governed by the rule of law.

Politics triumph over law

The Protocol is clearly a product of political expediency. The Member States were prepared to interfere with the constitutional and institutional balance of the

---

[30] Case 61/79 *Amministrazione delle Finanze dello Stato* v *Denkavit Italiana*, [1980] ECR 1205 at 1223, para 16.
[31] Case 43/75 *Defrenne* v *SABENA* [1976] ECR 455.
[32] *Supra*, n 29.   [33] Lenaerts, *supra*, n 27 at 28.

Community, in order to protect certain powerful interest groups, for political reasons. Curtin[34] describes this process as "hijacking the *acquis communautaire*"; an apt description of the triumph of politics over law in various respects in the TEU, of which the *Barber* Protocol is but one example.

The question then arises whether the assertion that the Protocol is an example of "hijacking" could be grounds for a challenge before the Court of Justice to the Protocol as "unconstitutional", that is to say, contrary to the fundamental norms of Community law. Such a contention has been advanced by several writers in the context of the Social Policy Protocol. On the one hand, such a challenge would be impossible, since Protocols to the TEU form part of the Treaty,[35] the Treaty is the primary source of Community law, part of the constitution of the EC and therefore cannot be subject to a challenge before the Court.[36] On the other hand, since the TEU expressly provides that the existing *acquis communautaire* be maintained, and since the Social Policy Protocol breaches the basic principles of the Community, such as uniformity of the legal order, fair competition and solidarity, the Social Policy Protocol is not consistent with the Community "constitution" and should be struck down.[37] Moreover some writers have asserted that the Court of Justice has already developed (or in the alternative, should now develop) an inherent jurisdiction as a constitutional court, even though the Treaties themselves do not expressly confer that jurisdiction. Therefore the Court of Justice could and should strike down the Social Policy Protocol as contrary to the scheme of the Treaty system and the spirit of the Treaty.[38]

Could similar assertions be advanced in respect of the *Barber* Protocol?[39] The answer is probably in the negative, since it is difficult to find sufficiently serious grounds upon which the Protocol might be said to be "unconstitutional". The unconstitutionality of the Social Policy Protocol goes to the very heart of the entire system of Community law – uniformity and cohesion. Such a breach may be sufficiently serious to overcome the problems of jurisdiction outlined above: in order to protect the Community itself a primary source of Community law could legally be overturned. The grounds on which the *Barber* Protocol may be held to be unconstitutional (breach of the separation of powers, destabilization of the institutional balance, promotion of intergovernmentalism), although undoubtedly part of the *acquis communautaire*, are, in my opinion, insufficiently fundamental to the Community as a whole to justify a ruling from the Court of Justice that the Protocol is invalid. After all, the separation of powers in the Community is not complete,[40] the institutional balance is constantly

---

[34] Curtin, *supra*, n 1.

[35] Art 239 EC, as amended.

[36] See Watson, *supra*, n 10 at 489–490. Watson draws an analogy with Annexes to the Acts of Accession of new Member States to the Community. The Court has held that these Annexes are provisions of primary law, and thus that the Court has no jurisdiction to consider their validity; Case 31/86 *Levantina Agricola Industrial SA CPC España* v *Council* [1988] ECR 2801.

[37] See, for example, Fitzpatrick, "Community Social Law after Maastricht" (1992) 21 ILJ 199–213 at 203; Whiteford, "Social Policy after Maastricht" (1993) 18 EL Rev 202–222.

[38] See Whiteford, *supra*, n 37; see also Arnull, "Does the Court of Justice have inherent jurisdiction?" (1990) 27 CML Rev 683–708.

[39] See Curtin, *supra*, n 1 at 63.

[40] See Lenaerts, *supra*, n 27.

developing,[41] and intergovernmentalism has always been a part of Community practice, and even provided for in Community treaties.[42]

However, the conclusion that the *Barber* Protocol might not be in such fundamental conflict with the *acquis communautaire* as to be in some sense "unconstitutional" does not in any way detract from the observation that the Protocol, as an example of the triumph of political considerations over integration through law, is a step in the wrong direction by the Member States.

Market forces triumph over the fundamental rights of individuals

There is one further possible ground upon which the assertion that the Protocol is unconstitutional might be upheld. The *Barber* Protocol could be said to be in breach of fundamental personal human rights.

The jurisprudence of the Court of Justice concerning fundamental rights establishes that fundamental rights are part of the general principles of law the observance of which the Court is charged with ensuring according to Article 164 of the Treaty of Rome.[43] Could it be argued that fundamental rights are therefore higher norms in the Community legal order than Treaty amendments, and that therefore Treaty amendments could be challenged on the basis of their inconsistency with such a higher norm?[44]

It should be stated by way of a *caveat* here that establishing the status of sex equality or non-discrimination as a fundamental personal human right in Community law is not straightforward. Sex equality provisions in Community law, since they limit the choices of market actors,[45] conflict with the principles of liberalism and free market economics upon which the single European market is founded. Interference in the market by enactment of rules providing for non-discrimination on grounds of sex is justified for two quite different reasons. One reason is the need to create a level playing field for all employers. The other is the promotion of the fundamental human right of equality, of which non-discrimination on grounds of sex is one facet. The fact that the concept of sex equality owes its position in Community law to these two purposes, which are held in constant tension, means that it cannot be regarded as settled that sex equality is a human right in the Community legal order. However, assertions that sex equality is a human right, and consequently a general principle of Community law, exist in the jurisprudence of the Court of Justice.[46]

---

[41] See Case C-70/88 *Parliament* v *Council (Chernobyl)* [1990] ECR I-2041, paras 23 and 26; Bradley, "Sense and Sensibility: *Parliament* v *Council* continued" (1991) 16 EL Rev 245–257 at 256.

[42] See, for example, Single European Act, Title III (OJ 1987 L169/1).

[43] See, for example, Case 29/69 *Stauder* v *City of Ulm* [1969] ECR 419; Case 11/70 *Internationale Handelsgesellschaft mbH* [1970] ECR 1125; Case 4/73 *Nold* v *Commission* [1974] ECR 491.

[44] See Whiteford, *supra*, n 37 at 220.

[45] In general, employers.

[46] For example, see Case 149/77 *Defrenne* v *SABENA (No. 3)* [1978] ECR 1365.

Accordingly, if sex equality can be accepted as a fundamental human right, then a challenge to the constitutionality of the *Barber* Protocol could perhaps be envisaged. The effect of the Protocol is to postpone equality between men and women in pension provision for 40 years or so. The Protocol might therefore be said to breach the right to equal treatment on grounds of sex, a human right, which is a higher norm than even Treaty amendments. In view of the various reservations expressed above, such a conclusion could only be tentatively advanced.

However tentative the conclusion concerning the constitutionality of the *Barber* Protocol, it remains the case that the Protocol is to be deplored as a triumph of market forces over the rights of individuals. The concept of legitimate expectations or legal certainty, and the cost (to certain market actors) of a decision that promoted equality, were used to justify the interpretations of Article 119 in the *Barber* case[47] itself and in the Protocol. The cost to employees or beneficiaries of pension funds for whom equality will be denied for another 40 years did not weigh heavily with the Court or the Member States. The underlying theme of both the decision of the Court of Justice and the Protocol is the favouring of the interests of powerful economic actors at the expense of the protection of rights of individuals. This, if nothing else, is a serious ground for criticism of the Protocol.

Conclusions

The precise legal status of the *Barber* Protocol must remain uncertain. It seems likely that the Court of Justice will uphold the substance of the Protocol in subsequent case law. In practice, a ruling that the Protocol is invalid on grounds of unconstitutionality is extremely unlikely, given the political ramifications that such a ruling would entail.[48]

However, it should be recognised that the Protocol exemplifies certain trends, such as a challenge to the rule of law, preference of intergovernmental rather than institutional solutions, and a lack of protection of human rights, which, in the new Europe after Maastricht, are indeed of grave concern.

TAMARA K HERVEY

---

[47] *Supra*, n 5.
[48] Whiteford, *supra*, n 37 at 220.

Part 10

The British and Danish Positions

Chapter 22
UK Constitutional and Parliamentary Aspects of the Maastricht Treaty

Introduction

The leaders of the 12 Member States of the European Community have sought to use the Maastricht Treaty or Treaty on European Union (TEU) as a reflection of their long term political and economic aspirations and objectives. But the reflection is distorted by the compromise required to find a text broadly acceptable to all the 12 Member States. The contemporaneous progression towards economic and monetary union and towards political union, which would lead to important constitutional changes, has been hemmed in by those who prefer greater intergovernmental co-operation within the Community and the retention of existing powers for national institutions. The deletion of the term "federal goal" during the negotiations on the draft text of the Treaty did not prevent the setting up of "a European Union founded on the European Communities, supplemented by the policies and forms of co-operation established by this Treaty."[1]

European Union

The title of "Treaty on European Union" may lead to the conclusion that there is a greater move towards a federal Europe, a United States of Europe, than an examination of the provisions of the Treaty would warrant. Such a move would have significant consequences for the British constitution in general, and in particular, would mean a weakening of the sovereign powers of Parliament, a fundamental principle of the constitution.

The adoption of the title confirms the use of a term which has been current for many years. Mr Leo Tindemanns was the author of a Report on European Union in 1975,[2] a Report which foreshadowed many of the later political developments in the European Community. The Stuttgart Declaration on

---

[1] Art A.3 TEU.
[2] Bull EC Supp 1/76.

European Union set out objectives for the development of the Community in its preamble. The Heads of State or Government:

"are resolved to continue the work of the Treaties of Paris and Rome to create a united Europe ... determined to work together to promote democracy on the basis of the fundamental rights recognised in the constitutions and laws of the Member States, in the European Convention for the Protection of Human Rights ... speaking with one voice in foreign policy, including political aspects of security ... recalling decisions ... concerning the progressive construction of European Union ... and reaffirming their will to transform the whole complex of relations between their States into a European Union."[3]

Two years later, in the Single European Act (SEA) there is frequent reference to the term "European Union", the opening preambular paragraph beginning with "the Member States being resolved to transform relations as a whole among their States into a European Union."[4]

The goals to be achieved in the above statements would undoubtedly affect the British constitution, but the use of the word "Union" has several connotations. It may range from the major constitutional changes which occurred in 1707 with the Union between England and Scotland to the Western European Union, identifying co-operation between sovereign States or even the Postal Union.

Radical changes

In order to assess the effects of provisions being introduced in the TEU, it is as well to observe the radical changes to British constitutional law which took place in 1972, with the passing of the European Communities Act.[5] On the accession of the United Kingdom to the European Economic Community on 1 January 1973, Community law thereby "became a source of the constitutional law of Britain."[6] Community Treaties, Directives, Regulations and Decisions, as well as rulings of the European Court of Justice take effect in British law. Further, the rulings and principles which are laid down by the Court have been accepted by the United Kingdom as binding,[7] and in accordance with decisions by the Court, Community law prevails over national law.

The SEA also introduced changes into the law-making powers of the United Kingdom, particularly by the extension of the use of the Qualified Majority Vote (QMV) under Article 100a EEC, on those matters relating to the creation of the single market and the opening of internal borders under Article 8a SEA. This had the effect of undermining the principle of a state's sovereignty over its own frontiers, the introduction of economic and monetary union under Article 102a and a structured form of European Political Co-operation in the sphere of

---

[3] Conclusions of the European Council, Stuttgart, 17–19 June 1983.
[4] SEA, 1986, first preambular para.
[5] European Communities Act 1972, chap 68.
[6] De Smith, Street and Brazier (eds) *Constitutional and Administrative Law*, 6th ed, (1992) 26.
[7] *Ibid.*

Foreign Policy, under Title III. Powers accorded to the European Parliament (EP) under the SEA included, for the first time, the possibility for the EP, not only to influence, but to have a direct input into European Community legislative texts under the Co-operation Procedure,[8] and to assent to and, consequently, to object to applications for membership to the European Community and ratification of certain international agreements.[9] These two last powers could lead to a clash with national Parliaments, though none has been recorded so far.

Constitutional significance of provisions of the TEU

There is no comparable quantum leap towards major change in the British constitution as at present envisaged, though there are some issues which require examination.

The granting of European citizenship on all nationals of the Member States of the European Community does not impose any duties or additional obligations on EC nationals, nor does it override national citizenship. The concept of subsidiarity, introduced in Article 3.b.2 TEU, acts as a brake on the powers of the Community institutions. The extension of competence in new policy sectors, not formerly included in the Treaties, now gives express, although limited, powers to the Community institutions. They have already been the subject of Community legislation, mainly under the general Articles 100 and 235. Lord Wilberforce pointed out during the debate on the Second Reading of the European Communities (Amendment) Bill in the House of Lords that, "it must be beneficial as diminishing the discretion of Brussels and setting down the position in black and white". He went on to say that:

"there is one small constitutional impact of the Maastricht Treaty. It may well be the case that having those points in black and white in the Maastricht Treaty will result in a different attitude on the part of the European Court .... Following Maastricht, everything is in black and white. One does not even have to look at the small print. It is all in small print, 133 pages of it. It may well be that in future the European Court may find itself much more engaged in scrutinizing what is in the book rather than trying to find principles and purposes on which to extend its jurisdiction."[10]

New powers granted to the European Parliament under Articles 138b–e, 144 and 189c TEU, as well as stronger control, in conjunction with the Court of Auditors, over Community expenditure, in Article 188c, do not represent transfer of power from national Parliaments. Even so, these new powers are subject to approval by Act of Parliament.[11]

---

[8] Art 18 SEA, Art 100a EEC.
[9] Arts 8,9 SEA, Arts 237,238 EEC.
[10] Official Report, 7 June 1993, at col 577.
[11] European Parliamentary Elections Act 1978 and see cl 1(2).

Future changes

There may not be major changes which will take immediate effect on ratification of the Treaty, but it must be recognised that the Treaty holds important consequences for the constitution in the future, subject in each case, to approval by Parliament.

The first and by far the most significant change is the intended introduction of a single currency, with the transfer of monetary policy to a System of European Central Banks. The move to a single currency will be subject to certain criteria set out in the Treaty and applicable to all Member States. The position of the United Kingdom is protected by a Protocol annexed to the Treaty, whereby the United Kingdom "shall notify the Council, whether it intends to move to the third stage before the Council makes its assessment under Article 109(3) of this Treaty."[12] This notification will be subject to approval by Act of Parliament.[13]

Secondly, matters currently to be dealt with by intergovernmental co-operation in the field of home and justice affairs, such as asylum and immigration, listed in Title VI, may be transferred, on the initiative of the Commission or of a Member State, subject to the unanimous agreement of the Council.[14] Unanimity ensures that Member States will have the power to agree or not, subject to their constitutional procedures, in the case of the United Kingdom, by Parliamentary approval.

Thirdly, in the Provisions on Common Foreign and Security Policy, all questions relating to security shall be included and also "the eventual framing of a common defence policy, which might in time lead to a common defence."[15]

Fourthly, under Article Q, "The Treaty is concluded for an unlimited period". A fundamental principle of the British constitution is the sovereignty of Parliament, and the rule that no Parliament can bind its successors. This rule remains. It was restated with admirable clarity by Lord Simon of Glaisdale, during the Committee stage of the European Communities (Amendment) Bill that, "It is a fundamental doctrine, that in the famous words of the common law, Acts derogatory of Parliament bind them not. Anything that is passed by one Parliament can be altered by a future Parliament."[16]

It is therefore understandable, with these measures set out in the Treaty, that proceedings in Parliament during the course of the European Communities (Amendment) Bill led to detailed discussion and debate.

---

[12] Para 1 Protocol on certain Provisions relating to the United Kingdom of Great Britain and Northern Ireland.
[13] Cl 2. European Communities (Amendment) Bill.
[14] Title VI, Art K.9.
[15] Title V, Art J.4.
[16] Official Report, 30 June 1993, at col 856.

The parliamentary process

Treaty-making powers in the United Kingdom are vested in the Crown and do not in general require parliamentary sanction, unlike in the United States where ratification of treaties must be approved by the Senate with a two-thirds majority. Only those Treaties which contain provisions affecting United Kingdom law must be considered by Parliament and the relevant legislation passed so that those Treaty provisions are honoured. It has been the practice, however, since 1924, under what is known as the Ponsonby Rule, for major treaties to be laid before Parliament for 21 days, after signature, but before ratification. There has been no precedent up to the present time for a Treaty not to be ratified by the United Kingdom following signature.

In the case of the TEU, unusually, on account of its critical importance, the Prime Minister reported to the House of Commons on the proceedings in the intergovernmental conferences on Economic and Monetary Union being held at Maastricht and sought the approval of the House for the negotiating position of the British Government, prior to the Treaty being initialled.

The vote in favour of the Prime Minister's proposals was 351–250.[17] The Prime Minister made a statement on the outcome of the negotiations on 11 December 1991, and a debate was held the following week to endorse the achievement of the negotiating objectives of the government and the agreement secured by the government at Maastricht. The vote was 339–253.[18]

The support of Parliament was essential. No government would normally entertain the prospect of negotiating the terms of a Treaty which would not be agreed by Parliament. That part of a Treaty affecting domestic law must receive the approval of Parliament. The original structure of the TEU responds to the constitutional requirements of the United Kingdom, Titles II, III and IV containing those parts of the Treaty which amend existing European Communities Treaties (EEC Treaty 1957, ECSC Treaty 1951 and Euratom Treaty 1957 as amended) and which as part of domestic law have been considered in Parliament in the European Communities (Amendment) Bill. But what was a workable government majority in 1991 was not to remain following the General Election in 1992. While all the major parties supported the Second Reading of the Bill held in May 1992, with a majority of 336 to 92,[19] this was not to be the case during the lengthy process of the Bill through the House of Commons.

The negative result of the Danish referendum on the Treaty, and the need for new proposals for Denmark, agreed at the Edinburgh summit in December 1992, led to the postponement of the Committee stage of the Bill's passage through the House of Commons until January 1993.

The passage of the Bill has been marked not only by the duration of the process, but also by consideration of two important constitutional issues, first, as regards procedure and the legal result achieved, and secondly, a demand by

---

[17] Official Report, 21 November 1991, at col 523.
[18] Official Report, 19 December 1991, at col 551.
[19] Official Report, 21 May 1992, at col 597.

some Members for a referendum, on the main ground that the people of Britain had not been consulted. The latter issue was considered to arise because the major parties had agreed to the provisions of the Treaty and it was not, therefore, a major matter of debate and discussion during the General Election held in April 1992.

Protocol on the Agreement on Social Policy

The crucial issue of the passage of the Protocol on Social Policy, annexed to the Treaty, has given rise to considerable debate and conflict of views on the constitutional position, with regard to the use of the Crown prerogative.

While the problem appears simple, its consequences do not have the same simplicity. The Protocol on Social Policy is an agreement between 11 Member States to pursue certain specific actions in the social field. The United Kingdom is not a party to the agreement, just as it was not a party to the Social Charter, agreed at the Strasbourg summit in December 1989. The Protocol therefore does not affect domestic law, and consequently there was no reference to it in the Bill before Parliament.

The Opposition wanted to have the Social Policy applicable to the United Kingdom, and with support from those who oppose the Treaty, an amendment was eventually adopted which excepted the Protocol on Social Policy from the definition of "the Treaties" and "Community Treaties". The exclusion of the Protocol on Social Policy from the Treaty was intended to require the government to negotiate with the other 11 Member States and to accept the Social Policy, or else be unable to ratify the Treaty. At first sight, the government's response to such an amendment was that, if it was adopted, the United Kingdom would not indeed be able to ratify the Treaty.[20] By February, there was new advice, to the effect that the inclusion of such an amendment would not impede ratification of the Treaty. As Mr Hurd explained, in a statement to the House:

"the amendment would not have any effect on the Treaty itself. It would not change the agreement among 11 to an agreement among 12. It would not bring the social chapter into effect in this country ... The legal question is therefore whether the United Kingdom could ratify the Treaty even if the protocol were not incorporated into domestic law."[21]

It would seem clear that no obligations arise from the Protocol which would affect English law, and although it might be desirable to have the Protocol incorporated, it does not impede ratification of the Treaty. Acts under the Protocol would not apply to the United Kingdom. Ratification of the Treaties being an act of the Executive, under the Crown prerogative, there is nothing to prevent ratification where the particular provision excluded from the Bill would not affect domestic law. On these grounds the government accepted the amendment during the Report stage of the Bill.[22] Reviewing the history of the Protocol on Social Policy, Mr Hurd stated that:

---

[20] Official Report, 20 January 1993, Garel-Jones, at col 403.
[21] Official Report, 15 February 1993, at col 27.
[22] Official Report, 5 May 1993, at col 207.

"In the pre-Maastricht debate on 20 and 21 November 1991, a Labour amendment, which called for, among other things, the inclusion of the social agreement in the Treaty of Rome, was defeated by 191 votes .... . In the debate on 18 and 19 December 1991, immediately after Maastricht, the Liberals tabled an amendment deploring the social opt-out. It was defeated by a majority of 364. On Second Reading of the Bill, on 20 and 21 May, in this Parliament, Labour moved that the Bill not be read a Second time, partly because of the opt-out on the social chapter. That amendment was defeated by 99 votes. There is no doubt about the judgment of the previous Parliament and of this Parliament on the question whether the Treaty should or should not include the social chapter."[23]

Nevertheless a new clause was inserted into the Bill to allow for a debate in both Houses of Parliament on the Social Policy, following Royal Assent, but before the Act comes into force.[24] The change in the composition of the House since the negotiations on the text of the Treaty were concluded was very evident.

It remains to be seen whether the Agreement on Social Policy by the 11 Member States and the adoption of Directives will have any legal effect in the UK courts.

The European Communities (Amendment) Bill eventually was passed by a large majority in the House of Commons at Third Reading, of 292–112,[25] one year after its second reading in May 1992, with three further amendments, including the requirement that elected representatives of local authorities be proposed for membership of the Committee of the Regions.

Passage of the Bill in the House of Lords

The Bill, having concluded the Committee stage by the end of June, with no amendments, the only contentious issue remaining was the amendment on the holding of a referendum. Debates held on the second reading of the Bill during the Committee stage have provided valuable material for clarification and inter-pretation of the text of the Treaty and the implications of the Bill on UK law.

With no amendments to the Bill, following Royal Assent, and the debate in both Houses on the Protocol on Social Policy, there still remains the promised judicial review process to be brought before the English courts, as well as major claims in the Danish court and the German Constitutional Court, which could block ratification of the Treaty. The difference in the role of the German consti-tution with a possible need to hold a referendum contrasts with the principle of the British constitution, that Parliament is sovereign.

Postscript

The last hurdle to be overcome was the case of *Regina* v *Secretary of Foreign Affairs, ex parte Rees-Mogg* (QBD, 30 July 1993), in which Lord Rees-Mogg attempted to thwart ratification by applying for judicial review of the Foreign Secretary's

---

[23] Official Report, 5 May 1993, at col 201.
[24] European Communities (Amendment) Bill, cl.7.
[25] Official Report, 20 May 1993, at col 468.

decision to proceed with ratification of the Treaty. Claiming that the issue was the most important constitutional case for 300 years – a view not supported by the court – Lord Rees-Mogg set out three major objections to the government's handling of the Treaty. First, the government would be in breach of section 6 of the European Parliament Elections Act 1978 as the Social Protocol would increase the powers of the European Parliament. It was argued that while the Treaty had been approved by Parliament that did not include Protocols because they were annexed to the Treaty of Rome. This argument was rejected by the court. The European Communities Amendment Act contained the approval required, the term Treaty including any Protocol or Annex to the Treaty.

The second objection was based on the argument that by ratifying the Protocol on Social Policy, the government would be altering Community law under the Treaty of Rome. This argument was also rejected by the court. Finally, it was claimed that the government could not lawfully transfer any part of the Crown's prerogative powers in relation to foreign affairs without Parliament's approval. The court held that Title V of the Treaty could not be read as a transfer of prerogative powers. It was, rather, an exercise of those powers.

Lord Rees-Mogg's application for judicial review was dismissed by the court and was not appealed.

Before the case opened, the Speaker had warned that the courts should not interfere with the proceedings of Parliament, citing Article 9 of the Bill of Rights 1689. Lord Justice Lloyd said that the issues of the case were within the sphere of judicial review, just as "questions of policy were within the sphere of Parliament".

Both the constitutional and parliamentary aspects of the Treaty were addressed in this case, and following the court's decision, the Treaty was ratified promptly on 2 August 1993.

DIANA ELLES

Chapter 23
Denmark and the Edinburgh Summit: Maastricht without Tears

Background

After it had been signed in February 1992, the Treaty of Maastricht[1] "only" needed to be ratified by the Member States "in accordance with their respective constitutional requirements", following which it would enter into force on 1 January 1993.[2] However, in their first referendum of 2 June 1992 the Danes made it painfully clear to "Brussels" that within the Member States such a thing as a *population* also exists; the electorate indicated by a slender majority of 50.7% of the votes that the limits of "public tolerance" had indeed been crossed. Although it is difficult to assess exactly what the Danish feelings of discomfort were based on, they would appear to concern matters which are difficult to grasp such as the fear of losing the national cultural identity and national sovereignty and freedom of action which the Union was seen to imply. Since the referendum a number of surveys have been published, most notably one conducted at the Institute of Political Science, Aarhus University,[3] which shed light on the motivations behind the vote.[4] The politically uncomfortable finding is that the vote was pertinent enough: it was a genuine vote against the expansion of the Community into foreign and defence policy and very much against the idea of the European Union as such.[5]

In any event, and whatever the precise motivation for the negative Danish result, it was painfully clear that the time was ripe for Europe's governing elite to adopt a less "detached" attitude towards the populations of the Member States. Initially, however, the political reaction was not to attempt to meet the Danish objections. On the contrary, Denmark was to be isolated and perhaps even forced to leave the Community. According to the Council of Ministers (of

---

[1] For discussion of the structure of the Union, see Everling, 'Reflections on the structure of the European Union', (1992) 29 CMLRev 1053–1077; Schmuck, 'Der Maastrichter Vertrag zur Europäischen Union' (1992) Europa-Archiv, 97–106; Kapteyn, 'Inleidende beschouwingen over het Verdrag betreffende de Europese Unie' (1992) SEW, 667–673; Curtin, 'The constitutional structure of the Union: a Europe of bits and pieces' (1993) 30 CML Rev 17–69.

[2] See Art R of the Treaty and – to the extent that the EC Treaties are amended – Arts 236 EEC, 96 ECSC and 204 EAEC.

[3] Siune, Svensson, and Tonsgaard, *Det blev et Nej*, Arhus (1992).

[4] See, in general, Petersen, 'Denmark and the Maastricht Treaty, a European problem' in *La communaute europeenne avant Edimbourg*, journee d'etudes, Bruxelles, 21 novembre 1992, 11.

[5] See Petersen, *ibid* at 22.

Foreign Affairs) – meeting in Oslo on 4 June 1992 – the ratification procedures were to proceed "as normal".[6] In Ireland this resulted in the referendum of 18 June 1992 which produced a clear "Yes" in favour of the Treaty, despite a very difficult campaign focused on the so-called "abortion issue". The French followed on 20 September 1992, albeit with a very guarded "Oui".

A change of strategy in respect of the unresolved Danish problem was adopted at the extraordinary meeting of the European Council in Birmingham on 16 October 1992. A Declaration issued at the conclusion of this Summit was replete with pious promises to bring the Community closer to its citizens.[7] Thus the European Council "solemnly declares" that it is necessary to demonstrate to the citizens of the Member States the benefits of the Community and the Maastricht Treaty, to make the Community more open to ensure a better informed public debate on its activities, to respect the history, culture and traditions of individual nations and to make clear that citizenship of the Union brings the citizens additional rights and protection without in any way taking the place of their national citizenship. In addition, special attention was given to the European Parliament which is to play "an important role in the democratic life of the Community"; this is followed by the recommendation to reinforce the ties between the European Parliament and the national parliaments.

In reaction to this, Denmark presented a "national compromise" on 30 October 1992, which was meant to be the answer of the most important Danish political parties to the problems caused by the people's rejection of the Maastricht Treaty. This compromise is laid down in the memorandum "Denmark in Europe".[8] It appears from this document that the Danish objections related primarily to the lack of openness and transparency in Community decision-making, defence policy, the third stage of Economic and Monetary Union (EMU), citizenship of the Union, co-operation in the fields of justice and home affairs, the effective application of the principle of subsidiarity and the combating of unemployment. The document explicitly rejects the "United States of Europe", emphasises national independence and sovereignty and stresses the *intergovernmental* character of the Community. It also specifically rejects Union citizenship and demands a partial exception for Denmark with respect to "the objectives of the Union set out in the common provisions of the Maastricht Treaty", namely in those areas where specific exceptions are demanded (citizenship, third stage of EMU, foreign and defence policy and justice and home affairs).

What, then, did the Danes actually wrest from their Community partners at the European Council Summit meeting of 11 and 12 December 1992? Which significant amendments could be brought to the attention of the Danish

---

[6] On this matter, see d'Oliveira, 'Maastricht en Kopenhagen', (1992) NJB, 784–785. On the possibilities of forcing Denmark to leave the Community, see Kapteyn, 'Denemarken en het Verdrag van Maastricht', (1992) NJB, 781–783.

[7] See the 'Birmingham Declaration on a Community close to its citizens' annexed to the Conclusions of the European Council (Annex I), Bull EC 10–1992, 7–11 and *Europe* of 18 October 1992 (Spec ed).

[8] *Europe*, 5 November 1992.

electorate, prior to the second referendum of 18 May 1993? The results are recorded in a separate Part B of the Edinburgh Conclusions, entitled "Denmark and the Treaty on European Union".[9] Was the Maastricht Treaty indeed amended in order to accommodate the Danish objections? And for how long after the second Danish referendum will the Danes be able to retain their "special position"? Furthermore, what is to be made of the fact that the Heads of State and Government meeting within the European Council apparently have assumed the power to take legally binding decisions? The rest of this article will consider some possible answers to these questions.

At this stage it need only be confirmed that the "concessions" made to Denmark to a large extent determined the outcome of the second Danish referendum of 18 May 1993. A healthy majority of 56.8% of the Danes voted in favour of the Maastricht Treaty despite strong – and sometimes religiously inspired – opposition.[10]

Conclusions of the Edinburgh Summit

General structure

The conclusions of the European Council summit meeting in Edinburgh are important, because they contain "solutions" for a number of highly sensitive problems. Part A of the Conclusions highlights the general areas on which agreement was reached,[11] including the opening of accession negotiations with Austria, Sweden and Finland at the beginning of 1993 on the basis of acceptance in full of the Maastricht Treaty and the *acquis communautaire*; more detailed consideration of certain major areas are found in a series of Annexes. Thus, Annexes 1 and 2 contain guidelines for the implementation of the subsidiarity principle and Annex 3 measures to increase transparency and openness in the decision-making process of the Community. Annex 4 to Part A contains a veritable "plan of action" to promote growth and to combat unemployment in Europe[12] and Annex 5 a declaration on principles governing external aspects of migration policy, a highly controversial and topical subject. Finally, Annex 6

---

[9] Probably because of its great political importance and its legal status, this part of the Conclusions was also published in the *Official Journal* (OJ 1992 C348/1). This publication was undoubtedly designed to underline the *Community* features of this decision. See further below.

[10] Thus we were informed by the media that a Copenhagen minister (of the Church) had called for 'a No to Maastricht and a Yes for Jesus'. There also were violent clashes (with firearms) between the police and opponents of 'Maastricht'.

[11] As well as the subjects mentioned below this includes an agreement in principle on the increase in the number of seats in the European Parliament, to reflect German reunification and in the perspective of enlargement. The formal Council Decision increasing the number of seats has already been adopted (OJ 1993 L33/15).

[12] See further, Conclusions of the European Council of Copenhagen, 21–22 June 1993, Bull EC 6-1993 where special attention was given to action aimed at tackling the economic and social problems faced by the Community and particularly the unacceptably high level of unemployment.

contains the text of a *decision* taken between the Representatives of the Governments of the Member States pursuant to Article 216 of the EEC Treaty on the definitive seats of the European institutions (and a number of other bodies).[13]

Part B of the Edinburgh Conclusions is entitled "Denmark and the Treaty on European Union" and merits the description "Columbus egg".[14] It consists of a general introduction, three annexes (a novum in the form of a "decision" of the Heads of State or Government, *meeting within the European Council*, declarations of the European Council itself and some unilateral declarations by Denmark) as well as a final overall declaration. The precise legal status and content of this part of the Conclusions will be considered in detail below.

Finally, Part C of the Conclusions contains an agreement on the financing of Community action and policies for the rest of this decade (the so-called "Delors II Package"),[15] and Part D miscellaneous declarations by the European Council in the field of external relations.

These multifarious subjects cannot possibly be done justice in the limited framework of this article with its focus on the specific problems arising from the negative outcome of the first Danish referendum.[16] Nevertheless, it is worth noting that Annexes 1–4 of Part A of the Conclusions (principles of subsidiarity and transparency as well as the promotion of co-operation between the Member States to combat unemployment) concern subjects which were discussed as giving rise to particular concern in the Danish "national compromise" referred to above.[17] Aside from the areas from which the Danes requested specific *exceptions* from the terms of the Maastricht Treaty (and which were ultimately dealt with in Part B of the conclusions and are considered in detail below), one area can be singled out as a matter of acute Danish preoccupation, namely the closed and impenetrable decision-making processes of the Community.

The objective explicitly and repeatedly stated in the Danish "national compromise" was that "the EC must be made more democratic so that, *inter alia*, there is greater openness and transparency in its decision-making procedures". Annex 3 of the conclusions of the Edinburgh Summit is devoted to this question of a more open and transparent Community. Concrete measures discussed, include, open orientation debates on relevant Presidency or Commission work programmes, regular open debates on major issues of Community interest, to be decided by unanimity and in cases where a formal vote is taken in Council, making the voting record public (including explanations of vote should delegations request this). In addition, various pointers towards making new

---

[13] This decision is itself not uncontentious. First, its title refers to the 'seats of the institutions' (plural) whereas Art 216 EEC refers to the singular. The European Parliament now appears to have at least two seats. Secondly, Art 216 EEC is not an adequate legal basis with regard to the provisions of the decision concerning the Economic and Social Committee and the European Investment Bank (since they are not 'institutions' within the meaning of Art 4 EEC). With regard to the Court of Auditors, Art 216 EC will be adequate once the Maastricht Treaty has entered into force.

[14] Apparently given to it by the Danish Foreign Minister, Mr Ellenmann-Jensen, see Petersen, *supra*, n 4 at 37.

[15] On which see, Jouret, 'Les conclusions d'Edimbourg sur le pacquet Delors-II', (1993) RMC 391.

[16] For a general discussion of these Conclusions, excluding the Danish question, see Verloren van Themaat, 'De Europese Raad van Edinburgh als goudmijn voor juristen' (1993) SEW, 423, 433.

[17] See, *supra*, n 8. See also introductory remarks to Part B of the Edinburgh Conclusions.

352

Community legislation clearer and simpler as well as more accessible to the citizen were given. That the measures discussed here were intended to produce consequences quite independently from the Maastricht Treaty itself is confirmed by the recent publication of a Commission Communication on transparency[18] and a related Council resolution on the quality of drafting of Community legislation.[19]

Despite the laudable improvements which the Commission communication entails in terms of transparency and access to information, the fact remains that on one very pivotal issue no progress whatsoever has been made: "negotiations on legislation in the Council must remain confidential" is explicitly underlined in the Edinburgh conclusions itself.[20] This is in contrast to the occasional and purely *ad hoc* use of *preliminary* open debates on "major new legislative proposals". The refusal to revise the general secretive nature of normal Council legislative deliberations constitutes a significant negative response to the Danish request that:

"European co-operation must be in line with the peoples justified desire to be involved in and play an active part in democratic decisions. Each country's arguments and votes in the Council of Ministers must therefore be public."

The explicit recognition by the European Council of the need for secrecy in Council debates underlines in rather formal fashion the regrettable fact that decisions on Community legislation will continue to be made in secret with each Member State free to pursue its own national interest in blatant disregard, as the case may be, of the binding objectives, principles and other provisions of the Community Treaties.[21] On the other hand national parliaments may now well be prompted in the name of the so-called "democratic deficit" to *insist* that their representative in the Council elaborates and defends the position they adopted during the secret Council debate.[22]

The legal status of the Danish decision

As already indicated, Part B of the Conclusions purports to regulate the "Danish question". Annex 1 contains a new departure in Community law: a "Decision of the Heads of State and Government, meeting within the European

---

[18] *Transparency in the Community*, Communication to the Council, the European Parliament and the Economic and Social Committee, COM (93) 258 def (OJ 1993 C166/4).

[19] Council Resolution of 8 June 1993 on the quality of drafting of Community legislation (OJ 1993 C166/1). A close reading of this resolution reveals exhortatory statements not to be repetitive, to use clear language *etc.* This seems to be such a matter of plain common sense that it is surprising to see it all piously enshrined in a formal resolution, translated into all the Community languages!

[20] See Annex 3 to Part A of the Conclusions under 'Access to the Work of the Council.' The full text of the Conclusions of the Edinburgh European Council is published in Bull EC 12–1992 and *Europe* of 13 December 1992 (Spec ed).

[21] See, in the same sense, Ver Loren van Themaat, *supra* n 16 at 426. The Member States have bound themselves under Art 5 EEC to co-operate loyally in the execution of their obligations and in the facilitation of the accomplishment of the tasks of the Community.

[22] In that event the interesting legal question arises as to whether the Council's Rules of Procedure (which mandates the secrecy of the legislative proceedings) overrides national legal provisions which enable national parliaments to call Government Ministers to account. See further, Ver Loren van Themaat, *supra*, n 16 at 426.

Council, concerning certain problems raised by Denmark on the Treaty on European Union." This decision[23] itself consists of five sections, the first four of which (A-D) contain the "derogations" from the Maastricht Treaty in favour of Denmark; section E contains the "final provisions" and relates to procedural matters. Annex 2 consists of two Declarations of the European Council, the first on social policy, consumer protection, the environment and the distribution of income, the second on defence. Annex 3 consists of two unilateral declarations of Denmark "to be associated with the Danish Act of ratification of the Treaty on European Union and of which the eleven other Member States will take cognizance." The first Danish Declaration concerns the citizenship of the Union, while the second relates to co-operation in the fields of justice and home affairs.

The Danish decision is, in particular, remarkable. It appears both from the fact that it is presented as a "decision" and from its content (section E states it explicitly), as well as the clearly indicated intentions of the respective states that it is meant to be legally *binding*. As a matter of public international law, it seems that Article 11 of the Vienna Convention on the Law of Treaties ("The consent of a State to be bound by a treaty may be expressed by signature ... acceptance, approval ... or by any other means if so agreed") is satisfied.[24] It is significant that the Decision does not provide that the consent of the Member States to be bound by it to be expressed by means of ratification. The implication clearly is that signature is sufficient.

It is explicitly provided that the decision "will take effect" on the date of the entry into force of the Maastricht Treaty and that it has been concluded for an unlimited period. It will, however, be considered at the Conference of the Representatives of the Member States to be convened in 1996 in order to examine the need for revising the Maastricht Treaty, whether the decision also needs to be revised.[25] In addition it is provided that Denmark may unilaterally and at any time inform the other Member States that it will effectively disapply all or part of the decision. This provision is implicitly premised on the fact that Denmark at that time will satisfy the prevailing *acquis* in the relevant areas.

It is, however, exceptional that the text of the decision (and relevant "declarations"), embedded as it is in European Council conclusions, were published almost immediately in the "C" series of the *Official Journal*.[26] The question of the binding nature of the results of European Council summit meetings has, of course, been raised by some authors in the past and been

---

[23] Referred to hereafter in abbreviated form as 'the Danish Decision'.

[24] For the purposes of the Vienna Convention 'treaty' is defined as 'an international agreement concluded between States in written form and governed by international law ... and whatever its particular designation' (Art 2(1)(a)).

[25] See the reference in para 1 of the Final Provisions to Arts Q and N(2) of the Maastricht Treaty. As the latter provision refers to the objectives of the Union (Arts A and B) as a point of reference for this revision, it is likely that the complete revocation of the Decision of the Heads of State and Government is envisaged.

[26] See, n 9, *supra*. It is quite usual however, that 'acts of the representatives of the governments within the Council' are published in the C-series of the *Official Journal* and are often signed by the President of the Council. See further as to the status of these acts, below.

given a negative answer.[27] It follows from the fact that the statements of the European Council, even if the term "decides" is present in the conclusions, are not adopted in accordance with the procedural rules of the EEC Treaty, no binding legal nature can *stricto sensu* be ascribed to such acts within the Community legal order as such.[28]

What, if anything, is different about the Danish decision? To begin with, it is important to stress the fact that the disputed decision does not purport to be a decision of the European Council as such. Rather, it is a decision "of the Heads of State or Government *meeting within the European Council*". This is the first such decision ever to be taken in the history of the European Communities and as such certainly merits detailed legal scrutiny. Effectively the Heads of State or Government utilised the European Council summit meeting as a convenient platform and meeting place to adopt this *sui generis* decision. Consequently, this decision is by no means identical with the acts of the European Council as such. The immediate analogy of the Danish decision is with the so-called "acts of the representatives of the governments of the Member States meeting *within the Council*", what the Dutch refer to in convenient short-hand fashion as "framework-decisions"(*kaderbesluiten*).[29] Such "acts of the representatives" emanate from a diplomatic conference and not from the Council as an institution of the European Communities. It follows from this fact that the rules in the treaties concerning the way in which decisions of the Community institutions are taken, their legal effects, implementation and judicial review, cannot apply to "acts of the representatives".[30] This conclusion applies with even greater force to the Danish decision, adopted within the framework of the *European Council*. The European Council is not an institution of the Communities. No new Community institution in a legal sense was created by providing a legal basis for the European Council under Article 2 of the Single European Act or, will be created upon entry into force of the Maastricht Treaty, under Article D thereof.[31]

Many of the (legally binding) framework decisions or "acts of the representatives" must be considered as international agreements which are designed to be *complementary* to the Treaties and to the institutional acts put in place by the Treaties (pursuant to Art 189 EEC *etc*). These acts do not fall under the compe-

---

[27] See, in particular, Dondelinger, *Le Conseil Europeen* (1975); Everling, 'Die Entwicklung der EG' in *Schriftenreihe des Arbeitskreises Europaische Integration*, Vol 32 at 21; Werts, *The European Council* (1992) at 134.

[28] However, under the Maastricht Treaty the matter may change somewhat in very specific areas. For example, real decision-making powers seem to have been transferred to the European Council under Arts 109j and 109k within the framework of a procedure organised under Community law. In the context of co-operation in Foreign and Security Policy, decisions of the European Council under Arts J.3 and J.8 will have binding legal force for the Council with regard to joint action and to the principles and guidelines of Foreign and Security Policy.

[29] This is effectively a translation of the fuller Dutch description which translates as 'acts of the representatives taken *within the framework* of the Council' (authors' emphasis). For the detailed consideration of these acts, *e.g.* Kapteyn and Ver Loren van Themaat, *Introduction to the law of the European Communities* (1990) at 204–208. See also the Burger Report, 12 March 1969, EC Doc 1968–1969 215.

[30] Kapteyn and Ver Loren van Themaat, *ibid.* at 204.

[31] Although the European Council does appear to get some decision-making powers in the Maastricht Treaty: see in particular, Arts 109J(3) EC and Art J.8 TEU.

tence of the Community as such but rather under the international competence of the individual Member States; it follows therefore that they constitute international agreements concluded in simplified form.[32] So far the analogy is apposite for the Danish decision which can fairly readily be classified as an international agreement in simplified form.[33] It can readily be distinguished from other acts of the representatives of the *Member States* which constitute the exercise of a power conferred jointly on the Member States and which find an explicit legal basis in the Treaties (*viz* Art 11 of the Merger Treaty, Arts 158, 167, 168a and 216 EEC).

Nevertheless, to classify some "acts of the representatives" as being in the nature of international agreements is by no means the end of the matter. These agreements do not stand by themselves. They pursue Community objectives; they are in one way or another, in a different intensity, linked with the Community legal order. For these reasons some authors have considered that they nevertheless form part of the *Community* legal order.[34] Opinions differ widely on this point.[35]

It is generally assumed that these "framework decisions" cannot alter the obligations for Member States under the Treaties and the decisions based thereon: only formal Treaty amendments pursuant to Article 236 EEC can do so.[36] The statement by the "Heads of State or Government meeting within the European Council" in the preamble to the Danish decision to the effect that the decision is "in conformity with the Treaty on European Union" merely states the obvious from the perspective of the hierarchy of norms. If it had indeed purported to amend the Maastricht Treaty or to provide legally-binding "opt-outs" not contained in the text of the Treaty itself then the Commission could possibly have brought an action against the Heads of State or Government for infringement of the Treaty![37] The principle of the hierarchy of norms mandates that in the event of a conflict between the provisions of the Treaty, on the one hand and the provisions of the decision, on the other, then this putatively complementary law can never prevail over the

---

[32] It is clearly possible to make some exceptions to this general rule depending on the type of act at issue in certain cases: see further, Kapteyn and Ver Loren van Themaat, *op cit*, n 29 at 205–206. These exceptions for 'acts of the representatives' in the classic sense can all be distinguished quite sharply from the nature of the *Danish* decision.

[33] See also Hartley, 'Constitutional and institutional aspects of the Maastricht Agreement' (1993) 42 ICLQ 213, 235.

[34] See, for example, Bebr, 'Acts of representatives of the Governments of the Member States taken within the Council of Ministers of the European Communities' (1966) SEW, 529, and Hartley, *The Foundations of European Community Law* (1988) at 97.

[35] See, Kapteyn and Ver Loren van Themaat, *op cit*, n 9 at 206.

[36] See Case 43/75 *Defrenne II* [1976] ECR 455 from which it appears that amendments to the EEC Treaty can only be made according to the procedure of Art 236 EEC (now Art N TEU).

[37] Quite apart from the politically unreal nature of such an infringement action which would certainly never have got off the ground, such an action could probably only refer to those parts of the Decision which purported to alter the (amended) provisions of the EC Treaty itself and could only be contemplated once the Decision entered into force (*i.e.* upon entry into force of the Maastricht Treaty). In such circumstances the failure in question would be a failure to follow the procedure provided for in Art N of the Maastricht Treaty. An action for annulment of the decision in question could not however be brought since such an action only lies in the case of 'acts of the Council and the Commission'. (It is by now also clear that certain acts of the European Parliament can also be reviewed by the Court of Justice).

terms of the Treaty itself. Only an amendment proper of the Treaty can have that result.

To move on to a different point, seperate from the status of the Danish decision under public international law and Community law: was approval of the legislative organ (or other State organ) constitutionally necessary at the *national* level as a condition precedent to the making of the international act? At the risk of being unduly simplistic it can be stated that in the vast majority of Member States, and as a matter of national constitutional law, parliamentary ratification will be necessary unless the decision can be considered as forming part of the Community legal order or other delegated powers.[38] We feel that whereas it may indeed be possible to argue that certain types of classic "acts of the representatives" or Council "framework decisions" must be considered as forming part of the Community legal order in a very wide sense, and thus that there was no need for a seperate national ratification process[39] this may not be the case for the Danish decision. Our reasons for tentatively suggesting this are threefold. First, the framework decision was not taken "within the framework" of a Community institution as such (the Council) but of the European Council whose decisions are not normally legally binding and which is not bound by the constitutional rules and obligations laid down in the Treaties. It can therefore be maintained that decisions of the European Council are not taken in accordance with the procedures of the Treaty (not to mind the framework decisions). There is therefore no organic link with the Community legal order. Secondly, it is arguable that there is no normative link between this decision and the Community legal order as such. Thus, a distinction can be made with all those decisions taken in common by the Member States, with an express legal basis in the Treaties.[40] That is, for example, the fundamental difference between the Danish decision and the other "decision" embedded in the Edinburgh conclusions on the seats of the institutions (Art 216 EEC). The latter plainly falls within the Community legal system. The former does not necessarily do so. That is why certain Treaty articles provide that decisions may be taken by common accord among the Member States without making provision for ratification by Member States in accordance with their respective constitutional requirements. They don't need to be subject to national (parliamentary) ratification because of their express normative link with the Community legal system as such.[41]

On the other hand, it seems that the Member States intended the Danish decision to constitute a type of "implementation agreement" of the Maastricht Treaty itself and as such would not require a *new* ratification procedure.[42] This view was premised on the fact that the Danish decision constituted part of the

---

[38] See, for example, Art 29.4.3 of the Irish Constitution and Art 53 of the French Constitution.

[39] Many of the 'acts of the representatives' concerned matters such as customs or transport tariffs areas where national executives enjoy considerable discretion.

[40] For example, Art 158 (nomination of the members of the Commission), Art 167 (nomination of the Judges and Advocate-Generals of the Court of Justice), Art 168A (nomination of the members of the Court of First Instance) and Art 216 EC (fixing the seats of the Institutions of the Community).

[41] See Treaty articles, *ibid.*

[42] See, for example, comments made to the Dutch Parliament by the Secretary of State for European Affairs, TK, 16 December 1992, 2842, left column.

"context" of the Maastricht Treaty itself, within the meaning of Article 31 of the Vienna Convention on the Law of Treaties.

Finally, the question arises whether the terms of the decision are justiciable by the Court of Justice. No express jurisdiction is conferred upon the Court over disputes concerning the application and interpretation of the provisions of the Danish decision. Almost certainly the Danish decision, like its inspiration the Council "framework decision", cannot fall within the term "acts of the institutions of the Communities" whose validity and interpretation may be the subject of a preliminary ruling of the Court.[43] By relying on a broad interpretation of Article 164 EEC the Court could, however, regard the Danish decision as entering into the *system* or *context* of the Community (Union) Treaty as part of "the law" which it has a duty to ensure is respected. This can fairly readily be envisaged with regard to Sections A and B of the Danish decision as they concern "interpretations" of the EC Treaty itself. Much less obvious are Sections C and D which constitute clarification of the two intergovernmental pillars where the Court's jurisdiction was expressly excluded (Art L of the Maastricht Treaty).

An alternative view is that as a purely international legal agreement its correct interpretation and application does not fall within the purview of the Court of Justice at all but rather that of the International Court of Justice. This can hardly be considered a satisfactory solution from a constitutional point of view. Not only does this solution do nothing to further the "unity" of the whole, it could arguably only apply with regard to Sections C and D of the decision since Sections A and B can be considered as part of the "context" of the EC Treaty.[44]

Substantive analysis of the Danish "opt-outs"

Citizenship

Section A of the Danish decision concerns the citizenship of the Union as provided for in Articles 8–8e of the EC Treaty.[45] There is no reference to Denmark, far less to exceptions; it is simply established that the provisions relating to citizenship of the Union give nationals of the Member States *additional* rights and protection as specified in Part Two of the EC Treaty. They do not in any way take the place of *national* citizenship. The question whether an individual possesses the nationality of a Member State will be settled solely by reference to the national law of the Member State concerned. In Denmark's first unilateral Declaration in Annex 3, it is stipulated that citizenship of the Union in no way in itself gives a national of another Member State the right to

---

[43] Arts 177 EEC and 150 Euratom. Art 41 ECSC is phrased somewhat differently.
[44] This is suggested by Hartley, *supra*, n 33 at 235.
[45] The EC Treaty is the EEC Treaty as amended by Title II of the Maastricht Treaty (Art G TEU).

obtain Danish citizenship or any of the rights, duties, privileges or advantages that are inherent in Danish citizenship by virtue of Denmark's constitutional, legal and administrative rules.

It follows that Articles 8–8e of the EC Treaty are not to be understood as meaning that the Union has only power to settle questions relating to the nationality of a Member State. This clarification is fairly self-evident. The EC Treaty only provides that "every person holding the nationality of a Member State shall be a citizen of the Union" (Art 8(1)). The fact that this matter of nationality of a Member State is to be settled solely by reference to the national law of the Member State concerned repeats *verbatim* the first sentence to the second "declaration" annexed to the Maastricht Treaty itself.[46]

It is submitted therefore that the oft-repeated assertion that "Denmark does not accept the idea of European citizenship" is not correct. Denmark is fully bound by Articles 8–8e of the EC Treaty and consequently will have to grant rights of residence and political rights to the citizens of the Union. This is not a problem. In its first unilateral Declaration Denmark states that it "will fully respect all specific rights expressly provided for in the Treaty and applying to nationals of the Member States".[47] It is quite a different matter that many of these rights either already exist or may be of limited value to the citizens.[48] Section A of the Danish decision and Denmark's unilateral Declaration on citizenship, therefore, primarily serves a political purpose: it had to be made clear to the Danish population that the introduction of Union citizenship does not imply that the power to establish nationality (with all the rights and privileges adhering thereto) is to be transferred to "Brussels". If it is to be accepted that the second function of the decision and Declaration was to give a completely different meaning, in public, to Union citizenship – namely to suggest that Denmark was not bound in any way by the provisions on citizenship – this could be considered as quite a clever psychological tactic on the part of the "Yes-lobby" in the second Danish referendum.

The Danish unilateral Declaration on citizenship is more problematic where it states that nothing in the Maastricht Treaty implies or foresees an undertaking to create a citizenship of the Union in the sense of citizenship of a nation-state. Such a measure may conceivably be included in a future Council decision under Article 8b (or perhaps Art 8a). Yet, in that case, the unanimity requirement provides the guarantee that such a Council decision can only be adopted

---

[46] The 'Declaration on Nationality of a Member State'. It may be added that, in its judgment of 7 July 1992 in Case C-369/90 *MV Micheletti*, (1993) 30 CML Rev 623–637 (with comment by Jessurun d'Oliveira), the Court of Justice indicated that certain limits relating to the exercise of the basic rights under the EEC Treaty (such as the freedom of establishment in the case in hand) do exist in this respect.

[47] It declared that nationals of the other Member States will enjoy the right in Denmark to vote and stand as a candidate in municipal elections and that Denmark intends to introduce legislation granting nationals of the other Member States the right to vote and to stand as a candidate for elections to the European Parliament in good time before the next elections in 1994. These are precisely the voting rights which, according to Art 8b of the EC Treaty, are to be granted to citizens of the Union!

[48] The scope *ratione materiae* and *ratione personae* of Union citizenship has been analysed extensively elsewhere: Van Dijk, 'Free movement of persons: towards European citizenship', (1992) SEW, 277–307; Closa, 'The concept of citizenship in the Treaty on European Union', (1992) 29 CML Rev 1137–1169.

with Denmark's consent.[49] Denmark's declaration underlines its firm opposition to any progress in this direction.

Economic and Monetary Union

One of the most important arrangements undoubtedly concerns the exemption granted to Denmark from participating in the third stage of EMU. This final stage of the process towards economic and monetary integration in Europe will be characterised *inter alia* by a single currency and the functioning of a European System of Central Banks (ESCB).[50] In justifying this important opt-out, reference is made in Section B of the Danish decision to the "Protocol on certain provisions relating to Denmark".[51] The content of this Protocol is considerably less neutral than its title suggests. The core provision of the Protocol is that the Danish Government shall notify the Council of its position concerning participation in the third stage of EMU, before the Council makes its assessment as to whether or not the conditions for the adoption of a single currency are fulfilled.[52] In the event of a notification that Denmark will not participate in the third stage, this Member State shall have an *exemption*. The effect of the exemption shall be that all articles and provisions of the EC Treaty and the Statute of the ESCB referring to a derogation shall be applicable to Denmark.

In Section B of the Danish decision it is noted that Denmark has given notification that it will *not* participate in the third stage. The legal consequences of this notification are set out explicitly: Denmark will not participate in the single currency and will not be bound by the rules concerning economic policy which apply only to the Member States participating in the third stage of EMU. Denmark will retain its existing powers in the field of monetary policy according to its national laws and regulations, including powers of the National Bank of Denmark in the field of monetary policy.[53]

Given the fact that the 12th Protocol speaks of a derogation (following the granting of an exemption), it may be assumed that Denmark must now be treated as a "Member State with a derogation" within the meaning of Article 109k of the EC Treaty. As a consequence of this derogation the

---

[49] Schuster, 'Der Sonderstatus Dänemarks im Vertrag über die Europäische Union', (1993) EuZW, 177–180 believes that this part of the Danish Declaration might have '*Sprengkraft*' if it is accepted that it can limit Art 8e of the EC Treaty, in that the 'Schaffung einer echten Unions-Staatsbürgerschaft' (the creation of real Union citizenship) would not even be possible in the future. It should be recalled, however, that a Declaration – and *a fortiori* a unilateral Declaration – cannot limit the scope of a provision of the Treaty. See also, Toth, 'The legal status of Declarations annexed to the Single European Act', (1986) 23 CMLRev 803–812.

[50] On this subject see, *inter alia*, Smits, 'De monetaire unie van Maastricht – een overzicht van de Verdragsbepalingen inzake de economische en monetaire unie', (1992) SEW, 702.

[51] Annexed as the twelfth Protocol to the Maastricht Treaty.

[52] According to Art 109j(2) of the EC Treaty the Council (acting by a qualified majority) shall first assess for each Member State, whether it fulfils the necessary conditions for the adoption of a single currency; subsequently, it will be assessed whether a majority of the Member States fulfils these conditions.

[53] The notification will take effect upon the coming into effect of the Decision of the Heads of State and Government, which is the moment the Maastricht Treaty enters into force, 1 November 1993, *supra*, 353 of this volume.

special provisions of Article 109k(3)–(6) of the EC Treaty will apply to Denmark.[54]

It may be concluded that at the Edinburgh Summit Denmark "merely" made use of a *possibility* which was already contained in the 12th Protocol of the Maastricht Treaty. As a result of the notification that Denmark will not participate in the third stage of EMU, this twelfth Protocol will be activated, as it were, at an early stage, namely at the date of entry into force of the Maastricht Treaty itself (1 November 1993). Section B of the Danish decision, therefore, in fact has an entirely declaratory character. This "activation" of derogation status as and from the moment of entry into force of the Treaty is perfectly compatible with its terms which simply provide that Denmark exercises this right (at any time) *before* the Council makes an evaluation according to the terms of Article 109j(2).

The Danish exemption does not apply to the second stage of EMU. Denmark is therefore fully bound by the provisions which, as from 1 January 1994, should be in force in this transitional stage (Art 109e *et seq* of the EC Treaty). It is further stated in the decision of Heads of State and Government that Denmark will continue to participate in exchange rate co-operation within the European Monetary System (EMS). It would seem that by agreeing to this, Denmark has assumed more obligations than EMS rules strictly require.[55]

Defence Policy

One of the thorniest problems occurs in the so-called second pillar of the Maastricht Treaty concerning the – preponderantly intergovernmental – co-operation in the field of foreign and security policy (Title V). This common foreign and security policy includes all questions related to the security of the European Union, including the eventual framing of a common defence policy, which might in time lead to a common defence (Art J.4(1)). The Western European Union (WEU) – which is an "integral part of the development of the Union" – is requested to elaborate and implement decisions and actions of the Union which have defence implications (Art J.4(2)). In a Declaration attached to the Maastricht Treaty the – then – nine Member States of the Union which are also members of the WEU express their willingness to undertake the tasks the WEU is requested to perform.[56]

However, the creation of such close links between the European Union and WEU gives rise to substantial problems. At the time of the negotiations in Maastricht, three members of the European Union were not members of the WEU; at present, Denmark and Ireland are not members of the European security organization.[57] But does the envisaged interlocking of the two organizations

[54] It may be observed that the opting-out Protocol of the UK contains much wider exemptions. See the eleventh Protocol annexed to the EU Treaty which has the meaningless – but for lawyers suspect – title 'Protocol on Certain Provisions Relating to the United Kingdom of Great Britain and Northern Ireland'.

[55] See, Schuster, *supra*, n 49 at 177–178.

[56] See the thirtieth Declaration annexed to the EU Treaty, the 'Declaration on Western European Union', which in fact consists of two declarations of the 9 members of the WEU.

[57] In the meantime, Greece has acceded to the WEU; Denmark and Ireland have been given 'observer' status.

imply that all members of the European Union must also be members of the WEU? The text of the Maastricht Treaty – and particularly Title V on Foreign and Security Policy – indeed does not impose any explicit obligation on the Member States to join the WEU. In the Declaration on Western European Union, the States which are members of the European Union are "invited" in a rather non-committal way to accede to the WEU or to become observers "if they so wish".[58] Moreover the statement in Article J.4(4) that "the policy of the Union shall not prejudice the specific character of the security and defence policy of certain Member States" seems to indicate that non-membership was expressly contemplated. The question may, however, be raised as to whether the general obligation of the Member States "to support the Union's external and security policy actively and unreservedly in a spirit of loyalty and mutual solidarity" (Art J.1(4) TEU), does not make WEU membership imperative for all Member States. In contrast with the situation in respect of Article 5 of the EEC Treaty, which is comparable to this provision, no legally binding answer can be provided by the Court of Justice on this point.[59] In weighing the arguments for and against, the conclusion must be that the wording of the Maastricht Treaty is too general and too vague to be able to derive such a concrete obligation as compulsory membership of the WEU for the Member States.

In Section C of the Danish decision it is observed that nothing in the Maastricht Treaty commits Denmark to become a *member* of the WEU. Denmark will therefore not participate in the elaboration and the implementation of decisions and actions of the Union which have defence implications (Art J.5); neither will it prevent the development of closer co-operation between Member States in this area. This seems to follow implicitly from the terms of Article J.4(2) of the Maastricht Treaty itself. In a Declaration of the European Council in Annex 2, the European Council takes note, that Denmark will renounce its right to exercise the Presidency of the Union (Art J.5 TEU) in each case involving the elaboration and implementation of decisions and actions of the Union which have defence implications. The normal rules for replacing the President, in the case of the President being indisposed, shall apply.

It is questionable, however, whether simply renouncing the right to exercise the Presidency whenever matters which have defence implications are under discussion, is sufficient; it can be argued that in such cases Denmark ought to adopt a completely passive attitude. It may further be queried whether the arrangements agreed upon in respect of the Danish Presidency will have any consequences for Ireland, the other Member State which is not a WEU member? As no specific arrangements have been made in respect of this Member State, it would seem that Ireland will be able to exercise the half-yearly Presidency "normally", even when decisions of the Union which have defence implications are under discussion. Yet it is submitted that the reasoning of Section C of the Danish decision is equally apposite in the case of Ireland. Ireland is not a member of the WEU and is not obliged to become one. As it is

---

[58] See, the thirtieth Declaration annexed to the Maastricht Treaty.
[59] See Art L TEU.

the WEU which will elaborate and implement the decisions and actions of the European Union with defence implications, Ireland will not participate in this elaboration and implementation. Once more it appears that the Danish decision merely clarifies or "interprets" the content of the Maastricht Treaty itself.

Justice and Home Affairs

The so-called third pillar of the Maastricht Treaty (Title VI) concerns the – mainly intergovernmental – co-operation in the fields of justice and home affairs. The "matters of common interest" which are the subject of this co-operation include asylum policy, the conditions of entry to and residence in the Union by nationals of third countries, combatting unauthorised immigration, combatting drug addiction and judicial co-operation in civil and criminal matters (Art K.1). As Denmark did not insist on an exception on this point during the negotiations in Maastricht, the provisions of Title VI are fully applicable to this Member State. This is also recognised in Part D of the decision of the Heads of State and Government in the following terms: "Denmark will participate fully in co-operation on Justice and Home Affairs on the basis of the provisions of Title VI of the Treaty on European Union."

The background to this – rather unremarkable – statement becomes clearer on reading Denmark's second unilateral Declaration. This emphasizes the fact that Article K.9 TEU requires the *unanimity* of all the Members of the Council of the European Union for the adoption of decisions to apply Article 100c of the EC Treaty to action in areas referred to in Article K.1(1) to (6). Before it enters into force such a unanimous decision will, moreover, have to be adopted by each Member State in accordance with its constitutional requirements. As in the case of the unilateral Declaration on citizenship, it is again made clear here that, in the case of a transfer of sovereignty, the Danish constitution requires either a majority of five-sixths of the Members of the *Folketing* or both a majority of the Members of the *Folketing* and a majority of voters in a referendum.[60]

Social Policy, consumers, environment and distribution of income

The Conclusions only contain a Declaration of the European Council in respect of these areas of Community policy (Annex 2). The Declaration states explicitly that the Maastricht Treaty does not prevent any Member State from maintaining or introducing more *stringent* protection measures compatible with the EC Treaty. The EC Treaty indeed leaves room to the Member States to conduct a stricter national policy in these areas (see, Arts 118a(3), 129a(3) and 130t of the EC Treaty and – as far as Social Policy is concerned – Article 2(5) of the Agreement on Social Policy between the Member States of the European Community with the exception of the UK). The Declaration further confirms

---

[60] The question remains, however, whether Denmark (and the other Member States) under the procedural requirements of Art K.9 of the Maastricht Treaty have full control over the supervisory role of the Court of Justice in view of the fact that the areas mentioned in Art K.1(1) to (6) may overlap considerably with areas in which the EC is competent. See, O'Keeffe, 'The free movement of persons and the single market', (1992) EL Rev 3–19.

that the provisions introduced by the Maastricht Treaty, including the provisions on EMU, permit each Member State to pursue its own policy with regard to distribution of income and maintain or improve social welfare benefits.

No tears but constitutional heartache?

The tremendous problem which arose with regard to the ratification of the Maastricht Treaty following the first Danish referendum, was solved in a most ingenious way at the meeting of the European Council in Edinburgh. In a decision of the Heads of State and Government, legally binding under public international law, a "special position" was created for Denmark in order to deal with those aspects of the Maastricht Treaty which were thought to encounter objections on the part of the Danish population. Danish ministers rejoiced at their success and most commentators agreed that Denmark had succeeded in obtaining important concessions. The true situation is different, however.[61] The reason why the Maastricht Treaty did not need to be adapted is that it was not amended at the Edinburgh Summit. The texts presented to the Danish population on 18 May 1993 were exactly the same the electorate had already rejected on 2 June 1992. The Edinburgh summit merely "interpreted" or "clarified" which rights and obligations Denmark has under the Maastricht Treaty in relation to citizenship, defence and justice and home affairs. In addition, the latent right, already present in the Maastricht Treaty, not to participate in the third stage of EMU was "activated". The fact that 11 of the Member States[62] glossed over any necessity for *national* parliamentary ratification while proclaiming its binding nature under public international (as opposed to Community) law, illustrates that in substance they too were of the view that it did not give Denmark anything other than that contained in the Maastricht Treaty itself. Denmark's much discussed "special position" is therefore a legal mirage.

More fundamentally however, the Danish decision confirms the perception which the "Heads of State or Government" have of their role in the integration process. One of the main criticisms levelled against the Maastricht Treaty itself was the deepening of the "democratic deficit", in the sense that the parallel extra-EC pillars (the Union to the extent that it does not overlap with the three Community Treaties) which were created were taken out of the national systems and *intergovernmentalised*, but not within the Community democratic system. This inevitably leads to a democratic retrogression since the role of national parliaments is greatly reduced and the role of the European Parliament is effectively *nihil*. Another criticism is the fact that several limitations were in practice placed on the jurisdiction of the Court of Justice. Finally, it can be argued that

---

[61] See also, Mortimer, 'Same deal as before', *Financial Times*, 28 January 1993 and Curtin, 'A European solution to a Danish problem', *Irish Times*, 15 December 1992.

[62] Excluding Denmark because the Danish decision was placed before the people in the second referendum.

the *acquis communautaire* was effectively hijacked by the intergovernmental conference (in the composition of the Heads of State or Government) in certain respects despite the lip-service to its maintenance in the preamble to the Maastricht Treaty.[63]

The Danish decision brings these three threads together in a type of post-Maastricht frenzy. Indeed it confirms that the Heads of State or Government feel themselves competent to give "legal interpretations" of the Maastricht Treaty. This was first done in a little remarked "declaration" added to the Maastricht Treaty on 1 May 1992.[64] Here, they gave what was explicitly termed a "legal interpretation" of Protocol 17 to the Maastricht Treaty (on the Irish abortion issue). In the Danish decision they went one step further in that they also gave an "interpretation" of the terms of the Maastricht Treaty, but this time as a legally binding (intergovernmental) agreement under public international law. This trend is disturbing because it aggravates problems of democratic accountability and judicial control and ignores certain basis premises of the theory of the seperation of powers. With regard to the Danish decision, it can be said that the role which national parliaments in 11 Member States could (should) have played in the ratification of the decision, as a matter of national constitutional law was completely glossed over by the governing elite. Moreover, some suggestions have been made that the Court of Justice may not be competent to adjudicate upon questions of interpretation and application of the Danish decision as such, but possibly the International Court of Justice, a construction which, even if it remains purely theoretical, stands to damage the unique nature of the EC. Finally, to the extent that the whole purpose of the Danish decision was to copperfasten certain "opt-outs" for Denmark, it can hardly do otherwise than confirm the non-unitary, "bits and pieces", nature of the European Union exercise, a facet which was already firmly enshrined in the Maastricht Treaty itself.[65]

The lesson is that political pragmatism is indeed endlessly inventive and disrespectful of perceived legal and constitutional niceties. The risk is, however, not only of constitutional heartache but of possible chaos. That is why news of the possible creation of a Committee of "wise men"[66] as the platform for a new constitutional debate about the future of the EC is very heartening.[67] In this context the "draft Constitution", which is in the process of finalization by the European Parliament's Committee on Institutional Affairs, can furnish a constructive starting block.[68]

DEIRDRE CURTIN
RONALD VAN OOIK

---

[63] See further, Curtin, *supra*, n 1, on all these points.

[64] OJ 1992 C191/109.

[65] It appears that in the context of the current enlargement negotiations all four candidate states (Austria, Norway, Finland and Sweden) have formally tabled a demand for an explicit provision in their Accession agreement similar to Protocol 1 (Danish) to the Maastricht Treaty. If successful, this would enable all candidate countries to discriminate *indefinitely* against individuals of other Member States regarding the acquisition of so-called 'second homes'. This really illustrates the 'turbo' effect such 'special provisions' can have.

[66] It is apparently not considered that women are ever 'wise'...

[67] See, *Financial Times*, 15 July 1993.

[68] See the draft Report on the Constitution of the European Union, parts A and B, 9 September 1993 (rapporteur F Herman).

Index